CHURCH BUILDING AND SOCIETY
IN THE LATER MIDDLE AGES

The construction of a church was one of the most demanding events to take place in the life of a medieval parish. It required a huge outlay of time, money and labour, and often a new organisational structure to oversee design and management. Who took control and who provided the financing was deeply shaped by local patterns in wealth, authority and institutional development – from small villages with little formal government to large settlements with highly unequal populations. The later middle ages was a period of great economic and social change as communities managed the impact of the Black Death, the end of serfdom and the slump of the mid-fifteenth century. This original and authoritative study provides an account of how economic change, local politics and architecture combined in late-medieval England. It will be of interest to researchers of medieval social and architectural history.

DR GABRIEL BYNG is Research Fellow in History at Clare Hall, Cambridge University, and Director of Studies in History of Art at Clare College. He is a member of the Council of the British Archaeological Association, sits on the Fabric Advisory Committee of St George's Chapel, Windsor, and is a trustee of Caius House and the Mausolea and Monuments Trust. He is also co-Principal Investigator on the Digital Pilgrim II project. He won the Reginald Taylor and Lord Fletcher Essay Prize in 2014.

Cambridge Studies in Medieval Life and Thought
Fourth Series

General Editor
ROSAMOND McKITTERICK
Emeritus Professor of Medieval History, University of Cambridge, and Fellow of Sidney Sussex College

Advisory Editors
CHRISTINE CARPENTER
Emeritus Professor of Medieval English History, University of Cambridge
MAGNUS RYAN
University Lecturer in History, University of Cambridge, and Fellow of Peterhouse

The series *Cambridge Studies in Medieval Life and Thought* was inaugurated by G.G. Coulton in 1921; Professor Rosamond McKitterick now acts as General Editor of the Fourth Series, with Professor Christine Carpenter and Dr Magnus Ryan as Advisory Editors. The series brings together outstanding work by medieval scholars over a wide range of human endeavour extending from political economy to the history of ideas.

This is book 107 in the series, and a full list of titles in the series can be found at:
www.cambridge.org/medievallifeandthought.

CHURCH BUILDING AND SOCIETY IN THE LATER MIDDLE AGES

GABRIEL BYNG
University of Cambridge

CAMBRIDGE
UNIVERSITY PRESS

University Printing House, Cambridge CB2 8BS, United Kingdom

One Liberty Plaza, 20th Floor, New York, NY 10006, USA

477 Williamstown Road, Port Melbourne, VIC 3207, Australia

314-321, 3rd Floor, Plot 3, Splendor Forum, Jasola District Centre, New Delhi - 110025, India

79 Anson Road, #06-04/06, Singapore 079906

Cambridge University Press is part of the University of Cambridge.

It furthers the University's mission by disseminating knowledge in the pursuit of education, learning and research at the highest international levels of excellence.

www.cambridge.org
Information on this title: www.cambridge.org/9781108827454
DOI: 10.1017/9781316661765

© Gabriel Byng 2017

This publication is in copyright. Subject to statutory exception and to the provisions of relevant collective licensing agreements, no reproduction of any part may take place without the written permission of Cambridge University Press.

First published 2017
First paperback edition 2020

A catalogue record for this publication is available from the British Library

Library of Congress Cataloging in Publication data
NAMES: Byng, Gabriel Thomas Gustav, author.
TITLE: Church building and society in the later Middle Ages / Gabriel Thomas Gustav Byng, University of Cambridge.
DESCRIPTION: New York : Cambridge University Press, 2017. | Series: Cambridge studies in medieval life and thought. Fourth series | Includes bibliographical references and index.
IDENTIFIERS: LCCN 2017029980 | ISBN 9781107157095 (alk. paper)
SUBJECTS: LCSH: Church buildings – England – Design and construction – History – To 1500. | Building – Social aspects – England – History – To 1500. | Building – Economic aspects – England – History – To 1500. | Architecture and society – England – History – To 1500. | England – Social conditions – 1066–1485. | England – Economic conditions – 1066–1485.
CLASSIFICATION: LCC BV604 .B96 2017 | DDC 246/.9509420902–dc23
LC record available at https://lccn.loc.gov/2017029980

ISBN 978-1-107-15709-5 Hardback
ISBN 978-1-108-82745-4 Paperback

Cambridge University Press has no responsibility for the persistence or accuracy of URLs for external or third-party internet websites referred to in this publication, and does not guarantee that any content on such websites is, or will remain, accurate or appropriate.

CONTENTS

List of Figures		*page* vii
List of Tables		ix
Acknowledgements		x
List of Abbreviations		xi
	INTRODUCTION	1
	The Social Significance of Church Construction	3
	Economic and Social Change in England, c. 1300–1500	10
	Changes in Cost and Money Supply	26
	Church Building and the Economy	33
	Sources	45
	Plan of the Work	47
1	FINANCING CONSTRUCTION I: THE PARISH	51
	Introduction	51
	Assessing the Evidence	52
	Fundraising Techniques	65
	Case Study: Cambridgeshire	95
	Conclusion	108
2	FINANCING CONSTRUCTION II: GENTRY AND CLERGY	110
	Introduction	110
	Tombs, Arms and Inscriptions	111
	Wills, Contracts and Accounts	118
	Affordability	122
	Rectors and Vicars	127
	Conclusion	134
3	ORGANISING CONSTRUCTION I: THE CHURCHWARDENS	136
	Introduction	136
	'Strong' and 'Weak' Wardenship	137

Contents

	Case Studies	139
	Organisation	159
	Conclusion	172
4	ORGANISING CONSTRUCTION II: CONTRACTING COMMITTEES AND FABRIC WARDENS	174
	Introduction	174
	Contracting Committees	175
	Fabric Wardens	185
	Authority and Autonomy	204
	Conclusion	212
5	ORGANISING CONSTRUCTION III: ARISTOCRACY, CLERGY AND INSTITUTIONS	214
	Introduction	214
	Aristocratic Projects	215
	Clerical and Institutional Projects	231
	Conflict and Cooperation	242
	Conclusion	245
6	APPROACHES TO BUILDING WORK	246
	Introduction	246
	'Simple Economy'	247
	Managerial Strategies	250
	Financial Planning	264
	Conclusion	276
	CONCLUSION	278
Bibliography		282
Index		318

FIGURES

I.1	Ten year moving average for building wages (all professions), 1208–1500	page 27
I.2	Ten year moving average for building wages (carpenter, thatcher, tiler and mason), 1208–1500	27
I.3	Ten year moving average of finished materials prices, 1265–1500	29
I.4	Ten year moving average of raw materials prices, 1260–1500	30
1.1	Revenue for building work at All Hallows, London Wall (1528–29)	57
1.2	Revenue for building work at Louth, Lincolnshire (1501–15)	57
1.3	Revenue for building work at Thame, Oxfordshire (1443)	58
1.4	Revenue for building work at Swaffham, Norfolk (1507–08)	59
1.5	Revenue for building work at Ludlow, Shropshire (1469–72)	60
1.6	Revenue for building work at Leverton, Lincolnshire (1498)	61
1.7	Parish church building work in Cambridgeshire	98
2.1	Harlestone nave (Keltek Trust)	123
3.1	Thame from the northwest, showing the Trinity aisle (© anonymous)	143
3.2	Ludlow tower (© Keltek Trust)	145
3.3	Great Dunmow tower (© Keltek Trust)	147
3.4	Louth tower (© David Traish LRPS)	149
4.1	Arlingham tower (© Roger Smith)	178
4.2	The east end of Long Melford, with an inscription to John Clopton (© Gabriel Byng)	186
4.3	Totnes tower (© John Ward)	188
4.4	Bodmin, Cornwall, from the southwest (© Tim Jenkinson)	194
4.5	Bridgwater tower and spire (© Graham Shaw)	195
4.6	Hedon from the southwest (© Keltek Trust)	196

List of Figures

4.7	North Petherwin, showing the south aisle and porch (© Roy Reed)	198
4.8	Berry chapel tower (© Tim Jenkinson)	202
5.1	Fotheringhay nave and tower (© Jonathan Ward)	217
5.2	The west doorway of Bolney (© Gabriel Byng)	223
5.3	Bolney fabric accounts, Par 252-9-1 #09 ff. 5v–6r (© Sussex Record Office)	224
5.4	Helmingham tower (© Gabriel Byng)	227
5.5	Biddenham north aisle (© Gabriel Byng)	229
5.6	Adderbury interior (© A. McRae Thomson)	234
5.7	Merton College Chapel, Oxford (© Gabriel Byng)	238

TABLES

I.1	Cambridgeshire chapels	page 37
I.2	Estimated quantities of building work styles	38
I.3	Parish church building as a proportion of the English economy	38
I.4	Medieval parochial building contracts summary	41
I.5	Bequests to church building in West Kent	43
I.6	Bequests to church building in Somerset	44
1.1	Large collections for building work	74
1.2	Incomes per parish I: Early fourteenth century	85
1.3	Incomes per parish II: Fifteenth century	91
1.4	Cambridgeshire taxpayers (1327) and building work	101
1.5	Cambridgeshire taxpayers (1524–25) and building work	104
1.6	Cambridgeshire taxable wealth (1524–25) and building work	105
1.7	Cambridgeshire per capita tax payment (1524–25) and building work	105
2.1	Building work in Cambridgeshire and the 1291 *Taxatio*	129
4.1	Arlingham, Gloucestershire, members of the 1372 contracting committee	179
4.2	Wardens of the building of Totnes tower (1449–52)	190
6.1	Contractor masons' hometowns	254

ACKNOWLEDGEMENTS

Much of the research for this book was carried out for my PhD at Cambridge University with the tireless encouragement, support and guidance of Professor Paul Binski. I am also deeply grateful to Professor Christine Carpenter, Dr Julian Luxford, Professor Mark Bailey and Professor Richard Marks, who gave essential advice during the redrafting and editing process. Professor Beat Kümin, Professor Katherine French, Dr Rosemary Horrox, Dr John Munns, Dr Joanna Mattingly, Professor Christopher Dyer, Dr Alex Sapoznik, Professor John Hatcher, Professor Paul Crossley, Dr Ian Forrest, Dr Clive Burgess, Dr Chris Briggs, Maria Black, Jeremy Musson and Dr Stephen Priestley kindly answered questions or provided ideas and guidance during research. I would also like to thank the many vicars, rectors, churchwardens and other parishioners who have facilitated my visits and provided useful and entertaining guides. Above all else I cannot begin to express my gratitude and debt of thanks for the help, support and generosity of my parents and sister.

ABBREVIATIONS

AHEW	*Agrarian History of England and Wales*
BCM	Berkeley Castle Muniments
BL	British Library, London
BLA	Bedfordshire and Luton Archives and Records Service, Bedford
BLO	Bodleian Library, Oxford
CA	Cambridgeshire Archives
CCA	Canterbury Cathedral Archives
CCCC	Corpus Christi College, Cambridge, Archives
CRO	Cornwall Record Office, Truro
CUL	Cambridge University Library
CWAs	Churchwardens' Accounts
ERO	Essex Record Office, Chelmsford
ERYA	East Riding of Yorkshire Archives, Beverley
ESRO	East Sussex Record Office, Brighton
HALS	Hertfordshire Archives and Local Studies, Hertford
HCA	Hereford Cathedral Archives
LA	Lincolnshire Archives, Lincoln
LMA	London Metropolitan Archives
LSE	London School of Economics and Political Science Archive
NRO	Norfolk Archives Centre, Norwich
OHC	Oxfordshire History Centre, Oxford
SkRO(IB)	Suffolk Record Office (Ipswich branch)
SRO	Somerset Record Office, Taunton
TNA	The National Archives, Kew
VCH	*Victoria County History*
WLHC	Walsall Local History Centre

INTRODUCTION

In 1536, John Bolney decided to start work on a new tower for his local church. He faced a stiff organisational and financial challenge. First, he requested an estimate and sold some land that had been in the family for generations in order to build up the necessary capital. He sought out a well-qualified architect with good references from a nearby town and met with the village leadership in order to convince them that the project was worthy of their support. It would, after all, turn the centre of the village into a building site, and, besides, he could not afford the work alone. Whether under pressure from Bolney, who was also their lord, or from enthusiasm for the new project, they agreed to fund the timberwork of the project. Some wealthy, pious men promised to labour for free. John negotiated the contract with the architect and began discussing designs. Meanwhile, the parish authorities started fundraising in earnest, holding parties, taking collections and selling unwanted items. They found and instructed their own contractor. Plans were produced, and stone bought from quarries and transported. Complex pieces were cut in the workshop, while others were finished on site. The architect sent two of his men to oversee the building site and occasionally visited himself, to make sure the project was running smoothly (and, of course, not over budget). John had calculated that he could save money by purchasing much of the materials and labour himself, so he kept his own account books, jotting down every transaction he made to monitor costs and payments. No doubt he met with the architect and authorities every so often to monitor progress, expenditure and the quality of the work. Under his rigorous and time-consuming oversight, it took only a few months for the new tower to top out. By Lent the following year, John could survey the realisation in stone and mortar of his family's worldly success, finished off with his arms over the main entrance, visible whenever the church was entered. The parishioners might have seen it somewhat differently. Nearly half a millennium later, the tower of St Mary

Introduction

Magdalene, Bolney, in West Sussex remains as witness not only to the craftsmanship of the masons but also to the wealth and managerial talents of John Bolney and the parishioners.[1]

The construction of England's parish churches required great achievements not only in art and engineering but also in organisation and finance. While cathedrals and abbeys could draw on substantial landed wealth for their building projects, parishes had to depend upon more varied and unpredictable resources. Careful management was required to convert the revenues of a multitude of peasant or urban families into a reliable income stream for an often lengthy building project, and to ensure projects were completed quickly and to budget. Such organisation was inflected by social and economic structures, local customs and cultural expectations. The distribution of land and wealth, the availability of employment and money, and the vagaries of weather and plague determined on a short- and long-term basis which parishioners could provide the funds for church building and the length, cost and ambition of their project.

At the heart of this book is a simple but important contention: that the financing of parish church construction was closely tied to the social fabric of medieval parishes, and was run and financed by comparatively wealthy groups of peasants or townsfolk, smaller and more distant in some places, larger and less polarised elsewhere. They carefully chose managerial structures, using special committees or existing institutions, which, contrary to the claims of some historians, acted with flair and competence, to reduce costs, eliminate fraud and speed completion.[2] The parish gentry could and did take on the management of their own projects, but their contributions were often made in collaboration with other wealthy parishioners; indeed building work was often less affordable to them individually than it was for wealthier peasants acting collaboratively.[3] Ecclesiastical institutions and the nobility were occasionally involved in architectural work on parish churches, but when they were, they delegated it to junior officials or local agents.

This book will also set building work in a changing economic context, showing how the proportion of parishioners who could contribute to building work contracted and expanded, affecting the quantity and ambition of church construction, the development of fundraising techniques and the significance of architectural patronage in defining and justifying the position of wealthier peasants and townsfolk during periods of social change.[4] Changes in prices, wages and the availability of money

---

[1] Chapter 5, section b.ii, pp. 221–26. [2] Chapter 6, section b, pp. 247–49.
[3] Chapter 2, section d, pp. 122–25. [4] Chapter 1, section c.vii, pp. 92–95.

were mediated by cultural and social expectations to determine not only what could be built but also by whom. Participation in the parish, and its cultural patronage, will be shown to be structured and unequal, and used by families and groups to both claim authority and demonstrate their position. These conclusions create a nuanced picture of church construction that is dominated neither by the manor or monastery nor by a monolithic parochial or civic 'community'.

A) THE SOCIAL SIGNIFICANCE OF CHURCH CONSTRUCTION

In the last three decades, scholarly attention on the social and religious life of the late medieval and Reformation parish has been concerned with demonstrating that it was inclusive, flourishing and highly focused on the parish church. A common premise in this argument has been to note the energy and money expended on church buildings and furnishings, reflecting the devotion of the parishioners and their engagement with the life of the church, and involving, critically, the whole 'community', if strictly ordered by status, and sometimes excluding members of the aristocracy. Clive Burgess, for example, may be taken as representative when he notes the 'vitality' of parish life 'as indicated ... by the unequivocal, if unquantifiable, physical testimony of medieval church building'.[5] Eamon Duffy makes a related point: 'at its most obvious this continuing and indeed growing commitment to corporate Christianity [in late medieval England] is witnessed by the extraordinary and lavish spate of investment by lay men and women in the fabric and furnishing of their parish church'.[6] Similar conclusions have also been reached by other historians.[7]

Collaboration across the parish has been a centrepiece of these arguments: Colin Richmond argues that 'most [church towers] were constructed co-operatively';[8] Christopher Harper-Bill found that 'this architectural revolution [of the late middle ages] was normally the result of concerted communal effort';[9] Christopher Dyer agrees that 'late

---

[5] Clive Burgess, 'The Benefactions of Mortality: The Lay Response in the Later Medieval Urban Parish', in *Studies in Clergy and Ministry in Late Medieval England*, ed. D. Smith (York, 1991), 66–67 n. 2.
[6] Eamon Duffy, *The Stripping of the Altars: Traditional Religion in England, c. 1400–c.1580* (New Haven, 1992), 131–32. This is, in many ways, the *locus classicus* of this argument.
[7] E.g. Richard Morris, *Churches in the Landscape* (London, 1989), 373; Christopher Harper-Bill, *The Pre-Reformation Church in England 1400–1530* (London, 1989), 72; Christopher Haigh, *Reformation and Resistance in Tudor Lancashire* (Cambridge, 1975), 67.
[8] Colin Richmond, 'The English Gentry and Religion, C. 1500', in *Religious Beliefs and Ecclesiastical Careers in Late Medieval England*, ed. Christopher Harper-Bill (Woodbridge, 1991), 133–35.
[9] Harper-Bill, *Pre-Reformation Church*, 72.

Introduction

medieval church building must be attributed in most cases to ... the collective contributions of the community of parishioners';[10] Beat Kümin characterises late medieval church building as 'thousands of collaborative efforts';[11] and Katherine French entitles one chapter 'The Architecture of Community' and writes that 'building and furnishing the parish church bound the parishioners together through shared discussions of expectations, fundraising, work, and building use'.[12] Individual examples are described as a 'community enterprise',[13] 'a genuinely communal achievement',[14] 'a vast communal effort',[15] 'the people's creation',[16] or 'an effort of collective devotion of all sections of the community'[17] or of 'the whole community of the parish', even when evidence exists to the contrary.[18] Popularising works have argued too that the 're-building or enlargement of a Parish Church was testimony to the enthusiasm and generosity of a whole community'.[19]

Many have specifically noted the contributions of poor parishioners: Colin Platt, rather romantically, argues that 'it was not just the wealthy who had been called on [for contributions], but the widow to contribute her mite';[20] Colin Richmond notes the gifts of a 'great multitude of far humbler folk';[21] Norman Pounds writes of 'the small man' who invested in church building because he could not afford land;[22] and Gerald Randall adds that payments were made by 'ordinary members of the congregation including the poor'.[23] Richard Morris notes the contribution of gentry and merchants but also that 'enthusiasm for building seems to have been as strong among poor parishioners as among rich', as it was

---

[10] Christopher Dyer, 'The English Medieval Village Community and Its Decline', *Journal of British Studies* 33, no. 4 (1 October 1994): 413.

[11] Beat A. Kümin, 'The English Parish in a European Perspective', in *The Parish in English Life*, ed. Katherine L. French, Gary G. Gibbs, and Beat Kümin (Manchester, 1997), 29.

[12] Katherine L. French, *The People of the Parish: Community Life in a Late Medieval English Diocese* (Philadelphia, 2001), Chapter 5; cf. Katherine L. French, 'Parochial Fund-Raising in Late Medieval Somerset', in *The Parish in English Life*, ed. Katherine L. French, Gary G. Gibbs, and Beat Kumin (Manchester, 1997), 117.

[13] T. A. Heslop, 'Swaffham Parish Church', in *Medieval East Anglia*, ed. Christopher Harper-Bill (Woodbridge, 2005), 246, cf. 260–61. Heslop notes that a tenth of the adult population may have contributed to the church rebuilding.

[14] Gervase Rosser, *Medieval Westminster: 1200–1540* (Oxford, 1989), 271.

[15] David Lloyd, Margaret Clark, and Chris F. Potter, *St. Laurence's Church, Ludlow: The Parish Church and People, 1199–2009* (Little Logaston, 2010), 42.

[16] Colin Richmond, *John Hopton: A Fifteenth Century Suffolk Gentleman* (Cambridge, 1981), 179.

[17] Peter Brandon, *Sussex* (London, 2006), 186.   [18] Harper-Bill, *Pre-Reformation Church*, 72.

[19] Christopher Steed, *Let the Stones Talk: Glimpses of English History Through the People of the Moor* (Milton Keynes, 2011), 99.

[20] Colin Platt, *The Parish Churches of Medieval England*, 2nd ed. (London, 1995), 47.

[21] Richmond, *John Hopton*, 175.

[22] Norman Pounds, *A History of the English Parish* (Cambridge, 2000), 462.

[23] Gerald Randall, *The English Parish Church* (London, 1988), 46.

'an enterprise from which no one was excluded'.[24] About Louth, Reginald Dudding wrote that 'from the richest to the poorest all seem to have been affected with a like zeal'.[25] Norman Scarfe similarly described the democratic nature of fund raising, writing that 'most people contributed what they could'.[26] Others have been doubtful of the role of the gentry: Richmond argued that 'where the building effort was communal ... I believe it is non-gentry contributions which need to be stressed';[27] and Andrew Brown posits that, although aristocratic patronage could be 'overwhelming' in some churches, it was 'diluted in most', and replaced by 'a much wider group of parishioners' as part of a 'collective initiative'.[28]

Although these arguments have graduated to the centre of recent academic debates, they are not new: in the 1950s, G. H. Cook was willing to claim that 'it were almost as if democracy was claiming the last phase of Gothic architecture as its own'.[29] Earlier historians made similar points: in the 1920s, Sidney Dark mourned 'the fine co-operation in church building that existed in the Middle Ages';[30] a century ago Cardinal Gasquet noted that 'all were eager to have a part in the work of building up their church';[31] and, in the 1870s, J. J. Wilkinson recorded that 'every one seems to have given [to building Bodmin church] according to his means and up to his means'.[32] Referring to the same church in 1913, John Charles Cox wrote of the 'marvellous unanimity' of its reconstruction and doubted it was exceptional.[33] The sentiment can be found in Tudor sources: writing in 1598, John Stow found, at St Andrew Undershaft, London, in 1520–32, 'every man putting to his helping hand, some with their purses, others with their bodies';[34] and Thomas Bentley, commenting on his extracts from the St Andrew, Holborn, churchwardens' accounts in 1584, wrote that the steeple was 'builded by money given of devotion of good people ... in boxes, at ales, shootings, etc ... as by their accounts, yet remaining, may and doth appear' in 1446–68.[35] Parishioners could describe building work like this themselves – John Leland wrote that the church of Mells, Somerset, for

---

[24] Morris, *Landscape*, 373, 355–56.
[25] Reginald C. Dudding, *The First Churchwardens' Book of Louth, 1500–1524* (Oxford, 1941), xviii.
[26] Norman Scarfe, *Suffolk in the Middle Ages* (Woodbridge, 1986), 161.
[27] Richmond, 'Gentry and Religion', 133–35.
[28] Andrew Brown, *Church and Society in England, 1000–1500* (Basingstoke, 2003), 92.
[29] G. H Cook, *The English Mediaeval Parish Church* (London, 1954), 55.
[30] Sidney Dark, *London* (London, 1924), 111.
[31] Francis Aidan Gasquet, *Parish Life in Mediaeval England*, 3rd ed. (London, 1909), 30.
[32] J. J. Wilkinson, *Receipts and Expenses in Building Bodmin Church, 1469–1472* (London, 1874), v.
[33] John Charles Cox, *Churchwardens' Accounts from the Fourteenth Century to the Close of the Seventeenth Century* (London, 1913), 82.
[34] John Stow, *A Survey of London*, ed. Charles Lethbridge Kingsford (Oxford, 1908), 138–50.
[35] Quoted in Cox, *Churchwardens' Accounts*, 81.

Introduction

example, was built 'in time of mind ... by the whole parish', c. 1540, presumably based on the testimony of those he met.[36]

The parish church takes a rather different, often smaller but still far from infrequent, role in studies of gentry families and culture in the late middle ages.[37] Architectural and artistic evidence has been employed in biographical studies, rather as gentry biographies feature in art historical approaches, often emphasising building work as an expression of a patron's political or social ambitions and loyalties, and religious practice.[38] The seigniorial, martial qualities of towers and battlements, for example, have been associated with the emulation of great lordship.[39] Architectural patronage has been interpreted ambiguously: sometimes as indicating local domination and other times parochial commitment; sometimes worldly concerns and the display of wealth; other times pious devotion or altruistic inclinations.[40] These divisions are often mapped onto the question of the 'privatisation' of gentry religion, split between those who cite the building of private chapels alongside the use of confessors, prayer

---

[36] John Leland, *The Itinerary of John Leland in or about the Years 1535–1543*, ed. Lucy Toulmin Smith, vol. 5 (London, 1910), 105.

[37] E.g. Peter R. Coss, *The Foundations of Gentry Life: The Multons of Frampton and Their World, 1270–1370* (Oxford, 2010), Chapter 9; Eric Acheson, *A Gentry Community: Leicestershire in the Fifteenth Century, c. 1422–c. 1485* (New York, 1992), 189; Christine Carpenter, *Locality and Polity: A Study of Warwickshire Landed Society, 1401–1499* (Cambridge, 1992), 235–36; Christine Carpenter, 'The Religion of the Gentry of Fifteenth-Century England', in *England in the Fifteenth Century*, ed. D. Williams (Woodbridge, 1987), 66; Malcolm Graham Allan Vale, *Piety, Charity, and Literacy among the Yorkshire Gentry, 1370–1480* (York, 1976), 10–11; K. B McFarlane, *The Nobility of Later Medieval England: The Ford Lectures for 1953 and Related Studies* (Oxford, 1973), 95; Richmond, *John Hopton*, 156–57; Richmond, 'Gentry and Religion', 134. Andrew Brown, *Popular Piety in Late Medieval England: The Diocese of Salisbury, 1250–1550* (Oxford, 1995), 121.

[38] See particularly the work of Nigel Saul: 'Chivalry and Art: The Camoys Family and the Wall Paintings in Trotton Church', in *Soldiers, Nobles and Gentlemen: Essays in Honour of Maurice Keen*, ed. Peter R. Coss and Christopher Tyerman (Woodbridge, 2009); 'Shottesbrooke Church: A Study in Knightly Patronage', in *Windsor: Medieval Archaeology, Art and Architecture of the Thames Valley*, ed. L. Keen and E. Scarff (Norwich, 2002), 264–81; *Scenes from Provincial Life: Knightly Families in Sussex 1280–1400* (Oxford, 1986), Chapter 5; cf. Kate Heard, 'Death and Representation in the Fifteenth Century: The Wilcote Chantry Chapel at North Leigh', *Journal of the British Archaeological Association* 154, no. 1 (1 January 2001): 134–49; Eamon Duffy, 'The Disenchantment of Space: Salle Church and the Reformation', in *Religion and the Early Modern State: Views from China, Russia, and the West*, ed. James D. Tracy and Marguerite Ragnow (Cambridge, 2004), 325–26. Professor Saul's recent *Lordship and Faith* (Oxford, 2017) arrived too late for inclusion in this book.

[39] See (among his other works): Charles Coulson, 'Hierarchism in Conventual Crenellation: An Essay in the Sociology and Metaphysics of Medieval Fortification', *Medieval Archaeology* 26 (1982): 69–70.

[40] Gabriel Byng, 'Patrons and Their Commissions: The Uses of Biography in Understanding the Construction of the Nave of Holy Trinity, Bottisham', in *Writing the Lives of People and Things, AD 500–1700: A Multi-Disciplinary Future for Biography*, ed. R. F. W. Smith and G. L. Watson (Farnham, 2016), 227–43.

books and family pews,[41] and those who emphasise its parochial, if hierarchical, nature, occasionally using church construction as evidence.[42] These options are not mutually exclusive – Nigel Saul describes the fruits of the Walsh family's patronage at Wanlip, Leicestershire, as 'a communal witness to an act of charity' and 'a showcase for lordly power'.[43]

Although this is the first systematic study of the administration, management and financing of parish church construction, these are not wholly uncharted waters. The scholar who has given the most attention to the effect of economic change on regional church building is John James. His research into correlations between patterns of church construction in the Paris basin and the contemporary climate of economics and politics is the most wide-ranging of its kind.[44] The most comparable works in England are by Richard Morris, whose much-repeated graph of great church building has, for example, been set next to John Hatcher's of English demography.[45] Chapter 2 of Morris's *Churches in the Landscape* remains the most thoroughgoing analysis of the organisation of parish church building in the later middle ages.[46] The most thorough survey of the organisation and financing of major church construction in Europe is by W. H. Vroom, who has built on the work of many earlier scholars, including the well-known historians and editors of English cathedral and royal building accounts.[47] The work of Knoop and Jones on the

---

[41] John Bossy, 'The Mass as a Social Institution 1200–1700', *Past & Present*, no. 100 (1 August 1983): 29–61; Colin Richmond, 'Religion and the Fifteenth Century English Gentleman', in *The Church, Politics, and Patronage in the Fifteenth Century*, ed. Barrie Dobson (Gloucester, 1984), 193–208; C. Pamela Graves, 'Social Space in the English Medieval Parish Church', *Economy and Society* 18, no. 3 (1989): 317.

[42] Christine Carpenter, 'Religion', in *Gentry Culture in Late Medieval England*, ed. Raluca Radulescu and Alison Truelove (Manchester, 2005), 134–50; Carpenter, 'Religion of the Gentry'; Duffy, *Stripping*, 121–23; Saul, *Provincial Life*, 156–58; Nigel Saul, 'The Religious Sympathies of the Gentry in Gloucestershire, 1200–1500', *Transactions of the Bristol and Gloucestershire Archaeological Society* 98 (1980): 103–04.

[43] When describing, respectively, their brass and the building: Nigel Saul, 'Language, Lordship, and Architecture: The Brass of Sir Thomas and Lady Walsh at Wanlip, Leicestershire, and Its Context', *Midland History* 37, no. 1 (1 March 2012): 9.

[44] John James, 'Impact of Climate Change on Building Construction: AD 1050 to 1250', *AVISTA Forum Journal* 20, no. 1/2 (Fall 2010): 43–49; John James, 'How Many Built All the Churches?', *AVISTA Forum Journal* 13, no. 2 (2003): 23–24; John James, 'Funding the Early Gothic Churches of the Paris Basin', *Parergon* 15 (1997): 41–82; John James, 'An Investigation into the Uneven Distribution of Early Gothic Churches in the Paris Basin, 1140–1240', *The Art Bulletin* 66, no. 1 (March 1984): 15–46; John James, *The Pioneers of the Gothic Movement: Interim Report* (Wyong, N.S.W., 1980).

[45] Richard Morris, *Cathedrals and Abbeys of England and Wales: The Building Church, 600–1540* (London, 1979), Figures 7 and 8; John Hatcher and Mark Bailey, *Modelling the Middle Ages: The History and Theory of England's Economic Development* (Oxford, 2001), 29.

[46] Morris, *Landscape*.

[47] W. H. Vroom, *Financing Cathedral Building in the Middle Ages: The Generosity of the Faithful*, trans. Elizabeth Manton (Amsterdam, 2010).

Introduction

administration of building work, sadly largely overlooking parochial projects, is one of the two pillars on which all later study of masonry rests, the other being the research of L. F. Salzman.[48] Both conducted most of their work in the interwar period but published later. A more qualitative approach, encompassing the parish church, has combined social history and archaeology, particularly in works by Colin Platt.[49] Norman Pounds similarly includes an account of architectural development, and patronage, in his history of the parish.[50] Heather Swanson has perhaps done the most to set medieval workmen in their urban environment.[51] Few art historians have taken economic change as a central aspect of their study of medieval church building, and of these, Paul Binski is the most important recent example.[52] However, particular periods of building work in some regions have been associated by architectural historians with new wealth – expressed in phrases such as 'wool Gothic' – and popular histories of the parish church have long shown awareness of the broad contours of cultural and economic change.[53] Some such interpretations when applied to parish churches are, in fact, erroneous or overly simplistic, and tend to paint patrons as passive victims of economic change. This point will be discussed further in the section[54] 'Church Building and the Economy' in this chapter.

One important, and still far from resolved, scholarly debate has been over the effects of church building on the contemporary economy, largely focusing on towns in continental Europe, and is split between the 'optimists' – von Simson, Owen and Saltow[55] – and the 'pessimists' – Lopez and Williams.[56] Barbara Abou-El-Haj has described medieval

---

[48] Douglas Knoop and G. P. Jones, *The Mediaeval Mason*, 3rd ed. (Manchester, 1967), Chapter 2; L. F. Salzman, *Building in England down to 1540: A Documentary History*, 2nd ed. (Oxford, 1967).

[49] Colin Platt, *Medieval England: A Social History and Archaeology from the Conquest to A.D. 1600* (London, 1978); Colin Platt, *The Architecture of Medieval Britain: A Social History* (New Haven, 1990); Platt, *Parish Churches*; Gladys May Durant, *Landscape with Churches* (London, 1965).

[50] Pounds, *English Parish*, 408–12.

[51] Heather Swanson, *Medieval Artisans: An Urban Class in Late Medieval England* (Oxford, 1989); Heather Swanson, 'Artisans in the Urban Economy: The Documentary Evidence from York', in *Work in Towns*, ed. P. Corfield and D. Keene (Leicester, 1990), 42–56; Heather Swanson, *Building Craftsmen in Late Medieval York* (York, 1983).

[52] Paul Binski, *Gothic Wonder: Art, Artifice and the Decorated Style 1290–1350* (New Haven, 2014), 87–90; see also Henry Kraus, *Gold Was the Mortar: The Economics of Cathedral Building* (London, 1979).

[53] A good early example is J. Charles Cox and Charles Bradley Ford, *The Parish Churches of England* (London, 1935), Chapter 1.

[54] See pp. 33–45.

[55] Otto G. von Simson, *The Gothic Cathedral* (London, 1956); Virginia Lee Owen, 'Gothic Cathedral Building as Public Works', in *Essays in Economic and Business History*, edited by James H. Soltow (East Lancing, 1979); Virginia Lee Owen, 'The Economic Legacy of Gothic Cathedral Building: France and England Compared', *Journal of Cultural Economics* 13, no. 1 (1989): 89–100.

[56] Robert S. Lopez, 'Economie et Architecture Medievales, Cela Aurait Il Tue Ceci?', *Annales; Economies, Societes, Civilisations* 7 (1952): 433–38; Jane Welch Williams, *Bread, Wine & Money: The*

church building, for example, as a 'history of social burden and dislocation in towns with limited resources', likening it to exploitation by contemporary landlords.[57] There is also a group of less well-known writers that could reasonably be described as 'neutrals': Pacey, Johnson and Berecea et al.[58] This book will touch upon this debate, finding evidence in English towns and counties that church building acted as a stimulus to economic growth rather than a drain on local finances.[59]

A distinctive challenge for all these authors, and for this book, is defining the financial, political and social boundaries of the parish when it comes to church construction. Collections for building work stretched over neighbouring parishes, so accounts include money collected as 'devotion gathered at diverse churches'[60] or donations from other parishes' churchwardens,[61] while churchwardens attended one another's ales, donating sums in the name of their parish.[62] Testators often left money to churches outside their parish, usually where they were born or held property, with a concomitant loss to the potential income of their home parish, although it might also benefit from the gifts of non-resident donors.[63] Wealthier testators, even below the gentry, often left money to multiple churches – a tendency possibly mirrored in life.[64] Others had a career in court or trade but built up estates in a rural parish or returned to a childhood home for burial.[65] Meanwhile, rural parishioners often maintained links to their nearest town, where they bought and sold goods, even becoming members of urban guilds.[66] The transference of certain rites to chapels could mark a loss of income as well as of other resources, even though parochial

---

Windows of the Trades at Chartres Cathedral (Chicago, 1993); cf. Coulson, 'Crenellation', 79; Vroom, *Cathedral Building*, 134–39.

[57] Barbara Abou-El-Haj, 'The Urban Setting for Late Medieval Church Building: Reims and Its Cathedral between 1210 and 1240', *Art History* 11, no. 1 (1 March 1988): 17.

[58] Arnold Pacey, *The Maze of Ingenuity: Ideas and Idealism in the Development of Technology* (Cambridge, 1992); T. Thomas Johnson, 'Cathedral Building and the Medieval Economy', *Explorations in Entrepreneurial History* 4 (1967): 191–211; T. Thomas Johnson, 'The Economic Effects of Cathedral Building in Medieval England: A Rejoinder', *Explorations in Entrepreneurial History* 6 (Winter 1969): 170–74; Brighita Bercea, Robert B. Ekelund, and Robert D. Tollison, 'Cathedral Building as an Entry-Deterring Device', *Kyklos* 58, no. 4 (2005): 453–65.

[59] See Chapter 6, section c.iii, pp. 262–64.

[60] Charles Welch, *The Churchwardens' Accounts of the Parish of Allhallows, London Wall, in the City of London* (London, 1912), 57.

[61] E.g. at Swaffham: NRO PD 52/71, f. 42.

[62] Edmund Hobhouse, *Church-Wardens' Accounts of Croscombe, Pilton, Yatton, Tintinhull, Morebath, and St. Michael's, Bath: Ranging from A.D. 1349 to 1560* (London, 1890), 80.

[63] A. K. McHardy, 'Some Late-Medieval Eton College Wills', *The Journal of Ecclesiastical History* 28, no. 4 (1977): 391.

[64] J. J. Scarisbrick, *The Reformation and the English People* (Oxford, 1984), 4.

[65] See, for example, the case of Elias de Beckingham in Byng, 'Patrons and Their Commissions'.

[66] Gervase Rosser, 'Communities of Parish and Guild in the Late Middle Ages', in *Parish, Church and People. Local Studies in Lay Religion 1350–1750*, ed. S. J. Wright (London, 1988), 33.

Introduction

building projects could call on parishioners dwelling in chapelries for contributions.[67] Local churches also had to compete with shrines, cathedrals, monasteries, friaries, charities and hospitals for their parishioners' expendable income, although funding could flow in the opposite direction when ecclesiastical institutions donated to parochial building work.

These trends do not point to a single effect: one tends to balance another or, perhaps, to redistribute resources from wealthier to poorer parishes. Examples of sums explicitly donated from or to other villages or towns are, in fact, typically modest. Nevertheless, there are two important conclusions that must be stated: first, that many recent scholars have emphasised the parish as a source of group identity and religious commitment; but, secondly, that its boundaries were porous and its forms varied. There was the parish as a territory, with regularly beaten bounds; as an economic unit, imposing demands for tithes, rates or collections; as part of the institutional church and subject to oversight by archdeacon and bishop; as a set of institutions, interacting, occasionally, with crown or manor; and as a place of religious practice, although often with a number of centres. It is useful to think of these as different but overlapping parishes, in which only those with the greatest wealth and status participated fully. One man or woman might be part of the economic and geographic parish but excluded from the political parish; another might participate in the latter, through guild membership, say, and attend church occasionally but not be a resident or pay tithes; yet another might be too poor to contribute to collections, while still owing tithes to the rectory and attending an outlying chapel. Cultural, commercial and political bonds outside the parish have also been a focus of recent research.[68] The 'parish', then, played different parts in different identities. Indeed, in this book, 'parochial' architecture will figure most often as a symbol not of parochial but of group identity.

B) ECONOMIC AND SOCIAL CHANGE IN ENGLAND, C. 1300–1500

This section provides a short introduction to those aspects of late medieval social and economic change that most profoundly affected the ability of parishes to fund and organise church construction.

---

[67] Emma Mason, 'The Role of the English Parishioner, 1100–1500', *The Journal of Ecclesiastical History* 27, no. 1 (1976): 19; Nicholas Orme, 'Church and Chapel in Medieval England', *Transactions of the Royal Historical Society* 6 (1 January 1996): 92–93.

[68] E.g. Phillipp R. Schofield, 'England: The Family and the Village Community', in *A Companion to Britain in the Later Middle Ages*, ed. S. H. Rigby (Oxford, 2003), 26–28.

Economic and Social Change in England, c. 1300–1500

The Rural Economy before the Black Death

The earliest periods of church building touched on in this book took place at the culmination of a remarkable period of economic and demographic expansion in England. By c. 1300, the English population may have reached 4.5–6 million, having grown from 1.75 to 2.25 million in Domesday, 1086.[69] To supply this increased population, and a growing number of urban dwellers, the area of land under cultivation also rose sharply, from some 5.9 million acres in Domesday to about 10 million by the early fourteenth century.[70] Prices soared: the cost of clothing and feeding the average person more than doubled during the thirteenth century, while some rent charges rose by as much or more.[71] Demand peaked in the early fourteenth century, when medieval agriculture was at its most intensive and pressure upon the land at its greatest. The effects of these changes on parishioners, including those who would be involved in the financing of church construction, are controversial. The economic experience of rural dwellers was varied, but it is likely that a growing number suffered extreme hardship. It has been estimated that by c. 1300, two-thirds of peasant holdings in many parts of England were of half a virgate, typically fifteen acres, or less, leaving their owners 'close to the bare margin of subsistence'.[72] Tenancies had proliferated in many areas because of both subdivision and colonisation, and holdings tended to reduce in size as they increased in number. In regions with high levels of freedom, low regulation or partible inheritance, fragmentation could be extreme: in some densely and anciently populated east Norfolk manors, average holdings were of just three to five acres by the later thirteenth century, with no substantial tenants and little evidence of inter-manorial holdings.[73] Most smallholders had to rely on by-employment where

---

[69] See the discussion in Stephen Broadberry, Bruce M. S. Campbell, Alexander Klein, Mark Overton and Bas van Leeuwen, *British Economic Growth, 1270–1870* (Cambridge, 2015), Chapter 1 and especially Section 1.3; higher estimates are given in John Hatcher, *Plague, Population, and the English Economy, 1348–1530* (London, 1977); the causes and effects of these changes have been the subject of widespread dispute among scholars since the 1960s, for a useful introduction to these debates see Hatcher and Bailey, *Modelling*.

[70] Bruce M. S. Campbell, 'The Land', in *A Social History of England, 1200–1500*, ed. Rosemary Horrox and W. M. Ormrod (Cambridge, 2006), 183.

[71] Jim Bolton, 'The English Economy in the Early Thirteenth Century', in *King John: New Interpretations*, ed. S. D. Church (Woodbridge, 2003), 109–10; cf. John Hatcher, 'English Serfdom and Villeinage: Towards a Reassessment', *Past & Present*, no. 90 (1 February 1981): 7–10.

[72] R. H. Britnell, *Britain and Ireland, 1050–1530: Economy and Society* (Oxford, 2004), 172; Hatcher and Bailey, *Modelling*, 45.

[73] Bruce M. S. Campbell, 'Population Pressure, Inheritance and the Land Market in a Fourteenth-Century Peasant Community', in *Land, Kinship and Life-Cycle*, ed. R. M. Smith (Cambridge, 1984), 103; cf. Bruce M. S. Campbell, 'The Complexity of Manorial Structure in Medieval Norfolk: A Case Study', *Norfolk Archaeology* 39 (1986): 243–44.

available, but nominal wages were low, and real wages fell significantly during the thirteenth century.[74] Cottagers, commoners and subtenants bore the brunt of famine, plague and economic instability. In periods of sustained dearth, as in 1315–22, distressed peasants had little option but to sell small plots of land in order to feed themselves.[75] It will be argued that in typical years these groups, a growing majority of tenants in many places, could probably afford to give little or nothing to major communal projects – and indeed were not expected to.[76] Communities were also burdened with sustained and heavy royal taxation from the 1280s to the 1340s that would have depleted their available spare income for construction work.[77]

This experience was not universal, however. Areas with strong lordship, high regulation or impartible inheritance, as in much of the midlands and central south of England, restricted the fragmentation and sale of land. In Halesowen, Worcestershire, for example, the land market was relatively muted, and large holdings tended to pass within families, maintaining their size. Here, poorer families were much less likely to maintain their holdings and could be compelled to sell them to wealthier neighbours.[78] Where the land market was freer, as in East Anglia, economic differentiation was often the result of wealthier families benefitting from sales forced on poorer neighbours. It has been calculated that by 1279–80, in certain parts of England, 60 per cent of directly tenanted land was held by the top 20 per cent of tenants, those with a yardland or more; and 90 per cent was held by the top 40 per cent of tenants, those with at least a half-yardland.[79] Disparities in landholdings do not necessarily relate to differences in wealth, especially when comparing arable and pastoral farming, but similar inequalities can be found in taxation records, peasant housing and animal ownership: it has been estimated that around 10 per cent of rural taxpayers in Bedfordshire held almost half of the county's total sheep wealth, for example, and two-thirds of oxen wealth in 1279.[80]

---

[74] B. M. S. Campbell, *English Seigniorial Agriculture, 1250–1450* (Cambridge, 2000), 5.

[75] Ian Kershaw, 'The Great Famine and the Agrarian Crisis in England, 1315–1322', in *Peasants, Knights and Heretics*, ed. R. H. Hilton (Cambridge, 1976), 85–132; Zvi Razi, *Life, Marriage and Death in a Medieval Parish: Economy, Society and Demography in Halesowen 1270–1400* (Cambridge, 1980), 37; Campbell, 'Population Pressure', 114.

[76] Chapter 1, section c.vi, pp. 83–86.

[77] Stuart Jenks, 'The Lay Subsidies and the State of the English Economy (1275–1334)', *Vierteljahrschrift Für Sozial- Und Wirtschaftsgeschichte* 85 (1998): 4–7.

[78] Zvi Razi, 'Family, Land and the Village Community in Later Medieval England', *Past & Present*, no. 93 (1 November 1981): 4–5.

[79] Junichi Kanzaka, 'Villein Rents in Thirteenth-Century England: An Analysis of the Hundred Rolls of 1279–1280', *The Economic History Review*, 55, no. 4 (1 November 2002): 599.

[80] Kathleen Biddick, 'Missing Links: Taxable Wealth, Markets, and Stratification among Medieval English Peasants', *The Journal of Interdisciplinary History* 18, no. 2 (1 October 1987): 287; Harry

Wealthier peasants were able to capitalise on high prices, cheap labour and a rising demand for land. The poorest consumed much of what they produced and had little more that they could market, but their wealthier neighbours could pursue relatively commercial strategies: planting valuable crops, hiring labour, selling at larger markets and competitively marketing their goods.[81] This relatively small, and diminishing, group will often be the subject of this book where it seeks to identify who in the parish was able to contribute to building projects.[82]

The Rural Economy after the Black Death

From the later fourteenth century, the profile of those who could and did contribute to parish church construction changed profoundly. Up to half the population, perhaps more, died in the Black Death of 1348–49 and in further bouts over the following quarter-century. In fact, it was not until the final decades of the fifteenth century that there were the first signs of a demographic recovery, which was not fully fledged until the early sixteenth.[83] From the 1370s, a shortage of tenants led many landlords to make significant tenurial concessions to reduce emigration, attract newcomers and encourage the take-up of vacant or decaying holdings.[84] Serfdom, which was probably the typical tenure of about half of rural dwellers and nearly a half of peasant land, withered away from the late fourteenth century and was replaced with forms of contractual tenure.[85] Demesnes were also available for lease, although not only to peasants, as many lords, struggling with low prices and high wages, gave up farming them directly.[86] These trends substantially released the markets for land and labour. Determining the effects of these changes on social differentiation and communal wealth is difficult, not least because the economic experience of different areas varied greatly. Some scholars have postulated

---

Kitsikopoulos, 'Standards of Living and Capital Formation in Pre-Plague England: A Peasant Budget Model', *The Economic History Review*, 53, no. 2 (1 May 2000): 251–52.

[81] R. H. Britnell, *The Commercialisation of English Society, 1000–1500*, second edition (Manchester, 1996), 120–23; Kathleen Biddick, 'Medieval English Peasants and Market Involvement', *The Journal of Economic History* 45, no. 4 (1985): 828–30.

[82] E.g. Chapter 1, sections c.vi and d.ii, pp. 83–86 and 98–99.

[83] Broadberry et al., *British Economic Growth*, 3.

[84] Phillipp R. Schofield, 'Tenurial Developments and the Availability of Customary Land in a Later Medieval Community', *The Economic History Review*, 49, no. 2 (1 May 1996): 261–64.

[85] Bailey has argued that villein tenure declined in many places as early as the 1350s to the 1380s; the usual chronology is around 1370–1410: Mark Bailey, *The Decline of Serfdom in Late Medieval England: From Bondage to Freedom* (Woodbridge, 2014), 4–5, 287; Bruce M. S. Campbell, 'The Agrarian Problem in the Early Fourteenth Century', *Past & Present* 188, no. 1 (1 August 2005): 36.

[86] Christopher Dyer, *An Age of Transition? Economy and Society in England in the Later Middle Ages* (Oxford, 2005), 195–97.

Introduction

a general trend to larger holdings at all levels of peasant society,[87] but others identify a widening of economic divisions as the upper peasantry benefitted disproportionately from low land values and an active land market, if perhaps not until the later fifteenth century.[88] Jane Whittle has demonstrated that, by the early sixteenth century, landholdings in some east Norfolk manors were highly differentiated, with a small elite of one or two farmers with exceptionally large holdings (over 100 acres) at one end of the economic spectrum and a majority with under twenty acres at the other.[89] One such wealthy farmer was Robert Bisshop, who owned over sixty-five acres of customary, freehold and leasehold land in thirty-nine pieces across six manors, as well as leasing a demesne.[90] In some parts of England, these men, and their families, appear regularly in the archaeological and documentary record of donations to church construction, especially from the later fifteenth century.[91]

However, it is by no means exclusively this group that was able to fund architectural patronage, especially before the later fifteenth century. In many places the upper and middling peasantry below this 'yeoman' class grew too, both in quantity and in the size of their holdings. Even among economically polarised communities in east Norfolk, most had a large core of tenants with holdings of twenty to fifty acres in the early sixteenth century. Nevertheless, the number and proportion of wealthier tenants varied widely across the country, and large holdings could take several generations to appear.[92] In Lawrence Poos' study of Essex manors, the proportion of holdings over forty acres doubled to 4 per cent between the early fourteenth and early fifteenth centuries,[93] but on one Leicestershire manor holdings of over thirty acres increased sevenfold between 1341 and 1477, forming a majority of holdings.[94] Evidence of better housing, diets and clothing, and more leisure pursuits also indicate the increasing wealth of some peasants.[95] Nevertheless, larger holdings were often

---

[87] M. M. Postan, *The Medieval Economy and Society: An Economic History of Britain in the Middle Ages* (London, 1972), 139–42.

[88] Jane Whittle, *The Development of Agrarian Capitalism: Land and Labour in Norfolk, 1440–1580* (Oxford, 2000), Chapter 4; Christopher Dyer, *Standards of Living in the Later Middle Ages: Social Change in England, C. 1200–1520* (Cambridge, 1989), 142.

[89] Whittle, *Agrarian Capitalism*, 190.   [90] Ibid., 186–88.

[91] See Cambridgeshire examples in Chapter 1, section d.iii, pp. 106–07. Men such as Robert Parman in Chevington: Christopher Dyer, 'A Suffolk Farmer in the Fifteenth Century', *The Agricultural History Review* 55, no. 1 (1 January 2007): 12.

[92] Campbell, 'Population Pressure'.

[93] From 14/672 holdings to 11/316: L. R. Poos, *A Rural Society After the Black Death: Essex 1350–1525* (Cambridge, 1991), Tables 1.1 and 1.2, p. 16.

[94] Dyer, *Standards*, Table 11, p. 141; Christopher Dyer, 'Tenant Farming and Farmers. The West Midlands', in *AHEW*, ed. Edward Miller, vol. 3 (Cambridge, 1991), 636.

[95] Dyer, *Transition*, 147–57; Dyer, *Standards*, 166–69.

unstable, breaking up as a result of financial loss or failure of heirs, and it was not until the end of the fifteenth century that they were widely preserved intact.[96] In fact, increasingly stable large holdings and lengthy tenures, especially of demesne lands, when combined with demographic recovery, reducing wages and increasing prices probably created an Indian summer for parish church construction in the decades before the Reformation. The next section[97] will suggest that, from around this time, there is evidence of a resurgence in parochial and great church building projects. This book will argue that the growing number of yardlanders and half-yardlanders in many places enabled a larger proportion of the parish to contribute to building work and provided greater expendable wealth among wealthier groups, thus facilitating large amounts of church construction during the long fifteenth century.[98] Not all those able to donate did so, however. Rather, growing prosperity among middling groups sharpened ideas about who should finance architectural work.[99]

Within many parishes there were still large numbers who could afford, or were expected, to contribute little or nothing to communal projects. Smallholdings reduced in number in many places but did not disappear, despite the availability of land: Poos found that the proportions of holdings under five acres in some Essex manors were roughly the same in the early fifteenth as in the early fourteenth century,[100] and, Britnell's survey of manors in eastern England revealed that holdings under ten acres contributed a substantial majority of tenancies, although the size of the smallest holdings had risen since the pre-Black Death era.[101] Elsewhere, however, numbers and proportions of smallholders fell dramatically: on the same Leicestershire manor cited earlier, holdings of less than eleven acres declined from 52 per cent in 1341 to 16 per cent in 1477.[102] Some tenants were undoubtedly restricted by the cost of entry fines and rents, but smallholders were also able to attract better wages. Rates improved considerably from the 1370s until the late fifteenth century, as did fringe benefits such as clothing and food.[103] The

---

[96] Dyer, *Standards*, 142–43; Christopher Dyer, 'Changes in the Size of Peasant Holdings in Some West Midland Villages 1400–1540', in *Land, Kinship and Life-Cycle*, ed. Richard M. Smith (Cambridge, 1984), 292–93; Mark Bailey, *Medieval Suffolk: An Economic and Social History, 1200–1500* (Woodbridge, 2007), 251.

[97] See pp. 36–45. [98] Chapter 1, sections c.iii, pp. 74–75.

[99] Chapter 1, section c.vii, pp. 92–94.

[100] Poos, *Rural Society*, Tables 1.1 and 1.2.

[101] R. H. Britnell, 'Tenant Farming and Farmers: Eastern England', in *AHEW*, ed. Edward Miller, vol. 3 (Cambridge, 1991), Tables 7.1–7.2, pp. 614–15.

[102] Dyer, *Standards*, 141.

[103] However, the availability of reliable high-waged employment and increases in income are disputed: John Hatcher, 'Unreal Wages: Long-Run Living Standards and the "Golden Age" of the Fifteenth Century', in *Commercial Activity, Markets and Entrepreneurs in the Middle Ages*, ed. Ben Dodds and C. D. Liddy (Woodbridge, 2011), 9–11; see the review in Christopher Dyer, 'A

Introduction

tide may have begun to turn around the end of the fifteenth century as competition for land and work increased – indeed evidence for large collections for building work is considerably more plentiful before 1500 and includes the largest, at Bodmin in 1469–72 (Table 1.1).[104] Where accounts run for long periods, increasingly exclusive financial models for building work can be found from the later fifteenth century.[105]

The relationship between economic and social differentiation among peasants is difficult to assess. How distinct wealthier groups were, their sense of group consciousness and their relationship to formal power structures are controversial topics. Historians from the Toronto School divided the peasantry into strata based on the regularity with which they held office – usually ranked across several levels from 'A' downwards.[106] Families from the 'A' group, probably those chiefly involved in running and financing church construction, dominated livestock ownership, involvement in the land market and ale brewing, the employment of servants and labourers, and access to credit. Group-consciousness may be indicated by high levels of intragroup cooperation and intergroup friction (although friction between 'A' families could be high too). These properties may have been essential to both corporate fundraising and organisational delegation, not least in building work.[107] The critique of this school is well-known, particularly concerning the problems of tracing families through time and of assigning individuals to groups over lengthy time periods, but their work does point to the tendency of wealthy peasants to dominate the civic life of the parish and to conflict with other, poorer groups – findings consistent with both the central arguments of this book and the work of more recent scholars.[108]

Golden Age Rediscovered: Labourers' Wages in the Fifteenth Century', in *Money, Prices and Wages: Essays in Honour of Professor Nicholas Mayhew*, ed. M. Allen and D. Coffman (2014), 180–95; Broadberry et al., *British Economic Growth*, Chapter 6.3.3.

[104] N.B. these examples are nearly all from urban settings. Broadberry et al., *British Economic Growth*, 276, Figure 6.07.

[105] Gabriel Byng, 'The Chronology and Financing of the Perpendicular Work at Saffron Walden, Essex', *Essex Archaeology and History*, 6 (2016), 329–43, 338–39.

[106] Of the many publications of the Toronto School, the following are foundational: J. A. Raftis, *Tenure and Mobility: Studies in the Social History of the Mediaeval English Village* (Toronto, 1964); J. A. Raftis, 'Social Structures in Five East Midland Villages: A Study of Possibilities in the Use of Court Roll Data', *The Economic History Review*, 18, no. 1 (1 January 1965): 83–100; J. A. Raftis, 'The Concentration of Responsibility in Five Villages', *Mediaeval Studies* 28, no. 1 (1 January 1966): 92–118.

[107] Stephen H. Rigby, *English Society in the Later Middle Ages: Class, Status and Gender* (Basingstoke, 1995), 47–49.

[108] Zvi Razi, 'The Toronto School's Reconstitution of Medieval Peasant Society: A Critical View', *Past & Present*, no. 85 (1 November 1979): 141–57; Keith Wrightson, 'Medieval Villagers in Perspective', *Peasant Studies* 7 (1978): 203–16. For accounts of wealthier peasants in visitations and juries, see Ian Forrest, *The Detection of Heresy in Late Medieval England* (Oxford, 2005), 70–75; R. B. Goheen, 'Peasant Politics? Village Community and the Crown in Fifteenth-Century England', *The American*

There were, of course, enormous variations between regions, manors and farms, based not only on social and economic structures but also on climate and topography. Many of these factors were no doubt of critical importance to building work but their net effect is hard to account for. For example, some virtues useful to the management and financing of church building – 'order, hierarchy and neighbourliness' – are associated with nucleated villages.[109] However, in a polyfocal village, the church building may have acquired heightened importance as a site for socialising and for demonstrating civic and religious solidarity. Did closed and stable communities encourage the necessary neighbourliness and local pride for communal fundraising, or did open and expanding ones provide an influx of managerial talent, ambitious outsiders and architectural awareness, as well as newcomers keen to demonstrate their local commitment and piety? Did divided lordship spur aristocratic patronage or discourage it? Did ecclesiastical or noble lords help forge links to cathedral or castle masons, or were lords of a single manor more effective allies, enjoying a closer intimacy with the villagers and their church? Did competition between pious institutions dilute the donations of the faithful or stimulate it? Did proximity to towns or markets encourage the spread of styles and improve access to workmen or raise the cost of materials and labour? Did peasant resistance find a corollary in communal building projects on 'their' church, or was the fabric understood as being a place for cooperation with the manor? This book will make some inroads into these questions but provide few complete answers.

The Urban Economy and the Governance of Towns

The number, size and distribution of towns in England grew for about three centuries into the later thirteenth century. At least 170 were founded between the late eleventh and early fourteenth centuries, largely as lords granted borough status to existing settlements.[110] Estimates for the percentage of the English population that lived in towns in 1300 vary from around 10 to 20 per cent, perhaps twice the equivalent figure in

---

Historical Review 96, no. 1 (1 February 1991): 47; for an earlier period, see, for example: Phillipp R. Schofield, 'Endettement et Credit Dans La Campagne Anglaise Au Moyen Age', in *Endettement Paysan et Crédit Rural Dans l'Europe Médiévale et Moderne*, ed. M. Berthe (Toulouse, 1998), 69–97.
[109] Campbell, 'The Land', 209.
[110] R. H. Britnell, 'Boroughs, Markets and Trade in Northern England, 1000–1216', in *Progress and Problems in Medieval England*, ed. Richard Britnell and John Hatcher (Cambridge, 1996), 46–49; Maurice Beresford, *New Towns of the Middle Ages: Town Plantation in England, Wales and Gascony* (London, 1967), 336 and Table XI.2.

Introduction

1086.[111] Scholarship regarding the following two centuries has been divided on the question of urban decline. Certainly the number of urban dwellers fell between 1320 and 1520, but the proportion of England's population living in towns may have changed little.[112] A network of markets survived, most people lived within a few miles of a town, and, indeed, there was a considerable amount of urban church building.[113] The economic experience of individual towns, and so their capacity to build, was highly varied, depending on patterns in emigration, trade, geography, commerce and the impositions or investments of lords.[114] While London, home to several case studies in this book, and some other large towns showed signs of economic and demographic success, many experienced severe decline by the early sixteenth century, as at York, Coventry and Lincoln.[115] Some smaller towns, and many rural settlements, grew with the clothing industry after the mid-fifteenth century, often concentrating wealth in the hands of merchants. As in villages, economic performance was mediated by social structure in freeing expendable income for church construction. The economic success of Lavenham in Suffolk from the 1460s, for example, stimulated high levels of personal wealth among some residents, as is evidenced in wills and housing.[116] This created sufficient expendable income to finance an exceptional church building programme. Indeed, because of the greater document survival rate of sources for urban church construction, the examples covered in this book are drawn largely from small towns with fewer than 2,000 inhabitants, of which there were about 600 in this period.[117] It will be noted that some, but not all, of these projects can be shown to have been in places which experienced economic and demographic growth over the late middle ages.[118]

Towns had a complex family of governing structures that could oversee communal projects such as church construction. Urban government was increasingly organised under elected councils, with a hierarchy of

---

[111] Christopher Dyer, 'How Urbanised Was Medieval England?', in *Peasants & Townsmen in Medieval Europe*, ed. Jean-Marie Duvosquel and Erik Thoen (Gent, 1995), 172–78.

[112] Alan Dyer, 'Urban Decline in England, 1377–1525', in *Towns in Decline AD 100–1600*, ed. T. R. Slater (Aldershot, 2000), 281–82; see Rigby's review of Dyer's methodology: Stephen H. Rigby, 'Urban Population in Late Medieval England: The Evidence of the Lay Subsidies', *Economic History Review* 63, no. 2 (May 2010): 393–417.

[113] Christopher Dyer, 'The Hidden Trade of the Middle Ages', in *Everyday Life in Medieval England* (London, 1994), 288–89.

[114] Christopher Dyer, *Making a Living in the Middle Ages: The People of Britain 850–1520* (New Haven, 2002), Chapter 9.i.

[115] Alan Dyer, *Decline and Growth in English Towns 1400–1640* (Cambridge, 1995), 25–27.

[116] Bailey, *Medieval Suffolk*, 285.

[117] Christopher Dyer, 'The Archaeology of Medieval Small Towns', *Medieval Archaeology* 47, no. 1 (1 June 2003): 87–88.

[118] See pp. 52–53.

offices held by wealthier inhabitants and headed by the mayor and bailiffs.[119] The privileges held by individual boroughs varied considerably, from those where the burgesses were able to elect officers, to those where the town's overlords controlled the courts, collected fines and tolls, and appointed officers.[120] When managed by an agent of their aristocratic or ecclesiastical overlord, burgesses might have little autonomy.[121] Indeed, the smallest towns were no bigger than villages, with as few as 300 inhabitants. However, the case should not be overstated: many small towns gained control of parts of their administration or revenues, especially after the later fourteenth century, through guilds and through leasing parts of the borough.[122] The ways in which urban government could be involved in church construction were varied, depending above all on the development of both civic and parochial institutions. It will be argued that, in smaller towns, coterminous with a single parish, civic bodies tended to initiate and oversee parochial projects. The example of Totnes, where church construction was carried out by a specialised administration under the ultimate instruction of the mayor, will be discussed, as will towns where the civic government staffed fabric committees (Louth) or instructed churchwardens over building projects that they were notionally running (Bridgwater).[123] In cities, as in villages, local parochial leaders probably directed church building projects, although, in the former, typically with some oversight from civic institutions.

The social and economic restrictions which applied to some rural parishioners in contributing to building projects were also found in towns. The wealth and power of the mercantile elite of the largest settlements has been widely discussed in the debate on urban 'oligarchy' but is rarely relevant to this book, in which most case studies are found in small towns.[124] Historians of the latter have tended to emphasise their

---

[119] For the relationship between the development of government and urban topography see Sarah Rees Jones, *York: The Making of a City 1068–1350* (Oxford, 2013), Chapter 6.

[120] Stephen H. Rigby, 'Boston and Grimsby in the Middle Ages: An Administrative Contrast', *Journal of Medieval History* 10 (1984): 60.

[121] Stephen H. Rigby and Elizabeth Ewan, 'Government, Power and Authority 1300–1540', in *The Cambridge Urban History of Britain*, ed. D. M. Palliser, vol. 1 (Cambridge, 2000), 291–312; R. H. Hilton, 'Medieval Market Towns and Simple Commodity Production', *Past & Present*, no. 109 (1985): 13–15.

[122] Mark Bailey, 'Self-Government in the Small Towns of Late Medieval England', in *Commercial Activity, Markets and Entrepreneurs in the Middle Ages*, ed. Ben Dodds and C. D. Liddy (Woodbridge, 2011), 1–24.

[123] Chapter 4, section c.ii, pp. 192–93.

[124] E.g. Susan Reynolds, 'Medieval Urban History and the History of Political Thought', *Urban History Yearbook*, 1982, 14–23; Stephen H. Rigby, 'Urban "Oligarchy" in Late Medieval England', in *Towns and Townspeople in the Fifteenth Century*, ed. J. A. F. Thomson (Gloucester, 1988), 62–86.

Introduction

relatively flat economic structure, evident in the occupation of civic offices by retailers and craftsmen, in taxation returns and in the material culture of urban houses.[125] In towns such as Bodmin, with relatively low per capita wealth, the financial burden of building work had to be shared widely, through large collections. Nevertheless, even small towns had a large body of wage earners, unemployed or indigent, and richer families dominated civic institutions.[126] Indeed, it will be argued that Bodmin was exceptional – most urban building projects surveyed in this book were in towns with individually wealthier inhabitants, and indeed smaller populations, and responsibility for financing and commissioning new architecture was concentrated in the hands of a wealthy few who also participated in civic government.[127] The fear of urban conflict as well as the ideal of a united but tightly structured urban society may have encouraged donations to building work, particularly by the wealthy: a disproportionately large number of urban contracts compared to rural ones name the 'whole parish' as contractee – even when it is demonstrably untrue – while construction displayed the generosity, piety and good governance of civic leaders.[128]

The Aristocracy

Lords great and small benefitted from rising rents and the growing area of cultivation up to, and in some places after, the early fourteenth century. Many scholars have argued that the aristocracy in general, and the gentry in particular, demonstrated, and augmented, their social ascendancy and sense of group identity in building work on parish churches.[129] These social changes find their corollary in knightly tombs, brasses and windows, for which antiquarian and archaeological evidence begins to survive from this period.[130] Nevertheless, lords' ability to exploit the increasing demand for land financially was constricted by custom: increases in rent and entry fines rarely kept up with land values.[131] The gentry, who feature most often in the history of parish church

---

[125] Dyer, *Standards*, 24–25; Susan Reynolds, *An Introduction to the History of English Medieval Towns* (Oxford, 1977), 173–77; James Davis, *Medieval Market Morality: Life, Law and Ethics in the English Marketplace, 1200–1500* (Cambridge, 2011), 296–97; Dyer, 'Small Towns', 102–03.

[126] Hilton, 'Medieval Market Towns', 15–17; for an earlier period see R. H. Hilton, 'Small Town Society in England Before the Black Death', *Past & Present* 105, no. 1 (1 November 1984): 67–68.

[127] Chapter 1, section c.iii, pp. 74–75.   [128] Chapter 4, section d.i, pp. 204–05.

[129] Saul, *Provincial Life*, 152; R. H. Hilton, *A Medieval Society: The West Midlands at the End of the Thirteenth Century* (Cambridge, 1966), 50–51; Brown, *Popular Piety*, 115–32.

[130] Nigel Saul, *English Church Monuments in the Middle Ages: History and Representation* (London, 2009), 207–08.

[131] Hatcher, 'Serfdom and Villeinage', 15; Dyer, *Making a Living*, 141–42; Campbell, 'Agrarian Problem', 54.

construction, tended to have smaller and less valuable manors than those of nobles, royalty or the great ecclesiastical institutions.[132] The more minor figures among them often held one of several manors within a parish, which may have encouraged competition between lords, stimulating gifts to the church. Indeed, they were important figures locally, probably knowing and known by their tenants and directly involved in local agriculture and their manor court, and as a result were better able to encourage, coerce or support architectural endeavours.[133] They would have had a close connection to their parish church, the site of marriages and burials as well as of regular worship. Nevertheless, most had limited means, if larger than any other household in the locality, and, as will be shown, few would have been able to afford architectural patronage single-handedly.[134] Cooperation between gentry and tenants in building projects, perhaps underlined by deference and coercion as well as common purpose, is the subject of Chapters 2 and 5.

From the later fourteenth century, both noble and gentry landlords began to adapt to an era of high wages, low prices, stagnant rents and a scarcity of tenants. The move to leasing demesnes or whole manors, the rise of contractual tenure and the commutation of any remaining labour services have already been noted.[135] Many were compelled to offer better conditions of tenure or lower rents to encourage the take-up of land: a half-yardlander on the Worcester manor of Hanbury paid as little as half the rents and services in 1400 that he would have done a century before, and entry fines in some places became little more than a nominal payment in recognition of lordship.[136] Leasehold and demesne rents were also likely to fall during the first seventy years of the century. This was not uniformly the case, however, and the move from customary to various forms of fixed-term tenure allowed some lords the freedom to raise rents.[137]

Generalising about the impact on the gross incomes of individual families and institutions is very difficult, however. Many lords found that their lands declined in value during the first half of the fifteenth century, although proportions varied substantially in different parts of the country – by modest amounts in economically successful counties such as Cornwall but by as much as a third on some northern estates by the

---

[132] Campbell, 'The Land', 204–06.
[133] R. H. Britnell, 'The Pastons and Their Norfolk', *The Agricultural History Review* 36, no. 2 (1988): 141–42.
[134] See e.g. Chapter 2, section d, pp. 122–24.
[135] Mark Bailey, *The English Manor, C. 1200–1500* (Manchester, 2002), 108.
[136] Christopher Dyer, *Lords and Peasants in a Changing Society: The Estates of the Bishopric of Worcester, 680–1540* (Cambridge, 1980), 243–44.
[137] Bailey, *Decline of Serfdom*, 32–35.

Introduction

1460s.[138] Nevertheless, some gentry, nobles and even ecclesiastical institutions were able to acquire more land, recouping losses through marriage, purchase, patronage or inheritance.[139] Enterprising landlords leased or bought land from other manors for commercial pastoral farming and launched industrial initiatives.[140] Others lived off their rents and tried to dissuade tenants from leaving. Monasteries appropriated parish churches – where they could – and new collegiate churches were founded, occasionally with large estates.[141] H. L. Gray's analysis of the gross incomes of lay aristocratic society in 1436 will be given later and contrasted with the changing cost of architecture.[142] There were signs of a recovery after about 1470, as revenues increased through rising rents and prices, intensifying in the early decades of the next century. The following section will use Richard Morris's figures on great church construction to argue for a modest upswing in building work after the 1470s. Some gentry worked successfully in the service of others. Sir John de Wingfield, for example, made his fortune in the service of the Black Prince and funded the rebuilding of Wingfield parish church.[143]

The Parish Officers

The identity and powers of the lay administrators of the parish were locally variable. The most universal were the churchwardens, referred to by a host of different names, whose history has been well told elsewhere and will be briefly summarised here.[144] The earliest evidence for the appointment of permanent officers in England begins in the thirteenth century. Peter Quinel's Exeter statutes of 1287 were the first to lay out the responsibilities of 'five or six worthy parishioners', making them accountable 'for the defects of the church'.[145] Quinel may have been trying to standardise existing practice: there were '*procuratores*' at All Saints, Bristol,

---

[138] Dyer, *Making a Living*, 337–38.
[139] Carpenter, *Locality and Polity*, 55; Simon Payling, *Political Society in Lancastrian England* (Oxford, 1991), 9; S. M Wright, *The Derbyshire Gentry in the Fifteenth Century* (Chesterfield, 1983), 26–27.
[140] Robert C. Allen, *Enclosure and the Yeoman* (Oxford, 1992), 43–47; Whittle, *Agrarian Capitalism*, 199; Carpenter, *Locality and Polity*, Chapter 5.
[141] The new parochial nave added to Fotheringhay College in 1434, founded in 1411, is discussed in Chapter 5, section b.i, pp. 216–18. R. M. Serjeantson and W. R. D. Adkins, eds., *VCH Northamptonshire*, vol. 2 (London, 1906), 170–77.
[142] Chapter 2, section d, pp. 124–26.
[143] Mark Bailey, 'Sir John de Wingfield and the Foundation of Wingfield College', in *Wingfield College and Its Patrons: Piety and Patronage in Medieval Suffolk*, ed. Peter Bloore and Edward A. Martin (Woodbridge, 2015), 44–45.
[144] The foundation work on this subject is: Charles Drew, *Early Parochial Organisation in England: The Origins of the Office of Churchwarden* (London, 1954), 6.
[145] F. M. Powicke and C. R. Cheney, eds., *Councils and Synods, 1205–1313*, vol. 2 (Oxford, 1964), 1008.

for example, in 1261, and similar arrangements can be found in some twelfth-century parishes.[146] These changes have been associated by many scholars, following Charles Drew, with the development of new legal responsibilities for nave repair and, subsequently, the provision of liturgical equipment by the laity in some dioceses from the 1220s.[147] Around the end of the century, statutes passed in first Canterbury (1279–92) and then York provinces (c. 1306) indicate that the practice was universal.[148] Although determining a chronology for the sophisticated and lively political world evident in late medieval churchwardens' accounts is difficult, the increase in per capita wealth among many levels of local society evident from the later fourteenth century is suggestive. Other authors have noted the rise of the equity courts, especially the growth in petitions to Chancery and the creation of the Court of the Star Chamber and the Court of Requests, enabling parishes to take corporate action over property, thefts and loans.[149]

The parochial body with the greatest authority was the parish masters, often termed 'the six or eight men', 'council', 'chief men', 'goodmen', 'substantial men' or even 'the parish'. The masters were usually made up of four to twelve wealthy men who had often already served in more junior parochial offices, and were probably the precursor of the sixteenth-century vestry.[150] It remains unclear how widespread these bodies were, what control they had over the churchwardens and other bodies, how formally their powers were constituted and what the chronology of their development was. However, examples can be found in both urban and country parishes, from London to rural Devon, in the long fifteenth century.[151] They had their own funds and accounts, and had a role in

---

[146] E. G. C. F. Atchley, 'Some Documents Relating to the Parish Church of All Saints, Bristol', *Archaeological Journal* 58 (1901), 163.

[147] Drew, *Early Parochial Organisation*, 15–16.

[148] Powicke and Cheney, *C&S*, 1964, 2:1122–23, c. 7; 497–98, c. 44.

[149] French, *People*, 38–43; Beat A. Kümin, *The Shaping of a Community: The Rise and Reformation of the English Parish, C. 1400–1560* (Aldershot, 1996), 17–20.

[150] For evidence of the operation of Elizabethan vestries see Ian W. Archer, *The Pursuit of Stability: Social Relations in Elizabethan London* (Cambridge, 1991), 69–74; P. Seaward, 'Gilbert Sheldon, the London Vestries, and the Defence of the Church', in *The Politics of Religion in Restoration England*, ed. T. Harris, P. Seaward, and M. Goldie (Oxford, 1990); Clive Burgess, 'Pre-Reformation Churchwardens' Accounts and Parish Government: Lessons from London and Bristol', *The English Historical Review* 117, no. 471 (1 April 2002): 331; Paul Kissack, 'The London Parish Vestry, C. 1560–1640' (MPhil Thesis, Cambridge, 1998).

[151] On the 'masters' see the following foundational works: Clive Burgess, 'Shaping the Parish: St Mary at Hill, London, in the Fifteenth Century', in *The Cloister and the World: Essays in Medieval History in Honour of Barbara Harvey*, ed. John Blair and Brian Golding (Oxford, 1996), 264–69; Clive Burgess, *The Church Records of St Andrew Hubbard, Eastcheap, C. 1450-C. 1570* (London, 1999), xxvii–xxix; Burgess, 'Lessons'; Eamon Duffy, *The Voices of Morebath: Reformation and Rebellion in an English Village* (New Haven, 2001), 24–27.

Introduction

appointing, instructing and auditing the churchwardens. It is likely that they did not develop consistently in all localities and were varied in organisation and authority. It will be suggested later that they were supplanted in small towns by municipal bodies.[152] Chapters 3 and 4 will also discuss the powers of the parish assembly – typically an annual meeting of some or many of the male householders (and perhaps others) which in many places oversaw or approved the appointment of officers – and the auditors, a senior committee often identical with the parish masters, who reviewed the churchwardens' accounts when this was not done at the assembly.[153]

Individual lights, chantries, altars and stores had their own wardens, sources of income and accounts, which are occasionally discernible in surviving accounts and which contributed, both directly and indirectly, to church building.[154] Some parishes had sidesmen, groups of parishioners who would support the wardens during visitations or synods and assist with other parish business. Larger parishes could also have rent or rate collectors.[155] Ad hoc temporary bodies could also be created, such as those that ran church construction, which are termed in this book, for convenience and in line with the terminology used on many major building sites, 'fabric committees', and their officers, 'fabric wardens'.[156] The complexity of parish government was highly variable, both between places and across time: greatest, of course, in larger and richer parishes with more business and greater resources to be organised, whether in town or village. Several scholars, however, have noted differences in the financial regimes of urban and rural parishes and particularly the large rental incomes that attached to the former and active fundraising required by the latter.[157] Major building projects in both, however, would require new sources of income.[158]

Of these lesser parochial and inter-parochial bodies, it is religious guilds and more informal social groups that figure most regularly in both archaeological and documentary evidence for church patronage.[159] Eamon Duffy gives a three-part account of guild functions: the maintenance of lights, attendance at funerals, and the holding of a communal feast.[160] The distribution of guilds varied considerably – found in about half of parishes in East Anglia, three-quarters in Cambridgeshire and as many as six per parish in Cornwall – and authors have found little

---

[152] See Chapter 4, section c.ii, pp. 192–93.   [153] Kümin, *Shaping*, Chapter 6.2.
[154] E.g. the new aisle roofs at St Mary-at-Hill, London, in 1526: Chapter 3, section c.ii, p. 153.
[155] E.g. Chapter 1, section c.iii, p. 76.   [156] Chapter 4, section c.i, pp. 185–200.
[157] See particularly: Clive Burgess and Beat Kümin, 'Penitential Bequests and Parish Regimes in Late Medieval England', *The Journal of Ecclesiastical History* 44, no. 4 (1993): 610–30.
[158] Chapter 1, section b.iii, pp. 62–63.
[159] Chapter 1, sections b.i–ii and c.v, pp. 82–83, 201–02.   [160] Duffy, *Stripping*, 143.

correlation with population, wealth or economic activity.[161] Guilds with wealthy members, such as the Holy Trinity Guild at Wisbech, could build up substantial property portfolios and current accounts, lending money for profit, holding ales and receiving legacies – as well as charging entrance fees – although they also tended to have greater demands on their income.[162] Most, however, were not especially wealthy, with regular income and possessions worth a few pounds, and made modest donations to fabric accounts. Five guilds at Swaffham contributed £8 over eleven years to the new steeple, for example.[163] However, financing was only one way in which guilds aided church construction: they also trained parochial officers, ran ales and collections, or, in exceptional circumstances, took charge of building work directly (as for the Berry chapel in Bodmin, Cornwall).[164] The careers of men who passed through the ranks of guild government and into positions where they ran church construction will be reconstructed later.[165] Building on the work of Gervase Rosser, recent historians have tended to emphasise that guilds did not undermine parochial integrity but rather intensified or extended it.[166] This model of subordination to parochial authority suggests that they would have led projects only with the assent and oversight of local authorities. The guild of St Mary at St Cuthbert, Wells, for example, contracted for a new reredos in 1470 but agreed the iconography with the master of the town.[167]

Characterising parochial government as an executive pyramid that ran from master or municipality, to churchwarden, then out to a host of junior stores and guilds, with a participatory assembly offering ultimate if occasional oversight probably implies greater formality, hierarchy and uniformity than existed in many cases, perhaps especially in smaller rural parishes. A functionalist analysis is equally misleading – masters could be auditors, for example, while wardens often shared responsibilities with other institutions. Chapters 3 and 4 will argue that one activity, church building, could be run as easily by churchwardens or fabric wardens, who

---

[161] Ken Farnhill, *Guilds and the Parish Community in Late Medieval East Anglia, C. 1470–1550* (Woodbridge, 2001), 30–34; Virginia R. Bainbridge, *Gilds in the Medieval Countryside: Social and Religious Change in Cambridgeshire, c.1350–1558* (Woodbridge, 1996), 25–33; J. Mattingly, 'Medieval Parish Guilds of Cornwall', *Journal of the Royal Institution of Cornwall* 10, no. 3 (1989): 308.
[162] R. B. Pugh, ed., *VCH Cambridgeshire*, vol. 4 (London, 2002), 255–56.
[163] Farnhill, *Guilds*, 120.
[164] Chapter 4, section c.iv, pp. 201–02; cf. St Mary and Holy Cross guilds at Abingdon, Gervase Rosser, *The Art of Solidarity in the Middle Ages: Guilds in England 1250–1550* (Oxford, 2015), 196–97.
[165] Chapter 3, section d.i, pp. 162–63.
[166] Rosser, 'Parish and Guild', 42; cf. Farnhill, *Guilds*, 18–19; French, *People*, 81; Kümin, *Shaping*, 102; Duffy, *Stripping*, 149; Rosser, *Solidarity*, 48–49.
[167] Wells City Records, Wells Convocation Book I, f.89; French, *People*, 201.

Introduction

in turn could be appointed or instructed by the masters, assembly or municipal government, according to custom or institutional development. Rather, parochial government consisted of a collection of mutually dependent institutions, each customarily identified with a certain, locally variable core of tasks and subset of parishioners, but which engaged with one another with considerable flexibility in order to take decisions, manage income and carry out a wide and varying range of functions.

The managerial and financial structures surveyed in this book had considerable continuity until the Edwardian Reformation, although increasing pressure on guilds and chantries, however variable and discontinuous, is evident a decade before their dissolution.[168] Limitations on land given for the benefit of parish churches in the 1530s, and a possible decline of ales and gift-giving after the 1540s, coincided with new costs for royal administration and worship, and tightening parish budgets, at least in some places.[169] Nevertheless, the most important parochial institutions surveyed in this book would remain at the centre of parish life. The office of churchwarden continued to handle building maintenance and liturgical items, and was held by wealthy parishioners in many places, while, even if novel in its Elizabethan form, the vestry bore a considerable resemblance to the masters.[170] Indeed, parochial organisation became increasingly sophisticated as parishes took on new responsibilities, and junior positions multiplied.[171] The latest examples surveyed in this book, of the 1530s and later, point to the strength and flexibility of parochial organisation through this period.

C) CHANGES IN COST AND MONEY SUPPLY

The economic environment in which churches were constructed was transformed by changes in the price and availability of labour, materials, transport and coin.[172] Variations in building costs were highly local – a church near a good quarry, wood or waterway would be much cheaper to construct than one at some distance, for example – but there were also national trends in prices and wages. Sources available for the eighty years before the Black Death indicate that the nominal wages of building labourers, masons and carpenters were low and stable (Figures I.1–I.2).

---

[168] Robert Tittler, *The Reformation and the Towns in England: Politics and Political Culture, c. 1540–1640* (Oxford, 1998), 68–69; Caroline Litzenberger, *The English Reformation and the Laity: Gloucestershire, 1540–1580* (Cambridge, 2002), 51–53.
[169] Kümin, *Shaping*, 204–08, 213–17.
[170] Keith Wrightson and David Levine, *Poverty and Piety in an English Village: Terling, 1525–1700* (Oxford, 1995); J. S. Craig, 'Co-Operation and Initiatives: Elizabethan Churchwardens and the Parish Accounts of Mildenhall', *Social History* 18, no. 3 (1993): 363–65; Kissack, 'Vestry'.
[171] Archer, *Pursuit of Stability*, 58–99.   [172] Cf. pp. 83–92.

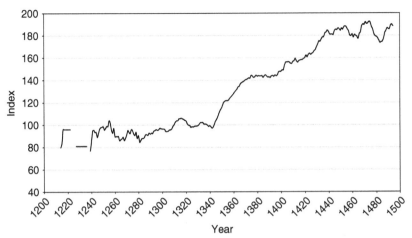

Figure I.1 Ten year moving average for building wages (all professions), 1208–1500. Source: Based on David Farmer, *AHEW*, II and III (Cambridge, 1988 and 1991).

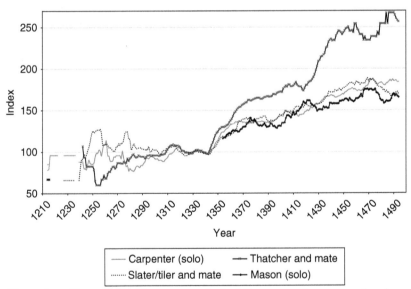

Figure I.2 Ten year moving average for building wages (carpenter, thatcher, tiler and mason), 1208–1500. Source: Based on David Farmer, *AHEW*, II and III (Cambridge, 1988 and 1991).

Introduction

There was a slight increase in labourers' day wages from the 1310s to the 1330s, rising from 1½d to 2d.[173] Caution is necessary, however: source material is available from only a few locations, largely in the south of England, often with little information about rank or skill, while nominal wages disregard often substantial payments in food, accommodation or clothing.[174] For the price of finished and raw building materials, no subsequent survey has replaced the work, now much out of date, of James E. Thorold Rogers. Again, the records are patchy, averages suspect and regional variety is not taken into account. A further serious problem is that Rogers tabulated together sale and purchase prices, and assumed a uniformity of weights and measures. He identified a period of price stability from 1265 to 1300, and a rise in the period 1300–20, especially during the famine years.[175] A graph of his figures is broadly supportive – prices are stable, or even inconsistently falling, in the last four decades of the thirteenth century but rise during the first two decades of the fourteenth (Figures I.3–I.4).[176] After 1320, the price of raw materials dropped back, but those of finished materials remained relatively high.

In the eighty years before the Black Death, therefore, low and stable wages and prices created a predictable and relatively inexpensive economic environment for construction, one exploited by great and local churches alike.[177] Anticipating the total cost of construction and budgeting for it would have been comparatively straightforward. High money supply in the 1310s to 1330s made saving, finding credit and running collections relatively easier.[178] Nevertheless, periodic shortages of coin reduced the liquidity of building projects, especially in the 1290s and again in the 1330s and 1340s, making it difficult to stockpile money, find credit or pay workmen and suppliers.[179] The cost of even highly worked architectural features would be relatively low thanks to cheap and

[173] See the summary in Bruce M. S. Campbell, *The Great Transition* (Cambridge, 2016), 161–66; E. H. Phelps Brown and Sheila V. Hopkins, 'Seven Centuries of Building Wages', *Economica*, 22, no. 87 (August 1955): Figure 1; D. L. Farmer, 'Prices and Wages', in *AHEW*, ed. H. E. Hallam, vol. 2 (Cambridge, 1988), 769; Gregory Clark, 'The Long March of History: Farm Wages, Population, and Economic Growth, England 1209–1869', *Economic History Review* 60, no. 1 (2007): 97–135; Knoop and Jones, *Mediaeval Mason*, Appendix I, Table I; Salzman, *Building in England*, 71; Gustaf Fredrik Steffen, *Studien Zur Geschichte Der Englischen Lohnarbeiter*, vol. 1 (Stuttgart, 1901), 107–122, see Tabelle II.
[174] John Hatcher, 'England in the Aftermath of the Black Death', *Past & Present*, no. 144 (1994): 20; Jim Bolton, *Money in the Medieval English Economy 973–1489* (Manchester, 2012), 265–67.
[175] James E. Thorold Rogers, *A History of Agriculture and Prices in England*, vol. 1 (Oxford, 1866), 96; cf. Farmer, 'Prices and Wages', 720.
[176] Cf. price rises around the 1310s in LSE Beveridge Price History W9.
[177] Introduction, section d, pp. 34–35.
[178] Martin Allen, *Mints and Money in Medieval England* (Cambridge, 2012), 343–45; Broadberry et al., *British Economic Growth*, 227–29.
[179] Bolton, *Money*, 183–84. Cf. pp. 269–72 in this volume.

Changes in Cost and Money Supply

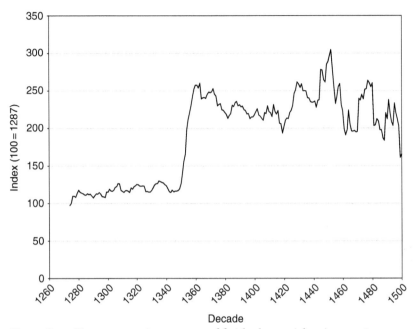

Figure I.3 Ten year moving average of finished materials prices, 1265–1500. Source: Based on James E. Thorold Rogers, *A History of Agriculture and Prices in England* (Oxford: 1866).

plentiful labour, although stone remained an expensive material used only for high-status work.[180] In this way, it is possible to explain one factor of how parishes were able to afford building work: reducing the quantity of stone even as it required more working – introducing slimmer walls, piers and arches, better ashlar masonry, longer lancet windows, and pointed arcades spanning wider bays with fewer piers. These trends continued with the introduction of large bar-traceried windows and complex pier plans. High-quality coloured glass could be expensive, but new windows could be filled, at least in the immediate term, with inexpensive white glass.[181] Lead production increased and prices stabilised in 1240–70 after a long period of rises, and iron prices were probably stable or falling for the

---

[180] Morris associates the same trend with the ready availability of silver coin: Morris, *Cathedrals and Abbeys*, 214.
[181] J. R. Hunter, 'Glass Industry', in *Medieval Industry*, ed. D. W. Crossley (London, 1981), 147.

Introduction

Figure I.4 Ten year moving average of raw materials prices, 1260–1500.
Source: Based on James E. Thorold Rogers, *A History of Agriculture and Prices in England* (Oxford: 1866).

last forty years of the century.[182] The rich decorative forms of the Decorated style also tended to be labour intensive but small in scale. The commercial exploitation of quarries, the spread of horse-haulage and the improvement of roads made high-quality stone from more distant quarries increasingly accessible, reduced the cost and risk of transport and the speed at which ashlar blocks could be produced.[183]

In the wake of the Black Death, David Farmer's research indicates that average summer building wages grew by about 40 per cent in the quarter century after 1349, and they stayed at that level until the turn of the fifteenth century (Figures I.1–I.2). They rose again until, in the mid-1430s, they were around 80 per cent higher than they had been in the

---

[182] Ian Blanchard, *Mining, Metallurgy, and Minting in the Middle Ages: Continuing Afro-European Supremacy, 1250–1450*, vol. 3 (Stuttgart, 2005), 1458–59.

[183] Martin S. Briggs, 'Building Construction', in *A History of Technology*, ed. Charles Joseph Singer and Richard Raper, vol. 2 (Oxford, 1956), 427; John Langdon, 'Horse Hauling: A Revolution in Vehicle Transport in Twelfth- and Thirteenth-Century England?', *Past & Present*, no. 103 (1 May 1984): 37–66.

second quarter of the fourteenth century.[184] In practice, this meant a rise in carpenters' and masons' day wages from around 3d or 4d to 6d. For the next sixty years, wage rates were largely stagnant before drifting downwards at the end of the century. To this may be added increased benefits such as drink, food and clothing, which were used to circumvent wage regulation.[185] Increases varied across trades, with the greatest being in the wages of unskilled labourers: craftsmen earned around 120 per cent more in the first half of the fourteenth century and only 40 per cent more in 1430–1500.[186] It was through employment that building projects met a source of external regulation in the form of statutes concerning the use of sureties and maximum wage levels, eventually enforced with increasing uniformity under Justices of the Peace.[187] They were probably most effective in the two decades after the Black Death and again in 1495 and 1514, when they may have aided in stabilising wage rates – otherwise many employers broke the rules, apparently quite freely.[188] Wealthy peasants who employed agricultural labourers benefitted from the statute, and this group stood to profit too in their capacity as architectural patrons.[189]

The rise in material prices after the Black Death was, if anything, even sharper than that of wages: around double for finished materials in the 1350s and 1360s.[190] However, prices then fell gradually by around a fifth until the end of the fifteenth century, except for a slight recovery in the 1430s to 1450s. The rise in the price of raw materials is even greater: around 70 per cent in the 1350s and, after rising in the 1380s to 1390s, peaking at around 150 per cent more than the pre–Black Death period. However, like finished materials, they subsequently decreased by around a fifth, mostly over the second half of the fifteenth century. The

---

[184] Campbell, *Transition*, 257–61; Hatcher, *Plague, Population, and the English Economy*, 48.
[185] Hatcher, 'England in the Aftermath', 14.
[186] D. L. Farmer, 'Prices and Wages, 1350–1500', in *AHEW*, ed. E. Miller, vol. 3 (Cambridge, 1991), 478–79, Table 5.10.
[187] W. M. Ormrod, *Edward III* (New Haven, 2011), 359–62; P. R. Cavill, 'The Problem of Labour and the Parliament of 1495', in *'Of Mice and Men': Image, Belief and Regulation in Late Medieval England*, ed. Linda Clark (Woodbridge, 2005), 154–55; Bertha Haven Putnam, *The Enforcement of the Statutes of Labourers During the First Decade After the Black Death, 1349–1359* (New York, 1908).
[188] Simon A. C. Penn and Christopher Dyer, 'Wages and Earnings in Late Medieval England: Evidence from the Enforcement of the Labour Laws', *The Economic History Review* 43, no. 3 (1 August 1990): 372; P. Booth, 'The Enforcement of the Ordinance and Statute of Labourers in Cheshire, 1349 to 1374', *ARCHIVES*, no. 127 (2013): 6; Donald Woodward, *Men at Work: Labourers and Building Craftsmen in the Towns of Northern England, 1450–1750* (Cambridge, 1995), 182–83; Swanson, *York*, 27.
[189] L. R. Poos, 'The Social Context of Statute of Labourers Enforcement', *Law and History Review* 1, no. 1 (1983): 27–52; Elaine Clark, 'Medieval Labor Law and English Local Courts', *The American Journal of Legal History* 27, no. 4 (1983): 330–53.
[190] M. M. Postan, *Mediaeval Trade and Finance* (Cambridge, 2002), 177; Mavis Mate, 'Agrarian Economy after the Black Death: The Manors of Canterbury Cathedral Priory, 1348–91', *The Economic History Review*, 37, no. 3 (1984): 347.

Introduction

price of transport is not widely studied but probably underwent a significant increase after the Black Death — by as much as 40 per cent in some cases, although just 20 per cent in others — caused substantially by rises in wages.[191]

It is possible to draw some general conclusions from this outline, although local effects may have varied widely. The rising cost of labour and materials after the Black Death probably increased the like-for-like cost of building work by at least double by the early fifteenth century, with much of that rise in 1350–75.[192] This created a generally hostile environment for building work: the sharp rise in wages and prices not only made construction less affordable but also rendered budgeting and financial planning difficult for a project of any length.[193] Another challenge was finding coin to save or pay for labour and materials, which would have been difficult during the silver scarcity of the mid-fifteenth century.[194] The large number of building projects and donations calculated in multiples of 6s 8d, the value of a gold noble or angel, is possibly telling.[195] The evolution of sophisticated managerial and financial strategies for church construction may be related to the triple challenge of handling an increasing quantity of donations, negotiating an uncertain economic environment and meeting a greater demand for oversight. However, effective financial planning for long-term projects was aided by the relative reduction in direct taxation after the early 1340s.[196] All this points to two conclusions, germane to the focus of this book: that the large amount of Perpendicular building work that did take place required both radical changes in the distribution of wealth in many parishes as well as considerable financial acumen by project managers.[197]

---

[191] Rogers, *Agriculture and Prices*, 1:657.   [192] For the cost of comparable projects see: p. 89–90.
[193] This may have stimulated contracting as well as reducing quantities of work: pp. 250–56 in this volume.
[194] The following section will argue that it contributed to a reduction in building projects. Peter Spufford, *Money and Its Use in Medieval Europe* (Cambridge, 1988), 339–62; Allen, *Mints and Money*, 336–45; Martin Allen, 'Silver Production and the Money Supply in England and Wales, 1086–c. 1500', *Economic History Review* 64 (2011): 114–31; for the impact of a reduction of coinage on building work in an earlier period, see Richard Gem, 'A Recession in English Architecture during the Early Eleventh Century and Its Impact on the Development of the Romanesque Style', *Journal of the British Archaeological Association*, XXXVIII (1975): 28–49.
[195] Dunster tower, built for 13s 4d a foot, in 1442 is a good example: Salzman, *Building in England*, 514–15.
[196] G. L. Harriss, *Shaping the Nation: England, 1360–1461* (Oxford, 2005), 59–61; W. M. Ormrod, 'The English State and the Plantagenet Empire, 1259–1360: A Fiscal Perspective', in *The Medieval State: Essays Presented to James Campbell*, ed. John Robert Maddicott and D. M. Palliser (London, 2000), 203–05.
[197] For the latter point see: Chapter 6 in this volume.

D) CHURCH BUILDING AND THE ECONOMY

The period covered by this book spans the development of two distinctive architectural styles in England. As is usual, the terminology of Thomas Rickman will be used in identifying these as the 'Decorated' and the 'Perpendicular'.[198] In parish churches, the first is characterised by its varied window tracery, use of micro-architecture and rich moulding profiles. The largest and most developed examples of the type, Patrington in Holderness or Heckington, Lincolnshire, for example, can show a profusion of highly worked niches, tombs and canopies, large windows with extraordinary flowing tracery compositions, and substantial buttressing. The simpler tracery forms of the turn of the fourteenth century, generally termed geometric and intersecting, although often highly varied, became increasingly rich. Curvilinear tracery types, with inventive combinations of daggers and mouchettes, were common after the 1320s, as was the net-like 'reticulated' form. Most parish churches of this period, however, are relatively simple with slender octagonal piers, double-chamfered arcades, simply moulded capitals and less sumptuous tracery. In nearly every case construction took place on a site already occupied by a church and constituted the rebuilding or extension of a part of the fabric, so Decorated aisles, towers and windows are more common than Decorated churches.

The transition to the Perpendicular style was slow, and churches with Decorated features can be found up to the end of the century or later. The south transept and presbytery at Gloucester Cathedral of the 1330s, then an abbey, is usually recognised as being the first large-scale essay in Perpendicular architecture. Perpendicular in many parishes was rather more austere than Decorated. The multitude of varied, curvilinear tracery forms was condensed down into a narrower range of varieties that changed relatively slowly over the next two centuries, even as windows grew in size, filling the available wall space. Window and door arches were increasingly flattened, and the 'four pointed' arch became common, evolving into the characteristic 'Tudor' arch. Nevertheless, additions to parish churches could be highly refined, in some cases with extraordinary decorative roofs and large west towers. The greatest Perpendicular churches were exceptional in size – for example, Lavenham, Suffolk, or Cirencester,

---

[198] Thomas Rickman, *An Attempt to Discriminate the Styles of English Architecture* (London, 1817); for parish church architecture through the middle ages, see Platt, *Parish Churches*; Morris, *Landscape*; Randall, Pounds, *English Parish Church*; for the Decorated style see Binski, *Gothic Wonder*; N. Coldstream, *The Decorated Style: Architecture and Ornament, 1240–1360* (London, 1994); J. Bony, *The English Decorated Style: Gothic Architecture Transformed, 1250–1350* (Oxford, 1979); for the Perpendicular style, important works include: Christopher Wilson, 'Origins of the Perpendicular Style and Its Development to C. 1360' (PhD, University of London, 1979); John Harvey, *The Perpendicular Style, 1330–1485* (London, 1978).

Introduction

Gloucestershire. Piers could be very slender, often lozenge-shaped in plan, and buttresses correspondingly large. Mouldings became wider but shallower. The style would dominate into the sixteenth century, and buildings in versions of the Perpendicular continued to be constructed even after the Reformation brought a near cessation to church construction across England. This summary is necessarily brief, and there are many texts well able to set the scene for this book with regard to the development of the Gothic style in England in the later middle ages, but there is much less clarity regarding the pace or quantity of construction.

Measuring patterns in medieval building work is challenging for three principal reasons: the first is the size of the object domain, including some 8,000–9,000 parish churches; the second is the rate of losses, both during the medieval period, as older parts of churches were built over, and later; and the third is the difficulty of dating what remains. Great church building, with fewer structures but which are more readily dated, is less subject to these problems. Quantifications of building work on English great churches have been compiled by Richard Morris and provide a useful yardstick against which parish church construction can be measured.[199] His calculations demonstrate that, after a long period of growth from the mid-twelfth century, both the number of projects commenced and the number in progress began to decline from the middle decades of the fourteenth century. In 1220–1350 there was an average of nineteen building projects in progress on great churches each decade and never fewer than fifteen.[200] For the eighty years following the Black Death, there was an average of only seven building projects in progress each decade. If the first period was one of uninterrupted growth, then the second is of interrupted decline. The nadir was reached in 1430–70, when the average was fewer than three a decade. Indeed, three of the five lowest decade totals for the entire period 1070–1530 are 1430–60. In 1470–1530, the average recovers slightly to more than six a decade. Morris's figures for projects commenced are similar: more than six per decade in 1350–1440 and 1470–1530; fewer than three in 1440–70. In 1220–1350, the average was almost ten. Such brute totals are not entirely satisfactory: totalling building projects is a crude measure of 'quantity' and scholars have also tried calculating projects completed,[201] volume,[202]

---

[199] Morris, *Cathedrals and Abbeys*, Figures 7 and 8.
[200] Pace John Langdon and James Masschaele, 'Commercial Activity and Population Growth in Medieval England', *Past & Present* 190, no. 1 (2006): 74.
[201] John James, *The Template-Makers of the Paris Basin: Toichological Techniques for Identifying the Pioneers of the Gothic Movement with an Examination of Art-Historical Methodology* (West Grinstead, 1989), 96.
[202] Johnson, 'Cathedral Building and the Medieval Economy'; B. W. E. Alford and M. Q. Smith, 'The Economic Effects of Cathedral Building in Medieval England: A Reply', *Explorations in Entrepreneurial History* 6 (Winter 1969): 161–62, Table C.

ground plan area,[203] membranes of accounts,[204] 'superficies',[205] labourers' annual wages,[206] a 'magisterial quotient' (namely, height),[207] and arbitrary units of cost such as man-years per cubic yard[208] or 'bulkbilling units'.[209]

Quantifying building work is quixotic; any unit is crude, whether disregarding size, complexity, expense, changes in prices and wages, the cost of transport and quarrying, or the evolution of building technology and commercialisation. Nevertheless, changes in the size and ambition of architectural projects give impressionistic strength to a pattern of greater building work in the decades around 1400 and 1500, and less in the period between. Several important building projects were in hand at Beverley, York, Westminster, Sherborne and Winchester in the early fifteenth century. To this could be added cloisters at Chichester, Worcester and Hereford; towers at York and Canterbury; chapter houses at Canterbury and Exeter; and the west front at Norwich, as well as several substantial windows. They were, however, largely over by the 1440s. The next most important architectural projects would remain unfinished until towards the end of the century or later, at King's College, Cambridge, Eton College and the Oxford Divinity Schools. Similarly, the generation of great architects following Yevele and Wynford largely disappear from the records by or during the early 1440s. None of William Colchester, Robert Playser, John Thirsk, Robert Winchcombe or Thomas Mapilton survived for long after 1440, and many had died before then. The reason for the lack of successors was practical – with a reduction in great projects, there was also a reduction in the number of leading architects required to design them and in the number of opportunities they had for experimentation.

These observations provide a useful timeline against which changes in parish church construction can be measured. No similar quantification has been attempted for parish churches, for the reasons given above. Indeed, no contemporary source lists every parish church and chapel in medieval England and no comprehensive modern survey has been attempted. The 1291 *Taxatio* listed 8,085 parishes and 457 chapels but excluded those valued at below 6 marks. The *Valor Ecclesiasticus* of 1535 recorded 8,838 benefices, which Richard Morris estimates as equivalent to 9,000–11,000 local churches – parish churches and chapels

---

[203] Brighita Bercea, Robert B. Ekelund, and Robert D. Tollison, 'Cathedral Building as an Entry-Deterring Device', *Kyklos* 58, no. 4 (2005): 453–65.
[204] Douglas Knoop and G. P. Jones, 'The Impressment of Masons in the Middle Ages', *The Economic History Review* 8, no. 1 (November 1937): 64.
[205] Robert Willis, *The Architectural History of York Cathedral* (London, 1848), 55–57, Note A.
[206] Vroom, *Cathedral Building*, 85.   [207] Bercea, Ekelund, and Tollison, 'Entry-Deterring', 461.
[208] Johnson, 'Cathedral Building and the Medieval Economy', 199.
[209] James, 'Funding the Early Gothic Churches', 48–52; James, 'Impact of Climate Change'.

Introduction

together.[210] The larger quantity will be used in this book as an estimate of the total number of church buildings in medieval England. Morris estimates that 6 to 10 per cent of medieval churches are lost.[211] In southeast Wiltshire, Davidson calculated that evidence exists for approximately 70 per cent of medieval churches, while about 45 per cent survive relatively intact, although the level of rebuilding in the county may have been unusually high.[212] In Cambridgeshire, fifteen medieval churches have disappeared entirely[213] and others exist only in ruins.[214] Particularly serious is the loss of chapels.[215] In Cambridgeshire, documentary and archaeological evidence can demonstrate the existence of almost forty parochial chapels, roughly a quarter of the county's churches, of which seven are extant (usually as parish churches) – a survival rate of about a fifth (Table I.1).[216] This broadly supports the upper limit of Morris's estimate of the total number of local churches.

Nevertheless, in contrast to the decline noted in Morris's figures for great churches, guides to medieval architecture almost universally note the proliferation of parochial building projects in the late middle ages, often attributing it to the wealth that wool generated for the English economy, a crisis of faith brought about by repeated plagues or a national shift in the focus of patronage from religious houses to parishes.[217] Data from the *Buildings of England* series suggests this interpretation is correct. Some three-quarters of surviving medieval churches surveyed by Pevsner have at least one example of Perpendicular work,[218] while the equivalent figures for Decorated and Early English work are 56 and 50 per cent respectively (Table I.2).[219] It was an economic historian, M. M. Postan, who sounded a note of caution, however, noting that measurement

---

[210] Richard Morris, 'The Church in the Countryside: Two Lines in Inquiry', in *Medieval Villages*, ed. Della Hooke (Oxford, 1985), 50–51.
[211] Ibid., 55.
[212] Carol Foote Davidson, 'Written in Stone: Architecture, Liturgy, and the Laity in English Parish Churches, c. 1125–c. 1250' (PhD, University of London, Birkbeck College, 1998), 39.
[213] Based on my own calculations and Alison Taylor, 'Churches out of Use in Cambridgeshire', *Proceedings of the Cambridge Antiquarian Society* LXXII (March 1982): 31–38.
[214] Robert Halliday, 'The Churches of Ashley and Silverley', *Proceedings of the Cambridge Antiquarian Society* LXXIII (1984): 37–41.
[215] Dorothy Mary Owen, *Church and Society in Medieval Lincolnshire* (Lincoln, 1971), 8.
[216] Willingham, Barway, Caldecote, Coton, Newton, Parson Drove and, possibly, Little Childerley. Ashley was a private chapel, later used as a parish church; Bainbridge, *Gilds*, 25.
[217] Stephen Friar, *A Companion to the English Parish Church* (Stroud, 1996), 285; Platt, *Parish Churches*, 90; Morris, *Landscape*, 227–315; Randall, *Parish Church*, 46; Platt, *Medieval England*, 138; Edwin Smith, Graham Hutton and Olive Cook, *English Parish Churches* (London, 1976), 117–24; Philip Ziegler, *The Black Death* (Stroud, 1990), 267–70.
[218] Cf. estimate of two-thirds in Scarisbrick, *Reformation*, 13.
[219] Estimate compiled using data from Michael Good, ed., *A Compendium of Pevsner's Buildings of England on Compact Disc* (Oxford, 1995).

Table I.1 *Cambridgeshire chapels*

Chapel	Parish church	Earliest record
Redreth	Guilden Morden	1100
Newton★·★★	Hauxton	1150
St. Margaret	Isleham	1163
Barway★	Soham	1189
Coton★	Grantchester	1198
Stunteney	Holy Cross, Ely [described as chapel to St Mary in 1291]	pre-1200
Caldecote★	Bourn	pre-1200
Little Childerley★	Great Childerley	pre-1200
	Ditton Camoys	1200s
St Nicholas, Landwade	Burwell	1200s
Quy	Stow	1200s
St John, Reach	Burwell	1200s
Eadike	Tydd St Giles	1251
Kilhus	Wisbech St Mary	1252
Emneth (Norfolk)★★	Elm	1275
Kneesworth	Bassingbourn	1275
Howes	Girton	1279
Holy Cross, Ely★★	St Mary, Ely	1291
Barnwell Chapel★★	Barnwell Priory	1291
St George, Thetford	Stretham	1300s
St Botolph	Upwell	1300s
Parson Drove★	Leverington	1300s
St Edmund★★	St Mary the Less, Cambridge	1300s
St Swithun	Steeple Morden	1300
All Saints, Newmarket	Wood Ditton	1336
Guyhirn	Wisbech St Mary	1337
St Christopher	Outwell	1348
Murrow	Wisbech St Mary	1376
Hauxton Bridge	Hauxton	1391
Chettisham	St Mary, Ely	1400
St Anne, Whittlesford Bridge	Hinxton	1401
Eastrea	Whittlesey	1403
St Etheldreda	Swaffham Prior	1440
Eldernell	Whittlesey	1525
Willingham★	Carlton	1540
Manea	Coveney	1646

★ indicates a modern day parish church
★★ indicates it was taxed in 1291

Sources: Thomas Astle, Samuel Ayscough, and John Caley, eds., *Taxatio Ecclesiastica Angliae Et Walliae, Auctoritate P. Nicholai IV, Circa A.D. 1291* (London, 1802); J. H. Denton, 'The 1291 Valuation of the Churches of Ely Diocese', *Proceedings of the Cambridge Antiquarian Society* XC (2001): 69–80; C. L. Feltoe and Ellis H. Minns, eds., *Vetus Liber Archidiaconi Eliensis* (Cambridge, 1917); and the Victoria County History volumes for Cambridgeshire.

Introduction

Table I.2 *Estimated quantities of building work styles*

Style	Number of surviving examples	% of Perpendicular	% of benefices (1535)
Romanesque	3830	59	43
Early English	4401	68	50
Decorated	4921	76	56
Perpendicular	6470	100	73

Source: M. Good, *A Compendium of Pevsner's Buildings of England on Compact Disc* (Oxford, 1995).

Table I.3 *Parish church building as a proportion of the English economy*

Period	Number of examples	Estimated average unit cost	Total expenditure on architecture	Average annual expenditure	% of nominal GDP (c. 1300/c. 1500)
1290–1360	4,921	£5	£24,605	£352	0.007%
1290–1360	4,921	£15	£73,815	£1,055	0.020%
1290–1360	4,921	£30	£147,630	£2,109	0.040%
1360–1540	6,470	£10	£64,700	£359	0.009%
1360–1540	6,470	£30	£194,100	£1,078	0.027%
1360–1540	6,470	£60	£388,200	£2,157	0.053%

Sources: M. Good, *A Compendium of Pevsner's Buildings of England on Compact Disc* (Oxford, 1995); S. N. Broadberry et al., *British Economic Growth, 1270–1870* (Cambridge, 2015), Table 5.04.

Note: This table is highly speculative: total quantities of projects are estimates that do not distinguish between size of project or survival rate, and estimated average cost is based on the discussion in Chapter 1, section 'Fundraising Techniques', with a large range given. It suggests that parish church construction formed a small proportion of the English economy throughout this period and that it may have increased slightly in the long fifteenth century.

through time is almost impossible, given rates of overbuilding, and denying any link between national affluence and the quality of construction.[220] Indeed, although highly speculative, calculating total expenditure on church building suggests there may have been relatively little increase between the Decorated and Perpendicular periods, given rates of overbuilding (Table I.3). R. B. Dobson and Alan Dyer similarly warned that assuming large building projects indicated a wealthy parish was unreliable

---

[220] M. M. Postan, *Essays on Medieval Agriculture and General Problems of the Medieval Economy* (Cambridge, 1973), 46.

Church Building and the Economy

without knowing who paid for the work.[221] In other words, during periods of economic contraction, some people can become exorbitantly wealthy. Indeed, two very expensive parochial building projects of the late middle ages, at St Margaret, Westminster, and Swaffham, Norfolk, have been associated by their historians with periods of falling wealth.[222] Christopher Dyer, however, argues that 'as fundraising was frequently a collective effort', new architecture 'reflects not just the wealth of a few individuals but of the whole community'.[223] This question will form the context for Chapter 1. Both a will and a way were necessary, and Richard Morris has pointed to areas that were economically successful but did not build – the Lincolnshire Wolds, for example.[224]

Treating the Perpendicular period as one of uniformly intensive building work is as short-sighted as assuming that earlier periods were not. The fifteenth century was not an age of invariable prosperity and nor was wool or cloth always a shortcut to wealth. In some regions, little building work took place at all or, when it did, was limited to small renewals or replacements. At a national level, temporal changes in the quantity of church building can be observed. The dip in great church construction identified in Morris's figures c. 1430–70 is roughly coterminous with the mid-century 'slump', a correlation that suggests causation.[225] Postan identified a similar decline in parish church building from 1425 to 1475, which Morris rejects.[226] Few scholars of late medieval architecture have identified a similar pattern in national building work, with an important exception in John Harvey, although his highly qualitative periodisation fits only inexactly with those of Postan and Morris. Harvey's model of architectural change placed the monarch and nobility at its centre, while the prosaic question of economic change took on only a secondary importance. The parish is largely absent from his analysis, reduced to an 'iconoclastic rabble'.[227] The earliest account was given in *Gothic England*,

---

[221] R. B. Dobson, 'Urban Decline in Late Medieval England', in *The English Medieval Town: A Reader in English Urban History, 1200–1540*, ed. Richard Holt and Gervase Rosser (London, 1990), 273; Dyer, *Decline and Growth*, 34–35.

[222] Rosser, *Medieval Westminster*, 264; Farnhill, *Guilds*, 106; cf. Derek Keene, *Survey of Medieval Winchester*, vol. 1 (Oxford, 1985), 126–27; a similar, but more general point is made in Morris, *Landscape*, 328.

[223] Dyer, *Making a Living*, 300.   [224] Morris, *Landscape*, 357.

[225] John Hatcher, 'The Great Slump of the Mid-Fifteenth Century', in *Progress and Problems in Medieval England: Essays in Honour of Edward Miller*, ed. Richard Britnell and John Hatcher (Cambridge, 1996), 237–72; R. H. Britnell, 'The English Economy and the Government, 1450–1550', in *The End of the Middle Ages? England in the Fifteenth and Sixteenth Centuries*, ed. J. L. Watts (Stroud, 1998), 89–116.

[226] Postan, *Essays*, 46.

[227] Cf. John Harvey, *An Introduction to Tudor Architecture* (London, 1949), 10–12; John Harvey, *The Gothic World, 1100–1600: A Survey of Architecture and Art* (London, 1950), 74.

Introduction

published 1947, in which late medieval history was divided into five periods with suitably evocative names, including 'The Great Slump' under Bolingbroke; the 'Indian Summer' under Henries V and VI; and the 'Pregnant Winter' of 1455–71.[228] In 1978 this was clarified in *The Perpendicular Style*, when the period after the fall of Richard II and before c. 1460 is identified as one of 'relative depression and mediocrity', although the fall in quantity and quality was not universal.[229]

Documentary evidence of parish church construction, albeit modest in quantity and drawn largely from small towns, is consistent with a slackening of building work during the economic slump of the middle decades of the fifteenth century followed by steady increase as economic conditions for church building improved – described in the previous section as culminating in an 'Indian summer' that finished c. 1530.[230] Suggestive evidence can be found in parochial building contracts: nine survive from 1410–42 but only one for 1443–75, for a roof (Table I.4). Recovery had to wait until the sixteenth century: four contracts survive from 1476–1508 and six from 1508–40. The only significant building projects in churchwardens' accounts from the middle decades are at its bookends: in Thame, Oxfordshire (c. 1442–43), and Walsall, Staffordshire (c. 1462–66). The others tend to be later, although this might suggest an increased survival rate of documents as well as intensive building work in the late fifteenth and early sixteenth centuries.[231] Examples of parochial fabric committees are also from either the early decades of the century (Hedon) or later ones (Bodmin, St Mary-at-Hill, London, Saffron Walden and Bolney).[232] Wills also indicate a slackening of work in the middle decades: just 17 per cent of the bequests to medieval building projects that Leland L. Duncan published for West Kent were of 1420–67 (Table I.5).[233] The majority are later, but the sharp difference between the 1440s (no projects receiving bequests), 1450s (one), 1460s (three) and 1470s (seven) is suggestive that the endurance of documents cannot entirely explain the increasing quantities of bequests. Although varying from decade to decade, bequests continue in similar quantities into the 1520s. In Somerset, Frederic Weaver recorded bequests to seven building projects in 1401–38, twelve in 1469–1500 and just two between these periods (including one in London; Table I.6).[234] In other words, less than a tenth of his abstracts of fifteenth-century bequests for building work are from 1438–69. In Eamon Duffy's sample of East

---

[228] Harvey, *Gothic World*, 94–95. [229] Harvey, *Perpendicular*, 160–62, 199.
[230] Cf. Dyer, *Decline and Growth*, 17. [231] Chapter 1, section b.ii, pp. 55–61.
[232] Chapter 1, section b.i, pp. 52–55.
[233] L. L. Duncan, *Testamenta Cantiana (West Kent)* (London, 1906), vi–ix.
[234] Frederic William Weaver, ed., *Somerset Medieval Wills, XIVth and XVth Centuries*, vol. 1, 3 vols (London, 1901).

Table I.4 *Medieval parochial building contracts summary*

Location	Unit	Language	Date	Named contractees	Whole parish?	Parson?	Aristocracy?	Institution?	Reserved responsibilities
Southchurch	Chapel	Latin	1293	1	No	No	Yes	No	Materials and other things necessary for the work
York	*Houses*	*Latin*	*1335*	*3*	*'ac interceteros parochionos'*	*No*	*No*	*No*	*None*
Sandon	Chancel	Latin	1348	2	No	No	No	Yes	None
Etchingham	Five windows	Latin	1363	1	No	No	Yes	No	Food
Arlingham	Tower	Latin	1372	19	*'et omnes parochianos'*	Yes	Yes	No	All materials except tools; board and lodging
St Dunstan, London	Aisle and porch	French	1381	1	No	No	Yes	No	None
Edinburgh, Scotland	Five chapels	English	1387	2	'and the Communite of the ylke'	No	Yes	No	All 'great' tiles
Hornby	South aisle	English	1410	1	No	No	Yes	No	A fother of lead
Catterick	Church	English	1412	2	No	No	Yes	No	Carriage of stone; lime, water and sand
Halstead	Roof	Latin	1413	1	No	No	No	Yes	None
Wyberton	Church and tower	French	1419	2	No	No	No	No	Unknown
Surfleet	Chancel	Latin	1420	2	No	Yes	No	No	None
Walberswick	Tower	English	1425	4	No	No	No	No	Materials, equipment, lodgings
Chester	Chapel	English	1433	1	No	No	Yes	No	Materials, scaffolding, windlass, necessaries
Fotheringay	Nave	English	1434	2	No	No	Yes	No	Materials, transport, appointment

Table I.4 (cont.)

Location	Unit	Language	Date	Named contractees	Whole parish?	Parson?	Aristocracy?	Institution?	Reserved responsibilities
Dunster	Tower	English	1442	0	Yes	No	No	No	Materials, transport, equipment, labour, a lodge
St Bene't's, Cambridge	Roof	English	1452	2	No	No	No	No	Not specified
Broxbourne	Chapel	English	1476	1	No	No	Yes	No	Materials
Wolverhampton	Tower	English	1476	0	'the Gentilmen Wardens Yomen and Comyns'	No	No	No	Iron, lead
Thornham Parva	Steeple	English	1485	3	No	No	No	No	None
Helmingham	Tower	English	1488	4	No	No	No	No	Materials, equipment, transport
Wycombe	Tower	English	1509	6	No	No	Yes	No	Materials
Great Sherston	*Church House*	*English*	*1511*	*4*	*'ut all the wole p'ysch'*	*No*	*Yes*	*No*	*Materials, quarrying, transport*
Tempsford	Wooden chapel	English	1512	1	No	Yes	No	No	None
Biddenham	North aisle	English	1522–23	1	No	No	Yes	No	Transport, materials, pulling down the old wall
Orby	Battlements	English	1529	2	No	No	No	No	Iron, carriage of stone

Source: L. F. Salzman. *Building in England Down to 1540: A Documentary History* (Oxford, 1952). The references for contracts omitted by Salzman are given in the bibliography.

Note: Entries in italics are for parochial projects carried out on buildings other than the parish church.

Table I.5 *Bequests to church building in West Kent*

Parish	Work	Date of first bequest to the project
Orpington	Porch	1370
Crayford	Tower	1406
Cliffe	Roof	1413
Ightham	Church	1420
St Margaret, Rochester	Tower	1457
Woldham	Tower	1460
Snodland	Porch	1461
Bromley	Aisle	1467
Lewisham	Tower	1471
High Halstow	Chapel	1472
Hoo	Nave	1473
Hartley	Buttresses	1473
Deptford	Tower	1476
Dartford	Tower	1477
Stoke	Tower	1479
Cudham	Roof	1487
Cowden	Window	1487
Hadlow	Window	1488
Westerham	Seats	1490
East Peckham	Window	1491
Yalding	Nave	1493
Shorne	Arch	1496
Shipbourne	Window	1496
Lewisham	Window	1498
Kemsing	Buttresses	1499
Lewisham	Chapel	1500
Strood	Chapel	1501
Chevening	Tower	1506
West Wickham	Aisle	1509
Seal	Tower	1510
Hunton	Chapel	1513
Hunton	Porch	1513
Bromley	Seats	1513
Burham	Covering of High Altar	1516
St Clement, Rochester	Church	1517
Strood	Chapel	1517
Lee	Church	1518
Keston	Seats	1521
West Farleigh	Tower	1523
Leigh	Tower	1525
Erith	Chapel	1525
Stone	Chapel	1526
Beckenham	Chancel	1535

Source: L. L. Duncan, *Testamenta Cantiana (West Kent)* (London, 1906).

Introduction

Table I.6 *Bequests to church building in Somerset*

Parish	Work	Date of first bequest to the project
Wells	Window	1401
Whritlyngton	Porch	1407
Wells	Work	1409
Nyenhide	Aisle	1410
Porteshede	Glass	1411
Bruton	Glass	1417
Staverdale	Work	1438
London	Steeple	1454
Lapford	Belfry	1457
Brimpton	Aisle	1469
Aisheton	Glass	1483
Compton Passfort	Aisle	1485
Yevilton	Tower	1486
Combe St Nicholas	Ceiling	1486
Welington	Paving	1486
Henton	Tower	1486
Taunton	Tower	1488
Taunton	Tower	1490
Taunton	Tower	1492
Taunton	Tower	1493
Taunton	Tower	1494
Tickenham	Tower	1497
Taunton	Tower	1497
St Decuman	New work	1498
Taunton	Tower	1499
Beaminster	Tower	1499
Vyncalton	Aisle	1500

Source: Frederic William Weaver, ed., *Somerset Medieval Wills* (London, 1901).

Anglian parishes, the decade with the lowest number of parishes carrying out work on rood screens was the 1450s, followed by a sharp increase, with very high quantities in 1490–1520,[235] a trend mirrored in Kent.[236] In Kent, Somerset and East Anglia there are relatively low numbers of bequests for the 1480s too, mirroring, perhaps, a drop in cloth exports in the middle years of the decade.

---

[235] Twelve in the 1450s, twenty-four in the 1460s and fifty-two in 1500–09: Eamon Duffy, 'The Parish, Piety, and Patronage in Late Medieval East Anglia: The Evidence of Rood Screens', in *The Parish in English Life, 1400–1600*, ed. Katherine L French, Gary G. Gibbs, and Beat Kümin (Manchester, 1997), Table 8.1.
[236] Duncan, *Testamenta Cantiana (West)*, x.

Sources

Together these suggest that the pattern of parish church building followed that of great church building in one respect: flourishing at the beginning and end of the century but experiencing a reduction in c. 1440–70. A contraction in money supply and the profitability of large holdings in this period provides a powerful economic explanation. However, relying on documentary evidence, with small samples, inconsistent survival rates and complex functions is clearly hazardous. It is important to contrast this with the evidence of considerable vernacular building work for which dating evidence flourishes in the middle third of the century.[237] Moreover, Richard Morris lists several famous parish churches that were constructed in this period.[238] Not everyone was equally affected by recession, of course, and some were able, even in straitened times, to find ways to continue with building work – increasing timescales, moving to a part-contract system or tightening the regulation of fundraising structures.[239] A central argument of this book is that patrons were not the passive victims of economic change but balanced their ambitions against changes in income.

E) SOURCES

The temporal boundaries of this book are determined by the availability of sources. The earliest contract for parochial building work is from the 1290s, but, as with churchwardens' accounts, examples are rare before the fifteenth century. The first fabric accounts are from the 1430s. Examples continue into the 1530s or later. Problematically, surviving examples are overwhelmingly from the south of England and from urban contexts, unlike the distribution of medieval parishes, populations and building projects. They are also typically from parishes of above average wealth.[240] Given the small sample size and large quantity of Perpendicular building work in rural parishes across England, this can safely be assumed to reflect

---

[237] Sarah Pearson, 'Tree-Ring Dating: A Review', *Vernacular Architecture* 28, no. 1 (1 June 1997): 25–39; Sarah Pearson, 'The Chronological Distribution of Tree-Ring Dates, 1980–2001: An Update', *Vernacular Architecture* 32, no. 1 (1 June 2001): 68–69; Dyer, 'Small Towns', 111–13; John Langton, 'Late Medieval Gloucester: Some Data from a Rental of 1455', *Transactions of the Institute of British Geographers*, 2 (1977): 259–77.

[238] Morris, *Landscape*, 352–55; cf. Brown, *Popular Piety*, 113.

[239] For timescales see Chapter 6, section d.i, pp. 267–68; for tightening the regulation of fundraising for major projects in the 1450s, see Byng, 'Saffron Walden'; for peasant farming strategies and exposure to the market in the mid-fifteenth century, see Christopher Dyer, 'Peasant Farming in Late Medieval England: Evidence from the Tithe Estimations by Worcester Cathedral Priory', in *Peasants and Lords in the Medieval English Economy: Essays in Honour of Bruce M.S. Campbell*, ed. Maryanne Kowaleski, John Langdon, and Phillipp R. Schofield (Turnhout, 2015), 83–109.

[240] Andrew Foster, 'Churchwardens' Accounts of Early Modern England and Wales', in *The Parish in English Life, 1400–1600*, ed. Katherine L French, Gary G. Gibbs, and Beat Kumin (Manchester, 1997), 77–85.

Introduction

only the survival rate of documents rather than record-keeping practices. Indeed, this book will rarely lack for a single example from a village or northern settlement to provide some contrast. In fact, organisational and financial differences between large and small, or rich and poor, towns and villages are often more striking than those between urban and rural examples. Testamentary evidence provides some of the earliest sources, but most examples relevant to this book, particularly those of multiple bequests to a single project, are drawn from the fifteenth century or later. The evidence of inscriptions and heraldry exists throughout this period, although it has to be used with considerable caution.[241]

Medieval building agreements survive in a number of different forms.[242] Many are indentures, where the text of the agreement was copied out twice before being divided by a wavy line, and different halves kept by the contractee and contractor.[243] Others survive in the form of memoranda or registered copies, where scribal errors or summarising may have taken place. In one case, considered later, a draft indenture survives.[244] They will be described as 'contracts' through this book, not unproblematically.[245] Parochial examples, drawn largely from the fifteenth century, are typically in English, but some Latin or French contracts, typically by members of the aristocracy or of ecclesiastical institutions survive, often with some English vocabulary (Table I.4). Discussion could, of course, take place in English or French before being rendered into Latin for the contract. The survival of contracts often depended on institutional archives – not least in chancery when plaintiffs brought pressure to bear on either contractees or contractors for failing to meet the terms of the contract. The chronology and purpose of building contracts will be discussed later.[246]

It is salutary to recall that no complete surviving working accounts exist for a single piece of medieval parochial architecture. Even exceptional survivals like the Bolney fabric accounts are damaged or decayed and can be shown to have many missing details – in this case including most of the project's revenue.[247] When accounts survive at all, they are nearly always summaries compiled for audit or commemoration, either of fabric

---

[241] Chapter 2, section b, pp. 111–18.
[242] A more extensive discussion of these documents can be found in Alexandrina Buchanan, 'Vestiges of Conversations? The Medieval Building Agreement and Architectural Language', in *Language in Medieval Britain: Networks and Exchanges*, ed. Mary Carruthers (Donington, 2015), 7–32.
[243] Alfred William Brian Simpson, *A History of the Common Law of Contract: The Rise of the Action of Assumpsit* (Oxford, 1975), 19; Robert L. Henry, *Contracts in the Local Courts of Medieval England* (London, 1926), 208; Frederick Pollock and Frederic William Maitland, *The History of English Law: Before the Time of Edward I*, 2nd ed., vol. 1 (Cambridge, 1923), 210.
[244] Chapter 5, section b.iii, pp. 228–32.
[245] John H. Baker, *An Introduction to English Legal History*, 4th ed. (London, 2002), 317–19.
[246] Chapter 6, section c.i, pp. 250–61.   [247] Chapter 5, section b.ii, pp. 221–26.

Plan of the Work

accounts, as at Bodmin, or, much more commonly, of churchwardens' accounts, where it is all but certain that some entries are missing or misleadingly described.[248] The wardens often recorded only what was required to cover shortfalls in the expenditure of other bodies, disregarded sums that were fully spent on their object or inadvertently disguised or omitted an entry in the auditing process.[249] Even then, few of these annual versions run, in good condition, for the duration of construction. In churchwardens' accounts, furthermore, distinguishing income raised for building projects from that intended for other duties is often difficult, although 'building' years can be compared to 'normal' years. To these problems it must be added that churchwardens could run separate accounts for discrete projects, such as church construction (the 'lytell qware' at St Mary-at-Hill, London, will be described later), or share responsibility with other bodies, such as guilds, stores or masters, who may have entered some expenditure into their accounts.[250] At Bardwell, Wiltshire, for example, the townwardens' accounts include expenditure on church repair,[251] and at Chagford, Devon, expenditure on the building in the early sixteenth century appeared in the accounts of the Blessed Virgin Mary store (run since 1500 by two female wardens), the church receivers and the churchwardens.[252] Indeed, the flexible relationship between fabric wardens, churchwardens and other bodies is the subject of Chapter 4.

F) PLAN OF THE WORK

The first two chapters of this book concern the financing of parochial building projects, beginning with those funded by the parishioners themselves. Chapter 1 will establish how corporate architectural patronage depended upon the distribution of wealth and the degree of economic polarisation in local society. This will provide the basis for an outline of how changes in the structure of local society in one county, Cambridgeshire, affected church construction across the later middle ages. Chapter 2 will assess evidence for patronage by ecclesiastical institutions and members of the aristocracy, arguing that the nobility did not often take on parochial building work, while only relatively wealthy

---

[248] Chapter 4, section c.iii, pp. 199–200; and Chapter 3, section c.i, pp. 139–50.
[249] Charles Drew, ed., *Lambeth Churchwardens' Accounts, 1504–1645, and Vestry Book, 1610* (London, 1940), xv–xvi; Burgess, 'Lessons'; Duffy, *Morebath*, 21; Betty R Masters and Elizabeth Ralph, eds., *The Church Book of St. Ewen's, Bristol 1454–1584* (Bristol, 1967), xxiii.
[250] Chapter 3, section c.ii, p. 153.   [251] Brown, *Popular Piety*, 138.
[252] Francis Mardon Osborne, ed., *The Church Wardens' Accounts of St. Michael's Church, Chagford 1480–1600* (Chagford, 1979), 42–46.

Introduction

gentry families could afford to build single-handedly and many or most would be obliged to work cooperatively with the parish. The following three chapters of this book concern the management of building projects, taking in turn churchwardens, parochial fabric committees and institutional and aristocratic patrons. Chapter 3 discusses how churchwardens were able to run church building campaigns, given their typically small incomes and limited authority. Indeed, it was often more appropriate for other authorities to take over expensive and demanding new projects, and these temporary committees and wardens are the subject of Chapter 4. Parishes appointed contracting committees, often drawn from the wealthier rungs of local society, and dedicated project managers ('fabric wardens'), probably under the watchful eye of the parish masters or the municipality. Chapter 5 discusses the evidence for the management of projects by institutions and the aristocracy. The parish gentry could run building work themselves but lords with many manors across many parishes, or institutions with the advowsons of many churches, would delegate to a manorial bailiff, an existing or purposely created institutional officer, or a reliable deputy. Lastly, Chapter 6 turns to the management of building projects: the financial, administrative and legal strategies used to reduce risk, avoid corruption and ensure the timely completion of building work, against claims of passivity and short-termism on behalf of project managers.

Although its subject is 'parish church construction', this book will include bells, belfries, screens and even movable furnishings when their financing can shed light on more obviously 'architectural' work. Any distinction risks anachronism: a church tower or aisle were probably understood to be just one part of a set of works required to prepare a parish church for worship and which together were the proper object of lay donations.[253] More problematic is trying to distinguish between repair and construction in the documentary, and even in the archaeological, record. Contemporary terminology was imprecise: '*reparare*' meant to raise as well as to repair, while neither the phrase 'new reparation' nor wills for 'making' and 'repair' of the same object were uncommon.[254] Subsequent sections will attempt to focus only on examples that were demonstrably the latter.

This book is concerned with questions of management and financing, and only tangentially with motivation – the 'how' rather than the 'why' of church construction. The concerns that would inspire so many men and women to part with their expendable income for church building projects are hard to recover, individually variable and beyond the

---

[253] Binski, *Gothic Wonder*, 45.
[254] E.g. A. Hussey, ed., *Testamenta Cantiana (East Kent)* (London, 1906), 220.

Plan of the Work

purview of this inquiry. Historians have tended to privilege one motive above others, however: namely the desire to speed the passage of the soul through purgatory, where it was absolved of sins before achieving eternal salvation.[255] Church building was a good work – one that would 'purchase prayers' from those impressed by 'the act of giving'.[256] This was made clear in penitentiaries and the granting of indulgences.[257] Patrons may have said this of themselves: the phrase '*orate pro animabus*' is familiar from many inscriptions. Many new works were created to provide space for burials or chantries – a regular mass celebrated for the souls of the founder, her family and anyone else she chose to name. Less wealthy men and women might endow an obit, an annual celebration of the mass, or join a guild for the same purpose. Nevertheless, commentators were cynical. In *Dives and Pauper*, Pauper despaired: 'I dread me that men do it more for the pomp and pride of this world to have a name and worship thereby.'[258] Indeed, motivations could be complex, multiple and varying: civic pride, social competitiveness, corporate solidarity, familial loyalty, votive offering, aesthetic pleasure, memorialisation, the display of wealth, the expectations of contemporaries, religious injunctions and the desire for assimilation, popularity or reputation.[259] Each overlapped and informed the other, and their interaction and relative importance would depend on the individual and the locality.[260] The most accurate conclusion is probably that 'each man's motives are mixed and the mixture is a little different in each case'.[261] Although a drop-off in architectural projects in the 1530s has been mooted, several examples in

---

[255] E.g. Pounds, *English Parish*, 465; Platt, *Parish Churches*, 106; Platt, *Medieval England*, 138; Morris, *Landscape*, 360–61; whether purgatory was a fearful prospect for late medieval people has been the subject of scholarly revision: Clive Burgess, '"A Fond Thing Vainly Invented": An Essay on Purgatory and Pious Motive in Late Medieval England', in *Parish, Church and People: Local Studies in Lay Religion, 1350–1750*, ed. S. J. Wright (London, 1988), 56–84; Duffy, *Stripping*, Chapter. 10; for a more recent contribution to the debate, see Peter Marshall, *Religious Identities in Henry VIII's England* (2013), Chapter 3; for the history of purgatory in medieval thought, see Jacques Le Goff, *The Birth of Purgatory* (London, 1984); Jerry L. Walls, *Purgatory: The Logic of Total Transformation* (Oxford, 2011), Chapter 1.

[256] For noble philanthropy see Joel Thomas Rosenthal, *The Purchase of Paradise; Gift Giving and the Aristocracy, 1307–1485* (London, 1972), 10.

[257] Brown, *Popular Piety*, 124.

[258] G. G Coulton, *Art and the Reformation* (Oxford, 1928), 216.

[259] Ford argues that donors of 'art' were more religiously conservative, requesting burial services and obits, although they may simply have been wealthier: J. A. Ford, 'Art and Identity in the Parish Communities of Late Medieval Kent', in *The Church and the Arts* (Oxford, 1992), 237.

[260] For example, Margery Kempe's relationship with her parish seems to have changed in accordance with her perception of her economic and social status and the development of her spiritual life: Katherine L. French, 'Margery Kempe and the Parish', in *The Ties That Bind: Essays in Medieval British History in Honor of Barbara Hanawalt*, ed. Linda Elizabeth Mitchell, Katherine L. French, and Douglas Biggs (Farnham, 2011), 159–74.

[261] Michael Baxandall, *Painting and Experience in Fifteenth Century Italy*, 2nd ed. (Oxford, 1988), 2.

Introduction

this book are drawn from that decade (and occasionally later) as radical preaching and publishing against purgatory intensified. Royal limitations on images, lights and pilgrimage in the late 1530s must have been a sign of things to come. That church construction did endure in some places must indicate the continued, if increasingly qualified, affirmation of prayer for the dead before the Chantry Acts of the late 1540s, its enduring popular appeal (which would last in some quarters for decades to come), the strength of the medieval tradition of architectural patronage and the financial and organisational structures that underpinned it.[262]

---

[262] Marshall, *Religious Identities*, 44–46; Duffy, *Stripping*, Chapter 11; Ethan H. Shagan, *Popular Politics and the English Reformation* (Cambridge, 2003), 242–44; G. W. Bernard, *The King's Reformation: Henry VIII and the Remaking of the English Church* (New Haven, 2005), 494–97.

Chapter 1

FINANCING CONSTRUCTION I
The Parish

A) INTRODUCTION

The organisation of a major building project was one of the most taxing enterprises undertaken by any late medieval English parish. Of the many tasks it necessitated, probably the most challenging was to raise large and consistent sums of money over the many years of its duration, given the unreliable and often strained incomes of many peasants and townsfolk.[1] The objective was not simply to raise as much as possible from as many as possible, but to adjust financial necessity to social and economic inequalities and cultural expectations, and to balance these against architectural ambition, the availability of credit and the security of future income and costs. Gradations of payment had to be judged, donors consulted, responsibilities delegated, accounts kept and the machinery of collections, levies, parties and plays implemented and monitored.

This chapter will take an empirical approach to the financial evidence, asking who in the parish paid and through which mechanisms. Fundraisers needed to strike a delicate balance between long-term sources and short-term requirements. The manner in which the burden of responsibility was distributed would profoundly affect the position of church construction – and its patrons – in local society. The next chapter will point, for example, to the social significance of cooperation between the gentry and groups of senior parishioners in organising church construction. Forms of patronage were distributed along a broad spectrum – from the whole community, where all who could gave as much as they were able, to less democratic models dominated by small groups and individual families drawn from the parish's upper ranks. Of course, different parishes would organise in different ways according to custom and convenience, but

---

[1] See Introduction, section b, pp. 11–20.

Financing Construction I: The Parish

common patterns in economic stratification and widely shared norms provided models or standards in many places, which themselves altered over time and according to economic and social trends.

B) ASSESSING THE EVIDENCE

i) Fabric Accounts

This section will examine the two most common types of documentary evidence for the funding of parish church construction in the middle ages in turn, namely fabric accounts and churchwardens' accounts, starting with the former. Just five sets of parochial fabric accounts have survived: for two campaigns of building work at North Petherwin, Cornwall (on a series of often damaged membranes of 1505–07 and 1518–24),[2] the rebuilding of Bodmin church, Cornwall (bound in a decaying book, covering 1469–72, perhaps including only the south aisle and porch),[3] the tower at St Augustine, Hedon, East Yorkshire (five damaged rolls, covering 1428–38),[4] and the spire of Bridgwater, Somerset (one roll of annual accounts of 1366–67).[5] Although spread across 150 years, these examples are otherwise somewhat limited in range: three-quarters are taken from the southwest, and three-quarters from towns – a sample representative of documentary survival rates rather than patterns in building work.[6] The towns were all small, with between 1,000 and 2,000 inhabitants, and include some experiencing dramatic growth, as at Bodmin, and some in the midst of decline, as at Bridgwater – although perhaps not at the time that building work was underway.[7] The surviving examples at Hedon

---

[2] CRO P167/5/1 mm. 42–44, 73, and mm. 35–37, 48 respectively; Joanna Mattingly has transcribed the accounts and established their chronological order in Charles Johns, J. Mattingly, and Carl Thorpe, *St Paternus' Church, North Petherwin: A Watching Brief Report* (Truro, 1996), Appendices 2 and 3. The church was in Devon at the time of construction.

[3] CRO BBOD/244; the accounts have decayed further since Wilkinson made his transcription, and this book will follow his text where there is uncertainty; J. J. Wilkinson, 'Receipts and Expenses in the Building of Bodmin Church, A.D. 1469 to 1472', *Camden New Series* 14 (1875): 1–41.

[4] J. R. Boyle, *The Early History of the Town and Port of Hedon* (Hull, 1895), note x; Edward Herbert M. Ainslie, *The Church of St. Augustine, Hedon* (Hedon, 1926), 7.

[5] SRO D/B/bw 23a; Thomas Bruce Dilks, ed., *Bridgwater Borough Archives, 1200–1377* (Yeovil, 1933), 159–64.

[6] Introduction, section e, pp. 45–46.

[7] Bridgwater had a population of 1,700 in 1377, using a multiplier of 1.9, and 1,200 in 1524, using a multiplier of 6.5; the figures for Bodmin were 1,500 and 1,900. There is little scholarly consensus on which multipliers to use; these are taken from Alan Dyer's work and must be treated as approximate only, perhaps especially in rural areas. See the discussion in Rigby, 'Urban Population', 399–401; Carolyn C. Fenwick, ed., *The Poll Taxes of 1377, 1379, and 1381: Bedfordshire-Leicestershire*, vol. I (Oxford, 1998), 250; Carolyn C. Fenwick, ed., *The Poll Taxes of 1377, 1379, and 1381: Lincolnshire-Westmoreland*, vol. II (Oxford, 2000), 420; Carolyn C. Fenwick, ed., *The Poll Taxes of 1377, 1379, and 1381: Wiltshire-Yorkshire*, vol. III (Oxford, 2005), 459, 166; John

Assessing the Evidence

and North Petherwin are, therefore, of particular value in assessing similarities and differences between the financial and organisational approaches of the south-west and the north-east, and town and village respectively. North Petherwin was a highly developed rural parish with a large population of about 600 and at least fourteen guilds and stores. Nevertheless, the 1524 lay subsidy returns suggest it had very low per capita wealth: taxpayers paid less than 2s each on average.[8] Parochial contributions in the much smaller village of Bolney, where work was carried out under the direction of the lord of the manor in the 1530s, will also be surveyed.[9] It was a quarter of the size of North Petherwin, but taxpayers here paid over three times as much per head.[10] The urban case studies were not invariably wealthier, in fact per capita payments were scarcely higher in Hedon and Bodmin than in North Petherwin.[11] Indeed, the need to raise income from a large number of relatively poorer parishioners may help explain why these parishes, both urban and rural, chose to introduce specialist administrative bodies to oversee building work.

The advantage of using fabric accounts is, of course, that, unlike churchwardens' accounts, they notionally record all and only the income raised for and spent on building work. Nevertheless, the challenges they pose for quantitative analysis were discussed earlier.[12] Furthermore, in two of the best surviving examples, which are taken from very different contexts, the wardens relied on other institutions to carry out most of the fundraising. At Bodmin, three-fifths of the total recorded income in 1469–71 (almost £262) came from forty guilds and other groups, and a third from collections and bequests, while much of the remainder was raised from sales of materials. At North Petherwin, the only recorded income for the 1505–07 work is also from guilds and stores – twelve in total paying sums from under £1 to over £14 (the latter in fifteen instalments), in addition to smaller amounts that feature in the expense accounts.[13] Much is missing from the surviving accounts: expenditure exceeded income by some £20. The fabric wardens in both places were

---

Sheail, *The Regional Distribution of Wealth in England as Indicated in the 1524/5 Lay Subsidy Returns*, ed. R. W. Hoyle, vol. 2 (Kew, 1998), 41, 105, 301, 402; Dyer, *Decline and Growth*, 64.

[8] Sheail, *Distribution of Wealth*, 2:51; the problems with using these returns have been rehearsed elsewhere – both in terms of the atypical features of that year and the limitations of the documentary sources – and must be taken as indications of population and wealth only. E.g. John Sheail, *The Regional Distribution of Wealth in England as Indicated in the 1524/5 Lay Subsidy Returns*, ed. R. W. Hoyle, vol. 1 (Kew, 1998), 7.

[9] Chapter 5, section b.ii, pp. 221–26.

[10] Julian C. K. Cornwall, ed., *The Lay Subsidy Rolls for the County of Sussex, 1524–25* (Lewes, 1957), 89–90.

[11] Sheail, *Distribution of Wealth*, 2:51, 41, 402.   [12] Introduction, section e, pp. 46–47.

[13] CRO P167/5/1 m. 43; Johns, Mattingly, and Thorpe, *North Petherwin*, 35.

Financing Construction I: The Parish

evidently appointed less to fundraise than to coordinate largely guild-financed projects and the fundraising approaches the guilds adopted were not recorded in either parish.

Similarly, at Hedon there are records of just £36 being raised for the building work. Assuming similar quantities were raised in the missing accounts, this probably represents less than half the total cost of the tower. Boyle suggests that levies were the most important source of funding here, and well-organised collections did raise up to £10 a year, but it was donations by the churchwardens which funded the greater part of the building work, both through directly paying wages and costs, and in donating to the fabric fund.[14] The sources used by the wardens are unknown, but it seems inevitable that they must have arranged further fundraising and not relied on their usual income. Lastly, at Bridgwater, Somerset, 96 per cent of the recorded funds for the new tower came from a levy, recorded on tallies ('*per talliam*'), and reaching a substantial total of over £137.[15] Just 3 per cent came from bequests and 1 per cent from gifts. Sadly, the identity of those to whom the levy applied is lost.

However, there are several sets of fabric accounts that are not strictly the subject of this chapter but provide useful information – from a city, a town and a village all towards the end of the middle ages. The Berry chapel, Bodmin, is not a parish church but rather a detached guild chapel.[16] Nevertheless, the fabric accounts of c. 1501–10 for its tower have been included here as a similar example that is able to shed greater light on locally run corporate projects than the strictly parochial accounts can. The accounts are too badly decayed for any quantification of income to be attempted, but the surviving lists of receipts are made up of gifts, supported by an indulgence, from individual donors and guilds and occasionally numbering as many as thirty or more in a year. Surviving donations range from 1d to 30s or more, but the amounts are usually lost, even when the names survive.[17]

The partially decayed private accounts kept by the lord of the manor for the tower at Bolney in 1536–37 are also enlightening, even though they are largely concerned with expenditure and not income, and the sum given by the chief funder, John Bolney, was never recorded. The communal sources of which record survives were various, but the greatest quantities were from the hognel warden, an ale and the parish collection.[18] Smaller sums came

---

[14] It is possible that Boyle was able to use a more complete version of the accounts, however. Boyle, *Hedon*, 121.
[15] SRO D/B/bw 23a; Dilks, *Bridgwater Borough Archives, 1200–1377*, 159–64.
[16] See Chapter 4, section c.iv, pp. 201–02.   [17] CRO BBOD/314/1/1-14.
[18] See Chapter 5, section b.ii, pp. 221–26; Gabriel Byng, 'The Construction of the Tower at Bolney Church', *Sussex Archaeological Collections* 151 (2013): 101–13; 'hogling' was probably an

Assessing the Evidence

from offerings to a cross, the sale of broken silver in London, direct gifts, debt repayments, money lending and equipment rental. Sadly, however, the donors to all of these are unrecorded. Most useful, however, are the fabric accounts for the construction of a new house in St Ewen, Bristol, in c. 1493. Here, the most important sum was more than £7 in direct gifts, which made up almost a third of recorded income, followed by a loan of £5, which made up a fifth. After these were more than £3 from ales (14 per cent); and slightly smaller sums from the churchwardens (12 per cent), collections (10 per cent) and old debts, possibly to the churchwardens (9 per cent). Sales of building materials (5 per cent) and rents (3 per cent) make up the remainder.

ii) *Churchwardens' Accounts*

Churchwardens' accounts provide the most plentiful sources for determining the income for parochial building projects. The following discussion is based on instances, drawn from a survey of churchwardens' accounts from counties across England, where wardens can be found raising, and spending, large additional sums for parochial building work.[19] Leaving aside London examples, these are again largely drawn from small towns – Saffron Walden, Halesowen, Louth, Ludlow, Swaffham and Thame.[20] The towns are comparable to those of the previous section, stretching in size from Ludlow and Saffron Walden with over 2,000 inhabitants to Thame with as few as 650. The others fall somewhere between, with populations of around 700–1,500.[21] Two village projects are also surveyed: Croscombe in Somerset and Leverton in Lincolnshire, with populations, in the 1520s, of roughly 230 and 120 respectively.[22] Demographic differences were exceeded by financial ones: Croscombe, a wealthy clothing village, paid almost £32 in 1524–25 but Leverton, less than £2.[23]

---

entertainment led by the parochial elite and churchwardens, and given around the Christmas to Easter period in return for money: Christine Peters, *Patterns of Piety: Women, Gender and Religion in Late Medieval and Reformation England* (Cambridge, 2003), 26–27; J. Stokes, 'The Hoglers: Evidences of an Entertainment Tradition in Eleven Somerset Parishes', *Somerset and Dorset N&Q* 32 (1990): 807–16; D. M. M. Shorrocks, 'The Custom of Hogling', *Somerset and Dorset N&Q* 28 (1967): 341–42; Uvedale Lambert, 'Hognel Money and Hogglers', *Surrey Archaeological Collections* 30 (1917): 54–60; Peters, *Patterns of Piety*, 26–27.

[19] For further discussion of this survey see: pp. 139–40 [20] Introduction, section b, pp. 17–20.
[21] Sheail, *Distribution of Wealth*, 2:198, 224, 265, 280, 315; Farnhill, *Guilds*, 104; Poos, *Rural Society*, 126.
[22] Sheail, *Distribution of Wealth*, 2:183, 307.
[23] The Leverton assessment is from the 1525 survey, but values had changed little in other places surveyed in the Wapentake of Skirbeck.

Financing Construction I: The Parish

It is worth pointing out the vast variation in mean payments this suggests: from Croscombe, with over 17s per taxpayer, through Louth, Swaffham and Thame with some 4–5s each, to Leverton, with little more than 1s. The geographic spread is more varied than the fabric accounts of the previous section, but still omits the north and south-east, and is heavily weighted to the later fifteenth and sixteenth centuries, perhaps reflecting, as was argued earlier, an increase in building work in that period.[24]

Even allowing for problems with quantification, as discussed earlier, it is easy to find churchwardens radically increasing their annual income for major building work: for a new aisle at All Hallows, London Wall, for example, it rose from £2–£4 in normal years to more than £33 in 1528–29, a tenfold increase.[25] The difference was largely financed by borrowed money, which formed a third of the total (Figure 1.1). In this relatively poor parish, extra gifts, a play and sales were used only to bolster income, while torches, lights and oblations, largely for funerals and obits, could not, of course, be easily increased. Similarly, in Louth, the wardens managed to increase their annual income from £16 to almost £60 when building work on the tower began in earnest in 1501.[26] Regular Sunday collections increased by approximately half, but, again, payments for burial and tolling (which made up around two-fifths of the wardens' usual income) could for obvious reasons increase only unpredictably (or not at all). Instead it was direct donations and bequests that rose the most, by almost twentyfold. The wardens' total recorded income during building work in 1501–15 was dominated by these direct gifts and donations, followed by borrowed money and collections. Tolling, burials and sales made up the remainder (Figure 1.2).

Large, new absolute sums derived from direct donations, collections and borrowed money can be shown almost universally during building projects – even if their proportions can only be unreliably determined.[27] In 1442, in Thame in Oxfordshire, the first year from which accounts survive and when work on the Trinity Aisle was underway, the only recorded income is from seventeen named people.[28] This included one

---

[24] Introduction, section d, pp. 39–45. [25] Welch, *Allhallows CWAs*, 56–59.
[26] LA Louth St James Par/7/1 pp. 1–255, cf. p. 9 with p. 25; Reginald C. Dudding, *The First Churchwardens' Book of Louth, 1500–1524* (Oxford, 1941), xiv.
[27] Introduction, section e, pp. 46–47. In none of the examples in this section is there any explicit reason to suspect that any other body was involved in financing building work.
[28] OHC PAR273/4/F1/1 f. 2r; William Patterson Ellis, 'The Churchwardens' Accounts of the Parish of St. Mary, Thame, Commencing in the Year 1442', *Berkshire, Buckinghamshire and Oxfordshire Archaeological Journal* VII (1901): 115; William Patterson Ellis, 'The Churchwardens' Accounts of the Parish of St. Mary, Thame, Commencing in the Year 1442', *Berkshire, Buckinghamshire and Oxfordshire Archaeological Journal* VIII (1902): 24–27, 54–55, 75.

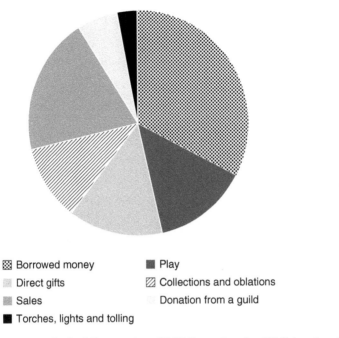

Figure 1.1　Revenue for building work at All Hallows, London Wall (1528–29)

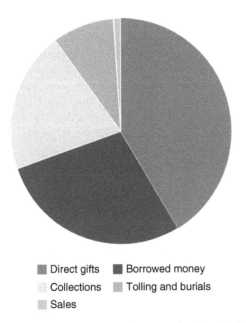

Figure 1.2　Revenue for building work at Louth, Lincolnshire (1501–15)

Financing Construction I: The Parish

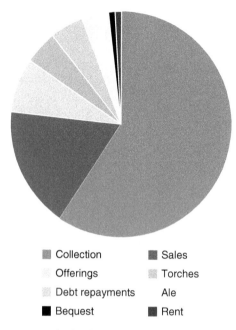

Figure 1.3   Revenue for building work at Thame, Oxfordshire (1443)

bequest and gifts from a 'gentleman' and a 'frankel', that is, a franklin or yeoman. The next year a collection 'to the work of the north aisle' raised almost £9 (three-fifths of that year's recorded total, Figure 1.3).[29] From 1444, by which point the aisle appears to be completed, annual receipts are of the order of £2–£4, suggesting that the wardens were able to increase their annual income by up to sevenfold, or even more, during the work. A similar, but more extreme, example can be given at Swaffham in Norfolk, where direct donations and bequests in 1507–08 made up nearly the entirety of the wardens' income (Figure 1.4).[30] The greater part of these sums was spent on the new tower. The late fifteenth-century benefactions recorded on the bede roll in the Black Book cannot be quantified, but the list of donations encompassed both large sums of money and, if it can be taken literally, the creation of whole units (transepts and chapels). They indicate the absolute, and suggest the relative, importance of large individual gifts.

[29] OHC PAR273/4/F1/1 f. 4r–5v.   [30] NRO PD52/71.

Assessing the Evidence

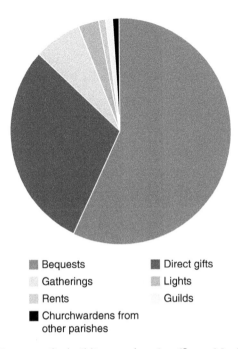

Figure 1.4   Revenue for building work at Swaffham, Norfolk (1507–08)

The accounts at Ludlow during the building of the tower c. 1469–72 indicate how substantial temporal variation could be (Figure 1.5). At first, income was dominated by direct gifts, coming to over £12 or half of the recorded total, of which £5 came from a single donor, a bailiff.[31] In the next surviving accounts, total income had almost halved and the proportions had changed too, with bequests making up a third of the recorded total. Direct gifts fell to a tenth of total revenues. Some of this is probably to be expected: the fall in gifts and collections might be associated with a rise in sales (of gifts in kind), bequests and donations by guilds, most giving a standard 6s 8d, the value of a gold angel, as parishioners found alternative means of donating. The prominence of direct gifts in the earliest accounts, and the dearth of bequests, suggests that little saving took place before work began. The following year, revenues fell again, to

---

[31] The church is often said to have been built by the Palmers guild, perhaps based on the window of the north chancel chapel: Platt, *Parish Churches*, 114.

Financing Construction I: The Parish

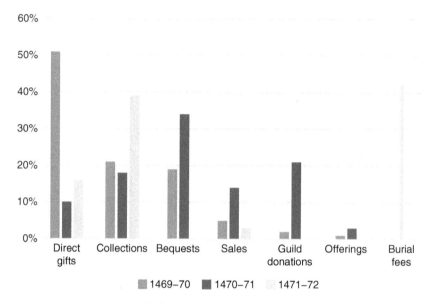

Figure 1.5 Revenue for building work at Ludlow, Shropshire (1469–72)

almost £8, and the greater part of the wardens' income came from burial fees, presumably granted to the wardens to aid the building work, and two collections. The rate of increase cannot be judged since no other accounts survive from around that time, but many direct gifts were given specifically for the new work.

Moving to the rural examples, the Lincolnshire village of Leverton seems to have followed a similar practice to urban churchwarden-led projects. In 1498, when work on the steeple was underway, the wardens' income was dominated by fifty-two weekly collections in church and direct gifts (Figure 1.6).[32] Total income that year was over £15, compared to revenues in normal years that rarely rose above £5. At Croscombe, however, there is no clear evidence that any special fundraising took place at the start of construction of the new chapel in 1506 but rather that the wardens of this unusually wealthy parish were able to rely on the parish stock.[33] This seems to have worked for a down payment of

---

[32] LA Leverton Par/7/1 ff. 3r–4v; extracts in Edward Peacock, 'Extracts from the Churchwardens' Accounts of the Parish of Leverton, in the County of Lincoln', *Archaeologia* 41 (1867): 338.
[33] Hobhouse, *Church-Wardens' Accounts*, 2, 29–32.

Assessing the Evidence

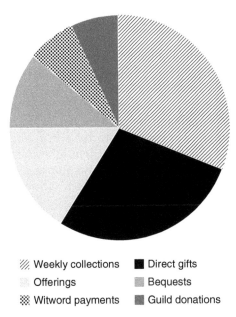

Legend:
- Weekly collections
- Offerings
- Witword payments
- Direct gifts
- Bequests
- Guild donations

Figure 1.6   Revenue for building work at Leverton, Lincolnshire (1498)

£8 to the mason John Carver at the start of the work in 1506–07, but two years later, further payments of 30s had to be made 'out of the box of the church money' and some fundraising activities increased, of which £3 for 'the coming in of Robin Hood', that year and the next, is notable. There was also a substantial increase in offerings to the 'croke box' (which Hobhouse identifies as being the processional cross), which continued into 1511–12. That year 'the whole sum of all the cost' was recorded at almost £28. It is at least possible here that the wardens were sharing financial responsibilities with another body. However, the wardens' recorded income was generally £5–£6 in this period, 1506–12 (around £2 higher than usual), while recorded expenses were 16s–30s – and this disparity may have enabled work to take place.

iii)   Modelling Fundraising

The above examples indicate significant variation in fundraising strategies but, throughout the period covered by these records, fabric wardens and churchwardens, certainly in towns and probably in the countryside too, were able to increase their income quickly and substantially for major building projects and did so using large rises in direct donations, whether of gifts from named individuals (both alive and dead), through collections or from guilds.[34] When this pattern was broken, in three cases, both urban and rural, the most likely causes were the economic circumstances and fundraising traditions of the parish. At All Hallows and Croscombe, the contrast is remarkable – in the former, collections and borrowing dominated, presumably as there were too few wealthy individual donors to provide direct funds, while the churchwardens of the latter appear to have been wealthy enough as an institution to create a considerable deposit account to draw upon. The early example of Bridgwater is also unusual in relying almost exclusively on a levy, but it will shortly be shown to have been a familiar, if controversial, technique in the parish at this time. Large parishes required more complex fundraising machinery – Bodmin used guilds and Hedon, the churchwardens – but Bridgwater was perhaps compelled to take more coercive measures. All Hallows, London, is the least remarkable of this group: in several other cases, alongside direct gifts and collections, borrowing was the other largest source of funding. The other active fundraising approach wardens could employ was sales, although these generally raised only small sums and were usually of gifts in kind made by parishioners and can be treated as donations. The death of Master Sheffett in All Hallows, London Wall, in 1527–28, for example, was a boon for the building work of that year – as well as receiving money for his knell and torches, and the payment of an old debt, the wardens also sold his 'best cross', which presumably had been left to them.[35]

Rents, knells, burial fees and so forth might provide large sums of money but could not easily be raised to accommodate the new burden of paying for building work (Ludlow, as we have seen, is a partial exception to this rule), neither were 'communal' activities, such as ales, invariably employed to fund major new projects, although some exceptions will be cited shortly. A rare example of a play, which raised over £5, explicitly used to fund a major building campaign can be found at All Hallows, although payments to Robin Hood at Croscombe have also been cited and an actor's wages were entered under the accounts for the new battlements of Heybridge, Essex, in 1516–17.[36] In urban parishes there is little evidence that offerings and

---

[34] See also the gilding of the rood loft at St Mary, Sandwich, c. 1508–12: Ford, 'Art and Identity', 233.

[35] Welch, *Allhallows CWAs*, 56.

[36] Samuel Pegge and John Nichols, *Illustrations of the Manners and Expences of Antient Times in England* (London, 1797), 156–57.

oblations increased significantly during building work, but the rural examples are less clear. Perhaps here collections were channelled through offering boxes to give the work an additional sense of spiritual purpose. Pilgrimage could also contribute significant sums to some church incomes, enough, perhaps, to make building work possible – as for the chapels at Sailholme and Rippingale, Lincolnshire, in the 1370s and the 1380s respectively.[37]

The primary importance of collections and gifts from individuals or guilds appears to be true of large non-architectural building projects too. Take, for example, the sums entered into the 1514–15 accounts for the new font cover at St Andrew, Canterbury: 37 per cent from a collection among the women of the parish, 13 per cent from the churchwardens and the rest, a half of the total, from a private donation by Paul Richmond, one of the wardens.[38] His position presumably contributed to his ability to attract a matched donation for the new cover – indeed, it is possible that the small donation by the wardens may have made up a shortfall. There was some contemporary understanding that direct donations were critical to building work, more so than communal sources such as ales or long-term ones such as rents. An undated memorandum at Eye, Suffolk, notes, appositely, that in 1470 the steeple was paid for 'partly with the plough, partly in church ales, partly in legacies given that way, but chiefly of the frank and devout hearts of the people the sum of £40 and little old money', along with loans of materials.[39] Elsewhere, an inscription gives credit to testators and organisers: 'pray for the good estate of all the township of Chelmsford that have been liberal willers and procurers of helpers to this work; and for ... them that first began, and longest shall continue'.[40]

There is little evidence for chronological developments in methods of fundraising, despite the economic and demographic changes of the long fifteenth century. It was suggested in the Introduction to this volume, for example, that declining real wages and stable large holdings made the financing of church building increasingly exclusive in the early sixteenth century, but the examples surveyed above indicate that collections continued while direct, named donations were dominant in some places in the mid-fifteenth. Importantly, however, it is only occasionally possible to discover who, or how many, were contributing to collections, and very few documents allow for

---

[37] Owen, *Church and Society*, 126–27.
[38] Charles Cotton, *Churchwardens' Accounts of the Parish of St. Andrew, Canterbury* (London, 1916), ii: 18.
[39] Bettey, *Church & Community*, 39.
[40] H. W. King, 'Historical Evidence of the Date of Erection of Certain Church Towers and of Church Restoration in Essex', *Transactions of the Essex Archaeological Society*, 1 (1878): 47.

comparisons over an extended period in one place. The former point will be addressed shortly, but one exception to the latter may be considered now.

The churchwardens' accounts of Saffron Walden, Essex, run for some sixty years from 1439 to c. 1490, and until the 1480s increases in ales and collections provided the greater part of recorded funds for a series of substantial projects – probably including the tower, the chancel clerestory, the south porch, the extensions of both aisles and some major new furnishings.[41] However, the last major project run by the churchwardens, in c. 1490, was the building of an aisle roof and for the first time the wardens moved to fund the work exclusively through direct gifts from no more than forty people (about 3 per cent of the population). The construction of the nave at this time was run by fabric wardens, whose accounts do not survive, but it is likely that they were under some pressure to move away from communal fundraising after decades of demanding work on the building during the recession of the mid-fifteenth century.[42] By the 1520s, Saffron Walden was a highly polarised town, with a larger number of wage earners than other nearby Essex hundreds, and a relatively substantial economic elite, and there is good reason to believe that this group were entrenching their position in the final quarter of the fifteenth century.[43]

Having established the significance of different types of income, the following section will evaluate the use and application of each. In conceptualising the range of donations they stimulated, the following models are useful, if often difficult to apply with certainty and admitting of alternatives:[44]

- 'Parish', where funding is shared between all or most parishioners according to their resources;
- 'Multiple patron and parish', where a few wealthy donors who led the financing also used sums from communal activities;
- 'Multiple patron', where building work is the responsibility of two or more wealthy families;

---

[41] Byng, 'Saffron Walden', 338–39.   [42] ERO D/DBy Q18, f. 143.
[43] Elizabeth Allan, *Chepyng Walden: A Late Medieval Small Town, Saffron Walden 1438–1490* (Saffron Walden, 2015), 107–08.
[44] French, for example, contrasts the 'group effort' to rebuild Bridgwater, Somerset, with St Michael, Bath, which 'reflected the interests of a few': French, *People*, 152. cf. Melo and Ribeiro's very different set of 'financing modes' for Portuguese towns: 'Construction Financing in Late Medieval Portuguese Towns', in *Nuts & Bolts of Construction History*, ed. Robert Carvais, André Guillerme, Valérie Nègre, and Joël Sakarovitch, vol. 2 (Paris, 2012), 306; Philippe Bernardi, *Bâtir Au Moyen Age* (Paris, 2011), 80.

Fundraising Techniques

- o A version of this model is 'guild', where a fraternity or semiformal social group acts as patron;
- 'Patron and parish', where there is a single outstanding patron but the fruits of collective activities also contributed to the work;
- 'Patron and multiple patron', where a single major patron, often of gentry status, combines with other wealthy families;
- 'Patron', where all the funding comes from a single donor.

The existence of each model is attested to by different forms of evidence: the 'patron' model is largely based on inscriptions and heraldry; the 'parish' models are usually taken from churchwardens' accounts. In other words, by its nature each source reveals more or less cooperative or exclusive aspects of a project's fundraising, often obscuring the work of other individuals and groups.

c) FUNDRAISING TECHNIQUES

i) Regular Income

Few churchwardens had large enough revenues to pay for a new project without extra fundraising: most surviving accounts record an income in the order of only a few pounds a year, of which the greater part was spent on the wardens' regular duties.[45] Although it may have been possible for them to call on other funds and stores within the parish, these would rarely have been sufficient to make up the necessary increase.[46] Rents, equipment leasing, fines, money lending and fees for burial or knells all provided useful, even large, sources of regular funding for the wardens' usual activities but were ill-suited to financing building work. Those that did not generate small or unpredictable sums were nevertheless typically dedicated to other responsibilities or were difficult or impossible to increase. Leasing out equipment and lending money might be pursued more rigorously, but the capacity of most churchwardens to increase these sources significantly was limited. Fees and fines were usually set by custom and, of course, depended upon parishioners' requirements for burials and other sacramental activities, which could not be artificially increased. Even in urban parishes with large and secure rental incomes, it is doubtful that much revenue was either expendable or could be easily increased. At St Mary-at-Hill, London, for example, the wardens had an

---

[45] Burgess and Kümin, 'Penitential Bequests', 612.
[46] Although in some cases the stocks received more than the wardens: Kümin, *Shaping*, 155; Alison Hanham, ed., *Churchwardens' Accounts of Ashburton, 1479–1580* (Torquay, 1970), 58–59; cf. St Andrew Hubbard: Burgess, 'Lessons', 318.

Financing Construction I: The Parish

exceptionally high and stable annual income which was substantially based on rents, but building projects were still carried out under a separate administration by members of the elite.[47] In many places the wardens were probably only able to contribute small sums to projects as and when they could, having discharged their usual obligations, as at Hedon or Bolney.[48] Croscombe, however, acts as a corrective to such generalisations and shows how wardens with quite modest incomes were, apparently, able to build up large enough surpluses, if spread over several years, to pay for building work, although even here some active fundraising was eventually necessary.[49]

ii) Ales and Plays

That communal activities were not more widely used might seem surprising. Contracts often described 'the community' (or a similar phrase, such as 'the parish' or 'parishioners') as financing the work.[50] Churchwardens sometimes identified their funding as communal – at Louth, for example, debts for the building of the steeple were to be paid back by 'the community' in 1501–02.[51] Modern authors have often highlighted their significance: Bishop Hobhouse described church ales as 'the most universal Churchwardens' resort for eliciting the bounty of the parish'[52] and Lawrence Blair's study of church ales found that 'before the Reformation, it was one of the chief sources of church revenue'.[53] It is possible that such sums were raised but not entered into the annual accounts or were abbreviated to the point of disappearance, but there is no reason to suspect so and there is good reason to assume it would be desirable for the wardens to record and commemorate such celebrations. Indeed, they do appear regularly, providing the examples that Hobhouse and Blair focused on. However, most parishes held no more than one or two ales a year, typically raising relatively small quantities, and probably associated with regular maintenance costs rather than with major new

---

[47] Chapter 4, section c.i, pp. 189–91.
[48] See previous section, pp. 54–55, and Chapter 5, section b.ii, pp. 224–25.
[49] Chapter 1, section b.ii, pp. 60–61.
[50] E.g. a contract at Edinburgh in 1387 agreed that 'the community as it is before spoken find all [the] cost' and 'the foresaid community shall give [600 marks] to the ... masons': George Hay, 'The Late Medieval Development of the High Kirk of St Giles, Edinburgh', *Proceedings of the Society of Antiquaries of Scotland* 107 (1976): 242–60.
[51] LA Louth St James Par/7/1 p. 22; Dudding, *Louth CWAs*, 17.
[52] Hobhouse, *Church-Wardens' Accounts*, xiii–xiv.
[53] Lawrence Blair, *English Church Ales* (Ann Arbor, 1940), 1; cf. J. R. Lander, *Government and Community: England 1450–1509* (London, 1980), 149; Johnston, 'Parish Entertainments in Berkshire', 335.

projects.⁵⁴ Francis Beaumont wrote in the sixteenth century: 'The churches must owe, as we all do know,/For when they be drooping and ready to fall,/By a Whitsun or Church-ale up again they shall go/And owe their repairing to a pot of good ale.'⁵⁵ Many parishioners probably could not afford to attend more ales or plays than the customary one or two, in addition to guild ales and other entertainments, so their number or profitability could not be easily increased for a new large project.⁵⁶

As a fundraising technique, ales were inefficient, charging all members of the community similar amounts irrespective of wealth and requiring large quantities of organisational input from the wardens, especially given the relatively small sums they tended to raise. For example, an ale held by the maids for the building of the Trinity aisle at Thame, Oxfordshire, in 1442 raised the not inconsiderable sum of 23s but required over 11s of investment.⁵⁷ It contributed just 4 per cent of that year's recorded total. An ale, unconnected with building work but for which accounts survive, at Bramley, Hampshire, raised over £5 in 1531–32 but cost more than £2 and was evidently an elaborate affair to organise.⁵⁸ Wardens tended to look to other sources for new funds. For example, the painting of the tabernacle at Cratfield, Suffolk, in 1494 cost the wardens £7, when expenditure was typically only about £3. Nevertheless, that year they ran only the usual number of ales which raised the usual amount, relying instead on an unprecedented number of bequests (six) and gifts (eight) to raise an extra £6 8s.⁵⁹ The remainder of the cost, as well as the wardens' other outgoings, were covered by their standard income.

Aside from Saffron Walden, Essex, discussed above, I have found only one example where building work was funded through ales: for the roof of Halesowen, Worcestershire, in 1531–34.⁶⁰ The greater part of additional

---

⁵⁴ Blair surveys numerous post-Reformation and some earlier examples of ales that raised much larger sums. At Wing, Buckinghamshire, ales raised twice as much in the 1560s as they did in the 1530s: Blair, *Ales*, 3–18; cf. Kümin, *Shaping*, 213–14.
⁵⁵ Quoted in John Gordon Davies, *The Secular Use of Church Buildings* (London, 1968), 165.
⁵⁶ Brown gives a counterexample at Wimborne, where ales in the run up to building work in the 1440s increased in profitability from £4–£5 to £9: Brown, *Popular Piety*, 119.
⁵⁷ Ellis, 'Thame CWAs', 1902, 27.
⁵⁸ This ratio, roughly 2:1, can also be found in the 1575 ale at Winterslow. However, even this may have been a good return, cf. Holy Trinity, Bungay, in 1568. In 1586, the inefficiency of the ale was acknowledged at Lacock, Wiltshire, when the village leadership agreed that 'if the dearness of the year suffer them [the vicar and parishioners] not to keep church ale in good and honest order that then every householder and others here underwritten shall pay towards the maintenance of the church as they are here ceased': Blair, *Ales*, 11, 25–26.
⁵⁹ William Holland, *Cratfield: A Transcript of the Accounts of the Parish, from A.D. 1490 to A.D. 1642*, ed. John James Raven (London, 1896), 24.
⁶⁰ At Yatton, Somerset, ales provided a large source of income during building work but they were held regularly and tended to raise similar amounts (£2–£4 per ale across three ales). Bequests and gifts provided more variable income. A. C. Edwards, 'The Medieval Churchwardens' Accounts of

Financing Construction I: The Parish

funding came from ales, which featured in the churchwardens' accounts only during and just before the building period, in 1530–34 (three in 1530–31, two in 1531–32, one in 1532–33 and two in 1533–34).[61] Receipts rose from an average of £2–£5 in the preceding years to more than £11. Ales probably became a vehicle for the extra donations that the community, or a segment of it, would need to provide in order to fund the new work. To this example may be added the inscription on the small timber gallery at Cawston, Norfolk: 'Be merry and glad what good ale this work made.'

The Bolney accounts also record gifts given during an ale, probably held on the day the contract for the tower was signed, and delivered to the lord of the manor, John Bolney, by the wardens.[62] A distinctive advantage of ales and plays for some project managers, such as Bolney, was that they could both demonstrate and encourage the approval of a broad cross section of the parish. Although several authors have noted that ales and plays (gifts from 'the living') were of greatest importance in rural parishes, there is little evidence of this when it came to raising funds for building work.[63] They were critical at Saffron Walden and Halesowen, and important at All Hallows, London Wall, but of negligible importance in the rural examples surveyed above, which are drawn from an admittedly small sample size.[64]

iii) Collections

Even without ales, plays or other communal activities, the prevalence of collections in fundraising accounts might appear to prove the general use of the communitarian 'parish' model given above, so popular with recent scholars.[65] Unlike ales or plays, collections allowed a wide range of sums to be donated, so anyone could give according to their wealth or income. They also required relatively little organisational effort or financial outlay by the wardens.[66] However, although these may have been advertised

---

St Mary's Church, Yatton', *N&Q for Somerset and Dorset* 32 (September 1986): 540; work carried out at St John, Glastonbury, in 1428 was funded by two plays and an ale: French, *People*, 151.

[61] Frank Somers, ed., *Halesowen Churchwardens' Accounts (1487–1582)* (London, 1952), 4 (Introduction by Margaret O'Brien), 60.

[62] Chapter 2, section c, p. 121; Byng, 'Bolney', 105.

[63] Kümin, *Shaping*, 116–17, 296–97, Figure 3.3.

[64] To these examples could be added the purchase of a new cross by St Ewen, Bristol, in 1454–55 for £24, of which £5 came from an ale. For the new church house of 1493, over £3 was raised from two ales: Masters and Ralph, *St Ewen, Bristol, CWAs*, 16.

[65] See Introduction, section a, pp. 3–6.

[66] Although a collection, probably for building work, at All Hallows, London, does note that the sum is 'clear and all charges born': Welch, *Allhallows CWAs*, 56; or they could appoint collectors: Margaret Aston, 'Iconoclasm at Rickmansworth, 1522: Troubles of Churchwardens', *The Journal of Ecclesiastical History* 40, no. 4 (October 1989): 525.

Fundraising Techniques

across the parish and organised street by street, it remains to be determined whether the number of donors does reflect a significant majority of the community, spread from the poorest to the richest.

There is good evidence for their efficacy. Early collection boxes for parish church fabrics were so successful that rectors complained and bishops restricted their use for fear of losing revenues at shrines.[67] The many examples of indulgences granted to encourage donations for building work suggest both the importance of collections for fundraising and their widespread appeal, on a par with offerings to a shrine.[68] At St Edmund, Salisbury, a collection backed by an indulgence was important enough for the church to spend 5d proclaiming the event, as well as 1s making six copies of the indulgence and 4d in distributing them in 1473–76, and paying 2s 4d to children who attended the declaration, presumably to encourage donations.[69] What these examples do not reveal, however, is whether the parish hoped to collect sums from almost every parishioner, according to their income, or only a few large gifts from the wealthiest, or some other combination between.

Some collections undoubtedly raised donations from large numbers of people. A collection for the rebuilding of Bodmin church (1469–72) in Cornwall is the surviving example with the greatest number of donors, 451 in total, usually claimed to comprise 'almost every adult in the parish'.[70] This claim is not without substance: the town's population has been estimated at 1,500 at the time of the Poll Tax of 1377 and 1,900 at the time of the lay subsidies of 1524–25.[71] Allowing for children, the collection represents perhaps only half the town's adult population but, therefore, a large number of households. Nevertheless, forty-nine donors are explicitly recorded as members of the same household as other donors and the actual number was no doubt higher. There were a considerable number of female donors, for example, a seventh of the total, although only a quarter of whom were specifically named as wives; these women usually gave a third as much as their

---

[67] Nevertheless, the venture was probably a failure, as was another printing of six copies of the indulgence in 1483. Drew, *Early Parochial Organisation*, 15.

[68] F. N. Davis, ed., *Rotuli Hugonis De Welles, Episcopi Lincolniensis, A.D. MCCIX–MCCXXXV*, vol. 2 (London, 1907), 253–54.

[69] Henry Swayne, *Churchwardens' Accounts of S. Edmund & S. Thomas, Sarum, 1443–1702* (Salisbury, 1896), 53; Cox, *Churchwardens' Accounts*, 29–30.

[70] CRO BBOD/244 ff. 29–37 (note, the folio numbering is unclear here); transcripts can be found in: A. R. Myers, *English Historical Documents 1327–1485* (London, 1996), 741; Wilkinson, *Bodmin Church*, 1874; cf. Randall, *Parish Church*, 46. Lander, *Government and Community*, 149; Cook, *Parish Church*, 58; Platt, *Parish Churches*, 94; Brown, *Church and Society*, 94.

[71] Dyer, *Decline and Growth*, 30–32, 64.

Financing Construction I: The Parish

husbands, or less.[72] Some were perhaps widows – Betty Trote gave 40s and William Trote, perhaps her son, just 3s 4d, for example.[73] Although impossible to calculate with accuracy, a sizeable number of households were evidently not obliged to donate even a penny.

The poorest are generally assumed to be those who gave animals, pots, pans, pennies and their labour to the works. This argument begs the question, however: the proof that those who gave 'small' donations were the poorest parishioners cannot be that they gave small donations. As noted earlier, in the 1520s, Bodmin had low per-capita taxable wealth, yet small gifts, admittedly made fifty years earlier, were rare: just 2 per cent of donors gave a penny, while 40 per cent gave a shilling or more.[74] Similarly, those who gave free labour were not the poorest: most also donated money and presumably gave the former as an act of piety.[75] Free time and spare energy were commodities enjoyed by wealthier inhabitants. Gifts in kind probably made little difference to the ability of poorer peasants to contribute: when labour, materials or accommodation are found in late medieval building accounts they were often the gift of wealthier parishioners who were perhaps coping with a period of reduced money supply.[76] Wealthier donors were expected to give large sums, while the handful who gave just a penny or two were either an exceptional few who decided to donate despite their poverty or else less generous but still relatively well-off parishioners. The former is more likely: since the names and contributions of all the donors were recorded, it seems likely both that those who felt obliged to give did, whether from personal conviction or social pressure, and that those who did not were understood to be exempt because of their poverty.

Collections were often entered on separate 'bills' or 'parcels' from the regular accounts and distinguished from large one-off gifts. For the aisle at All Hallows, London Wall, for example, there were ten donations in 1528–29, with none below 5s and one of 52s from the wives' guild, including gifts from the parson, a chantry priest and seven quondam churchwardens, most of whom also loaned money to the works and acted as auditors (in four cases) or collectors.[77] However, the accounts also record that a collection was taken 'in the parish' by William Stocks and Thomas Large, who were probably fabric wardens for the new work. Since such bills included large numbers of subscribers paying relatively small amounts, they would be unwieldy if copied into the regular

---

[72] Some first names are ambiguous as to gender.
[73] Alice and William Pole are a similar example; John Austel and his wife gave the same amount.
[74] Chapter 1, section b.i, p. 53.   [75] Cf. Bolney: Chapter 2, section c, p. 122.
[76] Cf. Dyer, *Standards*, 185.   [77] Welch, *Allhallows CWAs*, 59 cf. 57.

accounts. All Hallows, London Wall, had a separate 'gathering book' that recorded proceeds from the play and from collections at neighbouring parishes. Only occasionally do such lists survive, presumably retained as lasting evidence of the devotion of the community and the generosity of individual families. Indeed, it is possible that records of larger collections are more likely to survive, since more people had a vested interest in their preservation, while the memory of neighbours, for all its social significance, may have seemed less than reliable when so many people were involved. Where they exist, lists of subscribers to building work indicate both that Bodmin's was exceptional in reaching so far beyond the taxpaying population and that collections were usually limited to large minorities of the parish and consisted of few (or no) small gifts and many large ones.

At Great Dunmow in Essex, for example, the churchwardens' income regularly included large collections. The one taken for the making of the new steeple in 1526 had 165 subscribers (although some do not have a sum entered against their name), roughly the number of taxpayers in 1524–25.[78] The parish seems to have set a standard minimum of 4d (less than a tenth of donors gave less), the cost of a day's labour, but many gave considerably more. The collection was organised by street or quarter, but the accounts are headed by a group who was assessed not by where they lived but by social status. This social elite donated larger sums and was headed by current and former priests. Despite the major work going on, this was not an exceptional collection. The next year, 154 would give, probably for the bells, and were described as 'the whole town'.[79] Other collections took place for the organ, for new bells and for bell clappers in later years.[80] Dunmow provides a rare opportunity to compare donations to building work with the lay subsidy, taken just two years earlier, and Kate Cole has shown that the distribution of payments in the lay subsidy and to the collection was very similar.[81] She even makes the plausible argument that the subsidy roll was used to fix donations to the work – 4d, the most common donation, was the sum paid by those in the lowest tax band. Here, then, the 'whole town' and the group expected to fund new works was identified with the taxpaying population.

Although rarely so close in time to a usable tax record, in several other places the number of donors to a project was very similar to the parish's taxable population. The collection of 1443 for the new north aisle at Thame, Oxfordshire, for example, received 108 donations, with

---

[78] ERO D/P 11/5/1 ff. 2r–5v. [79] ERO D/P 11/5/1 f. 7.
[80] ERO D/P 11/5/1 ff. 12v–17v; 21v–22r; 25r–26r.
[81] Kate J. Cole, 'Great Dunmow's Local History: Henry VIII's 1523–4 Lay Subsidy Tax', http://www.essexvoicespast.com/henry-viiis-1523-4-lay-subsidy-tax/, accessed 20 July 2016.

only one gift of 1d and 15 of 2s or more.[82] Donations came from roughly the same number as the town's taxable population sixty years later, 100 people – perhaps a majority of its households, or, if limited to New Thame, which had responsibility for the north side of the church, even more.[83] Thame's population probably decreased slightly over the long fifteenth century.[84] This is also true of the Cambridgeshire village of Bassingbourn. Two collections for new bells in 1496–97 and 1499 garnered 109 and 85 gifts respectively, roughly the same as the parish's taxable population in the 1520s.[85] In the first there was just one gift of 2d, while 90 per cent were more than a shilling and seven were more than 10s; in the second the lowest gift was of 4d and three-quarters of gifts were more than a shilling.

These collections may have been exceptionally large, however. A collection at St Lawrence, Reading, in 1440, probably at tenements belonging to the church, raised almost £10 across eighty-four gifts. Only one person gave a penny, while almost a fifth gave more than 2s, and the highest gifts were of 6s 8d, the value of a noble.[86] Despite the relatively modest sums given, donations may have come from around a tenth of adults.[87] A later collection for repairing the bell tower in 1458 is now badly decayed, but twenty-six names survive. Where collections can be compared in a single place, smaller ones can sometimes be shown to raise higher mean sums – suggesting they were limited to wealthier parishioners. A collection ('sesse') for the new rood loft at St Andrew, Canterbury, in 1508–09, raised over £14 from forty-eight parishioners.[88] Here the smallest donation was of 7d and the largest of £2. The average gift increased for a collection four years later for new organs, raising more than £9 from twenty-eight parishioners. Another collection, for the font cover in 1514–15 raised over 7s from seventeen women, perhaps drawing on an association between motherhood and baptism. The church was situated on the High Street between Burgate and Newingate, which had 124 and 113 taxpayers respectively in 1524

---

[82] Following the parish's usual practice, these were entered as a list of names in the ordinary receipts: OHC PAR273/4/F1/1 ff. 4r–5v; Ellis, 'Thame CWAs', 1902, 24–27.

[83] In 1524–25 New Thame had seventy-eight and Old Thame twenty-two taxpayers, but around 510 and 140 inhabitants respectively: Sheail, *Distribution of Wealth*, 2:265.

[84] In 1377, Old Thame had 128 taxpayers (equivalent to about 240 people) and New Thame, 325 (about 620): Fenwick, *Poll Taxes*, 2000, II: 296.

[85] It was also the number of houses in the village at enclosure. CA P11/5/1; D. P. Dymond, *The Churchwardens' Book of Bassingbourn, Cambridgeshire 1496–c. 1540* (Cambridge, 2004), 152–55, 150–52; A. P. M. Wright, ed., *VCH Cambridgeshire*, vol. 8 (London, 1982), 12–30.

[86] Charles Kerry, *A History of the Municipal Church of St. Lawrence, Reading* (Reading, 1883), 12–13.

[87] Importantly, however, Reading had three parish churches, so the constituency of potential donors that St Laurence could call upon is uncertain: Ibid., 10.

[88] Cotton, *St Andrew, Canterbury, CWAs*, 43–45.

(about 800 and 740 people), indicating that subscribers, in the largest collection, made up as little as a tenth of the adult population.[89] As this suggests, on examination the distinction between a collection and a few direct 'named' gifts begins to dissolve in many places. Indeed, at St Margaret, Westminster, the donors to one collection were described as 'the worshipful and well-disposed people of this parish'.[90]

At Swaffham, Norfolk, the bede roll recorded in the Black Book suggest that a few wealthy families donated the majority of the funds for rebuilding the church. Some twenty-two donors are recorded as giving specifically to building or edifying the new church, including John and Catherine Chapman, who gave £120; John and Margaret Plumer, who gave £60; and John Walsingham and Simon Blake, who gave more than £40 each.[91] The parish may have had 600–1,000 inhabitants in the sixteenth century.[92] There were also payments specifically for substantial portions of the work: the Chapmans built the north aisle; the Taylors, the chancel roof; William Coo, the porch roof; Robert Payne, much of the nave and Trinity Chapel; John Payne, the Corpus Christi Chapel; and others glazed windows or gave large amounts of stone. The smallest donations were of 33s 4d and the names of thirty-one other donors to a collection are recorded, though the sums they gave are omitted. In the churchwardens' accounts, although one donation of 1d is noted, the majority donated more than 3s and one bequest was for £15, another for £5.[93]

Comparing this sample of large collections with the 1524–25 lay subsidy data suggests that the size of the former varied according to the capacity of the wealthiest local groups to cover the cost of building work themselves. When they could, collections were either not employed or were relatively small, resembling lists of named donors entered into regular accounts; when they could not, collections would stretch outside their number. At Reading and Canterbury, for example, with high per capita wealth, donors to the largest recorded collections numbered just a third and a fifth of the number of taxpayers respectively, and at Swaffham, also with reasonably high per capita wealth (and a few exceptionally generous donors), the figure is about 40 per cent (Table 1.1). However, at Thame, with middling per capita wealth, donors exceeded taxpayers, by a modest 10 per cent, and at Great Dunmow, with slightly lower per capita wealth, the figure is 20 per cent – again, these are in the largest collections. Bodmin had the lowest per capita taxable wealth of any urban

---

[89] Sheail, *Distribution of Wealth*, 2:166. [90] Rosser, *Medieval Westminster*, 268.
[91] J. F. Williams, 'The Black Book of Swaffham', *Norfolk Archaeology* 23, no. 3 (1964): 251–53; cf. Heslop, 'Swaffham'.
[92] Farnhill, *Guilds*, 104.   [93] NRO PD52/71, f. 10.

Financing Construction I: The Parish

Table 1.1 *Large collections for building work*

Collection	Year	Number of donors	1524–25 taxpayers	Mean 1524–25 payment (d)	Donors as a % of taxpayers
Bodmin	1469–72	451	311 *(1,900)*	32	145%
Great Dunmow	1526	165	139 *(900)*	41	119%
Thame	1443	108	*100 (650)*	45	108%
Bassingbourn	1496–97	109	116 *(700)*	25	94%
Swaffham	late 15C	53	123 *(800)*	59	43%
St Lawrence, Reading	1440	84	*245 (1,600)*	124	34%
St Andrew, Canterbury	1508–09	48	*237 (1,540)*	124	20%
Henley-on-Thames (rood loft)	1519	26	191 *(1,240)*	52	14%

Source: John Sheail, *The Regional Distribution of Wealth in England as Indicated in the 1524/5 Lay Subsidy Returns*, edited by R. W. Hoyle, Vol. 2 (Kew, 1998).
Note: Towns or parishes where populations are especially hard to estimate have been italicised.

example surveyed in this section so a major communal expense would need to be spread especially widely – and, indeed, here the number of donors exceeded the taxpayer population by 45 per cent.[94] This large figure points to the considerable number of people in some places who were able to donate to a collection but were nevertheless too poor to be taxed – those with under £1 per annum of goods or income. This in turn suggests the conclusion that, in towns with a wealthier and more exclusive economic elite, church architecture tended to be more distinctively their gift.

These data must be taken as rough indications only: the evidence of the lay subsidies is, of course, problematic in its own right and often dating from decades after building work was carried out, especially in Thame and Reading – although, when direct comparison is possible, at Great Dunmow, the link between donors and taxpayers is strong. Absolute taxable wealth was, of course, significant too. Bodmin was presumably only able to contemplate large-scale building work because it was a relatively larger town, with a large number of

---

[94] N.B. the time lag between building work and the Lay Subsidies means it can only be a rough comparison – Bodmin's population grew substantially between 1377 and 1524–25, from approximately 1,200 to 1,900.

taxpayers who would, in the 1520s, pay about twice as much together as those of Great Dunmow or Thame. A small parish with low individual taxpayer wealth would have had to trim its ambitions accordingly. A partial counterexample must be added: in rural Bassingbourn individual taxpayer assessments were even lower than in Bodmin, yet, as noted, the collection was equivalent to the number of taxpayers. The village was dominated by three very wealthy families, so perhaps here non-taxpayers were simply too poor to contribute.[95] The collection was made, of course, for the relatively modest purpose of purchasing new bells – the village's church was largely constructed a century and more earlier.

iv) Levies

Given that in many parishes collections applied only to a subset of parishioners, it is not surprising to discover that parish-wide levies were rarely employed for building work. The important exception is the Bridgwater tower, where almost the entire sum was raised in this manner and those who failed to pay were prosecuted. Although unusual when compared to other parishes, this practice was familiar to the people of Bridgwater: occasional levies were employed for repair work by early fifteenth-century churchwardens in the parish, incurring protests at unfair demands as well as summons for failure to pay by 'diverse persons'.[96] Indeed, a levy was used for the rebuilding of the chapel at Wembdon in the early fourteenth century, and defaulters were reported to the bishop.[97] Despite the large sums raised, Bridgwater demonstrates the risks and inefficiencies of relying on compulsory collections for building work. When the churchwardens stopped imposing levies, gifts rose considerably.

Hobhouse argued that the rarity of 'clear instances' of the imposition of levies is evidence of the willingness of almost all members of medieval parishes to contribute to building work.[98] However, the distinction between voluntary collection and compulsory levy may have been as unclear to contemporaries as it is to historians. When collections were organised street by street, raised by officers and

---

[95] Note the county's relative poverty at the time: Chapter 1, section d.iii, pp. 103–04.
[96] Thomas Bruce Dilks, ed., *Bridgwater Borough Archives, 1400–1445* (Yeovil, 1945), 46; sixteenth-century church rates have been linked to building or repair work: Anthony Palmer, *Tudor Churchwardens' Accounts* (Braughing, 1985), ix–x.
[97] Edmund Hobhouse, ed., *Calendar of the Register of John de Drokensford, Bishop of Bath and Wells (A.D. 1309–1329)* (London, 1887), 257–58.
[98] Hobhouse, *Church-Wardens' Accounts*, xiii.

Financing Construction I: The Parish

entered into rolls that were publicly audited, as at Bodmin or Great Dunmow, for those deemed eligible there may have been little choice but to donate, whether willingly or not. The obvious point of comparison would be the collection of tax, requiring 'machinery for choosing individuals to act on behalf of the community, to make assessments of neighbours and to cajole them into making financial contributions'.[99] Parishioners' incomes and their capacity for donating to corporate payments was a matter of public record, known to the parish authorities and so probably to those who were raising collections for building work – it has already been argued that the subsidy rolls were used to fix donations to the Great Dunmow collection. The beadles in the early fourteenth-century *Song of the Husbandman* warn the peasants as they collect tax 'you are written in my list, as you know very well'.[100] At St Mary-at-Hill, in 1490, one man agreed to pay 'as Mr Alderman will set him'.[101]

Nevertheless, the numbers of those who gave to collections could vary substantially. The last section gave examples of continuity in the number of donors to major projects at Bassingbourn and Great Dunmow, suggesting consistent social pressure to donate, but collections for different purposes at Thame in the 1440s achieved 108, twenty-two and sixty-one donors respectively.[102] At Great Dunmow, several later collections were considerably smaller.[103] Their profitability varied too: in just one year, 1498, weekly collections at Leverton, Lincolnshire, raised between 9d and 4s 8d.[104] Three collections at Ramsey, Huntingdonshire, in 1520–25 for an unknown purpose, recorded between 77 and 199 names.[105] The most plausible conclusion is that the expectation of who would give varied, both from place to place and from project to project, sometimes with considerable flexibility, but that collections affecting groups as large as, or larger than, the taxpayer population were not common even in those parishes that held them occasionally.

A sense of the semi-compulsory nature of some collections, for those eligible, is given in a few cases. In his will of 1432, one

---

[99] Dyer, 'Village Community', 412; Christopher Dyer, 'Taxation and Communities in Late Medieval England', in *Progress and Problems in Medieval England*, ed. John Hatcher and R. H. Britnell (Cambridge, 1996), 168–90; Goheen, 'Peasant Politics?', 50.
[100] M. T Clanchy, *From Memory to Written Record: England 1066–1307* (London, 1979), 46.
[101] Henry Littlehales, ed., *The Medieval Records of a London City Church (St. Mary at Hill) A.D. 1420–1559* (London, 1904), 157–58.
[102] OHC PAR273/4/F1/1 ff. 4r–5v; 10v–11r; 13v–14r.   [103] Chapter 1, section c.iii, pp. 71–72.
[104] LA Leverton Par/7/1 ff. 3r–4r.
[105] Anne Reiber DeWindt and Edwin Brezette DeWindt, *Ramsey: The Lives of an English Fenland Town, 1200–1600* (Washington, D.C, 2006), 33 nn. 38, 41.

parishioner promised to continue paying the '*customary* two pence every Sunday for four years promised by all the parishioners' to the building of Totnes.[106] At Bodmin more than £24 was raised from 'a grant *agreed throughout the town* [of] 1d a week of a man', although 'certain persons' gave a halfpenny instead. This collection was gathered by separate receivers and recorded on a paper account, now lost.[107] This appears to be distinguished from another grant given '*voluntarily* throughout the town', which was also recorded on a separate bill ('as it appears by the names') but which raised only a fraction as much. The terminology might be misleading: those recorded elsewhere in the accounts as being in arrears ('*qui sunt a retro*') usually owed large sums (over 2s) and are more likely to be slow in realising a pledge ('*plegius*') than in paying a levy. A variable rate was used elsewhere: parishioners at Ockbrook, Derbyshire, were charged 2d to attend an ale and cottars, 1d; and at Ashburton and St Petrock, Exeter, a levy was charged at 1d but ½d to 'every hire servant that takes wages' and a farthing for the unemployed.[108] Nevertheless, grants were regressive and inflexible compared to a collection. Few could afford 2d a week, a sum amounting to almost 9s a year. They risked raising less money than a collection and required more organisational effort, with little greater certainty of stability over time.

Charging parishioners according to wealth was not only a matter of pragmatism, necessity or social expectation; it was frequently enshrined in diocesan statute. Drew argues that by the late thirteenth century land became the basis of assessment in many parishes, requiring the wealthiest to take an increased share of the burden.[109] This definition was frequently expanded by the early fourteenth century to include property.[110] At St Andrew Hubbard, London, parish assessors were appointed to fix the rate for the parish clerk, and Burgess suggests this was used to peg other contributions to the parish.[111] More equitably, but apparently rarely,

---

[106] C. F. Rea, 'Building of Totnes Parish Church', *Transactions of the Devonshire Association* 57 (1925): 282.

[107] Over a year this would suggest over a hundred subscribers – many fewer than donors in the collection. Wilkinson, *Bodmin Church*, 1874, 32–33.

[108] Kümin, *Shaping*, 47; Hanham, *Ashburton CWAs*, 192; Gasquet, *Parish Life*, 129.

[109] Drew, *Early Parochial Organisation*, 12; cf. the tenth story of the sixth day in Boccacio's *Decameron*.

[110] E.g. '*secundum quantitatem terrarum et facultatum suarum*'; William Brown, ed., *The Register of Henry of Newark, Lord Archbishop of York, 1286–1296*, vol. 2 (Durham, 1913), 238; '*pro rata juxta suas possessiones et facultates*': A. W. Goodman, *Winchester Diocese: Register of Henry Woodlock*, vol. 1 (London, 1941), 472–73. See also the example of Wembdon given earlier; cf. Cox, *Churchwardens' Accounts*, 12.

[111] Clive Burgess, 'The Churchwardens' Accounts of St Andrew Hubbard, Eastcheap, and Their Implications', *London and Middlesex Archaeological Society Transactions* 50 (1999): xxviii.

parishes could use by-laws to enforce the carrying out of labour. At Brampton, Northamptonshire, tenants were compelled by a by-law to cart twelve loads of stone and sand from the common to mend the highway.[112] There are few surviving examples of such work being carried out on parish churches. However, in 1451, for example, parishioners at Totnes were ordered to dig stones for the tower and to bring horses if they had them.[113] The intuitive idea that contributions to communal funds should be proportionate to wealth, was sometimes explicitly extended to building projects. In 1490, at St Mary-at-Hill, for example, John Halhed gave £2 'upon condition that all the parish will contribute ... after their power, that may bear'.[114]

The essentially flexible and consensual nature of many 'levies' is revealed in some sources. An indication of the careful negotiations that preceded a decision to agree a levy and the level at which it would be set survive at the Totnes Mayor's Court of 1452, where the stewards were instructed to enquire how much the parishioners would be willing to give to building the tower before the levy was set.[115] At Wiverton, Nottinghamshire, the bishop instructed a levy for the repair of Langar church in 1298–99 to apply to all the parishioners 'according to the assessment of all of the parish community or the majority of their assembly (*consilium*) prudently decides'.[116] Some measure of consensus, if not unanimity, was required. Few records of defaulters survive, indicating that assessments were more flexible, carefully set and widely agreed than is suggested by the record.[117] Probably eligibility could be negotiated as it was for taxation.[118]

v) Corporate Donations

Wills do not provide quantitative evidence for the funding regime for an entire project but do suggest that substantial numbers of wealthy parishioners often collaborated in patronising architectural projects, giving widely varying sums, possibly according to wealth.[119] A time lag

---

[112] Warren Ortman Ault, 'Manor Court and Parish Church in Fifteenth-Century England: A Study of Village By-Laws', *Speculum* 42, no. 1 (1 January 1967): 58.

[113] Rea, 'Totnes', 282.   [114] Littlehales, *London City Church*, 157–58.   [115] Rea, 'Totnes', 282.

[116] '*juxta taxacionem de ipsorum omnium parochianorum communi vel majoris partis ipsorum consilio provide faciendam*'; Brown, *Register Newark (York)*, 2:238, 273–76.

[117] There are important exceptions, see French, *People*, 116.

[118] J. F. Hadwin, 'The Medieval Lay Subsidies and Economic History', *The Economic History Review*, 36, no. 2 (1 May 1983): 203–05; James F Willard, *Parliamentary Taxes on Personal Property, 1290 to 1334* (Cambridge, MA, 1934), 84–85.

[119] Cf. Brown, *Popular Piety*, 114; Peter Heath, 'Urban Piety in the Later Middle Ages: The Evidence of Hull Wills', in *The Church, Politics, and Patronage in the Fifteenth Century*, ed. Barrie Dobson (Gloucester, 1984), 211.

inevitably took place between the agreement to build and the time when the bequests would start to flow in: not only did testators have to die but their executors had to be trusted to carry out their instructions and to do so quickly. Occasionally, of course, a major bequest might occasion a new project. Some works were the recipients of large numbers of donations: in Kent, the steeple at Stoke received fourteen bequests and Lewisham, twenty-four. The sums varied widely: at Lewisham bequests to the steeple ranged between 12d and 10 marks, while, of the seven testators who left sums to the building of the new Lady Chapel at Cranbrook in the 1470s, one gave 65 per cent of the total.[120] The total number of donors to these projects and the balance of contributions between them must remain a mystery, and all would have required considerable further donations from the living, but the sums were sometimes substantial and consistent with a corporate fundraising model relying on direct gifts from wealthier parishioners.

Some wills, contracts and inscriptions give further information about the nature of cooperative fundraising. Several, for example, are collaborative ventures between one testator and an anonymous group of local donors – 'the parish'. In 1468, Thomas Forthe of Cockfield, Suffolk, offered to pay for the stone and labour for a new porch ('*vestibulum*') if the parishioners paid for timber.[121] Sir Walter Pauncefoot, the lord of the manor, left £20 for the aisle at Compton Pauncefoot, Somerset, in 1485, where he would be buried, but on condition that the parishioners were to finish it,[122] while Thomas Duffyn, the vicar, left £20 to the tower of Lyminge, Kent, 'if the parishioners will go on with the work' in 1508.[123] A Victorian copy of a painted board, itself evidently retrospective, at Steeple Ashton, Wiltshire, identified the Longs and Lucases as donors of the aisles in 1480–1500 and concludes that 'the rest of the church with the steeple was built at the cost and charge of the parishioners then living'.[124] Sometimes one gift depended upon another: Thomas Cowpar made the sum he would give to the nave at Cranbrook, Kent, in 1524 conditional on the amount William Lynch gave – 4 marks if he offered 20s, 40s if he did not.[125]

---

[120] Duncan, *Testamenta Cantiana (West)*, 45–46; Hussey, *Testamenta Cantiana (East)*, 87, 90.
[121] Peter Northeast and Heather Falvey, *Wills of the Archdeaconry of Sudbury, 1439–1474*, ed. D. P. Dymond, vol. 2 (Woodbridge, 2010), 205. Pevsner argues that this is the vestry.
[122] Weaver, *Somerset Wills*, 1:253.
[123] Hussey, *Testamenta Cantiana (East)*, 204. Cf. the patronage of William Preene there.
[124] John Britton, *The Beauties of Wiltshire*, vol. 3 (London, 1825), 204.
[125] Hussey, *Testamenta Cantiana (East)*, 90.

Financing Construction I: The Parish

In all these cases, in view of what has been said already, it can probably be assumed that 'the parish' or 'parishioners' encompassed only a relatively small number of residents.[126] This is represented more explicitly in some inscriptions. Screens, where they survive, provide particularly numerous evidence for collaborative patronage. That at North Repps, Norfolk, was patronised by the yeoman John Playford, his wife, 'and other benefactors', in 1460, while at Ludham, Norfolk, the inscriptions record that John and Cicely Salmon paid £14 in 1493. Those who made up the remainder, 'all other benefactors', were unnamed.[127] This probably reflected two pressures: the Salmons wished to demonstrate that their support was both financial and substantial but the other benefactors did not wish the Salmons to take undue credit. Inscriptions recorded benefactions by several patrons at Trunch, Norfolk ('all the benefactors')[128] and Stambourne, Essex ('the good benefactors').[129] The screens at Westhall, Suffolk, Wigginhall, North Burlingham and Aylsham, in Norfolk, and Llanfairwaterdine, Shropshire, all name two or more patrons.[130] At Wellingham and Methwold, both in Norfolk, the inscriptions distinguish between those families who paid for construction and those who funded the painting. Some were related, as with the chapel screen given by Robert and Thomas Walsh, and their wives, at Colby, Norfolk.[131] The rood screen at Attleborough, Norfolk, was donated by two parishioners and a fraternity, c. 1430s.[132] Such combinations could include the chaplain or vicar, as at North Weald Bassett, Essex; and Croxton and Weasenham, Norfolk.[133] In the latter case, the (decayed) inscription suggests that five men may have given the screen in memory of the vicar. The

---

[126] Clive Burgess, 'The Broader Church? A Rejoinder to "Looking Beyond"', *The English Historical Review* 119, no. 480 (1 February 2004): 12.

[127] 'et omnibus benefactoribus'; F. Blomefield, *An Essay towards a Topographical History of the County of Norfolk*, vol. 8 (London, 1808), 148–55.

[128] French, *People*, 144.

[129] W. W. Lillie, 'Medieval Paintings on the Screens of the Parish Churches of Mid and Southern England', *Journal of the British Archaeological Association* 9 (1944): 44.

[130] Simon Cotton, 'Medieval Roodscreens in Norfolk: Their Construction and Painting Dates', *Norfolk Archaeology* 40 (1987): 46–53; F. Blomefield, *An Essay towards a Topographical History of the County of Norfolk*, vol. 2 (London, 1807), 205; F. Blomefield, *An Essay Towards a Topographical History of the County of Norfolk*, vol. 6 (London, 1807), 279; Aymer Vallance, *English Church Screens* (London, 1936), 64–65; Duffy, *Stripping*, 160.

[131] Blomefield, *Norfolk*, 1807, 6:425. They probably also leave family brasses.

[132] Bede Camm, 'Some Norfolk Rood Screens', in *A Supplement to Blomefield's Norfolk*, ed. Christopher Hussey (London, 1929), 249.

[133] North Weald Bassett screen is now in Crimplesham, Norfolk. W. R. Powell, ed., *VCH Essex*, vol. 4 (London, 1956), 290–92; Blomefield, *Norfolk*, 1807, 2:153; F. Blomefield, *An Essay towards a Topographical History of the County of Norfolk*, vol. 10 (London, 1808), 75.

Fundraising Techniques

situation at the church of St Mildred, London, summarised by John Stow, was probably entirely typical. In 1455–57, the parson gave £32, three families had their arms in the east windows, and the churchwarden's arms were in the roof.[134] As will be argued in the following chapter, 'patronage' as recorded in inscriptions was by no means identical with financial patronage.[135]

Other collaborative projects divided the building into a series of units, each funded separately by wealthy families or guilds – Swaffham has already been cited. At St Mary, Beverley, in East Yorkshire, inscriptions record the gift of pillars by the guilds of good wives and minstrels, who are carved into the capital above, while John and Joanne Croslay gave two and a half pillars.[136] Thomas Bate and John Ingson are recorded as makers of pillars in inscriptions at Ropsley, Lincolnshire, in 1380, and at Grimsby in 1365, respectively.[137] At St Thomas, Salisbury, an inscription on a capital in the chancel reads 'the founder of this pillar ("peler") was … John Nichol', and adjacent capitals have the initials and merchants marks of two other important locals, both mayors.[138] Others contributed smaller sums to the same.[139] This was a parallel practice to the donation of individual panels to rood screens, as at Cawston and Aylsham, Norfolk, and Eye, Suffolk – sometimes of widely varying quality and spread over several decades.[140] Perhaps the most remarkable example of this was at St Mary-at-Hill, London, when 'certain of the parish' gathered before the parson and alderman in 1490, and five men promised to make an arch. Others contributed as executors or were commemorated in glass. Eight other men made cash donations, mostly of £2.[141] Similarly, the number of patrons, mostly wealthy clothiers and often giving large proportions of the church, recorded in the inscriptions at Long Melford, Suffolk, is famous – at least fourteen men are named as patrons of the late fifteenth-century work, along with thirteen wives (and other parents and children) and other 'well-disposed men'.[142] Such fundraising arrangements may have been more common than surviving inscriptions suggest, although few could have afforded an entire arch or pillar. Nevertheless, smaller units (such as a rood screen panel) would have

---

[134] Stow, *Survey of London*, 258–76.   [135] Chapter 2, section b, pp. 111–18.
[136] George Oliver, *The History and Antiquities of the Town and Minster of Beverley* (London, 1829), 351.
[137] It reads: '*at nomen factoris Thomas Bate*'. The inscription is often said to describe Bate as a mason. This interpretation is possible but unlikely, as is the case at Grimsby: '*Orate pro anima Johannis Ingson qui hanc culumnam fecit*'.
[138] C. Haskins, 'The Church of St Thomas of Canterbury, Salisbury', *The Wiltshire Archaeological and Natural History Magazine* 36 (1909): 4.
[139] Hussey, *Testamenta Cantiana (East)*, 195.
[140] Blomefield, *Norfolk*, 1807, 6:266; Duffy, 'Parish, Piety, and Patronage', 146.
[141] Littlehales, *London City Church*, 157–58.   [142] Chapter 4, section c.i, p. 186.

provided convenient objects of patronage for minor guilds or social groups.[143]

Indeed, where corporate donations did take place, it was often a guild or informal social grouping that was responsible, either alone or acting collaboratively. Some were even founded specifically to sponsor architectural improvements or build a guild chapel.[144] The young men paid for the roof at Garboldisham, Norfolk, the wives gave towards a window at Walberswick, Suffolk, in 1496, and the wives and young men at St Neot, Cornwall, gave windows in 1523 and 1528 respectively.[145] At Worstead, Norfolk, in 1501, the guild wardens are named in the inscription on a screen.[146] Six guilds are commemorated on the roof of Golant, Cornwall, along with wealthy local families.[147] Other examples can be found at Attleborough, Norfolk, by the fraternity of All Saints, and possibly at North Walsham, Norfolk.[148] In some cases, the donation was made with funds raised from sources outside the guild members: an inscription on the late fifteenth-century screen of Thorpe-le-Soken, Essex, reads: 'This cost is [by] the bachelors made[,] by ales this be there made'.[149] These examples tend to be small in scale, limited to a window or contributions to a larger project, although occasionally a wealthy guild could stretch to building a larger unit: a tower, aisle or chapel. The large sums donated at Bodmin in 1469–71 may have been exceptional.[150] Collaborative building projects can be found where construction costs were met partly by the wardens with parish income and partly by a guild (or family) who could then found a chantry in the new addition.[151] The guild might encourage gifts from its members but it may equally have been merely a channel, especially perhaps for smaller donations: one testatrix asked that her bequest be given with that of the widows' if they chose to make a window and individually if they did not.[152]

---

[143] A panel at Cawston cost one parishioner 4 marks: Duffy, 'Salle'.
[144] There are numerous examples in the Appendix of H. F. Westlake, *The Parish Gilds of Mediæval England* (London, 1919); Duffy, *Stripping*, 144–46; Rosser, 'Parish and Guild', 29.
[145] F. Blomefield, *An Essay towards a Topographical History of the County of Norfolk*, vol. 1 (London, 1807), 268–69; R. W. M. Lewis, *Walberswick Churchwardens' Accounts, A.D. 1450–1499* (London, 1947); J. Mattingly, 'Stories in Glass: Reconstructing the St Neot Pre-Reformation Glazing Scheme', *Journal of the Royal Institution of Cornwall* 3 (2000): 20–22.
[146] Cotton, 'Roodscreens', 52.   [147] Mattingly, 'Guilds of Cornwall', 294.
[148] Camm, 'Norfolk Rood Screens', 249.
[149] E. A. Wood, *A History of Thorpe-Le-Soken to the Year 1890* (Thorpe-le-Soken, 1975).
[150] This chapter, section b.i, p. 53; Wilkinson, *Bodmin Church*, 1874, vi.
[151] Farnhill, *Guilds*, 115; Duffy, *Stripping*, 146.   [152] Hussey, *Testamenta Cantiana (East)*, 91.

Fundraising Techniques

However, like many collections, gifts from guilds do not represent 'communal' patronage. By definition, guilds were sub-parochial bodies, limited to only a proportion of often wealthier parishioners and usually tightly controlled by a small elite of wealthy men (and occasionally women) who also held other local offices.[153] Membership was 'exclusive rather than integrative' and recognised by contemporaries as not including poorer parishioners.[154] Although there were informal groups, such as 'the wives' or 'young men', who contributed to windows or roofs, guilds that were wealthy enough to sponsor large scale building work received their income from a wealthy membership, probably as well as raising sums from money lending, property and other sources. Not all the guilds that donated to building work were as wealthy as, say, the Resurrection Guild, which contributed £49 to the tower, bells and Easter sepulchre at Chesterton, Cambridgeshire, during the later fourteenth century.[155]

vi) Affordability

Reconstructions of peasant budgets and populations in the decades before the Black Death indicate both that there was sufficient expendable wealth in the upper ranks of many rural parishes to fund church building even when the economy was at its most stretched and that few other villagers would have been able to contribute very much at all. Christopher Dyer estimates that a customary yardlander on the bishop of Worcester's manor of Bishop's Cleeve in c. 1300 may have had up to £1 of annual net income after paying tithes, rent, amercements and feeding a family of five, if there was no bad harvest, lay subsidy, cattle sickness or other demand.[156] The manor's customary half-yardlanders may have had a net income of just a few shillings each, while cotlanders and smallholders would have little or no leftover income. There were, however, a few freehold half-

---

[153] Introduction, section b, pp. 24–25.
[154] Duffy, *Stripping*, 152–53; Bainbridge, *Gilds*, 137; Rosser, *Medieval Westminster*, 287; Farnhill, *Guilds*, 131; Mattingly, 'Guilds of Cornwall', 217–18.
[155] William Mortlock Palmer, 'The Village Guilds of Cambridgeshire', in *Transactions of the Cambridgeshire and Huntingdonshire Archaeological Society*, ed. C. H. Evelyn White (Ely, 1904), 363; C. H. Evelyn-White and J. J. Muskett, *Cambridgeshire Church Goods: Inventories for the County and the Isle of Ely for Various Years, 1538–1556* (Norwich, 1943), 12.
[156] Dyer, *Standards*, 115–16; alternative sums two or three times larger have been estimated by Rogers, Granat, Gras and Bennett.; for a critical review see E. A Kosminsky, *Studies in the Agrarian History of England in the Thirteenth Century* (Oxford, 1956), 230–40; Kitsikopoulos estimates 18 acres would generate 7s 7d net a year: 'Standards of Living', 248; cf. J. Z. Titow, *English Rural Society, 1200–1350* (London, 1969), 90; John Langdon, *Horses, Oxen and Technological Innovation: The Use of Draught Animals in English Farming from 1066 to 1500* (Cambridge, 1986), 173.

Financing Construction I: The Parish

yardlanders on low rent who may regularly have enjoyed a surplus of 10s or more. The greater part of the payment for communal projects such as church building at this time would, therefore, have out of necessity fallen to the manor's yardlanders, rendering church building very difficult although not impossible, given time for stockpiling and the use of debt.[157]

Can anything be said about the affordability of church construction across England at the end of the thirteenth century? Extrapolating from the Hundred Rolls, which cover only part of the midlands and East Anglia, scholars estimate that there were probably some 150,000 freehold and villein yardlanders in England c. 1290, around seventeen per parish church (Table 1.2).[158] However, taking rural parishes alone, along with a large number of chapels, an average country church may have had sixteen to twenty-one yardlanders among its parishioners. There was an average of about twenty-two villein half-yardlanders per parish and, again, perhaps anywhere from eighteen to twenty-four per rural church. Nevertheless, on the basis of Dyer's figures, their collective net income per church would still be very little. It is doubtful that free half-yardlanders averaged more than six to eight per church. Smallholders, who may have made up 60 per cent of the tenantry, would have struggled to contribute anything at all.

There are few sources to measure the cost of pre–Black Death parochial building projects, but the Southchurch churchyard chapel in Kent, contracted for in 1293, offers a useful yardstick for a moderately sized parochial commission, akin to a chapel, aisle or even a chancel.[159] The patron, Sir Peter de Southchurch, was to provide transport and materials, and pay the mason 11½ marks (£7 13s 4d), a quarter of corn, a robe of his choosing and two 'smalls' of bacon. To provide a useful gauge of affordability a rough estimate of its total cost is needed: £15 is probably reasonable.[160]

---

[157] Chapter 6, sections d.ii–iii, pp. 269–76.
[158] Broadberry et al., *British Economic Growth*, 317–18; Campbell, *Transition*, 262; Campbell, 'Agrarian Problem', Table 1; Kosminsky, *Studies*, 216–23; Kitsikopoulos, 'Standards of Living', 248–54.
[159] Gabriel Byng, 'The Southchurch Chapel and the Earliest Building Contract in England', *Journal of the British Archaeological Association* 168 (2015): 131–41.
[160] It is impossible to provide a good estimate of the cash value of materials, transport and payments in kind at Southchurch but, for the purposes of comparison, roughly doubling the sum to £15 is probably a useful starting point for comparison through time. Ratios of materials to labour varied considerably between projects (2:3 at Ely, by my calculation, 3:2 at Savoy Hospital, 1:2 at Merton College. Many caveats are required regarding the quality of surviving documentation, differences in building type and temporal variation) and a range of £12–£18 or greater is plausible. £15 is consistent, at least, with the closest comparable project for which price evidence survives: the rebuilding of the chancel of Sandon, Hertfordshire, in 1348, for which the mason was to receive 20 marks (£13 6s 8d) and the materials of the old chancel. Salzman, *Building in England*, 437–38; F. R. Chapman, ed., *Sacrist Rolls of Ely, Notes*, vol. 1, 2 vols (Cambridge, 1908); Charlotte A.

Table 1.2 *Incomes per parish I: Early fourteenth century*

Household rank	Gross income bracket	Mean income (approx)	Quantity (approx, c. 1300)	Quantity per parish	Average income per parish	£15 as a % of mean income
Barons	£200–£500	£260	114	0.01	£3.35	6%
Noble women	£200–£500	£255	22	0	£0.63	6%
'Knights'	£40–£200	£40	925	0.1	£4.19	38%
Lower gentry	£5–£40	£15	8,500	0.96	£14.43	100%
Gentry women	£5–£40	£11	1,675	0.19	£2.08	136%
Total (gentry only)	£5–£40		10,175	1.15	£16.51	91% (per parish)
Yardlanders		£1 (net income)	150,000	17	£16.93	
Half-yardlanders		1–10s	193,000	22	£3.27	
Total			343,000	39	£20.20	75% (per parish)

Sources: S. N. Broadberry et al., British Economic Growth, 1270–1870 (Cambridge, 2015), 317–18; Bruce M. S. Campbell, The Great Transition (Cambridge, 2016), 262; Bruce M. S. Campbell, 'The Agrarian Problem in the Early Fourteenth Century', Past & Present 188, no. 1 (1 August 2005): Table 1 (see the note on sources).

Note: estimations have varied widely, this table shows lower estimates in order not to inflate the net wealth of parishes. Cottagers and labourers have been left out, as they would have been able to contribute little to church construction. The figures should have impressionistic value only.

Financing Construction I: The Parish

This would have consumed a little less than the total net annual income of an average-sized parish with some seventeen yardlanders – or, say, a fifth of this if spread over five years, of course. This assumes, however, that the hypothetical yardlanders in this parish received a comparable income to those of Bishop's Cleeve and were having a 'good' year. Additionally, they would, of course, have wished to spend a large proportion of this 'surplus' on clothing, housing and other costs.

More significant, therefore, is that the chapel would remain affordable even with many fewer, or much less affluent, yardlanders. To show this, the figures can be used in the opposite direction: to construct a chapel for some £15 would require, for example, half the net income of six yardlanders (or yardlanders who earned half as much as those in Cleeve) over five years. A small nave, costing perhaps three times as much, would require a substantially larger upper peasantry but of a size that is still close to the national average (say, half the net income of eighteen yardlanders over five years or of nine over ten years). This points to the affordability of moderately sized architectural additions in parishes with at least a small upper peasantry who were willing to part with a substantial amount of their surplus income, at least for a few years in a row. Although this does serve to emphasise the critical importance of collaboration among the upper peasantry, these percentages would of course reduce if some half-yardlanders or substantial free tenants also contributed.

Even as rough guides to affordability, these calculations must be used with caution, however. The Southchurch chapel is a single, possibly atypical, example, and its cost no more than an estimate. Its cost would have been very different if built in a different place or at a different time, and is a poor guide for the cost of a tower, nave, porch or screen. The distribution of yardlanders was far from even – with higher numbers in the midlands and central southern region, and greater fragmentation elsewhere. There was, of course, no 'average' peasant: differences in topography, proximity to towns, seigniorial obligations, family size, age, access to common land, rent, credit, employment and a host of other variables make any generalisation from budgets compiled for peasants on a single west-midland manor unreliable.[161] In good years, half-yardlanders and below were able to give more – they were occasionally

---

Stanford, *The Building Accounts of the Savoy Hospital, London, 1512–1520* (Woodbridge, 2015), 13; Rogers, *Agriculture and Prices*, 1:258–59.

[161] Shortcomings are well rehearsed by the compilers of peasant budget models; see also: Chris Briggs, 'Credit and the Peasant Household Economy in England before the Black Death: Evidence from a Cambridgeshire Manor', in *The Medieval Household in Christian Europe, C. 850–C. 1550*, ed. C. Beattie, A. Maslakovic, and Sarah Rees Jones (Turnhout, 2003), 231–48.

able to earn surpluses large enough to buy land, clothes or houses.[162] By the same token, in hard years, of which there were many in the early fourteenth century, they must have given nothing at all.[163] The relative reliability of the yardlanders' income, and their access to credit, may have been almost as important as its overall size in providing a reliable source of regular income in good years and lean.[164] Lastly, even the income of the yardlanders was far from regular. In addition to the vagaries of weather, taxation, harvest and sickness, holdings and income varied across a lifetime: members of the peasantry probably had access to unusually high levels of capital once children could contribute their labour but before accumulated holdings were divided between their offspring or they became too old to work their own land.[165]

A different measure of affordability can be made using the lay subsidies of the late thirteenth and early fourteenth centuries. The tax applied to citizens with movable goods valued above 10s, probably largely those with at least a half-yardland or reliable employment in a town, with several exemptions including equipment, coin and credit. Importantly, it probably affected only 'surplus' goods, those available to trade, thereby giving some indication of the sums which the wealthiest members of each community could raise at any one point, cash which would be necessary for paying building wages and purchasing materials.[166] These subsidies valued the nation's eligible goods at between £300,000 and £1.7 million, a substantial sum that ranges from £28 to £160 per church or chapel, or two to ten times the cost of the Southchurch chapel.[167] More revealing, however, are the quantities raised. The subsidies yielded between £25,000 and £80,000, working out at £2–£7 per church, but after 1295 the total was often close to £38,000, or £3 9s a church, suggesting the sum which wealthier peasants and townsfolk were able to surrender

---

[162] Dyer, *Standards*, 184–85.
[163] For the early fourteenth-century economy, see Introduction, section b, pp. 11–13.
[164] Chris Briggs, *Credit and Village Society in Fourteenth-Century England* (Oxford, 2009), 146–48.
[165] Richard M. Smith, 'Families and Their Property in Rural England 1250–1800', in *Land, Kinship and Life-Cycle*, ed. Richard M. Smith (Cambridge, 1984), 69–71.
[166] Pamela Nightingale, 'The Lay Subsidies and the Distribution of Wealth in Medieval England, 1275–1334', *The Economic History Review*, 57, no. 1 (February 2004): 2–9; Jenks, 'Lay Subsidies', 6–7; Willard, *Parliamentary Taxes*, 85; Robin E Glasscock, *The Lay Subsidy of 1334* (London, 1975), xxv–xxvi.
[167] Only the temporalities of the clergy were included on occasion before 1306, and they were wholly exempt afterwards. Westmorland, Cumberland and Northumberland were also exempt for most of the taxes under Edward II and Edward III – they had typically paid around £2,000. Once again, 11,000 has been used as an estimate for the number of churches and chapels.

without too much difficulty and which, in years when no tax was demanded, might be available for building work.[168] To employ the Southchurch chapel as a yardstick once again, it would have taken about five years to fund if the tax paid in an average year (c. £3) was available for stockpiling for building work. In fact, this may have been far from the maximum expendable wealth each parish could give up – standard prices, lowered valuations, minimised quantities, and legal and 'unofficial' exemptions meant that this 'surplus' was undervalued.[169] The early fifteenth of 1290, paid before customs of evasion and exemption had been developed but levied on the clergy too, brought in more than £116,000, more than £10 per church. It is, of course, unlikely that a similar sum was available every year for church building or otherwise – goods took time to accumulate and many parishes blamed high taxation for their impoverishment – but it evidently was possible sometimes and building projects were relatively exceptional events.[170] These sums are suggestive only but are consistent with the conclusions of the previous paragraphs: that those wealthy enough to be taxed were able to give up enough in good years, when there were enough of them, to fund church construction using savings and credit. These percentages would, of course, vary between parishes with greater or smaller numbers of taxpayers and according to the work planned – building a new nave would cost considerably more, or, rather, would take considerably longer to fund, than the Southchurch chapel.

After the early fourteenth century, opportunities for measuring affordability are reduced. The valuations of 1334 were largely ossified until the sixteenth century and parishes were granted relief in an ad hoc fashion. However, Dyer estimates that a yardlander in Bishop's Cleeve in 1475 was little better off than in 1300, some even being understood by contemporaries to be 'poor', albeit with lower taxes and fines, and mostly better harvests.[171] More recently, he has estimated that a customary yardlander in 1500 may have had around 7s of excess income to spend on clothes, shoes and household goods, as well as up to c. 20s from pastoral farming.[172] A greater change was enjoyed by the half-yardlander,

---

[168] Indeed, churchwardens were often able to raise more than tax collectors: Kümin, *Shaping*, 190–91; Willard, *Parliamentary Taxes*, 343–47.
[169] Hadwin, 'Lay Subsidies', 207.
[170] Alan R. H. Baker, 'Evidence in the "Nonarum Inquisitiones" of Contracting Arable Lands in England during the Early Fourteenth Century', *The Economic History Review*, 19, no. 3 (1966): 518–32.
[171] Dyer, *Standards*, 149.
[172] Christopher Dyer, 'The Agrarian Problem, 1440–1520', in *Landlords and Tenants in Britain, 1440–1660: Tawney's Agrarian Problem Revisited*, ed. Jane Whittle (Woodbridge, 2013), 23–24.

cottager and wage earner.[173] The former may have had a surplus of 15s or more as rents and taxes decreased, while the others benefitted from increasing wages.[174] Most significant, however, in Bishop's Cleeve was the redistribution of land. There were now half as many tenants as in c. 1300 but four times as many who held a yardland or more, including some with over 100 acres. Cooperative financing could be spread across a much larger proportion of the parish than was possible in 1299, when yardlanders made up just a few per cent of the manor's tenantry.

This was probably essential to the capacity of most parishes to engage in church building campaigns – the cost of construction had increased sharply. By way of comparison with the Southchurch chapel: an aisle at Hornby, Yorkshire, cost £40 in 1410, albeit including materials, the roof and some glazing, but an 'attached' chapel of similar proportions at Chester still cost £20 in 1433 with materials supplied.[175] A more appropriate contrast might, however, be a freestanding church house of similar proportions to the Southchurch chapel in Great Sherston, Wiltshire, that cost £10 in 1511, excluding water, materials, scaffolding and transport: a third more than the nominal cost of the Southchurch chapel.[176] A new Lady Chapel of 1425 at St Michael, Bath, may have cost £17.[177] If £15 was a useful benchmark for the total cost of an addition to a parish church on the scale of a chapel or an aisle in the early fourteenth century, £30 is probably a reasonable equivalent a century later.[178] Nevertheless, this represents the cost of only a modest addition – by contrast, the spire at Louth cost some £300 in 1501–15 and the magnificent chancel at Adderbury, £400, including roof and glazing, in 1408–18.[179] Building St Mary the Great, Cambridge, came to over £1,350 in 1478–1519, and St Margaret, Westminster, perhaps £2,000.[180] At St Mary the Great, the rood screen alone cost almost £100.

---

[173] Sear argues that the growing incomes of the lowest income group (smallholders, victualing trades, smiths, leatherworkers) and medium income group (yardlanders, tradesmen, merchants, lawyers, professionals) were largely absorbed in purchasing basic commodities: Joanne Sear, 'Consumption and Trade in East Anglian Market Towns and Their Hinterlands in the Late Middle Ages' (Unpublished PhD Thesis, University of Cambridge, 2015), Chapter 6.

[174] Cf. Hatcher, 'Unreal Wages', 19–20.   [175] Salzman, *Building in England*, 483, 503.

[176] Ibid., 561–62.   [177] Cox, *Churchwardens' Accounts*, 83.

[178] Introduction, section c, pp. 30–32, gives a rough estimate that the combined cost of materials and wages doubled between the early fourteenth and early fifteenth centuries. By comparison, midland peasant houses in 1400–60 cost around £4, although occasionally much more or slightly less, again emphasising the affordability of a chapel that cost only seven times as much. Nat Alcock and Dan Miles, *The Medieval Peasant House in Midland England* (Oxford, 2014), Table 6.1.

[179] J. E. Swaby, *History of Louth* (London, 1951), 98; T. F. Hobson, *Adderbury 'rectoria'* (Oxford, 1926), xxii.

[180] Another £100 was spent on St Mary the Great's tower in the 1570s. Samuel Sandars, *Historical and Architectural Notes on Great Saint Mary's Church, Cambridge* (Cambridge, 1869), 16; Rosser, *Medieval Westminster*, 263–71.

Financing Construction I: The Parish

As we have seen, changes in social structure were varied, and the situation in Cleeve cannot be extended universally, but in many places a greater availability of tenant land did lead to a larger number of large holdings in this period, which, when combined with increasing incomes for middling and poorer tenants, better harvests and less taxation, created a significant increase in collective expendable wealth.[181] Nationally, there may have been 160,000 with more than a yardland, about half of whom may have had over 50 acres, and another 110,000 with a half-yardland.[182] This would suggest an average of fourteen to sixteen yardlanders, and nine to eleven half-yardlanders, per local church (Table 1.3). Extrapolating from Dyer's figures for Cleeve suggests this would come to approximately £30–£37 of net income per parish – roughly equivalent to the ratio for the cost of an architectural addition on the scale of the Southchurch chapel that we found c. 1300. Similarly, bearing in mind the caveats above about late-medieval taxation, the 1524 lay subsidy raised £70,000, which was equivalent to the higher sums raised in the 1290s but was about twice the average amounts raised in the early fourteenth century, £6–£7 a church.[183]

Although this must be suggestive only, it indicates that affordability was relatively static despite the rise in prices, especially when combined with a reduction in taxation, mostly better harvests and the potential for contributions by smallholders and cottagers receiving better wages. At the bottom of parish society, of course, were many who could still afford to contribute nothing, and whose absence from even the largest collections was demonstrated earlier. At the other end of village society, larger farmers may have been able to afford small building projects singlehandedly with incomes in the order of the minor gentry.[184] All the same caveats regarding estimates of affordability made above must be repeated here, not least of which are the huge economic changes that took place during the Perpendicular period. Indeed, within a few decades of 1475, falling wages and rising prices may have forced more of the cost of church building onto the increasingly entrenched and enriched upper ranks,

---

[181] Introduction, section b, pp. 13–17.
[182] N. J. Mayhew, 'Population, Money Supply, and the Velocity of Circulation in England, 1300–1700', *The Economic History Review*, 48, no. 2 (1 May 1995): 249; N. Mayhew, 'Modelling Medieval Monetisation', in *A Commercializing Economy: England 1086 to c.1300*, ed. R. H. Britnell and Bruce M. S. Campbell (Manchester, 1995), Table 4.1; Dyer, *Standards*, 31. Correspondence with Professor Dyer.
[183] This excludes noble payments. Note, in 1525, despite the previous year's payments, £64,000 was raised. Sheail, *Distribution of Wealth*, 2:438.
[184] Introduction, section b, pp. 14 and Chapter 1, section d.iii, 106–07; cf. Byng, 'Saffron Walden'.

Table 1.3 *Incomes per parish II: Fifteenth century*

Households	Income bracket (gross)	Mean income (approx)	Total number (approx)	Number per parish	Average income per parish	£30 as a percentage of mean income
Barons	£300–£1000	£900	70	0.01	£7.11	3%
Knights	£100–£300	£210	180	0.02	£4.27	14%
Lesser knights	£40–£100	£60	750	0.08	£5.08	50%
Lesser gentry	£20–£39	£24	1,200	0.14	£3.25	125%
	£10–£19	£14	1,600	0.18	£2.53	214%
	£5–£9	£7	3,400	0.38	£2.69	429%
Total (poorer group) c. 1436	£5–£39	£12	6,200	0.70	£8.40	357% (of parochial income)
Large farmers		£2 (net income)	80,000	9.03	£18.06	
Yardlanders		£1	80,000	9.03	£9.03	
Half-yardlanders		15s	110,000	12.42	£9.31	
Smallholders			130,000	14.68		
Total (villagers only) c. 1470			450,000	50.80	£36.41	82% (of parochial income)

Sources: H. L. Gray, 'Incomes from Land in England in 1436', *The English Historical Review* 49, no. 196 (1 October 1934): 607–39; N. J. Mayhew, 'Population, Money Supply, and the Velocity of Circulation in England, 1300–1700', *The Economic History Review*, 48, no. 2 (1 May 1995): 249; N. J. Mayhew, 'Modelling Medieval Monetisation', in *A Commercialising Economy: England 1086 to C. 1300*, ed. R. H. Britnell and B. M. S. Campbell (Manchester, 1995), Table 4.1; Christopher Dyer, *Standards of Living in the Later Middle Ages: Social Change in England, c. 1200–1520* (Cambridge, 1989), 31.

Note: estimations have varied widely and lower ones are preferred here. Labourers have been left out as they could have contributed only small sums to church building. The table should give impressionistic strength only.

while any contribution coming from those with less than a half-yardland was reduced.

vii) Corporate Patronage and Social Change

The absence of levies, the modest size of many collections and the distinction between them and named gifts had a new significance from the later fourteenth century when an increasing number and proportion of parishioners were able to spare part of their income to communal projects. The non-appearance of poorer parishioners in collections taken in places with higher per capita wealth was probably not begrudged but expected – financing church construction was a privileged activity and a good work that had always been identified with wealthier groups and their voluntary largesse.[185] Gifts from the poorest would have undermined the highly stratified and relatively exclusive nature of architectural patronage: large donations both evidenced and constituted membership of the 'parish worthies'.[186] The lists of donors to collections codified the difference – especially if they were read aloud at the audit where their similarity to the bede roll would be noticeable. At Trowbridge the names of the benefactors to the 'newly built' church were to 'be comprised in a table hanging at the high altar of Jesu exhorting the people being present devoutly to say for them and for all Christian souls Pater Noster and the Maria'.[187] Twin desires to distinguish benefactors from the other ranks of the parish and to formalise and publicise their identity can be found in many parochial institutions – the bede roll, guild membership, office holding and membership of the 'good men' – as well as in documents such as the Arlingham contract or in the Long Melford inscriptions.[188]

Large voluntary collections on the scale of Bodmin or Thame had a rhetorical effect too: they proved and perhaps encouraged the broad and willing approbation given by middling groups to projects that were still led and dominated by the wealthy. The levy at Bridgwater is instructive – it could demonstrate neither the largesse of the wealthy nor voluntary support from the community, indeed levies here incurred some opposition

---

[185] Introduction, section f, pp. 48–49.
[186] R. N. Swanson, *Church and Society in Late Medieval England* (Oxford, 1989), 258.
[187] W. H. Jones, 'Terumber's Chantry at Trowbridge, with Deed of Endowment 1483', *Wiltshire Archaeological and Natural History Society* 10 (1867): 247–52, 248.
[188] Of these the bede roll may have been the most important for establishing parochial 'membership': Duffy, *Stripping*, 334–37; it was made explicit in the specific criteria (not exclusively financial) set down to define 'good doers', entitled to use a set of black vestments at their funerals, at St Nicholas, Bristol, in 1489: Burgess, 'Benefactions of Mortality', 75. For the Arlingham contract, see Chapter 4, section b.ii, pp. 178–80; for Long Melford, see Chapter 4, section c.i, p. 186.

Fundraising Techniques

and may not even have been as productive as collections.[189] However, it belongs to the 1360s, before the dramatic social and economic changes of the later fourteenth century had been realised: real wages were still comparatively low, and poorer parishioners were perhaps unwilling to part with their minimal expendable wealth, while the wealthier group felt less need to distinguish their contributions. Doubtless there was little choice – the parish leadership alone simply could not afford the work. Tellingly, Bridgwater would give up on levies by the mid-fifteenth century. In some places support was both encouraged and evinced by attendance at plays and ales. That these were not used more often may have been not only because they were cost inefficient but also because they would present the work as a communal project: ales probably included even poorer groups, who would pay similar amounts to the wealthy.

Greater differentiation in the nature and size of gifts probably became increasingly desirable for the wealthiest tenants as church building became a less exclusive endeavour and as greater mobility reduced the capacity for communal memory: three-quarters of the families in some villages changed every fifty years.[190] Inscriptions must be understood in this light when they record the value of the gift (as at Ludham, Norfolk), the role of the donor in organising construction (as with John Clopton and others at Long Melford, Suffolk), or the, usually large, proportion of the new work that was donated (an arch, a pillar, a panel in a screen). Another method of differentiation was to use forms of commemoration associated with the gentry or senior clergy – in glass and, particularly, brass – which moved down the social spectrum to be purchased by wealthy freeholders from the mid-fourteenth century.[191] Many showed a desire for greater individualisation in the record of their commemoration, often indicating trade or status: William Morys' brass at Great Coxwell, Berkshire, of c. 1500, for example, noted that he was 'sumtym fermer', probably of the demesne.[192] At the same time there was a general trend to greater social specification, as with the development of terms such as 'gentleman', 'esquire', 'yeoman' and 'husbandman'.[193] The naming of a donor demonstrated that their role in the building work was either important or generous – those who contributed smaller sums could be anonymised as part of 'the parish' or 'other benefactors'. The distinction between the 'named or unnamed' donor (to use the terminology of

---

[189] Chapter 1, section c.iv, pp. 75–76.   [190] Dyer, *Making a Living*, 342.
[191] Saul, *English Church Monuments*, 37–38, 58–59, 254–61; Richard Marks, *Stained Glass in England During the Middle Ages* (London, 1993), 5–8; Duffy, *Stripping*, 333–34.
[192] Geoffrey Tyack, Simon Bradley, and Nikolaus Pevsner, *Berkshire*, New ed. (New Haven, 2010), 314.
[193] Carpenter, *Locality and Polity*, 3.

Financing Construction I: The Parish

one late fourteenth-century contract)[194] may have been fundamental to the way in which corporate funding was understood by contemporaries: it was duplicated in inscriptions, wills and contracts, many of which distinguished between the main donor(s) and 'the parish' or 'the other benefactors'. Even accounts tended only to record the total raised by a collection or ale, and not the contributors, or to segregate the names of subscribers in a separate bill (usually lost) while retaining the names of larger donors in the audited copies. This kind of 'specific cataloguing' of names, so common in parish documents, was, after all, necessary for commemoration.[195] Even if the great mass of donors was remembered, it would be in paper and not in stone, timber or glass.

In all these ways church construction could help both to accommodate and to order social change stimulated by increasing wealth and mobility at all or most levels of the late medieval parish.[196] In the increasingly large and varied number of parochial activities carried out in the fifteenth century, which were often associated with a broad range of the parish participating in groups defined by gender, marital status, age or occupation, major building projects remained relatively, if decreasingly, exclusive.[197] To the historian this often appears as a crude tripartite division into a majority of non-donors, a core of often-anonymous donors and a few named leader-donors, but even if this is oversimplified, the existence of a major financial and organisational project would have rendered the economic and social axes of the parish highly visible. When most of the parish did not donate or contributed only small sums to projects funded by the elite, even as an increasing number developed the ability to do so, church building helped to define membership of wealthier groups and so to establish the dynamic between those who gave and those who received. Perhaps, like the rites themselves, 'they were used not only to promote harmony, but to impose hegemony, the dominance of particular families and groups within the parish and the wider community'.[198]

The near-complete absence of women from the management of church construction, except occasionally as executrix-fabric wardens or perhaps through their husbands, is also significant for this reason.[199] Although women do appear as contributors to collections and participants at ales, and as organisers in the case of Hocktide celebrations or through guilds and stores, as noted above these are the forms of donation

---

[194] '*tam non nominatos quam nominatos*', at Arlingham, see Chapter 4, section b.i, pp. 178–80.
[195] Duffy, *Stripping*, 334. [196] See Introduction, section b, pp. 13–16. [197] Ibid., pp. 22–26.
[198] Duffy, *Stripping*, 136.
[199] Katherine L. French, *The Good Women of the Parish: Gender and Religion after the Black Death* (Philadelphia, 2008), Chapter 1.

Case Study: Cambridgeshire

most likely to be rendered anonymously in the parish record.[200] In general, and despite the new economic opportunities available to women after the Black Death,[201] they were excluded from most senior managerial roles in the parish.[202] Female churchwardens, guild wardens and ale wardens have been found in some west country parishes at the end of the middle ages, but they tended to be widows of wealthy, even gentry, families, and so in an unusually powerful position.[203] The exception might be female guilds with their own chapels – the store of the Blessed Virgin Mary in Chagford, Devon, was run by female wardens who entered maintenance costs into their accounts in the early sixteenth century (paying any excess to the masters).[204] In a period of exceptional change, some things would remain the same.

D) CASE STUDY: CAMBRIDGESHIRE

i) Introduction

Sketching the experience of wealthier parishioners through the later middle ages in one region allows us both to define the pool of architectural patrons with greater accuracy, especially in rural areas which are otherwise poorly represented in the documentary evidence cited above, and to outline patterns of parish church construction over the course of time. We shall do so by looking at the evidence of just one county, Cambridgeshire.[205] The county had a relatively straightforward ecclesiastical and secular administrative structure, with a single diocese and

---

[200] In 1497, the Hocktide income of St Edmund, Salisbury, funded new windows for the church, and female guilds made contributions to building work at Walberswick and Bodmin: Katherine L. French, '"To Free Them from Binding": Women in the Late Medieval English Parish', *The Journal of Interdisciplinary History* 27, no. 3 (1 January 1997): 409; Katherine L. French, 'Maidens' Lights and Wives' Stores: Women's Parish Guilds in Late Medieval England', *The Sixteenth Century Journal* 29, no. 2 (1 July 1998): 402.

[201] From the extensive literature on the changing experience of women in late medieval England see Judith Bennett, 'Medieval Women, Modern Women: Across the Great Divide', in *Culture and History 1350–1600: Essays on English Communities, Identities, and Writing*, ed. David Aers (1992), 147–75; Judith Bennett, 'Confronting Continuity', *Journal of Women's History* 9, no. 3 (1997): 83–88; Caroline Barron, 'The "Golden Age" of Women in Medieval London', *Reading Medieval Studies* 15 (1969): 35–58.

[202] This may have changed slightly after the Reformation with the rise of rotational appointments: Peters, *Patterns of Piety*, 180–83.

[203] Katherine L. French, 'Women Churchwardens in Late Medieval England', in *The Parish in Late Medieval England: Proceedings of the 2002 Harlaxton Symposium*, ed. Clive Burgess and Eamon Duffy (Donington, 2006), 302–21; French, *People*, 86–88; Kümin, *Shaping*, 40.

[204] Osborne, *Chagford CWAs*.

[205] The 1831 county boundaries, as used in this book, are identical to the medieval ones except for Newmarket, Royston and Kentford, which were previously part of the county; and Heydon, Great and Little Chishill, and Papworth St Agnes, which were not.

Financing Construction I: The Parish

archdeaconry, both almost coterminous with the county. In the three hundreds of the Isle of Ely, administrative, judicial and fiscal immunity was held by the bishop, while in the south, the fourteen hundreds of the shire were under the sheriff and his bailiffs.[206] Its topography was likewise split: in the north were silt and peat fenland parishes, centred on clay 'islands' and sometimes larger than 20,000 acres and sparsely settled, while in the south, parishes in the clay uplands could be a tenth of this size, with nucleated settlements.[207] The majority of vills were identified with a single parish, although often with divided lordship, and their boundaries may not have matched exactly. Seven parishes had two churches.[208] The presence of both a major cathedral, Ely, and town, Cambridge, with its university and colleges, however atypical, also offer useful variables. It shared aspects of its economic and social structure with East Anglia and the east midlands, and even if the conclusions drawn are peculiar to the county, they might be typical in so far as conditions there are found elsewhere.

We must begin with a few words about cost and quantification. Destruction, restoration and rebuilding have affected the county's churches severely. The pace of destruction at the hands of sixteenth-century reform was quick: only 32 per cent of Cambridgeshire churches had brasses and only 1 per cent had unbroken stoups by 1600.[209] Cambridgeshire suffered badly at the hands of William Dowsing in the 1640s[210] and, although it is not certain whether he visited the north of the county or the churches in the south, 'local zealots, collaborators and looters' worked across the county.[211] Many churches experienced restoration or alteration during the nineteenth century, often on a substantial scale. More numerous are the lost chapels, surveyed earlier.[212] Attempts at quantification, then, should be taken as indicative only, although there is good reason to think that the pattern of destruction did not disproportionately affect different parts of the county while, as we shall see, relatively low rates of fifteenth-century construction mean that a reasonable attempt can be made at quantifying earlier periods.

---

[206] Fordham was in the diocese of Norwich. A. Hamilton Thompson, 'Diocesan Organisation in the Middle Ages: Archdeacons and Rural Deans', *Proceedings of the British Academy* 29 (1943): 165, 181 n. 3.
[207] H. C. Darby, *Medieval Cambridgeshire* (Cambridge, 1977), 1, 19, 29.
[208] Swaffham Prior, Histon, Duxford, Long Stanton, Burwell, Fulbourn and Wittlesey.
[209] Robert Whiting, *The Reformation of the English Parish Church* (Cambridge, 2010), 230, 224, 111.
[210] Julie Spraggon, *Puritan Iconoclasm during the English Civil War* (Woodbridge, 2003), 122.
[211] Robert Walker, 'William Dowsing in Cambridgeshire', in *The Journal of William Dowsing: Iconoclasm in East Anglia during the English Civil War* (Woodbridge, 2001), 34; Graham Chainey, 'The Lost Stained Glass of Cambridge', *Proceedings of the Cambridge Antiquarian Society* LXXIX (1990): 70–81.
[212] Introduction, section d, pp. 35–36.

Case Study: Cambridgeshire
ii) Before the Black Death

At first glance, the evidence of the Hundred Rolls would imply that the Cambridgeshire peasantry was in no condition to embark on ambitious building projects at the close of the thirteenth century. Three-quarters of villein holdings in the densely populated shire hundreds were of less than a half-yardland, compared to less than two-fifths in the other areas surveyed in the Hundred Rolls.[213] Indeed, half-virgaters outnumbered virgaters almost eight to one. Assarting in the fenlands reduced pressure on the land there but, on Ely Cathedral's manors, median holdings were small even in the mid-thirteenth century: five to twenty acres in the silt fens and one to three acres in the peat fens.[214] This was probably due to partible inheritance in some locations, relatively high levels of freedom on new land and opportunities for employment.[215] In several villages, particularly in the uplands, total holdings had more than quadrupled since Domesday, leading to a corresponding drop in median size and a rise in the proportion of holdings too small in themselves to provide for a family.[216] The conditions for these changes can be suggested: some 51 per cent of tenants were free, rather more than the east midlands counties, if less than in Norfolk and Suffolk, and of them some 80 per cent had holdings beneath a half-yardland.[217]

Nevertheless, although the economic and demographic trends of the long thirteenth century affected Cambridgeshire severely, they were concurrent with a period of intensive and widespread parochial building work (Figure 1.7). The relationship of church construction to the distribution of wealth in the county seems paradoxical: in a county of often impoverished peasantry and few wealthy gentry, how was it that almost every parish church engaged in some building work, frequently encompassing large projects to rebuild a nave, chancel, aisle or tower?[218] This was as true in the sparsely populated peat and silt fenlands in the north as it was in the densely populated clay and chalk upland in the south. The Hundred Rolls suggest the solution: a considerable number of substantial tenants remained in most manors and, unusually, the largest tended to be

---

[213] Kosminsky, *Studies*, 216–17.
[214] Ibid., 615; J. R. Ravensdale, *Liable to Floods: Village Landscape on the Edge of the Fens, AD 450–1850* (Cambridge, 1974), 154–56; Darby, *Medieval Cambridgeshire*, 7–8.
[215] Erin McGibbon Smith, 'Court Rolls as Evidence for Village Society', in *Town and Countryside in the Age of the Black Death: Essays in Honour of John Hatcher*, ed. Mark Bailey and S. H. Rigby (Turnhout, 2012), 256.
[216] Margaret Spufford, *Contrasting Communities: English Villagers in the Sixteenth and Seventeenth Centuries* (Stroud, 2000), 6–8; J. A Steers, ed., *The Cambridge Region 1965* (Cambridge, 1965), 142–43.
[217] Kosminsky, *Studies*, 216–17.
[218] Cf. C. H. Evelyn-White, *County Churches, Cambridgeshire and the Isle of Ely* (London, 1911), xxvii.

Financing Construction I: The Parish

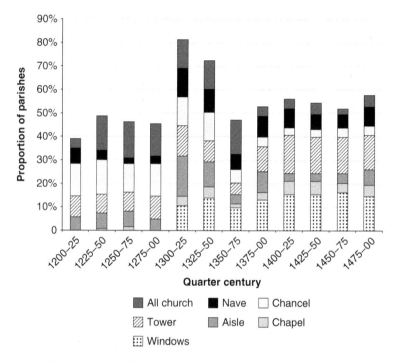

Figure 1.7   Parish church building work in Cambridgeshire

free.[219] In the shire, free virgaters outnumbered villein virgaters by three to one. There were 327 freeholdings of at least a half-yardland and sixty of more than a yardland across the hundreds surveyed by Kosminsky, an average of approximately nine free peasants with a half-yardland or more per parish church.[220] It was probably this group that was able to benefit from low wages and high prices, growing cash crops for sale through Cambridge markets and trading only small amounts locally.[221] Using Dyer's calculations for Cleeve it can be estimated that the average net income of the upper peasantry alone per parish church was around £12–£18. However, since at least four-fifths of this can be attributed to free tenants, the sum was probably significantly higher: a free virgater in

---

[219] J. A. Raftis, 'Social Structure. The East Midlands', in *AHEW*, ed. H. E. Hallam, vol. 2 (Cambridge, 1988).
[220] As noted earlier, the number of parish churches is unclear.
[221] Ravensdale, *Liable to Flood*, 146.

Case Study: Cambridgeshire

Cambridgeshire paid about a third of the rent per acre of a villein.[222] Church building could be driven by a small, largely free and relatively wealthy elite, while some four-fifths of the tenantry were able to offer little help as they struggled to raise subsistence levels of income from smallholdings and wage labour.[223]

Comparing a snapshot of rural society during a period of enormous change with construction that took place over decades presents methodological difficulties and must be taken as a rough guide only. Nevertheless, setting building work of the period c. 1250–1350 against the social stratification shown in the Hundred Rolls is revealing. Every parish with above twenty virgaters in 1289 carried out a major building project in this period, nearly always including the nave, aisles and/or tower, and five in six rebuilt almost the entire church. By contrast, a third of parishes with two yardlanders or fewer carried out no work, and a fifth carried out work on the chancel alone, presumably financed by clerical income. The middling tenantry were probably important too. Every parish with more than forty half-yardlanders and above carried out some building work: 64 per cent on the nave; 45 per cent on towers. Of those with fewer than twelve half-yardlanders, a fifth carried out no building work and another fifth carried out work on the chancel alone. Altogether, therefore, a correlation can be found between the absolute number of members of the upper peasantry and the likelihood of carrying out major building projects, particularly on the nave and tower. The point can be pressed home by calculating the annual total income of each parish, using Dyer's estimated peasant budget.[224] More than 70 per cent of parishes where the peasantry had a net income of at least £20 per annum rebuilt naves or aisles; almost a third, towers; while none built nothing at all. Of those with less than £2 per annum, a quarter built nothing at all.

The clay and chalk uplands of Cambridgeshire were badly affected by the economic, agricultural and demographic contraction of the decades after the Great Famine.[225] In 1340 the *Nonarum Inquisitiones* found that 5,000 acres in forty parishes were lying uncultivated, with the worst effects in the uplands.[226] Manorial accounts for a chalkland parish show 'a catastrophic fall in agrarian profits in the second quarter of the fourteenth century' from £80 a year in 1319–23 to £10 in 1333–46.[227] The royal demands of purveyance and taxation were high even though

---

[222] Kanzaka, 'Villein Rents', Table 2; Hatcher, 'Serfdom and Villeinage'; Kosminsky, *Studies*, Table 13.
[223] Kanzaka, 'Villein Rents', 612.   [224] Dyer, *Standards*, 115–16.
[225] Baker, 'Evidence in the "Nonarum Inquisitiones"', 525; Darby, *Medieval Cambridgeshire*, 16; L. F. Salzman, ed., *VCH Cambridgeshire*, vol. 2 (London, 1948), 71.
[226] Darby, *Medieval Cambridgeshire*, 16; Baker, 'Evidence in the "Nonarum Inquisitiones"', 525.
[227] Edward Miller, *The Abbey & Bishopric of Ely* (Cambridge, 1951), 105.

Financing Construction I: The Parish

numerous vills were granted exemptions.[228] Even fenland manors experienced a fall in profits.[229] This crisis, represented across several different sources, is, however, apparently mismatched with both Cambridgeshire's tax returns and church building programmes, which continued unabated. In 1334 the quantity of taxpayers and total assessments per acre in the shire were among the highest in England, although mean individual assessments were low.[230] Even when including the sparsely settled fenland, Cambridgeshire ranked eleventh wealthiest in the country. The area which had grown most significantly was the fertile silt fenland in the north, but in the peat fenland there had also been much absorbing of new cultivable land and the area was significantly wealthier than it had been a century before, if still lagging behind the uplands.[231] Although the fenlands had some of the lowest density of taxpayers and taxpayer wealth, the parishes were usually very large and thus equalled the shire parishes in absolute quantities of taxpayers and taxable wealth.[232]

To explain both this apparent wealth and extensive building programmes, it is necessary to turn again to the upper peasantry. Although the contraction probably represented crisis conditions for many smallholders, a sizable minority of substantial peasants may have been able to enlarge or improve their holdings as land became available after the famine.[233] Even in the context of near universal building work, there is a good correlation between taxpayer wealth and building work. The twenty parishes with the greatest overall tax revenue in 1327 (paying over £6 5s 9d) built seventeen major projects in c. 1300–50 and none did no building at all, while the twenty least wealthy parishes (paying less than £2 13s 4d) carried out eight major projects (on naves, aisles or towers) and six built nothing at all (Table 1.4). As already noted, only comparatively wealthy people with more than 10s of moveable goods were eligible for taxation before 1334, equivalent, perhaps, to less than 35–40 per cent of the

---

[228] W. M. Palmer and H. W. Saunders, *Documents Relating to Cambridgeshire Villages*, vol. 1 (Cambridge, 1926), 2.
[229] Miller, *Ely*, 105.
[230] Bruce M. S. Campbell and Ken Bartley, *England on the Eve of the Black Death: An Atlas of Lay Lordship, Land and Wealth, 1300–49* (Manchester, 2006), Map 18.15; John S. Lee, *Cambridge and Its Economic Region, 1450–1560* (Hatfield, 2005), 35; Mary Hesse, 'The Lay Subsidy of 1327', in *An Atlas of Cambridgeshire and Huntingdonshire History*, ed. Tony Kirby and Susan Oosthuizen (Cambridge, 2000), 36.
[231] Darby, *Medieval Cambridgeshire*, 8; the Bishop of Ely enjoyed a greatly increased income at the end of the thirteenth century due to reclaimed Fenland: Miller, *Ely*, 95–96.
[232] H. C Darby, *The Medieval Fenland* (Newton Abbot, 1974), 128–130 and Figure B; Darby, *Medieval Cambridgeshire*, 8; Campbell and Bartley, *England on the Eve*, Table 18.3.
[233] Kershaw, 'Great Famine'; Razi, *Life, Marriage and Death*, 39–40.

Case Study: Cambridgeshire

Table 1.4 *Cambridgeshire taxpayers (1327) and building work*

1327 Lay Subsidy	Twenty poorest parishes	Twenty richest parishes	Twenty smallest parishes	Twenty largest parishes	Twenty lowest mean	Twenty highest mean
All church	2	0	1	0	3	0
Nave	2	3	1	4	2	2
Chancel	3	8	4	7	2	8
Aisle	1	3	1	3	3	2
Tower	0	3	2	2	0	3
Windows	8	3	7	0	3	7
No work	6	0	5	3	6	1

Source: J. J. Muskett, 'Lay Subsidies, Cambridgeshire, I Edward III (1327)', *East Anglian Notes and Queries* X–XII. New Series (1903).

parish.[234] Mean tax returns and the number of taxpayers, although not the spread of wealth, both correlate with building work, suggesting, in accordance with the argument of this book, that the most important variable determining the capacity of a parish to afford construction work was the wealth and number of its wealthiest members.

iii) After the Black Death

The population of Cambridgeshire suffered typically uneven but often severe losses in the Black Death and the outbreaks of plague that followed.[235] The effects varied widely even between vills: mortality rates have been estimated from 43 to 70 per cent in some villages, while others were apparently unaffected, although these may be where landless and subletters were killed in higher numbers and have left no records.[236] Accounts of dilapidations, heriots, defaults and vacant plots indicate the toll of demographic contraction.[237] As in most of the country, during the

---

[234] Dyer, *Lords and Peasants*, 109; Barbara F. Harvey, 'The Population Trend in England between 1300 and 1348', *Transactions of the Royal Historical Society*, 16 (1966): 28.
[235] Salzman, *VCH Cambridgeshire*, 2:158, 210–17; Benedict Gummer, *The Scourging Angel: The Black Death in the British Isles* (London, 2009), 126–28; Ole Jørgen Benedictow, *The Black Death, 1346–1353: The Complete History* (Woodbridge, 2004), 364–68; John Aberth, 'The Black Death in the Diocese of Ely: The Evidence of the Bishop's Register', *Journal of Medieval History* 21, no. 3 (1995): 276–80.
[236] Darby, *Medieval Cambridgeshire*, 16.
[237] Ravensdale, *Liable to Flood*, 159; Frances Mary Page, *The Estates of Crowland Abbey, a Study in Manorial Organisation* (Cambridge, 1934), 120–25.

Financing Construction I: The Parish

third quarter of the century, little church building took place. This was especially marked in the densely populated shire, which was particularly badly affected by the plague (66 per cent of parishes carried out no work in the Isle in 1350–75; 76 per cent in the shire). Twice as many building projects comprising the insertion of new windows took place as involved the rebuilding of the entire church. This marks a relatively high proportion of parishes carrying out some building work compared to many other counties but still represents a fall of over half, relative to the preceding decades. Beyond the disruption caused by the plagues and their emotional and psychological effects, it is possible to be more specific as to the cause: the population of potential patrons and the supply of craftsmen and labourers had halved, while the cost of building work was soaring.[238] That demographic disaster impacted severely on the feasibility of repair can be shown in the union of All Saints and St Giles parishes in Cambridge in 1365, since most of the parishioners of the former were dead and the building in ruins.[239]

By the end of the century, landlords in Cambridgeshire, as in much of the rest of the country, had become collectors of rents, leasing out demesnes to tenants and giving up on the direct cultivation of land.[240] This process was completed at Soham by 1390, Chatteris by 1397 and Wilburton by 1415.[241] Tenants began to claim better terms, lower rents and fewer seigniorial charges, and accumulated larger holdings.[242] Building work began to recover in the final quarter of the century, with an increase in the proportion of parishes carrying out work on the nave, aisles and tower (Figure 1.7). However, construction remained relatively depressed throughout the late middle ages: rarely more than half of all churches carried out any work at all (compared with more than 80 per cent in the early fourteenth century). Small projects on windows outnumbered work on naves or aisles by 3:2 (compared to 1:2 in the early fourteenth century). Although many churches, of course, had been rebuilt relatively recently, by the fifteenth century this would have been outside any living memory, and the architectural styles of the early fourteenth century would have looked distinctively out of date.

---

[238] See Introduction, section c, pp. 30–32.   [239] Salzman, *VCH Cambridgeshire*, 2:158.
[240] See Introduction, section b, pp. 13–17, for a summary of events across England. Salzman, VCH Cambridgeshire, 2:71–72; R. H. Britnell, 'The Occupation of the Land', in *AHEW*, ed. Edward Miller, vol. 3 (Cambridge, 1991), 56; Frederic William Maitland, 'History of a Cambridgeshire Manor', in *Selected Historical Essays of F. W. Maitland*, ed. Helen M. Cam (Cambridge, 1957), 24–25, 32–33; Jim Bolton, 'The World Upside Down', in *The Black Death in England*, ed. W. M. Ormrod and P. Lindley (Stamford, 1996), 18.
[241] Ravensdale, *Liable to Flood*, 161; Britnell, 'Tenant Farming and Farmers', 614–17.
[242] Darby, *Medieval Cambridgeshire*, 18–19; Spufford, *Contrasting Communities*, 38–39.

Case Study: Cambridgeshire

It is important to reiterate that many counties (including neighbouring ones in East Anglia) experienced considerable levels of building work in this period, while economic circumstances were generally more favourable.[243] To explain why work stalled in Cambridgeshire, especially given so much construction was carried out during the tribulations of the early fourteenth century, it is necessary to turn again to the upper peasantry.[244] Taxation records suggest that most Cambridgeshire parishes, still dependent on grain farming in an era of depressed grain prices, did not develop an upper peasantry of the size of some Perpendicular counties.[245] In 1524–25, just 8 per cent of Cambridgeshire's taxpayers were assessed at £10 or more, and 3.5 per cent at £20 or more, compared to 10 per cent for the country as a whole.[246] Moreover, more than half of those assessed in 1524 were recorded as wage earners – many were probably cottagers – compared to a quarter to a third in most rural areas.[247] Evidence for the existence of yeoman farmers in some Cambridgeshire parishes from the end of the fifteenth century suggests that, if taxation rolls had been compiled some fifty years or more before the 1520s, they would show an even flatter economic structure for the county. Taxation reliefs of 20 to 30 per cent were not uncommon in Cambridgeshire during the two centuries after the Black Death. Indeed, the fact that some villages which had suffered devastating depletions in population were granted only small reductions indicates that they were not understood to be exceptional cases.[248] Cambridgeshire dropped from the eleventh wealthiest county in 1334 to twenty-first in 1515.[249] However, just as some building work did continue, so too did a reasonably sized upper peasantry exist in the county by the 1520s. Around a quarter of taxpayers had £2–£4 of goods, probably equivalent to between a half-yardland and a yardland, and a tenth had £5–£10, forming a prosperous group with 50–60 acres.[250]

As in the previous section, comparing a single year's tax revenue with building work over many decades is problematic. The unusually bad flooding of the fens in 1524 adds to the problems of using the 1524–25 returns. Nevertheless, even the relatively depressed building work of the long fifteenth century in Cambridgeshire still correlates well with the size and

---

[243] Introduction, section d, pp. 36–39.
[244] Cf. Simon Cotton, 'Perpendicular Churches', in *Cambridgeshire Churches*, ed. Carola Hicks (Stamford, 1997), 101.
[245] Britnell, 'Tenant Farming and Farmers', 612.   [246] Spufford, *Contrasting Communities*, 30.
[247] A. M. Everitt, 'Farm Labourers', in *AHEW*, ed. J. Thirsk, vol. 4 (Cambridge, 1967), 396–400; Spufford, *Contrasting Communities*, 33.
[248] Spufford, *Contrasting Communities*, 8–10.
[249] R. S. Schofield, 'The Geographical Distribution of Wealth in England, 1334–1649', *The Economic History Review*, 18, no. 3 (1 January 1965): Table 2.
[250] Spufford, *Contrasting Communities*, 35–36; cf. Whittle, *Agrarian Capitalism*, 218.

Financing Construction I: The Parish

Table 1.5 *Cambridgeshire taxpayers (1524–25) and building work*

Number of taxpayers	Parishes	No building work	Proportion
0–20	24	16	67%
21–30	21	10	48%
31–40	25	6	24%
41–50	18	9	50%
51–60	19	10	53%
61–100	18	7	39%
101–382	17	4	24%

Source: John Sheail, *The Regional Distribution of Wealth in England as Indicated in the 1524/5 Lay Subsidy Returns*, edited by R. W. Hoyle, Vol. 2 (Kew, 1998).

collective wealth of the most affluent groups in local society. Only a third of parishes with fewer than twenty taxpayers in 1524–25 carried out building work in c. 1450–1525, compared to three-quarters of those with more than 100 (Table 1.5). Indeed, of those with fewer than sixty, only a half carried out building work. This follows a similar pattern to rates of overall taxable wealth. More than two-thirds of parishes that paid less than £1 5s in total carried out no building work. The equivalent figure is less than a quarter for those paying more than £8 15s (Table 1.6). As suggested above, without a large yeomanry the correlation with mean taxpayer assessment is weak but it suggests that those with the lowest per capita wealth did struggle to build (Table 1.7). Although church building does correlate favourably with taxable wealth, it is striking that, apart from the smallest and poorest parishes, the differential is relatively small: parishes with twenty-one to thirty taxpayers were about as likely to build as those with fifty-one to sixty. All this indicates that even relatively small numbers of taxpayers were able to afford some building work in the early sixteenth century. Importantly, the nature of the building work is also not sharply differentiated between parishes; wealthy and poor were similarly likely to build anything from a window to a tower.

There is also qualitative evidence both for the range of patrons involved in church building in Cambridgeshire, and for an increase in work in the decades around 1500, after a fallow period in the middle of the fifteenth century. Indulgences, suggesting large-scale collections, proliferated from the middle decades of the century, when wealthier groups may have struggled to take on work: they were granted by the bishop of Ely for building work at Great Eversden (1466), Foxton (1456 and 1466) and Kingston (1488).[251] Testamentary

---

[251] Also at March in 1343; J. H. Crosby, *Ely Diocesan Remembrancer* (Cambridge, 1905), 128.

Case Study: Cambridgeshire

Table 1.6 *Cambridgeshire taxable wealth (1524–25) and building work*

Total tax (d)	Parishes	No building work	Proportion
0–300	16	11	69%
301–600	21	8	38%
601–900	21	7	33%
901–1200	16	7	44%
1201–1500	21	13	62%
1501–2100	16	7	44%
2101–4000	21	5	24%
4001–7500	9	2	22%

Source: John Sheail, *The Regional Distribution of Wealth in England as Indicated in the 1524/5 Lay Subsidy Returns*, edited by R. W. Hoyle, Vol. 2 (Kew, 1998).

Table 1.7 *Cambridgeshire per capita tax payment (1524–25) and building work*

Per capita payment (d)	Parishes	No building work	Proportion
0–10	6	4	67%
11–20	27	13	48%
21–30	62	27	44%
31–40	19	7	37%
41–50	16	5	31%
51–127	10	4	40%

Source: John Sheail, *The Regional Distribution of Wealth in England as Indicated in the 1524/5 Lay Subsidy Returns*, edited by R. W. Hoyle, Vol. 2 (Kew, 1998).

evidence for corporate patronage grows from the end of the century, reflecting not just an increase in surviving records but also the improving economic position of the upper peasantry.[252] There were bequests for building work at numerous parishes, for which evidence increases from the later fifteenth century, as at Melbourn (in the 1480s),[253] Soham (the 1490s),[254] Waterbeach (the 1510s to the 1520s),[255] Bottisham (1521)[256] and Barrington (the 1520s).[257] A donor

---

[252] Introduction, section b, p. 14.
[253] C. L. Feltoe and Ellis H. Minns, eds., *Vetus Liber Archidiaconi Eliensis* (Cambridge, 1917), 114–15.
[254] J. R. Olorenshaw, 'Some Early Soham Wills', *Fenland N&Q* 4 (1900 1898): 246–50; John Harvey, *English Mediaeval Architects: A Biographical Dictionary down to 1550*, Revised ed. (Gloucester, 1987), 319.
[255] William Keatinge Clay, *A History of the Parish of Waterbeach in the County of Cambridge* (Cambridge, 1859), 52–53.
[256] TNA: PRO PROB 11/20/152.   [257] BL Add. MS 5861, ff. 79, 88, 92.

Financing Construction I: The Parish

bequeathed £10 towards the chancel at Papworth St Agnes in 1539, provided the parishioners used the stone foundations already laid; he also gave timber for a new roof.[258] However, there is also earlier evidence, dating from the recession period, as at Meldreth in 1443.[259] The collections at Bassingbourn of the 1490s have already been noted, and at Leverington the churchwardens carried out several works using collections in 1518.[260] Guilds were responsible for building work at Chesterton, Gamlingay and Linton.[261] Evidence for gentry patronage also rose towards the end of the century (as at Grantchester, Isleham, Horseheath, Waterbeach and Linton), after a slump in the mid-century, when only one datable example (at St Mary, Swaffham Prior) took place. There are at least three surviving instances from the start of the century (at Grantchester, Hinxton and Newton, Wisbech).[262]

There is also evidence for a newly wealthy yeoman class acting as patrons in some places from the later fifteenth century.[263] In 1464, John Benet, a demesne lessee, 'caused to be made' the unusual rose window over Burwell chancel arch and the fine nave roof, and Walter Taylard (d. 1466), a freeholder and manorial steward at Gamlingay with extensive lands and tenants in numerous parishes, remodelled and furnished the north transept chapel where he was buried.[264] The earliest instance is in Harston, where a visitation noted that Adam Prat, probably a local farmer,[265] gave the large sum of £20 to the fabric of the church in c. 1370.[266] Such examples proliferate from the early sixteenth century onwards as large holdings became increasingly stable, prices increased and wages reduced.[267] John Gardener, who owned substantial property, bequeathed sums to repair Trumpington steeple and a buttress in

---

[258] TNA: PRO PROB 11/27/560.
[259] CUL Palmer MS A55, Meldreth church; TNA: PRO PROB 11/3/484.
[260] 'Leverington Parish Accounts', *Fenland Notes and Queries* 7 (October 1909): 189.
[261] TNA: PRO PROB 11/5/210; Palmer, 'Village Guilds', 363; Evelyn-White and Muskett, *Cambridgeshire Church Goods*, 12.
[262] Dating is often imprecise and other examples from the fifteenth century survive, as for example at Leverington, Barrington and Wittlesford.
[263] Introduction, section b, pp. 13–14.
[264] The Burwell inscription reads: '*Orate pro animabus Johannis Benet Johane et Alicie uxorum eius parentumque qui fieri fecerunt hunc parietem ac carpentariam navis*'; TNA: PRO PROB 11/5/2; *An Inventory of the Historical Monuments in the City of Cambridge*, vol. 1 (London, 1988), 100–01; Peter Alfred Taylor and Joseph Lemuel Chester, *Some Account of the Taylor Family (Originally Taylard)* (London, 1875), 4–5.
[265] Walter Rye, *Pedes Finium; or Fines, Relating to the County of Cambridge* (Cambridge, 1891), 83, 102, 136.
[266] Feltoe and Minns, *Vetus Liber*, 93.   [267] Introduction, section b, pp. 13–16.

1504.[268] Thomas Hitch, another yeoman and part of a parochial elite assessed at the highest amounts in 1524, left money for the construction of the Melbourn rood screen in 1508.[269] Symbols on the embattled parapet of the chancel of St Peter and Paul, Wisbech, include the monogram and rebus of Thomas Burwell, who was an official in the town's dominant guild in the early sixteenth century.[270] The windows at Comberton commemorate several sixteenth-century parishioners: Thomas and Margaret Baron; John Newman; John Baron; and John and Marion Auger/Angier.[271] They had all leased demesnes: Thomas Baron, who farmed demesne land from 1498, was assessed at £56 in 1524; John Baron succeeded him and was assessed at more than £27; the Angiers, who had farmed demesnes in the early sixteenth century, and three relatives paid tax on about £30.[272] The early sixteenth-century pews and stalls include the initials 'TB', suggesting that they were the gift of Thomas Baron.

Could the large quantity of building work taking place in Cambridge throughout the period have exacerbated a reduction in building work?[273] There are four important counterarguments. First, building work reduced even outside those parts of the county that were highly integrated with its capital. Secondly, there is little evidence that college building work was paid for by new or increasing demands on parishes or manors (take Adderbury where revenues came from the usual manorial income of an Oxford college),[274] which, in any case, would be difficult to impose, while voluntary donations or collections by parishioners for works on the colleges are unlikely. Thirdly, although it is possible that the work had an inflationary effect on local wages and prices, an increased supply of workmen and materials to the area may have made building work more affordable or convenient (as seems to have taken place during work at Ely Cathedral in the early fourteenth century).[275] Fourthly, craftsmen and labourers would have spent a proportion of their wages locally, providing some degree of economic stimulus.[276] The correct formulation is probably to wonder that more building work did not take place in parish churches despite the activity in Cambridge, not least as the colleges attracted new funds into the town, stimulated the urban economy and integrated the town into broader cultural circles.

[268] Wright, *VCH Cambridgeshire*, 1982, 8:248–67.
[269] CUL Palmer MS A55, Melbourn church; J. S. Brewer, ed., *Letters and Papers, Foreign and Domestic, of the Reign of Henry VIII*, vol. 3 (2) (London, 1867), 118.
[270] Pugh, *VCH Cambridgeshire*, 4:247–50, 255–56. [271] BL Add. MS 5861, f. 94.
[272] C. R. Elrington, ed., *VCH Cambridgeshire*, vol. 5 (London, 1973), 175–89.
[273] Simon Bradley and Nikolaus Pevsner, *Cambridgeshire* (New Haven, 2014), 9–13.
[274] Chapter 5, section c.ii, pp. 233–37. [275] Chapter 6, section c.iii, pp. 262–64.
[276] This argument belongs to the 'optimists' noted in the Introduction, section a, pp. 8–9.

Financing Construction I: The Parish

E) CONCLUSION

Although the medieval parish had several regularly employed and generally accepted communal fundraising techniques, these were rarely linked to building work. Ales, for example, often constituted part of the churchwardens' income but were reserved for their regular responsibilities and were, in any case, rarely profitable enough and too difficult to increase to a level where they could fund building work. Rather, direct gifts and bequests from relatively wealthy families, sometimes made through guilds, were necessary to provide the substantial funds needed for building work, often augmented by borrowed money. When collections were made, they can sometimes be shown to run into large numbers but did not inevitably represent 'communal' funding. Even those parishes that ran large-scale collections or levies cannot often be shown to have repeated them – Bodmin appears to have been a one-off; Bridgwater ended its levies once post-Black Death changes were truly underway. When wealthier inhabitants were able to fund building work without assistance, they did. Given their role in running such work,[277] and the large sums of capital it demanded, it is not surprising to find that it was the upper ranks who expected to provide large new funds, defrayed only slightly by revenue from property, ales, plays, sales and oblations.[278] Many parishioners had very little they could donate: in rural areas it was probably only half-yardlanders and above who could afford to share the cost of new building work.[279]

This observation nuances the link between the wealth of a 'community' and parish church construction: it was the social structure of each parish that controlled its capacity to build. Using this conclusion, it is possible to sketch a model for patterns in church construction during the high to late middle ages, which is explicated above in a regional study of Cambridgeshire. As the thirteenth century wore on, a decreasing proportion of most parishes could donate to church construction, and it became increasingly the responsibility of a dwindling upper and middling peasantry, with it being affordable only if they acted corporately. Profound changes to the structure of the English economy from the later fourteenth century meant that a growing proportion of many parishes could contribute to building work, at least into the early decades of the next century, after which trends might have begun to reverse. As a result, the wealthiest sought out new ways to distinguish their generosity from

---

[277] The subject of Chapters 3 and 4. [278] For their managerial approach see Chapter 6.
[279] Introduction, section b, pp. 11–16.

Conclusion

the limited contributions of the rest of the parish. Indeed, church construction maintained its association with wealthier parishioners even as parochial activities diversified to include a large range of inhabitants. Many or most still donated nothing, little or rarely, both from necessity and according to expectation.

Chapter 2

FINANCING CONSTRUCTION II
Gentry and Clergy

A) INTRODUCTION

'William caused this church to be rebuilt anew to the honour of God and of the Assumption of the Blessed Mary and of St Nicholas', so reads the elegant inscription on the brass of Sir William de Etchingham, 1389, in the Sussex church of the Assumption and St Nicholas in Etchingham.[1] Nigel Saul described him as 'head of one of the oldest and most distinguished knightly lineages in Sussex', and the church's windows were once filled with his family arms and those of his neighbours.[2] Even the tower's weather vane includes the Etchingham arms. Sir William's brass, and his church, are both unusually fine, but similar examples of aristocratic architectural patronage – or claims for it – can be multiplied across England, and many others are, of course, lost. How typical, then, were patrons like Sir William, and what was it precisely that they contributed to the building work they 'caused' to be made? Were all as closely involved in the work as Sir William, who contracted for five windows himself in 1363?

The economy of projects run by individual families and institutions should have been relatively straightforward – with funds issuing from a single source and passing directly to workmen or contractors. This kind of single-handed munificence is suggested by the archaeological, antiquarian and testamentary record of gentry patronage, but such an account faces three families of problems, which form the subject of this chapter. The first concerns the nature of this evidence – particularly the presence of tombs, arms and inscriptions in church buildings themselves, where the ambiguous cultural significance of commemoration muddies any straightforward

---

[1] It reads: '*iste Willelmus fecit istam ecclesiam de novo Reedificari in honorem Dei ac Assumpcionis Beate Marie et Sancti Nicholai*', Spencer Hall, 'Notices of Sepulchral Memorials at Etchingham, Sussex, and of the Church at That Place', *The Archaeological Journal* 7 (1850): 267; Saul, *Provincial Life*, 140–69; L. F. Salzman, 'Etchingham Church', *Sussex Notes & Queries* 3 (1930): 53–54.
[2] Saul, *Provincial Life*, 1, cf. 148–53.

interpretation of financial patronage. The second is the evidence for contributions from other local bodies to projects notionally carried out by wealthy families. The contrast between the archaeological and the documentary record is significant – the former often recorded only an element of a project's financing or leadership, while the latter could be considerably more expansive. The third concerns the challenge of raising the large sums of money required to pay for church building when most gentry kept little spare capacity in their accounts. This chapter is concerned, therefore, with the difference between causing a church to be rebuilt, and supplying the funds to do so.

B) TOMBS, ARMS AND INSCRIPTIONS

The presence of gentry tombs, heraldry and inscriptions provides the most considerable type of evidence for architectural patronage. To take one county as an example, in Cambridgeshire alone archaeological evidence survives for aristocratic building work in at least twenty-eight parishes, about a fifth of the county's churches, through heraldry or inscriptions, many now lost but recorded by antiquarians. The parish gentry dominate this group almost completely. The few exceptions are limited to bishops and nobles, who were usually overlords of the parish and where armorial evidence is likely to have been given in tribute or to suggest aristocratic bonds rather than as a record of direct donations.[3] Occasionally lawyers or officials patronised work, but they tended to have manors, or large holdings, in the parish.[4] There is little to suggest that the gentry regularly gave to parishes outside their own or to manors in which they were not resident. On only one occasion was the patron the lord of a different manor: the Burgoynes, lords of Impington, who owned only a tenement at Waterbeach but whose arms were once found in glass in the late fifteenth-century south aisle.[5] Although this sample must not be taken as representative of England as a whole, the county suggests the domination of many church interiors by records of gentry families and implies the local bonds that stimulated them. The ambiguity, and relative scarcity, of noble patronage will appear again when the documentary record is assessed in the following section. Partly, as the section entitled 'Affordability' will show,

---

[3] E.g. Saul, *Provincial Life*, 150–51, n. 32; Alexa Sand, *Vision, Devotion, and Self-Representation in Late Medieval Art* (Cambridge, 2014), 232.

[4] Elias of Beckingham was a judge who did not own the manor of Bottisham, Cambridgeshire, for example, where he was buried and may have contributed to building work: Byng, 'Patrons and Their Commissions', 230–37.

[5] Clay, *Waterbeach*, 47; A. P. M. Wright and C. P. Lewis, eds., *VCH Cambridgeshire*, vol. 9 (London, 1989), 257–62.

Financing Construction II: Gentry and Clergy

this must be a question of numbers – there were simply too few noble families, even allowing for their multiple residences and substantial incomes.

The greater part of this section will be concerned with inscriptions and heraldry, but, to begin with, tombs and brasses provide common but problematic evidence for financial patronage. Many are later additions to earlier aisles or chapels, and some were retained in later rebuildings. There was apparently little contemporary expectation that new tombs were to be matched by new architecture. Of the many wealthy testators who left instructions for the erection of their monuments, only a few also explicitly carried out building work: men such as the royal civil servant Sir Richard Fowler at St Romwold, Buckingham, in 1477, who willed that his brass should lie in the south aisle that he finished at his own cost and which should be supplied with a new shrine, and Sir Richard de Southchurch at Southchurch, Essex, in 1293, who built a churchyard chapel for his burial.[6] In some cases a partial refurbishment was evidently sufficient, as for William Ludlow (d. 1478), another royal civil servant, who 'ceiled and painted' the north aisle of St Thomas, Salisbury, with his arms before burial there.[7]

However, some tombs also bear an inscription recording the donor's building work, not only at Etchingham, but also, for instance, at Harlestone, Northamptonshire, on the tomb of the priest Richard de Hette of 1320,[8] and at Wimington, Bedfordshire, on that of John Curteys, mayor of the Calais staple, of 1391.[9] The brass of Sir Thomas and Katrin Walsh at Wanlip, Leicestershire, even gives the date of the building work in 1393 and not of its patrons' deaths some years later.[10] Inscriptions such as these provide the best evidence, in the greatest quantity, for the importance of architectural work by wealthy families, particularly members of the gentry. None, of course, can demonstrate that financing or organisation was single-handed, but there is no reason to doubt that these projects were led or substantially financed by the men

---

[6] Presumably the aisle at Buckingham had been commenced by others (Fowler writes of 'his friends' who were buried there too), but the inscription read: '*Ricus et Johanna hanc insulam in hac ecclesia fieri fecerunt*'; Nicholas Harris Nicolas, *Testamenta Vetusta*, vol. 1 (London, 1826), 344–45; Byng, 'Southchurch Chapel'.

[7] Thomas Tropenell, *The Tropenell Cartulary*, ed. John Silvester Davies, vol. 1 (Devizes, 1908), 274–75.

[8] It reads: '*orate pro anima Richardi De Hette, qui fecit cancellum cuius auxilio fuit Ecclesia facta*', Dorothy Willis, ed., *Estate Book of Henry de Bray* (London, 1916), 43.

[9] It reads: '*hic iacet Johannes Curteys dominus de Wymyton . . . qui istam ecclesiam de novo construxerut*'. William Page, ed., *VCH Bedfordshire*, vol. 3 (London, 1912), 117–22.

[10] It reads: 'here lyes Thomas Walssh knyght lorde of Anlep and dame Katine his wife whiche in her tyme made the kirke of Anlep and halud the kirkyerd', Saul, 'Language, Lordship, and Architecture', 5; Matthew Holbeche Bloxam, *The Principles of Gothic Ecclesiastical Architecture*, 10th ed. (London, 1859), 265.

Tombs, Arms and Inscriptions

and women recorded in them. Such inscriptions are not limited to tombs. A window at Buckland, Hertfordshire, for instance, records that Nicholas de Buckland built the church in 1348.[11] An example of female patronage was recorded in the window of Wolvey, Warwickshire, by Alice de Wolvey, whose effigy lies in the north aisle.[12] The stone screens to the Ridley Chapel in Bunbury, Cheshire, are inscribed: 'This chapel was made at the cost and charge of Sir Ralph Egerton Knight.' The common phrase 'cost and charge' reappears in his will of 1525, which leaves money for the chapel's completion, specifically that it is 'covered with lead, ceiled and drawn with knots gilded and the panels painted also two images either side of the altar within the Chapel and the Chancel'.[13] Lastly, an inscription above the door of the vestry at Halesworth, Suffolk, requested prayers for Thomas and Margaret Clement, 'who caused this vestry to be made'.[14]

The variation in these formulations is telling – from covering a project's 'cost and charge' or building 'anew', to 'causing' projects to be made or even, as we have seen, recording the precise cash value of patronage. When Curteys and Etchingham claimed to have built their churches 'anew' ('*de novo*'), they evidently wished to remove any ambiguity over the extent of their contribution – to have simply 'built' the church might suggest merely remodelling or adaptation. Similarly, Egerton's use of the tautologous phrase 'cost and charge', deliberately reminiscent of contracts and wills, indicates that he felt his financial patronage of the project was distinctive. Those who recorded that they 'paid' for new work, like the weaver John Albrede (d. 1444) and the painting of the rood screen at Woodbridge in Suffolk, were evidently intending to claim something different from those who 'built', 'made' or 'caused to be made'.[15]

However, even in these cases, such an inscription could prove hasty. An inscription at Steeple Ashton records: 'The North Aisle was rebuilt at the cost and charge of Robert Long and Edith his wife.' Work was still outstanding when Robert, a clothier, died in 1501, asking in his will that construction on the north side of the church be finished at his expense.[16]

---

[11] It reads: '*Nicholai de Bokeland qui istanc Ecclesiam cum Capella Beatiae Mariae construxit*'. Sir Henry Chauncy, *The Historical Antiquities of Hertforshire* (Bishops Stortford, 1826), 231.

[12] It reads: '*Domina Alicia de Wolvey que fecit fieri istam capellam*', Bloxam, *Principles*, 265.

[13] E. Ives, 'Patronage at the Court of Henry VIII: The Case of Sir Ralph Egerton of Ridley', *Bulletin of the John Rylands Library* 52, no. 2 (1970): 346; see also screens at Burford, 1431, and Worstead, 1512: Vallance, *Screens*, 63.

[14] It reads: '*qui istud vestiarium fieri fecerunt*', Judith Middleton-Stewart, *Inward Purity and Outward Splendour: Death and Remembrance in the Deanery of Dunwich, Suffolk, 1370–1547* (Woodbridge, 2001), 102.

[15] '*solverunt*'; he also left 20 marks to building the steeple. Vallance, *Screens*, 63–64.

[16] It is recorded on a Victorian copy of a painted board that had been fixed to the west gallery.

Nevertheless, there were problems with funding: Robert's widow was sued by the contractor's executrix for £49 unpaid, and in 1507, Robert Morgan willed that 'such works as be began by Robert Long in the North Aisle ... be performed'.[17] The inscription continues, probably more accurately, recording that: 'The South Aisle *for the most part* was built at the cost and charge of Walter Lucas and Matilda his wife'.[18] Thus, when John Sleaford ordered that his brass in Balsham, Cambridgeshire, should record that 'he built the church' ('*ecclesiam struxit*'), it is unclear what his financial or managerial contribution would have been, or what he would have expected his contemporaries to understand by the claim.[19] 'Patronage' was a special and distinctive, if ambiguous, relationship to new architecture – but not necessarily an act of single-handed munificence. Many may have believed that their contribution was considerably more exacting than merely providing the funds.

Of course, the funders of new projects did desire their arms or name to be included in the work: bequests can be found, for example, 'to make a window of glass ... with my arms in the said window'.[20] Contemporaries may have understood (or misunderstood) arms to imply financial patronage: early antiquarians regularly associated arms with funding, as for example at St Andrew Undercroft, London, where John Stow concluded that Steven Gennings had built the north arcade 'at his charge ... as appears by his arms over every pillar graven', and again in every window and pew.[21] Here, Stow notes also three other 'great benefactors' who presumably did not have their arms engraved. Indeed, the convention was familiar enough for the friar in *Piers Plowman* to link glazing with the inclusion of a name, when he tells Lady Meed: 'We have a wyndow in werchynge, wole stonden us ful hye;/Woldestow glaze that gable and

---

[17] TNA: PRO C 1/367/38; PROB 11/13/90; Brown, *Popular Piety*, 118; cf. John Leland, *The Itinerary of John Leland in or about the Years 1535–1543*, ed. Lucy Toulmin Smith, vol. 1 (London, 1906), 83.

[18] My italics. TNA: PRO PROB 11/10/518.

[19] It may have been only the south aisle: Nikolaus Pevsner, *Cambridgeshire*, 2nd ed. (Harmondsworth, 1970), 295; Herbert Haines, *A Manual of Monumental Brasses*, vol. 1 (1861), cxv; Charles Robertson Manning, *A List of the Monumental Brasses Remaining in England* (1846), 11; Rye, *Pedes Finium*, 61.

[20] Nicolas, *Testamenta Vetusta*, 1826, 1:161.

[21] Stow makes the same assumption about arms or inscriptions in numerous churches, e.g. John Bugge at St Dionys; John Brokeitwell, 'an especiall reedifier or new builder', at St Martin; John Barnes at St Thomas Apostle, Wringwren Lane; Sir John Hend at St Swithen; Sir John Crosby at the library of St Peter upon Cornhill; a Pophame at St Sepulchre, who had his arms in the glass and his image in the south porch; and for public houses and other buildings: Stow, *Survey of London*, 20–52, 138–50, 187–200, 200–05, 238–50, 303–10.

grave therinne thy name,/Sykir sholde thi soule be hevene to have' (3.48–50).[22]

That a range of different roles in new building work were conventionally recognised as 'making' or 'building' that did not necessarily, or even commonly, include a totality of financing can be shown through two further arguments. First, the price of creating a new inscription was detached from the actual cost of its installation and from the creation of any larger architectural setting for it. Donors were effectively purchasing the right to have their name recorded in a public place, and they were not necessarily paying for its actual execution, let alone the window, aisle or church that formed its architectural setting. This was reasonable – if their payment was only the cost of the paintwork, then the church would receive no net profit from the bequest. In his will of 1441, for example, William Wenard gave 8s 4d to nine abbeys and priories and to every parish church in Devon and Cornwall 'on condition that my name be written on a certain glass window or in a certain public place of each church'. He was not necessarily paying for new glass or windows, let alone an architectural addition, although the archaeological evidence, were there any, would have suggested otherwise (though surely these expensive and impractical bequests were never fulfilled).[23] In this sense, the inclusion of a name in the fabric of a church was a more exclusive version of the addition of a name on the bede roll, a list of benefactors regularly read aloud in church – a set sum given in return for memorialisation, whether written on parchment or glass.[24] Edmund Acombe, for example, specifically gave to the fabric of Thanet Minster 'so that my soul shall be kept in memory among the benefactors of the Church' in 1479.[25] It is not uncommon to find arms installed in pre-existing features, as on the screens of St Michael, Cornhill, London, where they may have commemorated maintenance work, now lost sculpture or paintwork, or some other involvement in parish life.[26] Archaeological evidence similarly shows that new glass was often added to old windows, just as new windows were regularly inserted in old walls.[27]

A second argument points to the social significance of inscriptions: units that relied on corporate sponsorship were often given in the name of a single patron. At Bolney, West Sussex, many parishioners contributed sums to building the new tower, but only the manorial lord's arms were

---

[22] William Langland, *The Vision of Piers Plowman*, ed. A. V. C. Schmidt (London, 1978), 25.
[23] Weaver, *Somerset Wills*, 1:148.
[24] Swayne, *Sarum, CWAs*, 13; Hobhouse, *Church-Wardens' Accounts*, xiii; Duffy, *Stripping*, 153–54.
[25] Hussey, *Testamenta Cantiana (East)*, 222.
[26] Nicholas Harris Nicolas, *Testamenta Vetusta*, vol. 2 (London, 1826), 466.
[27] E.g. the 1577 Callaway arms added to an older window at St Neot, Cornwall: Mattingly, 'Stories in Glass', 21.

included above the west doorway;[28] and at Biddenham, Bedfordshire, the parishioners paid for transport and materials, but only the arms of the gentry patron, Sir William Butler, were set into the aisle, and his grandson's monument in the chancel would mention him alone as its founder.[29] At St Mary, Devizes, an inscription in the nave roof records that William Smith (d. 1436) 'caused this church to be made' but a churchwarden's account of 1436 records much larger contributions of lead from men from another local family than that given by Smith (443lbs and 44lbs, respectively).[30] The rood screens at East Harling, Marsham and Garboldisham, all in Norfolk, attracted many benefactions, some large, but the inscriptions or heraldry commemorate just one family.[31] They were not necessarily the most generous donors: Eamon Duffy suggests that a lifetime of donations to the church fabric may have been as important as their local status or role in sponsoring the work. Equally, they may have been the driving force behind its organisation, as at Bolney and Biddenham, so that the work had become associated with them even if they had provided only a proportion of the funding. Occasionally, however, the archaeological record indicates that lords were engaged in some form of cooperative fundraising. At Mancetter, Warwickshire, and Carlton Scroop, Lincolnshire, for example, the advowson holder and local lord is shown in glass with the parish priest.[32]

Cambridgeshire churches suggest some trends in the archaeological evidence for gentry patronage. Most gentry arms or inscriptions are found in windows, in some cases where a new window had been added to an older wall at relatively low cost. At Shepreth, for example, the thirteenth-century aisle, probably remodelled, once contained the arms of Engaine, a family which held the manor in the late fourteenth century.[33] When lordly families took over a chapel or aisle this did not guarantee rebuilding – many made no changes that survive, while others made only modest or delayed alterations, as for example is probably the case with the fine Everard window formerly in the largely early-fourteenth-century chancel at Leverington (now in the Swaine chapel).[34] The window

---

[28] Joseph Dale, 'Extracts from Churchwardens' Accounts and Other Matters Belonging to the Parish of Bolney', *Sussex Archaeological Collections* 6 (1853): 244–52; Byng, 'Bolney', 107–11.

[29] TNA: PRO E41/318; Gabriel Byng, 'The Contract for the North Aisle at St James, Biddenham', *Antiquaries Journal* 95 (2015): 251–65.

[30] '*istam ecclesiam fieri fecit*'. The 'parishioners' also owed 400lbs of lead 'to the clerk of works of the castle': Edward Kite, 'Some Documents Relating to the Church of the B. V. Mary, Devizes, and Its Re-Founder, A.D. 1410–1458', *Wiltshire Notes and Queries* 7 (1911): 194–95.

[31] Eamon Duffy, 'The Parish, Piety and Patronage: The Evidence of Rood-Screens', in *The Parish in English Life*, eds. Katherine L. French, Gary G. Gibbs, and Beat Kumin (Manchester, 1997), 142.

[32] Marks, *Stained Glass*, 11; Peter R. Coss, *The Knight in Medieval England, 1000–1400* (Stroud, 1993), 90.

[33] Elrington, *VCH Cambridgeshire*, 5:251–63.   [34] Pugh, *VCH Cambridgeshire*, 4:186–97.

shows Sir Bartholomew Everard, who had married into the manor, and his son Lawrence, but it may have been patronised by John, Lawrence's son, given the reference in the inscription to John the Baptist. The majority of inscriptions are from chancel windows, as at Barrington, Burrough Green, Comberton, Grantchester, Horseheath, Lolworth, Orwell, Rampton, West Wickham and Wittlesford, suggesting that the architectural interests of such families were focused on the holiest part of the church.[35]

Some, of course, did build more substantially, adding a chapel, transept or aisle, but fewer took part in any general rebuilding. At Eltisley and Little Shelford, for example, family chapels are entirely out of keeping with the remainder of the church, leaving an asymmetrical composition where chapel and church are almost entirely disconnected, stylistically and spatially.[36] The patrons' munificence stopped short of rebuilding their parishioners' churches (although, in the case of Little Shelford, they gave furnishings and vestments), even at the cost of a finer setting for their chantry. These are important contrasts: the Frevilles dominated Little Shelford as the only manorial lords for three centuries, while manors in thirteenth-century Eltisley belonged to various families, none of whom can be identified with certainty with the contemporary knightly effigies in the north chapel.[37] However, in neither case did the family have the means or inclination to reconstruct the entire building – indeed, at Eltisley two further tomb recesses were cut into the chapel in the fourteenth century.

There are, however, examples where a chapel builder also added to the main part of the parish church: at Isleham, for example, Christopher Peyton (d. 1507), or his father Thomas, probably built the south chapel, which still contains his brass, but also recorded his gift of the roof and clerestory in an inscription.[38] The Peytons were almost exceptionally well suited to carrying out building work. Christopher had no issue and was only the second generation to own the manor – he would even include his predecessor's arms in the arcade spandrels.[39] Examples of

---

[35] Duffy, *Stripping*, 129; Nigel Saul, *Death, Art, and Memory in Medieval England: The Cobham Family and Their Monuments, 1300–1500* (Oxford, 2001), 75–76; Coss, *Foundations of Gentry Life*, 176.

[36] W. M. Palmer, *John Layer (1586–1640) of Shepreth, Cambridgeshire: A Seventeenth-Century Local Historian* (Cambridge, 1935), 84.

[37] Although members of the FitzErnis family are surely likely. Wright, *VCH Cambridgeshire*, 1982, 8:220–27; Elrington, *VCH Cambridgeshire*, 5:46–59; Palmer, *John Layer (1586–1640) of Shepreth, Cambridgeshire; a Seventeenth-Century Local Historian*, 84.

[38] He also left an antiphoner and wished to be added to the bede roll. TNA: PROB 11/15/532; Robinson, *A Short History of the Parish Church of S. Andrew, Isleham and the Priory Church of S. Margaret* (Ramsgate, 1961), 4; Feltoe and Minns, *Vetus Liber*, 88; Harvey, *English Mediaeval Architects*, 325.

[39] A. F. Wareham and A. P. M. Wright, eds., *VCH Cambridgeshire*, vol. 10 (London, 2002), 427–37.

patronage which extended beyond windows, aisles or chapels are not uncommon, however. Linton clerestory, St Mary, Swaffham Prior porch, and Whittlesford tower were all associated with gentry patronage.[40] It is hard to generalise about the wealth or status of gentry patrons in Cambridgeshire. However, around a third of surviving patronage examples were constructed by 'new' lords (defined here as those acquiring the manor within two generations or twenty years), and a seventh by lords without direct male issue, suggestively high fractions. As noted in the Introduction, interpreting these facts is a contentious point.[41]

c) WILLS, CONTRACTS AND ACCOUNTS

More useful evidence for the financing of building work may be found in documentary sources. A minority of testators provided for the entire construction of an architectural unit, as with John Baker, who built a new aisle at Folkestone, Kent, in 1464.[42] Smaller, more affordable items were also given with 'unlimited' funds, including windows,[43] arches[44] and pews.[45] These projects were exceptional, however. Most patrons would, presumably, rather build a new aisle, chapel or tower in life, rather than in death. This was, after all, more secure and gave the patron both control over the work and kudos for his or her generosity. Several wills do indeed include enough money to finish a project already in progress, as with Nicholas Norpice's chapel at Hawkhurst in Kent, in 1513.[46] Some executors became dilatory after the testator's death, and grand plans for monuments or tombs were not realised, John II Paston being a well-known example.[47] Some executors were probably not intended to spend the full amount: William Wykeham gave 2,500 marks to the nave of Winchester Cathedral in 1404, 'if so much be necessary to be expended', although this was hardly a typical bequest.[48]

Legacies of unlimited funds for building work do not remove the possibility that others in the parish contributed, however. Executors

---

[40] John Layer and William Cole, *Monumental Inscriptions and Coats of Arms from Cambridgeshire: Chiefly*, ed. William Mortlock Palmer (Cambridge, 1932), 107, 232; W. M. Palmer, *William Cole of Milton* (Cambridge, 1935), 118.
[41] Introduction, section a, pp. 6–7.   [42] Nicolas, *Testamenta Vetusta*, 1826, 1:306.
[43] Duncan, *Testamenta Cantiana (West)*, 48; Hussey, *Testamenta Cantiana (East)*, 220.
[44] Duncan, *Testamenta Cantiana (West)*, 68.   [45] Hussey, *Testamenta Cantiana (East)*, 116.
[46] TNA: PRO PROB 11/17/436; Hussey, *Testamenta Cantiana (East)*, 156.
[47] Colin Richmond, *The Paston Family in the Fifteenth Century: Fastolf's Will* (Cambridge, 1996), 156–57.
[48] J. Nichols, ed., *A Collection of the Wills Now Known to Be Extant of the Kings and Queens of England* (London, 1780), 766.

could encourage further donations, or the testator may have made agreements with other bodies in the parish without recording them in his or her will. When Sir William Fitzwilliam (d. 1534) desired to be buried in the chancel of Marholm, Cambridgeshire, 'which I have of late caused to be made and newly edified', the language is typically vague about his exact role in its construction, paralleling the inscriptions surveyed in the previous section.[49] Drawing quantitative conclusions about the proportion of gentry who left money to their own projects and to the projects of others is impossible since the surviving examples cannot be treated as representative. Nevertheless, members of the gentry and nobility did commonly bequeath fixed sums directly to building work in parish churches, like any other lay parishioner, with the remainder to be made up, presumably, through general fundraising.[50]

Contracts, even as they provide some evidence of the organisation of church building, are less useful than they might appear for understanding its financing. The contracts made by members of the aristocracy (Southchurch, 1293; Etchingham, 1363; St Dunstan's, London, 1381; Hornby, Yorkshire, 1410; Catterick, Yorkshire, 1412; St Mary-on-the-Hill, Chester, 1433; Fotheringhay, 1434; Broxbourne, Hertfordshire, 1476; and Biddenham, Bedfordshire, 1522) represent only a quarter of the total number of surviving medieval contracts for parochial work.[51] Although the contractee(s), and often their heirs and executors, are nearly always bound to pay, financial liability was not necessarily identical with financial patronage. A member of the gentry might contract for the work, agree the cost and bind himself to pay it, but seek funds from across the parish, as was probably the case at Bolney.[52] The 1522 draft contract for the north aisle at Biddenham, Bedfordshire, is unique in giving some details of financial cooperation between the main patron, Sir William Butler, and the parish ('parishioners and other the inhabitants of the said parish'), who were to pay for transport and materials.[53] Although the contractee was Butler, it had evidently been agreed that the parish would contribute substantial sums to his project. Such arrangements were probably not uncommon, even when not explicitly mentioned in contracts, and the Biddenham example will be returned to later.[54] As noted in the Introduction to this volume, family chapels were understood to be communal goods, which attracted further donations and

---

[49] Christian Steer, 'The Language of Commemoration', in *Language in Medieval Britain*, ed. Mary Carruthers (Donington, 2015), 243.
[50] E.g. Nicolas, *Testamenta Vetusta*, 1826, 1:63, 82, 168, 384. See Chapter 1, section c.v, pp. 79–80 in this volume.
[51] See Chapter 5, section b.i, pp. 215–21. There are also late examples at Exbourne, 1558–1579, and Heanton Punchardon, Devon, 1538–44: TNA: PRO C 3/138/92; and C 1/1074/18.
[52] Chapter 5, section b.ii, pp. 221–26; Byng, 'Bolney', 105.   [53] TNA: PRO E41/318, f. 2.
[54] Chapter 5, section b.iii, pp. 228–31; Byng, 'Biddenham', 262–63.

benefactions from the parish, and there is every reason to suppose that their erection was also funded from a broader sweep of parishioners.[55]

There are reports of early antiquarians, often accepted by historians, which gloss archaeological or testamentary evidence for cooperative fundraising as single-handed generosity. Leland's claim that Fairford, Gloucestershire, was rebuilt by John and Edmund Tame is undermined to some extent by the heraldic evidence, which includes record of at least seven trades on the tower in addition to the Tames' arms, all added some time after both the construction of the lower storeys and John's death.[56] Suggestively, neither man's will mentions the building work and Leland visited years after Edmund's death. At Newbury, Berkshire, Thomas Fuller reported in 1660 that John Winchcombe rebuilt the church west of the pulpit, but Winchcombe died in 1520 and the tower bears the date 1532.[57] Winchcombe's will indicates that the work was cooperative: he left £10 'towards building and edifying' the church. Similarly, scholars have tended to take at face value the inscription of the east window at Holme, Nottinghamshire, reconstructed by Nevile Truman and describing John Barton as 'Builder of this Church'. In the 1930s, Truman took the glass with 'Barton', 'JB', 'B', Barton's arms and rebus, and donor images from the northeast and northwest windows, to which they had possibly been moved by Victorian restorers.[58] Only parts of the inscription (*'mercatori'*, *'ville'*, *'nobis mortis implora pro'*) were in the east window and of different sizes from the text 'Barton'. An eighteenth-century account, however, found the inscription and images of Barton 'in east window of south aisle (sic)' and an inscription to a different couple, Thomas and Margaret Leek, in the east chancel window.[59] Truman describes no original glass with the word 'builder'. In fact, Robert Thoroton wrote in 1677 that Barton built 'a fair chapel like a Parish Church', almost certainly the south chancel chapel where he was buried, and Barton's will refers only to 'the chapel newly constructed by me'.[60] There are numerous other arms in the church's windows, indicating that the chancel and south aisle at least were probably cooperative ventures.

---

[55] Duffy, *Stripping*, 116.
[56] There are gloves for a glover, scissors for a tailor, and so forth. Anna Eavis, 'The Church', in *Fairford Parish Church: A Medieval Church and Its Stained Glass*, ed. Sarah Brown and Lindsay MacDonald, Revised (Stroud, 2007), 41.
[57] William Page and P. H. Ditchfield, eds., *VCH Berkshire*, vol. 4 (London, 1924), 130–55.
[58] Nevile Truman, 'Medieval Glass in Holme-by-Newark Church', *Transactions of the Thoroton Society* 39 (1935): 92–118; Nevile Truman, 'Medieval Glass in Holme-by-Newark Church, II', *Transactions of the Thoroton Society* 43 (1939): 27–32; Nevile Truman, 'The Barton Family of Holme-by-Newark', *Transactions of the Thoroton Society* 40 (1936): 1–17.
[59] Truman, 'Medieval Glass', 94.
[60] Thoroton in fact refers only to an ancestor of Thomas Barton. Thomas M. Blagg, *A Guide to the Antiquities of Newark and the Churches of Holme and Hawton* (Newark, 1906).

Wills, Contracts and Accounts

The accounts for Bolney tower, the only surviving private gentry building accounts for a parish church, which will be examined more fully later, allow a unique insight into the form that financial cooperation between lord and parish could take during a 'gentry' building project.[61] Scholarly opinion has been divided between claims that the work was made 'principally at the cost of John Bolney'[62] or that it was the result of 'collective devotion of all sections of the community'.[63] The accounts record no gifts from John Bolney himself, which makes quantification impossible, but he did undoubtedly provide some proportion of the total funding. The parish was not otherwise wealthy – the accounts record insufficient income for the tower's entire construction – and, although suggestive only, his arms are carved in the west doorway of the tower (once alone and once quartered with those of his mother's illustrious family, the St Legers).[64] Revealingly, however, Bolney appears to have agreed with the parish that the fundraising burden would be split: he refers to 'my grant of the said steeple' and 'my part of the steeple', and pays a mason 'for my part'. Probably the income recorded in the accounts was only that which came from external sources, the difference being made up by John and thus not requiring a record in his private accounts. The wording of the accounts suggests that he promised a total sum ('my grant' or 'part') and the parishioners were to pay for whatever excess was required. It is unlikely that the sums recorded in the heavily decayed accounts were sufficient for the entire project: slightly more than £13 in income and £34 in outgoings. The master mason had agreed to make the tower at 18s per foot, slightly over £59 in total, but this did not include payments for labourers, quarrying or materials, which appear separately in the accounts.

The other sources of income for the tower were surveyed in the previous chapter.[65] Many of these must have been sums received routinely by the churchwardens but granted to Bolney for the duration of the work. The accounts were audited on one occasion, an oddity for private fabric accounts that may have been the result of a condition laid down by the parish leadership in return for granting communal revenues to Bolney's project. The accounts' survival might also be explained as a

---

[61] See Chapter 5, section b.ii, pp. 221–26. The accounts are in WSRO Par 252/9/1; Dale, 'Bolney CWAs'; Byng, 'Bolney', 107.
[62] Mark Antony Lower, *A Compendious History of Sussex*, vol. 1 (Lewes, 1870), 62.
[63] Brandon, *Sussex*, 186.
[64] William Hervey, *The Visitations of Suffolk Made by Hervey, Clarenceux, 1561, Cooke, Clarenceux, 1577, and Raven, Richmond Herald, 1612* (Exeter, 1882), 127; Raphael Holinshed, *Holinshed's Chronicles of England, Scotland, and Ireland: England* (London, 1808), 301; Edward Hasted, *The History and Topographical Survey of the County of Kent*, vol. 5 (Canterbury, 1798), 385–96.
[65] Chapter 1, section b.i, pp. 54–55.

way of preserving a record of the parish's generosity – Bolney's contributions, after all, are not recorded in the accounts, and the book was discovered in the church chest in the 1850s (although it had previously been kept in a pub).[66] In addition to contributing money, the parish also contracted for the tower's timberwork: Bolney notes 'works made and covenanted between [Roger Frogbrook] and the parish'. Frogbrook was paid 'for making of the timber work of the steeple' and 'covering of the cock and wheel'. He writes also of 'the Parishioners' as donors, presumably through a collection. The donors noted in the accounts were usually wealthy enough to be taxed but few were assessed at the highest levels in 1524 and 1525, and many were also employed on the building site.[67] The account book is fragmentary, so donations by wealthier parishioners may have been lost, but perhaps they were unwilling to contribute to a project led so explicitly by John Bolney. Nevertheless, two wealthy locals, John Gaston and John Gratwick, laboured as an act of charity.[68]

This division of fundraising, whereby a single wealthy patron funded labour and stone work while 'the parish' funded the timberwork, was not unique to Bolney: testamentary evidence shows that it was used for the Cockfield porch in Suffolk too.[69] Similar divisions could be made between just a few wealthy locals. At Harlestone, Northamptonshire, in 1325, Henry de Bray, the owner of a sub-manor, noted in his estate book that he had supplied the stone and timber for rebuilding the church, probably the nave or a part of it; Roger de Lumley (a wealthy local), the iron and smith work; and John Dyve (Henry's son-in-law), the carpentry (Figure 2.1).[70] As noted in the previous section, the rector built the chancel and recorded on his tomb that he 'helped' ('*auxilio*') build the rest of the church. Although the exact form of financial cooperation at Bolney should not be generalised to building more widely, the nature of its division may not have been unusual. Splitting a project between a lordly patron and a larger group of parishioners including wealthy tenants as well as communal officers and sources would have been necessary for many gentry members to afford building work.

D) AFFORDABILITY

The conclusion that only the wealthiest gentry families were able to finance major building projects on their own is supported when their

---

[66] Cf. Burgess, 'Lessons', 326, 315.   [67] Cornwall, *Lay Subsidy*, 89–90.
[68] Ibid.; Dale, 'Bolney CWAs', 245; John Comber, *Sussex Genealogies – Horsham Centre*, ed. William Bull and L. F. Salzman, vol. 1 (Cambridge, 1931), 114–16.
[69] Northeast and Falvey, *Wills of the Archdeaconry of Sudbury, 1439–1474*, 2:205.
[70] Willis, *Bray's Estate Book*, 43.

Affordability

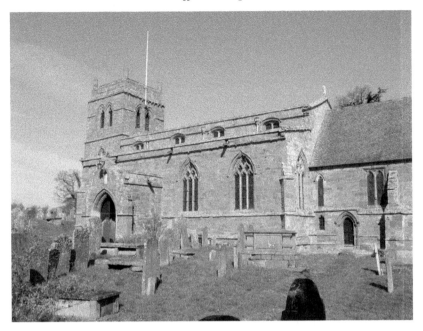

Figure 2.1 Harlestone nave (Keltek Trust)

incomes are considered. Dyer estimates that around 1300 there were some 1,100 knights, along with many who refused to be dubbed, with incomes above £40 and often much higher, about one for every ten churches and chapels, although, of course, the upper gentry and nobility owned manors in many parishes and could afford building work in more than one (Table 1.2).[71] By comparison, there were around 10,000 lower gentry families with incomes of £5–£40, almost one per local church or chapel, but with a mean income of c. £15. Bruce Campbell reduces these figures slightly to 925 knights with a mean annual landed income of £40 and 8,500 lesser gentry with an average income of just £11.[72] It is difficult to find useful yardsticks against which this could be measured but, as noted in the previous chapter, the Southchurch chapel, which cost almost £8 without materials and transport in 1293, perhaps £15 in total, is probably the most useful starting point.[73] Around 1300, this would be equivalent to about 100 per cent of the annual income of a member of the lesser gentry (using Dyer's figures) or 140 per cent (using Campbell's), but less than 40 per cent of that of the upper gentry. Of course, these percentages would increase

[71] Dyer, *Standards*, 29–30. [72] Campbell, 'Agrarian Problem', Table 1, p. 12.
[73] Chapter 1, section c.vi, pp. 84–86.

considerably for a larger project, and reduce when spread over several years using credit and savings, as will be discussed shortly.

Estimating affordability, particularly for the lower gentry, is, of course, highly speculative and individually variable. One useful, if impressionistic, method is to discuss a single example: for the poorer groups surveyed above, Henry de Bray is probably a suitable representative. He received £12 of rent annually and, as noted already, contributed stone and timber for construction at Harlestone.[74] Undoubtedly like many minor gentry, he was unable to afford major new work single-handedly but nevertheless had access to enough expendable income to make a critical difference to the feasibility of a collaborate venture. By working with two other wealthy locals, they were able to afford a new, aisled, three-bay nave. It is perhaps revealing that, in 1290, Henry was able to build a manor house for £12 excluding stone and beams, a total sum perhaps comparable to his expenditure on the church (there was a nearby quarry), and could spend another £54 over the next twenty years on various building works, often not including stone and timber, suggesting greater means than his rental income indicates.[75] Building work on the church, and the manor house, must have constituted a considerable burden on his income but indicates how much was achievable before the Black Death even by a minor landholder. It no doubt helped that Henry was both a canny manager and had a particular interest in his family's pedigree. By comparison, Nigel Saul estimates that William Trussell, with an annual income of up to £200 at his death, still had to borrow large sums of money in order to pay for the handsome collegiate church of Shottesbrooke, Berkshire, in 1337.[76] Generalising from Dyer's figures, therefore, we can probably conclude that around the turn of the fourteenth century, a small fraction of parishes may have had a resident (or occasionally resident) member of the upper gentry with sufficient income to carry out large-scale building work single-handedly, while many would have had a resident member of the lower gentry of whom it is doubtful that a considerable number could have afforded building work acting alone although their contribution to jointly-funded work could be essential.

A century later, the situation was very different. Extrapolating from the 1436 taxation accounts, H. L. Gray estimated that there was a leading group of around 180 actual or possible greater knights with £210 a year; 750 lesser knights with £40–£100 a year, an average of c. £60; and 1,200

---

[74] Willis, *Bray's Estate Book*, 43.
[75] This includes various agricultural buildings, but not cottages, water courses or mills. Stone was provided by a freed serf in lieu of rent. Ibid., xxiv–xxvii.
[76] Saul, 'Shottesbrooke', 271.

Affordability

lesser gentry with £20–£39, an average of c. £24.[77] Below them was a larger group of 1,600 with £10–£19 and 3,400 with £5–£9. The problems with these data have been assessed elsewhere and need not be repeated here, but they should be used to indicate rough totals only.[78] Gray's figures indicate there was now approximately just one family of knightly income for every twelve local churches and one member of the £5–£39 group to every two churches (Table 1.3). Even if many gentry families were wealthier, however, building costs had changed radically since the Black Death. The previous chapter suggested £30 as a useful comparison cost for a small new chapel or aisle in the fifteenth century, twice the cost of a similar unit, such as at Southchurch, a century before.[79] This would represent at best 75 per cent and at worst 600 per cent of the annual income of the poorer group (with £5–£39 a year), and three-quarters to a third of that of the lesser knights. Any improvement in income, therefore, was often far outstripped by increases in the cost of construction, with the result that affordability tended to be reduced, while the number of gentry families per parish had decreased substantially – although, of course, the wealthiest could finance building work on more than one church. Gray's calculations capture a snapshot in time, with the seigniorial economy generally weakening over the next few decades before improving at the end of the century, when building work may have become more affordable.[80] As before, gentry families could donate considerable sums to collaborative projects, perhaps greater in absolute terms than a century before but, in many places, nevertheless lower as a proportion of the total cost of building work. By inference, then, in an era of widespread church building, it would fall to non-gentry families and groups to make up an increasing shortfall.[81]

Comparing annual income with building costs is misleading, of course, as an absolute rather than relative measure of affordability. Nevertheless, a £30 project spread over, say, ten years would still come to 8–60 per cent of the annual income of the large £5–£39 group – affordability would depend upon individual circumstances, but the poorer half of this group (with £5–£9 a year) would surely find even this sum all but impossible. In order to spread the burden of payments, almost all gentry families would need to rely on saving, credit, and delayed and part-payment.[82] However, there is reason to doubt to what extent these could be

---

[77] H. L. Gray, 'Incomes from Land in England in 1436', *The English Historical Review* 49, no. 196 (1 October 1934): 621–29.
[78] Critiques have largely focused on the underestimation of baronial incomes, or the exclusion of some of the poorest members of the gentry. See the summaries in Payling, *Political Society*, 2–3; Carpenter, *Locality and Polity*, 50–55.
[79] Chapter 1, section c.vi, pp. 89–90. [80] Introduction, section b, pp. 21–22.
[81] See Chapter 1, section c.v, pp. 79–83. [82] See Chapter 6, section d.ii, pp. 269–76.

exploited, especially for relatively poorer families. The aristocracy were expected to spend their income, neither getting into debt nor hoarding.[83] Any savings would be especially limited for the lesser gentry, for whom reducing expenditure would save only small quantities in an economically run household where food might absorb half its income.[84] Wright argues that 'the concept of saving may have been foreign to the minds of the medieval aristocracy and large expenditures had of necessity to be financed by credit of some kind, for rent income was probably quickly consumed'.[85] This argument should not be taken too far, however – Henry de Bray is probably a good counterexample, and fungible assets such as plate could be purchased, for example, as a form of saving.[86] The gentry could call upon large amounts of credit, often from their peers, but there is little indication that this was used for major projects, like construction, rather than as an ad hoc measure to tide households through an unexpected shortfall.[87] There was a structural restriction too. For some members of the upper gentry, and the nobility, paying for parish church construction may not have been taxing but their contributions were spread over a large number of parishes, focusing perhaps on those where they were resident, or were diverted to high-status monastic or collegiate establishments.[88] The lord of a single manor, with close ties to his tenants and perhaps with other families in the parish to compete with, may have been willing to donate but unable to raise funds for more than furnishings, vestments or obits. One alternative of course was simply to build more slowly, but slow construction still represented an increased financial burden on household finances, was inadvisable for constructional reasons, delayed gratification and was liable to infuriate parishioners.[89]

Indeed, it is suggestive that so many men cited as architectural patrons in the two centuries after the Black Death can be shown to have had access to large amounts of expendable wealth, well beyond the normal run of the parish gentry: Thomas Spring at Lavenham, who left his wife 1,000 marks; John Clopton at Long Melford, who also left vast sums in his will; John Curteys at Wimington, who lent the king £20 and was mayor of the Calais staple; John Tame, the wealthy wool merchant, at Fairford; Sir Richard Fowler, the royal civil servant, at Buckingham; John Smallwood, a major clothier, at Newbury; Edward Lovekyn at Kingston upon Thames, Surrey, who was owed vast sums by the crown; and John Barton, a successful merchant of the Calais staple who

---

[83] Dyer, *Standards*, 91–92, 98–99. [84] Ibid., 106, 80–81; Dyer, *Making a Living*, 342.
[85] Wright, *Derbyshire Gentry*, 23. [86] Carpenter, *Locality and Polity*, Chapter 6.
[87] Wright, *Derbyshire Gentry*, 24. [88] Carpenter, 'Religion', 140.
[89] Chapter 6, especially pp. 265–68.

left 100 marks to his wife, at Holme.⁹⁰ These men were often newcomers who needed to stamp their authority or win popularity in a new parish, or were lawyers or merchants with exceptional amounts of surplus cash – 100 marks is more than twice the cost of a £30 chapel.⁹¹ For less exceptionally wealthy gentry members, it would have been necessary to defray the cost of building work by relying on other parishioners, for which there is in fact considerable evidence.⁹² There is also little indication that they used their manorial position by, for example, allowing labour services to be given to the work.⁹³ Yeomen and other newly wealthy groups outside the aristocracy must be treated slightly differently since their number grew considerably in the later fifteenth century but, given the challenges facing even the lesser gentry, it can be seen that very few could afford single-handed patronage.⁹⁴ We can follow a recent biographical study of a wool merchant in describing the donations of merchants to building work generally as 'helpful but not decisive'.⁹⁵

E) RECTORS AND VICARS

When rectors and vicars were responsible for church building, they cannot be easily distinguished financially from their lay peers. Even after Pope Gregory's reforms, lucrative rectories were typically held by members or acquaintances of the lordly families who owned the advowson, while poorer benefices were held by members of the lower social ranks, even including former villeins.⁹⁶ Architectural patronage by priests who were also members of a gentry or noble family was inseparable from lay gentry bequests, in so far as they drew on private resources as well as rectorial income. It is true that the same trends in archaeological evidence for gentry patronage, as surveyed in the previous section, apply here too. In Cambridgeshire, there are several inscriptions ascribing patronage to single clerics: Balsham was cited earlier in this chapter, but William de Longthorpe (c. 1352) at Fenstanton, Richard

---

⁹⁰ Page, *VCH Bedfordshire*, 1912, 3:109–17; William Page, ed., *VCH Buckinghamshire*, vol. 3 (London, 1925), 471–89; Barbara McClenaghan, *The Springs of Lavenham: And the Suffolk Cloth Trade in the XV and XVI Centuries* (Ipswich, 1924); William Parker, *The History of Long Melford* (London, 1873), 44; Page and Ditchfield, *VCH Berkshire*, 4:149; James Raine, ed., *Testamenta Eboracensia*, vol. 4 (London, 1869), 61; Nigel Saul, 'The Lovekyns and the Lovekyn Chapel at Kingston upon Thames', *Surrey Archaeological Collections* 96 (2011): 86–87.
⁹¹ Carpenter, 'Religion'; Carpenter, *Locality and Polity*, Chapter 6.
⁹² Chapter 5, section b.ii, pp. 222–31.
⁹³ However, parts of fines charged by manorial courts and municipal officers often went to building work: Ault, 'Manor Court and Parish Church'; Dyer, *Lords and Peasants*, 362.
⁹⁴ See Introduction, section b, pp. 13–15.   ⁹⁵ Dyer, *Country Merchant*, 215.
⁹⁶ M. J. Bennett, 'The Lancashire and Cheshire Clergy, 1379', *Transactions of the Historical Society of Lancashire and Cheshire* 124 (1972): 11–17; Peter Heath, *The English Parish Clergy on the Eve of the Reformation* (London, 1969), 136–37.

Financing Construction II: Gentry and Clergy

Anlaby (d. 1396) at Orwell and Thomas Patesley (d. 1418) at Great Shelford may be added.[97] The brass of the latter, a prebendary at Southwell Minster, credits to him the chancel, church and tower 'at his own expense', as well as books, vestments, stained glass and ornaments. Lastly, William le Busteler (1321–32), appointed by his own father, built the south chapel at Hildersham, probably as a chantry chapel for his parents.[98] The sums granted in wills could be substantial: Henry de Snaith bequeathed 100 marks to the making of a new east window of five lights and the roofing of the nave of Haddenham in 1382.[99] Clerics did not only donate to the chancel, for the upkeep of which they were legally responsible.[100] Leaving Cambridgeshire, gifts from vicars and rectors (just like those of lay patrons) to the repair of the church,[101] nave,[102] porch,[103] chapels[104] and screens[105] can be found in large numbers. Clergy could be as generous or as parsimonious as they pleased: at Farnham, Surrey, one incumbent gave stone worth £100 and left 100 marks in his will, but the former grant was purloined by his successor.[106]

The extent to which rectors and vicars may be treated differently from lay patrons in terms of their financial capacity depends on the income attached to their office. Although it is impossible to know what disposable wealth most parsons may have had, there is good reason to suppose that the income they received was not sufficient to sponsor significant architectural patronage single-handedly. Beginning with the pre-Black Death period, in 1291 the average benefice eligible for assessment in the *Taxatio* was valued at around £10, from tithes, mortuaries, oblations and the glebe, although in many appropriated churches either vicarial or rectorial income was not assessed.[107] The problems regarding the manuscript copies which have survived and the deficiencies of the printed versions are well known, as are the possibilities of evasion and inconsistency, and the many exemptions.[108] The sums were considerable, particularly from tithes, and fairly reliable but, however much

---

[97] Richard Marks, 'Brass and Glass: Rector Thomas Patesley and Great Shelford Church (Cambridgeshire)', http://vidimus.org/issues/issue-76/feature/, accessed 2 January 2017.
[98] Layer and Cole, *Monumental Inscriptions*, 79; A. P. M. Wright, ed., *VCH Cambridgeshire*, vol. 6 (London, 1978), 59–69.
[99] Cf. Duncan, *Testamenta Cantiana (West)*, 12.   [100] Introduction, section b, pp. 22–23.
[101] E.g. Hussey, *Testamenta Cantiana (East)*, 144, 212.
[102] E.g. Duncan, *Testamenta Cantiana (West)*, 37; Hussey, *Testamenta Cantiana (East)*, 210.
[103] Duncan, *Testamenta Cantiana (West)*, 56.   [104] Hussey, *Testamenta Cantiana (East)*, 17.
[105] E.g. Staunton, 1519, J. C. Cox and A. Harvey, *English Church Furniture* (London, 1907).
[106] T. F. Kirby, ed., *Wykeham's Register*, vol. 2 (London, 1896), 67.
[107] Warren Ortman Ault, 'The Village Church and the Village Community in Mediaeval England', *Speculum* 45, no. 2 (1 April 1970): 198; Hilton, *A Medieval Society*, 63; Heath, *English Parish Clergy*, 158–59; J. R. H. Moorman, *Church Life in England in the 13th Century* (Cambridge, 1945), 113, 136.
[108] J. H. Denton, 'The Valuation of the Ecclesiastical Benefices of England and Wales in 1291–2', *Historical Research* 66 (1993): 242–50; J. H. Denton, 'Towards a New Edition of the "Taxatio

Rectors and Vicars

Table 2.1 *Building work in Cambridgeshire and the 1291 Taxatio*

Ranking of clerical wealth (1291)	Chancel building work (1250–1350)	Any building work (1250–1350)	Chancels as % of work
1 to 20	10	19	53%
21 to 40	10	17	59%
41 to 60	11	19	58%
61 to 80	11	19	58%
81 to 100	8	14	57%
101 to 120	15	16	94%
121 to 140	8	15	53%
141 to 160	5	11	45%

Sources: J. H. Denton, 'The 1291 Valuation of the Churches of Ely Diocese', *Proceedings of the Cambridge Antiquarian Society* XC (2001): 69–80; Thomas Astle, Samuel Ayscough, and John Caley, eds., *Taxatio Ecclesiastica Angliae Et Walliae, Auctoritate P. Nicholai IV, Circa A. D.1291* (London, 1802).

underestimated, once depleted by the costs of assistants, hospitality, chancel maintenance and the household, would be insufficient to enable most rectors to carry out construction work without some personal wealth.[109] Vicars earned considerably less, the institutional patron usually taking the greater part of the income, and stipendiary chaplains and assistant clergy less still, an average of perhaps 6–7 marks.[110] The unbeneficed were typically the worst off.[111]

Returning to Cambridgeshire, at first glance, the *Taxatio* does appear to suggest a role for rectors. Of the twenty parishes in the county with the lowest clerical incomes in 1291, five carried out building work on the chancel in 1250–1350; of the twenty richest, the equivalent figure is double that, ten (Table 2.1). However, the correlation between rectorial income and chancel building is far from perfect, and nor can it demonstrate responsibility since wealthy rectors had wealthy parishioners and wealthy rectories tended to be held by men from important local families, who may have contributed.[112] The most that can be claimed on the basis

---

Ecclesiastice Angliae et Walliae Auctoritate P Nicholai IV circa AD 1291'", *Bulletin of the John Rylands Library* 79, no. 1 (1997): 67–79.

[109] However, labour legislation did restrict the wages of assistant clergy: H. G. Richardson, 'The Parish Clergy of the Thirteenth and Fourteenth Centuries', *Transactions of the Royal Historical Society*, 6 (1 January 1912): 116–17.

[110] Richardson, 'Parish Clergy'.

[111] A. K. McHardy, 'Ecclesiastics and Economics: Poor Priests, Prosperous Laymen and Proud Prelates in the Reign of Richard II', in *The Church and Wealth* (Oxford, 1987), 136.

[112] Schofield, 'Geographical Distribution', 507–08.

of these figures is that incumbents may have been responsible for building work in poorer parishes: at Coveney, a fenland church four miles west of Ely, for example, this reasonably large but poor parish was able to extend its chancel in the early fourteenth century and add windows with good, if varied, tracery. There is at any rate reason to believe that any clerical contributions to construction work were proportionate to the quantity of lay ones: no matter the wealth of the benefice, of those churches that carried out any building work, 50–60 per cent carried out building work on the chancel. The construction of chancels at Leverington (assessed at £85 in 1291 and 1341, rebuilt in the fourteenth century), Haddenham (£80, various late thirteenth-century features in the chancel and modern vestry), and Soham (£57, with reticulated traceried windows and some earlier features) may be suggestive, but then Coveney (£5) and Sawston (£5), with some of the poorest rectories, albeit lucrative enough to qualify for assessment, also managed to construct new stone chancels.

Although some could earn large sums, the poverty of many beneficed late medieval clergy is attested to in numerous sources, including tax returns and bishops' registers – especially for vicars, chaplains and assistant clergy.[113] The *Valor Ecclesiasticus* reveals a national elite of fewer than 900 rectors with more than £40 gross a year, while most received £5–£20, an average of around £10 each.[114] Peter Heath's study of vicars' household accounts argues that a vicar would require an annual income of £13, with no chaplain's fees, to cover his outgoings comfortably – building work would be limited to whatever excess remained. For most, this would be little or nothing: three-quarters of rectories and nine-tenths of vicarages in some dioceses were valued below this in the *Valor Ecclesiasticus*.[115] Unbeneficed or salaried priests were able to negotiate higher wages in areas or periods of scarcity – as, for example, after the Black Death.[116] However, despite these increases, few were well off, even in comparison with some of their parishioners. An indication of the relatively modest incomes of most appointments can be gathered from taxation brackets: the upper boundary for archiepiscopal levies was £10 and the lowest £5, while royal taxation of the church began at £8. Given

---

[113] Pounds, *English Parish*, 159; J. Pound, 'Clerical Poverty in Early Sixteenth-Century England: Some East Anglian Evidence', *Journal of Ecclesiastical History* 37 (1986): 393; M. L. Zell, 'Economic Problems of the Parochial Clergy in the Sixteenth Century', in *Princes and Paupers in the English Church, 1500–1800*, ed. R. O'Day and Felicity Heal (Leicester, 1981), 19–43; A. K. McHardy, 'Careers and Disappointments in the Late Medieval Church', in *The Ministry: Clerical and Lay*, ed. W. J. Sheils and D. Wood (Oxford, 1989), 124–25.

[114] Heath, *English Parish Clergy*, 173.

[115] Peter Heath, *Medieval Clerical Accounts* (York, 1964), 24 n. 102.

[116] Bertha Haven Putnam, 'Maximum Wage-Laws for Priests after the Black Death, 1348–1381', *The American Historical Review* 21, no. 1 (1915): 19–21.

Rectors and Vicars

the many charges on these sums, it is likely that few had sufficient expendable income to pay for repairs, let alone building work, even allowing for evasion and exemptions.

Nevertheless, revenues from the more valuable rectories and vicarages may have helped to top up other sources of income to make construction possible, as well as raising expectations that the incumbent would lead building work on the chancel. A sizable minority may have been able to fund a window, chapel, or other small but important architectural additions. However, like secular lords, many would have had to collaborate with lay parishioners in order to patronise building work, and evidence of this survives in testamentary records, building accounts and archaeological sources. Several examples have already been given of rectors, and some vicars, who bequeathed sums, often sizeable, to communally run projects in Cambridgeshire and elsewhere.[117] The accounts at Bodmin, Cornwall, show the vicar donating more than £20 'from the profits of the church' to the building work, as well as 18s personally.[118] Lastly, an inscription on the screen at Llanfairwaterdine, Shropshire, of c. 1485–1520, indicates it was given by the priest and a parishioner, for £10 each.[119]

Generalisations based on the *Taxatio* or *Valor* serve to hide the wealth that some could derive from holding numerous offices. Pluralism, leasing and work as a canon lawyer would have provided sources of income that, in some cases, could reach substantial sums. Nicholas de Braybroke, rector of Bideford in 1366, for example, probably did reside in his rectory there, worth £13 a year, but earned another £40 from four prebends.[120] Church legislation had succeeded in the late fourteenth century in reducing absentee rectors, but it remained common in 10–25 per cent of parishes even by the late fifteenth century.[121] However, it is doubtful that many pluralist rectors, often working in the highest echelons of the church, would have been minded to contribute to parochial building work.[122] Complaints that absentee rectors tended to shirk their pastoral responsibilities to their churches and

---

[117] See also, e.g. Hussey, *Testamenta Cantiana (East)*, 115, 204; L. A. Majendie, 'Dunmow Parish Accounts', *Transactions of the Essex Archaeological Society* 2 (1863): 231.
[118] '*de p[ro]ficuis eccl[es]ie*'; CRO BBOD/244 f. 19; Wilkinson, *Bodmin Church*, 1874, 30.
[119] Vallance, *Screens*, 65.
[120] C. J. Godfrey, 'Pluralists in the Province of Canterbury in 1366', *The Journal of Ecclesiastical History* 11, no. 1 (April 1960): 36.
[121] R. A. R. Hartridge, *A History of Vicarages in the Middle Ages* (Cambridge, 1930), 95, 175; Heath, *English Parish Clergy*, 56.
[122] C. J. Godfrey, 'Non-Residence of Parochial Clergy in the Fourteenth Century', *Church Quarterly Review* CLXII (1961): 443.

Financing Construction II: Gentry and Clergy

congregations were made by bishops,[123] popes[124] and in visitations.[125] They were often the subject of litigation or archidiaconal censure, and of numerous attempts to reduce the most outlandish examples.[126] One effect of absenteeism noted by many contemporaries was the dilapidation of buildings. Nevertheless, some pluralist rectors did carry out building work, as with Henry Trafford's chancel at Wilmslow, Cheshire,[127] and Ralph Lepton's rectory at Alresford, Surrey.[128] Contemporaries defended the practice of pluralism by arguing that an effective priest could ably manage numerous churches.[129] It has indeed been pointed out that only a small minority of churches with absentee rectors suffered from disrepair as reported by archdeacons and that those cases of neglect that ended up in court may have been atypical.[130] Moreover, resident clergy, both vicars and rectors, were also occasionally the subject of censure for failing to carry out repairs.[131] Indeed, members of the laity are to be found often among patrons of chancel building in the late middle ages.[132] Many pluralists, particularly those who combined jobs as a chantry priest, vicar and rector, were far from wealthy, however, and were more likely to be resident in their parish.[133] Some at least did take on building work and were trusted enough to receive bequests from lay testators for work on the chancel.[134]

In Cambridgeshire, appropriation cannot be straightforwardly shown to have affected the likelihood of carrying out building work. Of the churches which carried out work, 58 per cent were appropriated, while

---

[123] E.g. Robert Grosseteste and Oliver Sutton: Hartridge, *Vicarages*, 78; Thomas Gascoigne, Richard Swinfield and Thomas Cobham: G. G Coulton, *Five Centuries of Religion: Getting & Spending*, vol. 3 (Cambridge, 1936), 181, 173, 169.

[124] A. Hamilton Thompson, 'Pluralism in the Medieval Church', *Association of Architectural Society Reports and Paper* 33 (1915): 70–71.

[125] Christopher Harper-Bill, 'A Late Medieval Visitation – the Diocese of Norwich in 1499', *Proceedings of the Suffolk Institute of Archaeology and History* 34 (1977): 41; Margaret Bowker, *The Secular Clergy in the Diocese of Lincoln, 1495–1520* (Cambridge, 1968), 90–92.

[126] Platt, *Parish Churches*, 97–98.

[127] John Parsons Earwaker, *East Cheshire Past and Present*, vol. I (London, 1877), 88–89.

[128] Owen Manning and William Bray, *The History and Antiquities of the County of Surrey*, vol. I (London, 1804), 65.

[129] E.g. in the claims of Roger Otery: Godfrey, 'Pluralists', 24–25.

[130] Heath, *English Parish Clergy*, 67.

[131] E.g. CCA-DCc-ChAnt/M/356, 366; Cecil Deedes, ed., *Registrum Johannis de Pontissara Episcopi Wyntoniensis, A. D. MCCLXXXII-MCCCIV* (London, 1916), 166; Poos, *Rural Society*, 344, 160–63.

[132] E.g. At Great Chalfield; St Thomas, Salisbury; and St Laurence, Reading, the laity contributed to chancel building: C. R. Cheney, *From Becket to Langton; English Church Government, 1170–1213* (Manchester, 1956), 157.

[133] Heath, *English Parish Clergy*, 56; Godfrey estimates about a half of pluralists with parochial rectories were resident, rising to three-quarters among the poorest livings: Godfrey, 'Pluralists', 36.

[134] E.g. Hussey, *Testamenta Cantiana (East)*, 334.

of those which built chancels the equivalent figure is 55 per cent. This is roughly equivalent to the proportion of appropriated benefices in the county (based on data from the *Vetus Liber* of 1270 onwards, the 1291 *Taxatio* and the *Valor Ecclesiasticus*), indicating that appropriation made relatively little difference to the likelihood of carrying out building work, even of chancels, during this period.[135] This is significantly higher than the national average although lower than a few other regions.[136] Ecclesiastical institutions that owned benefices could finance building work, as, perhaps, with Ely Cathedral at Melbourn and Grantchester. Nevertheless, even unappropriated churches could lose money to larger institutions through the payment of portions and pensions that went to religious houses: Barnwell Priory, for example, took £30 from 21 parishes.[137] It was not unknown for vicars to have some personal wealth, although the 'Vicar de Beche', that is Waterbeach, who paid 13s 10d in tax in Swaffham Prior in 1326, despite the poverty of the vicarage (worth less than £5 in 1291), a sum equivalent to over £22 in moveable wealth and among the highest in the county, was exceptional.[138] This was almost certainly John of Staunton, who gave a set of vestments.[139] The next highest was the vicar of St Cyriac, who paid the substantial but not vast sum of 3s 5d.[140] Accordingly, low income did not invariably restrict architectural patronage: the vicar at Melbourn, whose vicarage was worth little more than £5 in 1291, an eighth of the rectory,[141] nevertheless gave windows and carvings in the early fourteenth century, but he must have been unusual.[142]

---

[135] J. H. Denton, 'The 1291 Valuation of the Churches of Ely Diocese', *Proceedings of the Cambridge Antiquarian Society* XC (2001): 74; R. M. Haines, 'Patronage and Appropriation in Ely Diocese: The Share of the Benedictines', *Revue Bénédictine* 108 (1998): 304; Feltoe and Minns, *Vetus Liber*; David Knowles, *The Religious Orders in England*, vol. 2 (Cambridge, 1948), 291; Hartridge, *Vicarages*, 79, 208; Edward Lewes Cutts, *Parish Priests and Their People in the Middle Ages in England* (London, 1898), 385, 394.

[136] J. E. Newman, 'Greater and Lesser Landowners and Parochial Patronage: Yorkshire in the Thirteenth Century', *The English Historical Review* 92, no. 363 (1 April 1977): 303; Moorman, *Church Life*, 4–5; Hartridge, *Vicarages*, 79–81.

[137] Haines, 'Patronage and Appropriation', 302–03.

[138] Barnwell owned the rectory and advowson, and after the Black Death appointed it's own canons as vicar who were probably resident. Ravensdale, *Liable to Flood*, 13; Wright and Lewis, *VCH Cambridgeshire*, 9:257–62.

[139] Possibly Fenstanton, fourteen miles west. Feltoe and Minns, *Vetus Liber*, 74–75.

[140] J. J. Muskett, 'Lay Subsidies, Cambridgeshire, I Edward III (1327)', *East Anglian N&Q*, 10–12 (August 1903): 385.

[141] Thomas Astle, Samuel Ayscough, and John Caley, eds., *Taxatio Ecclesiastica Angliae Et Walliae* (London, 1802), 266.

[142] Feltoe and Minns, *Vetus Liber*, 115.

Financing Construction II: Gentry and Clergy

F) CONCLUSION

Tombs, inscriptions, arms, contracts and wills provide good if not incontrovertible evidence that members of the gentry regularly led the (re)building of aisles, chapels and towers, and occasionally whole churches, in the later middle ages. However, none of these sources can show what proportion of the cost they paid for. The gentry arms that proliferate in parish churches, and were so assiduously collected by antiquarians, cannot demonstrate single-handed aristocratic patronage. Their insertion could be purchased for small sums of money, unconnected with significant building work or only with small adaptations. Inscriptions provide better evidence but their claims were often ambiguous with regards to finance, indeed many patrons probably believed that their relationship to the new work was more profound than the merely monetary. In both cases, collaborative ventures could be glossed as single-handed initiatives. Contracts rarely indicate where the money would come from, indeed some contractees can be shown to have raised money from their tenants, while wills show that members of the gentry regularly contributed to corporate projects. Many, like John Bolney or William Butler, can be shown cooperating with wealthy parishioners from lower social ranks (but rarely their peers) to construct new units which bore their arms alone or to make contracts in which they alone were bound.

Attempting to judge the frequency of cooperative projects is difficult, given the paucity of documentary sources, but three pieces of evidence can be adduced. First, the church was an institution used by all members of the parish and from the embellishment of which all stood to benefit. Secondly, work could take place only if the parish was agreeable, although it may sometimes have had little choice in the matter. Thirdly, building projects were demanding and complicated and required specialist knowledge that was best provided by locals: of transport routes, sources of materials, reliable craftsmen, available labourers, places for storage, and so forth. Above all, few members of the aristocracy had incomes sufficiently large, and sufficiently under-burdened, to afford significant building work alone, without considerably reducing their outgoings, running up debt or cooperating with others. Even if local lords were perhaps responsible for building the first parish churches, by the late thirteenth century it is doubtful that many outside the upper gentry and nobility had the economic capacity to rebuild significant proportions of their stone churches singlehanded. In the later middle ages, many gentry families enjoyed rising incomes but their ability to finance church construction probably did not keep up with the cost of wages and materials, while the contribution of England's few noble families was correspondingly limited.

Conclusion

Nevertheless, the significance of gentry leadership of and contributions to collaborative projects should not be discounted. In many cases, probably, their involvement was essential to a project's success: church architecture was a symbol not simply of dominance or largesse but also of negotiation and collaboration. Not only did building work encompass a range of more and less expensive units but it must also be contextualised as one of many good works that were essential to the celebration of religious services, such as the provision of images, lights, silverware and vestments. The gentry had many opportunities for funding local religion and large-scale, single-handed rebuilding was probably often both unaffordable and not required by either custom or social expectation. To this general conclusion may be added the income and interests of the village priest: those with substantial personal wealth (and probably a lucrative living or three) could behave just as their lay kinfolk, adding chapels or windows to their churches; those without would only rarely receive enough income from their benefice(s) to enable them to contribute. With the exception of a few pluralist rectors, it was probably through collaboration, both financial and organisational, with their parishioners that they contributed the most to church construction.

Chapter 3

ORGANISING CONSTRUCTION I
The Churchwardens

A) INTRODUCTION

In 1485, the churchwardens of Saffron Walden in Essex commissioned the designs for a spectacular new nave from some of the leading architects of their day, who were then working on King's College chapel in Cambridge. They travelled to the college to negotiate a price and when they returned a few days later with a contract, the parish leadership had to decide who would run the new work – the wardens, another local body or a new, temporary administration. During the previous half-century, the parish had been confronted with this decision on numerous occasions – for a new tower, chapels and porches – and had always picked the wardens. The new nave, however, was a more challenging prospect.

The making of decisions such as these reveals both the dynamic and the distribution of institutional power within medieval parishes. Recently, it has become an important part of scholarly debate regarding the authority of the churchwardens. At stake is the thesis that wardens were relatively junior administrators conducting a simple, boring and bureaucratic post as they tried to enter the parochial hierarchy and that, therefore, their contributions to an activity as taxing as church construction were limited. The alternative thesis gives them a significant managerial position in the parish as leaders and organisers, with church building as a key example of the important activities that they oversaw.

The question becomes particularly complicated around building work: as at Walden, parish churches were rarely built in a single campaign, and churchwardens could take on the construction of some units but not others, or of parts of a unit (the stone walls, timber roof, glass or furnishings) or a subset of tasks (purchasing labour and materials, organising transport, handling legal arrangements, fundraising). In Walden, the wardens would oversee the construction of an aisle roof but not the aisle, for example. To explain variations in the management of building projects between both places and periods, the range of factors under consideration must be as broad as the historical record will allow – the number of wardens, their experience, age and character, local precedent, the nature of the work, the powers of other institutions, practices of audit and oversight, and the local capacity for administrative adaptability. In every case the wardens worked as part of a network of parochial, sub-parochial and extra-parochial bodies: delegating tasks, submitting to audit and carrying out the instructions of the assembly, municipality or masters. The play of responsibility between them is often all but hidden in the accounts but forms one of the most important questions regarding parish church construction.

B) 'STRONG' AND 'WEAK' WARDENSHIP

The role of churchwardens in parochial administration has been the subject of scholarly dispute in the last two decades, with important implications for their role in the management of church construction. At its heart is the widely accepted thesis that wardens were significant local figures who acted as elected representatives and overall managers of the parish's public funds. In these works, sometimes implicitly, they take on important roles as local leaders and organisers of most, if not all, communal activities.[1] The wardens' mandate is usually understood as granted by the parish assembly, which Beat Kümin describes as 'the community's sovereign political institution'.[2] Some have gone so far as to describe the wardens' appointment as a form of rudimentary democracy: Colin Platt, for example, sees churchwardens as 'machinery for interpreting and then implementing the common voice'.[3] In this he is propagating the ideas of earlier scholars who imagined the assembly to be a kind of participatory parliament of equals involving every parishioner.[4]

Given the prime role often claimed for the churchwardens in parochial management, it is unsurprising to find authors arguing that it was typically the churchwardens who ran building projects.[5] Christopher Dyer, for example, writes that 'late medieval church building must be attributed in

---

[1] It is a thesis attributed to Beat Kümin and Ronald Hutton by Clive Burgess: Burgess, 'Lessons'; Kümin, *Shaping*, 100; Ronald Hutton, *The Rise and Fall of Merry England: The Ritual Year, 1400–1700* (Oxford, 1994), 49–50, cf. pp. 22–23 in this volume.
[2] Beat A. Kümin, 'Late Medieval Churchwardens' Accounts and Parish Government: Looking beyond London and Bristol', *The English Historical Review* 119, no. 480 (1 February 2004): 90.
[3] Platt, *Parish Churches*, 88.
[4] Gasquet, *Parish Life*, 43; Cox, *Churchwardens' Accounts*, 7; H. Maynard Smith, *Pre-Reformation England* (London, 1963), 124; cf. Kümin, 'Looking beyond', 90; Burgess, 'Shaping', 262–67.
[5] E.g. Richmond, 'Religion and the Fifteenth Century English Gentleman', 184.

most cases to the efforts of the churchwardens'.[6] Beat Kümin imagines a fictional town where a building project is initiated by a churchwarden, approved by the parish leadership and assembly, and funded jointly by a collection and a guild.[7] Such attributions are often implicit, with responsibility handed to the wardens as a matter of course when information about the patron does not survive, as, for instance, when J. H. Bettey gives the wardens credit for contracting for Dunster tower.[8] The contractees are, in fact, unnamed.[9] Some even give credit to the churchwardens when there is evidence to the contrary: the organisers of building work at Bolney, Sussex,[10] and Bodmin, Cornwall, have been described as churchwardens when, as will be shown in the following chapter, they were not.[11] There is a parallel tendency to ascribe corporate building projects to the entire parish (which are often represented by the churchwardens). Cardinal Gasquet, for example, wrote that 'all the parish [of Leverton, Lincolnshire] apparently contributed' to purchasing a new bell in 1495, when there were just twenty-two donations that year, several of which were for old debts or for lights, vestments or oblations.[12] As noted already, the evidential base is substantially drawn from towns, where parochial institutions were sometimes wealthier and more complex, and interacted with civic authorities, but a central role for churchwardens, and for collective fundraising more generally, has been identified in both urban and rural parishes – as it will be in this chapter.[13]

An alternative approach, led by Clive Burgess and focusing on London and Bristol, has recast the churchwarden as a mid-ranking, administrative figure whose accounts survive as testament to an otherwise thankless and forgettable, if necessary, task.[14] Its main virtue was as a brief step to senior parochial or manorial office, especially for those without the wealth or status to start at the top. Its origin was as an administrative solution to the problem of managing and raising continuous and varied sources of income to finance a limited number of necessary tasks. In some localities, the wardens' responsibilities might have been wider than those specified in diocesan or provincial statutes, but not sufficiently broad to constitute 'parish government' or the

---

[6] Dyer, 'Village Community', 413; cf. Dyer, *Standards*, 182; Dyer, *Country Merchant*, 215–16; Dyer, *Transition*, 76.
[7] Kümin, 'Looking Beyond', 93–94.
[8] J. H. Bettey, *Church & Community: The Parish Church in English Life* (Bradford-on-Avon, 1979), 40.
[9] The original contract is lost. Salzman, *Building in England*, 514–15.   [10] Brandon, *Sussex*, 186.
[11] J. H. Bettey, *The English Parish Church and the Local Community* (London, 1985), 18; *The Story of the Parish Church of St. Petroc, Bodmin*, Sixth ed. (Gloucester, n.d.), 7.
[12] LA Leverton Par/7/1 f. 2r; Gasquet, *Parish Life*, 35; Peacock, 'Leverton CWAs', 337.
[13] See Introduction, section e, pp. 45–46.
[14] Burgess, 'Shaping', 262; Burgess, 'Implications', 65 n. 7; Burgess, 'Lessons', 311; cf. Drew, *Early Parochial Organisation*, 14, 19.

Case Studies

totality of parochial activity. Many activities were funded by semi-autonomous junior bodies (including chantries, lights and stores), guilds or municipal government.[15] In some parishes the most important activities, such as church construction, were run by senior governing bodies, the 'masters', made up of a few leading parishioners.[16] It is relevant here that the duties devolved to the laity, and so to the churchwardens, in the thirteenth century made no mention of building rather than repair work.[17]

A useful scale for conceptualising this range runs from 'strong' to 'weak' wardenship, terms used by Katherine French to describe the membership, selection processes and powers of wardens in different parishes.[18] She associates strong wardenship with some smaller rural parishes, where the position was dominated by a small social elite who held office for a long time and so restricted popular control over decision-making. In such parishes, presumably, the masters, if they existed, had less need or ability to restrict the wardens' powers and autonomy, although, of course, some activities could still be financed and run by other bodies. When the wardenship changed hands regularly and was held by a broader range of parishioners, it was relatively 'weak'. In these places, however, it may have been the parish leadership rather than the assembly that was correspondingly more powerful – the weak wardens and powerful 'five men' at Morebath are a good example.[19] Indeed, it is necessary to recognise the churchwardens' authority and responsibilities as locally variable, and to admit ignorance in most places as to their relationship with other bodies, senior and junior, and the proportion of parochial activities they oversaw. Responsibility for church building has profound implications, therefore, for understanding not only formal power relations within the medieval parish but also the place of parish churches in local society – whether their construction was sanctioned and organised by a small elite, either directly by the 'masters', as argued by Burgess, or under 'strong' wardens, or by a democratically constituted assembly.

c) CASE STUDIES

i) Building Projects

From a survey of pre-Reformation churchwardens' accounts across twenty-nine counties, I found significant expenditure on major

---

[15] See Introduction, section b, pp. 24–25; Chapter 4, section c.i, pp. 185–92.
[16] See Chapter 4, section d.ii, pp. 209–11, and Introduction, section b, pp. 23–24; Kümin, *Shaping*, 31–41; Brown, *Church and Society*, 110; French, *People*, 75–79, 85–89.
[17] F. M. Powicke and C. R. Cheney, eds., *Councils and Synods, 1205-1-1313*, vol. 1 (Oxford, 1964), 128 c. 11; 512–3–3 c. 8; 600 c. 16; 367 c. 2; 148 c. 52.
[18] French, *People*, 81–83. [19] Duffy, *Morebath*, 28–31.

architectural projects, possibly for the entirety of the work, in almost a tenth of cases, in both urban and rural contexts. There are likely to be others in accounts not yet studied.[20] There is also evidence in an undated memorandum commenting on the churchwardens' accounts at Eye, Suffolk, where 'T. Harvey clerk Robert Anyell & John Fysk with William Hobert then being churchwardens' raised more than £40 and 'built up' the steeple in 1470.[21] Litigation at Kilmersdon, Somerset, indicates that the warden Richard Jamys ran work on the new aisle in c. 1538–44.[22] Although bequests to church fabrics, almost universal in medieval wills, do not invariably appear in churchwardens' accounts, many examples survive where they do, especially when the latter were running projects, while some wills name them specifically as recipients.[23] Robert Pert left £20 to the churchwardens of St Peter Mancroft, Norwich, for a new gable in 1445, for example;[24] at Yeovilton, Somerset, the wardens probably ran building work on the tower in 1486, when the rector gave five marks to them and left ten to the fabric in his will;[25] and, at Tunbridge in 1488, John Fane left them five marks for work on the screen.[26] It is possible, but doubtful, that their role was to aggregate the income and pass it on to another authority to spend. The following section will discuss to what extent these accounts can be taken as a representative sample but, whatever the conclusion, the survival of several such examples indicates that it was not uncommon for churchwardens to play an important role in church building, even as the main organising body. This could include exceptionally large projects, such as the reconstruction of St Margaret, Westminster, in c. 1487–1523, which may have cost some £2,000. Annual income rose as high as £190, a vast quantity by comparison to any other parochial project, and which suggests they did not share responsibilities with another body.[27] Given the rarity with which churchwardens' accounts survive, particularly for extended periods, and the exceptional nature of building work, the examples cited below can be taken to represent a significant quantity.

---

[20] These include every published account as listed in the appendix of Hutton, *The Rise and Fall of Merry England*. In addition are numerous unpublished accounts pursued either because they were contemporary with building work, referenced in secondary sources as containing building work, or suggested to the author by archivists or other researchers. Others were serendipitously chosen. There is no reason to think this is a representative sample.
[21] Bettey, *Church & Community*, 39. [22] TNA: PRO C 1/1014/48–49; French, *People*, 73.
[23] E.g. Dudding, *Louth CWAs*, 32; Ellis, 'Thame CWAs', 1901, 115.
[24] Norman P. Tanner, *The Church in Late Medieval Norwich, 1370–1532* (Toronto, 1984), 129.
[25] Weaver, *Somerset Wills*, 1:261. [26] Nichols, *Collection*, 392.
[27] The case is well surveyed by Rosser and will not be examined again here: Rosser, *Medieval Westminster*, 263–71.

Case Studies

Because of the nature of the documentary record, examples of churchwarden-run building projects considered in this chapter are largely taken from towns in the midlands and south of England.[28] As noted earlier, the largest of these, excluding Westminster, was Ludlow, with over 2,000 inhabitants in the 1520s.[29] The others, Thame, Walsall, Great Dunmow, Swaffham and Louth, probably had populations of fewer than a thousand. Smaller projects at Bishop's Stortford, Tavistock, Ashburton and Halesowen, are also all in market towns.[30] Several London examples are included here: the poor parish of All Hallows, London Wall, and the wealthier parishes of St Andrew Hubbard, St Peter Westcheap and St Mary-at-Hill.[31] Again, the large and wealthy clothing village of Croscombe and the smaller, poorer one of Leverton are included. Examples will also be taken from the village of Morebath and the large and growing fishing settlement of Walberswick, which had a population on the scale of a small town.[32] As noted in previous chapters, there is enough variation between urban examples, and uniformity between them and rural ones to suggest that differences between town and village were of less significance for organisational practice than local differences in precedence, institutional development and the authority of the churchwardens. These will be discussed in the next section. The limitations of the temporal and geographic range of the examples was noted when they were introduced in Chapter 1.[33]

As will be shown below, their accounts reveal churchwardens to be closely involved in the day-to-day, or at least week-to-week, organisation of building projects: purchasing and transporting a wide variety of materials; paying large and varied workforces to carry out a multitude of tasks both directly and indirectly related to building work; raising funds; travelling to acquire materials and craftsmen; and making contracts. Although there are examples of wardens contributing funds and running certain activities when other bodies were in charge of building work, there is little indication that, when the wardens were in control, they shared direct managerial oversight with other bodies. However, as always, the relatively small sample size, especially of rural examples, and

---

[28] Introduction, section e, pp. 45–46.
[29] Chapter 1, section b.ii, pp. 55–56; Westminster paid over £113 and had a population of about 3,000 in the parishes of St Margaret, St. Martin-in-the-Fields and St Clement Danes. Mean assessments, however, were comparable to those of the market towns: a little over 5s: Sheail, *Distribution of Wealth*, 2:211, 204–08.
[30] Sheail, *Distribution of Wealth*, 2:149, 62, 63; Razi, *Life, Marriage and Death*, 45.
[31] Sheail, *Distribution of Wealth*, 2:205–08.
[32] Ibid., 2:324; Duffy, *Morebath*, 4–5; Bailey, *Medieval Suffolk*, 283; Peter Warner, 'Walberswick: The Decline and Fall of a Coastal Settlement', *Medieval Settlement Research Group Annual Report* 16 (2001): 12.
[33] See Chapter 1, section b.ii, pp. 55–56.

Organising Construction I: The Churchwardens

the potential for the hidden involvement of other bodies, particularly municipalities, guilds and masters, are important caveats.[34] Some wardens did pay for advice, and delegated individual organisational tasks and decision-making to other parishioners, probably when they had particular expertise (from working as a mason or lawyer, for example, or simply as an influential local), or to the master mason. The accounts are silent on responsibility for deciding designs and recruitment. For accounts that run over several years, the growth, improvement and adaptation of managerial and accounting systems can occasionally be determined, as wardens responded to the challenges of managing large incomes and complex outgoings. Problems with arithmetic, grammar and spelling, so familiar generally from churchwardens' accounts, all reappear here, but the overriding impression in most places is of a highly disciplined and rational approach to running projects, based on careful forethought and critical improvement.[35] There are only rarely examples of unforeseen costs, litigation or external censure.

The construction of the Trinity aisle at St Mary, Thame, Oxfordshire, (c. 1442–43) may be taken as a good early example of a churchwarden-run project (Figure 3.1).[36] In 1443, it was organised by the New Thame churchwardens, Thomas Bunce and John Manyturn, but the introduction to an earlier and fragmentary set of accounts has disappeared. There is no evidence of contracting out (except for the roof, which was built and erected by a single man, John East) or of sharing responsibilities with other parish bodies. The first author to identify the accounts even described the men as 'in the true sense of the word, the architects of the work'.[37] Expenses for materials, wages (including food, drink and lodging) and transport were all entered into the largely intact regular accounts, along with other everyday purchases. The entries are for small, often repetitive, sums. For example, John Lavender was paid on five occasions for carrying stone from Headington in 1442, suggesting that the wardens were summarising numerous individual payments they had made to him. Most wages were paid for two to six days of labour but never more (some are for task work, most notably on the window), indicating that the wardens kept weekly paper accounts, now lost, from which the surviving annual

---

[34] Evidence for the leadership of municipal bodies will be given on Chapter 4, section c.ii, pp. 192–93.

[35] More generally on this topic, see Chapter 6 below.

[36] OHC PAR273/4/F1/1, ff. 1–7a; the Latin accounts on f. 1 are fragmentary and undated; f. 2 begins with a closing list of receipts given in a new hand in English, probably of 1442. The expenses from f. 2v onwards are complete. The next set of accounts (still in English but in a new hand) begins with receipts on f. 4r and are dated 1443; Ellis, 'Thame CWAs', 1901; Ellis, 'Thame CWAs', 1902.

[37] Payne, 'The Building of the Trinity Aisle, or North Transept, of Thame Church, Oxfordshire, A.D. 1442, et Seq', *The Gentleman's Magazine* XVIII (June 1865): 177.

Case Studies

Figure 3.1   Thame from the northwest, showing the Trinity aisle (© anonymous)

accounts were compiled. Their role was more significant than that of accountants or administrators: they visited the quarry at Teynton and travelled to woods to choose stone and timber.

The accounting system remained fairly basic – without subheadings, a formalised entry system or totals – and with large amounts of extraneous detail. Although a section of the accounts is headed 'Expenses of the same year as to the Trinity aisle' (in 1442), some other transactions (the purchase of land and the sale of grain) are mixed in with building costs. In receipts, although direct gifts are calculated first, they are not formally separated from other sources of income. Manyturn kept the accounts himself, occasionally using the first person singular, and it is possible he wrote them (and probably the paper accounts) too.[38] The work was not insignificant: the 'aisle' is the substantial north transept, with two large, five-light traceried windows, one probably reinserted from the old aisle. It was largely a remodelling of an earlier transept, of which the east and west walls were retained, albeit heightened. Recorded expenditures came to almost £29, while the total raised in 1442 came to more than £33 and almost £10 the next year, probably itself only a part of the total.

[38] Julia Carnwarth, 'The Churchwardens' Accounts of Thame', in *Trade, Devotion and Governance*, ed. Dorothy J. Clayton, Richard G. Davies, and Peter McNiven (Gloucester, 1994), 183.

Organising Construction I: The Churchwardens

A similar accounting procedure was used in a near-contemporary project: the tower, now demolished, of St Peter, Westcheap, London, in 1437–40.[39] Included in the neat accounts for audit is a rare surviving wage list, formed into weekly tabulations generally of around seven workmen for six days' work each. As at Thame, and in many other examples, the wardens contracted out some work, paying John Garter more than £6 'as it appears by a bill', presumably a contract, but they also paid wages and purchased a wide range of materials directly. Again, there is no evidence that oversight was shared with other authorities. Over the three years for which accounts survive the wardens spent more than £81. The accounting system was a little more sophisticated than at Thame: sums spent on the tower were entered into a separate section of the accounts with its own heading.

Where churchwardens' accounts run for several years together, as during the building of Ludlow's substantial tower, in c. 1469–72 (but perhaps 1453–1500), the improvement and adaptation of accounting and managerial systems can be traced (Figure 3.2). Here the churchwardens in the earliest undated accounts took an unusual and impractical approach, noting only gifts to the work, following each entry by what it was spent on, rather than including a separate expenditure section.[40] Their successors in 1469–70 created separate expenditure and income sections, and listed their outgoings in much greater detail. This arrangement was evidently preferred since it was followed by their successors two years later. The auditors had perhaps found the previous system wanting. However, records of bequests survive from 1453 and 1466 (and earlier), so it is possible that the improved accounting system was adopted only after several years of construction.[41] Certainly the income recorded in the churchwardens' accounts – £20, £12 and £7 successively – indicates that they show only a fraction of the work.

A more developed alteration to the management of major building work can be found during the reconstruction of All Saints, now St Matthew, Walsall, in c. 1462–69.[42] The churchwardens until 1466 were Richard Curtis and Thomas Fletcher, who organised the work directly.[43]

---

[39] LMA P69/PET4/B/006/001, ff. 27–33.

[40] Llewellyn Jones, 'Churchwardens' Accounts of the Town of Ludlow', Transactions Shropshire Archaeological Society, 1 (1889): 235–84.

[41] It is, of course, possible that the earlier donations were stockpiled before work began. Quarrying was continuing and a bequest to the 'vault of the steeple' was made as late as 1500. Lloyd, Clark, and Potter, *St. Laurence's Church, Ludlow*, 40–41, 45–46.

[42] Rebuilt 1819–21.

[43] WLHC 276/62* pp 3–37. Note the pages are numbered sequentially, not as folios. The earliest date can be found on page 7 (2 Edward IV), but fragmentary text suggests the earlier pages are probably of that year too. There is no reason to think that there were no earlier accounts which are now lost. The accounts from 1469–73 are missing. A transcription and partial translation can be

Case Studies

Figure 3.2   Ludlow tower (© Keltek Trust)

Their usual responsibilities continued, at first intermingling records of liturgical items with building costs. However, 1465–66 seems to have been a watershed year: expenses reached almost £16, and payments dominate the accounts. William Wotton, who ran the works as master

found in G. Mander, 'Churchwardens' Accounts, All Saints' Church, Walsall', *Collections for a History of Staffordshire* 52 (1928): 175–267.

Organising Construction I: The Churchwardens

mason, appears for the first time.[44] To handle these changes, Curtis retired and was replaced by William Ford, and the wardens took on a third parishioner, John Woodward, who seems to have worked for them as project manager, a role analogous to the fabric wardens surveyed in the next chapter but who appear typically to have worked for the parish leadership not the churchwardens.[45] Woodward paid Wotton large lump sums for 'the old chancel' (remodelled as part of the nave) and 'the body of the church', and charged almost £4 in expenses as well as receiving large payments from parishioners.[46] In 1467–68, Woodward accounted separately, although the wardens also paid him large sums in numerous instalments (on one occasion in Worcester Cathedral). Woodward disappears from the accounts in 1468–69, although payments to him and on the building work continued, probably because he was now running work independently, perhaps under the leadership of the parish masters: in 1473, when Fletcher and Ford were still churchwardens but building work had ceased, Woodward accounted separately alongside the churchwardens and the wardens of the Blessed Virgin light.[47]

Another example of delegation to a project manager is recorded for the tower at Great Dunmow, Essex, which was rebuilt in 1526 (Figure 3.3).[48] One of the four churchwardens, Thomas Savage, was paid 'to purvey such stuff as the workmen should need and to set them at work and help to stage' and rode to find stone at Cambridge and Ditton. Trips were made to find lime and to fetch an 'expert' in 'staging'. Savage was among the elite of the parish and is likely to have been the driving force behind the work – he gave the highest sum in the collection. The other churchwardens were not uninvolved, however. They entered receipts under a separate subheading and expenses under 'laid out for the steeple' (other headings were 'for the church' and 'for the bellframes and the bells'). When they purchased new bells with frame and wheels, they travelled to

---

[44] He may or may not be the same 'William Mason' of 1463 but there is no doubt a new phase of work begins in 1466, WLHC 276/62★, p. 12
[45] WLHC 276/62★ p. 16.
[46] 'pro veteri cancella', 'pro corpore ecclesie', WLHC 276/62★ p. 21. These items were scored through and 'W' written in the margin – perhaps because they were reentered in Woodward's own accounts. The letter does not appear next to other deletions.
[47] In this period the church was almost completely remodelled, the aisles widened, chapels added and a lofty chancel of three bays with large windows was built. Richard William Gillespie, *Walsall Records: Translations of Ancient Documents in the Walsall Chartulary at the British Museum* (Walsall, 1914), 26; M. W. Greenslade, ed., *VCH Staffordshire*, vol. 17 (London, 1976), 226–39; Frederic W. Willmore, *A History of Walsall and Its Neighbourhood*, New (Wakefield, 1972), 140; Pounds argues that the wardens were only rebuilding the chancel, citing the purchase of centering, if so this would be unusual: Pounds, *English Parish*, 405.
[48] ERO D/P 11/5/1 ff. 2r–5v; Majendie, 'Dunmow Parish Accounts'; *An Inventory of the Historical Monuments in Essex: North West*, vol. 1 (London, 1916), 118–20.

Figure 3.3   Great Dunmow tower (© Keltek Trust)

London to see the founder.[49] The total cost was less than £14, including more than £8 to the mason, however, although materials were reused.

That the practice was not, apparently, used more commonly is surprising: it had the considerable advantage of giving the project a dedicated overseer while freeing the wardens of any additional organisational burden.

---

[49] Majendie, 'Dunmow Parish Accounts', 234–35.

Organising Construction I: The Churchwardens

A version of this arrangement can be found at Croscombe in Somerset, where the wardens assumed responsibility for financing the addition of the chapel of St George, and possibly other rooms, to the north of the chancel in 1506–12, even though their role was probably only to contract it out.[50] At St Clement, Sandwich, the wardens similarly contracted out 'the spear of the steeple' for 25 marks, including a £7 advance.[51] The mason contractor thus took on all or most organisational responsibilities, with the churchwardens acting as contractees and moneymen only.

When the work was not delegated in full, the allocation of certain responsibilities to other parishioners was no doubt more common than the surviving records show, particularly for large and complex projects. At Ludlow, many other parishioners were involved: two men held a collection; another was paid to 'fetch home' the mason; money was received from one donor through Sir John Hoper and Robert Barbor, presumably executors; and at other times through 'the warden'. The mason Robert Karver was apparently brought in as a consultant and was paid 4d for 'seeing the work of the steeple'.[52] Clearer examples of important tasks delegated to parishioners with specialist knowledge survive for the erection of the magnificent steeple at Louth, Lincolnshire, in 1501–15 (Figure 3.4).[53] Several senior or specialist parishioners were involved: in 1500–01, William Nettleton, a mason and donor; John Chapman, the previous year's warden, a guild alderman and an important donor; William Johnson, the following year's warden; and two other unnamed men travelled to the quarry to choose stone. The following year, the wardens delegated to Nettleton the task of finding the master mason, recognising Nettleton's specialist knowledge. He would subsequently work for the new master mason, John Cole. That year Nettleton was again involved with Chapman, Johnson (now a warden), Cole and another warden (Robert Beverley and 'his fellows') in choosing stone and handling payments to the quarrymen.[54] Johnson, a weaver and constable, and Cole continued to be responsible for taking payment to the quarry, sometimes with Chapman, until their deaths. Johnson also arranged with a bailiff to allow passage for the stone (1502–03), as did a warden in 1511–12, who also built a house for the stone at the quarry. In 1508–09, a warden was paid 'for an obligation making', probably the indenture for three bells.[55] When this was broken the following year, the wardens hired others to

---

[50] Note: the originals are lost and it is unclear from Hobhouse's transcription whether the pages are fragmentary, so entries could have been lost. Hobhouse, *Church-Wardens' Accounts*, 2, 29–32.
[51] William Boys, *Collections for an History of Sandwich in Kent* (Canterbury, 1792), 11, 364.
[52] Jones, 'Ludlow CWAs'.
[53] LA Louth St James Par/7/1 pp. 1–255. Note: the pages are numbered sequentially. The leaves are incorrectly ordered: pages 76–77 follow from page 7; Dudding, *Louth CWAs*, xiv, xviii.
[54] Ibid., 20.   [55] Ibid., 111.

Figure 3.4 Louth tower (© David Traish LRPS)

litigate. No indication of the authors of other indentures that appear in the accounts are mentioned, however.

Proof of the resilience of the organisation may be found in the terrible events of c. 1505. Chapman, Johnson, Nettleton and Beverley all died, along with members of their families, the vicar, and other former wardens and wealthy donors, while Cole and the other main masons, Wilkinson and Stobard, disappeared from the record. This was probably linked to an outbreak of a plague at that time.[56] Nevertheless, the accounts, and the work, continued without evident break under new wardens and a new master mason (Christopher Scune, who brought his own 'servants' and apprentices). John Thomson (a warden), William Robinson, John Kechyng (a future warden) and Scune took over paying the quarry and liaising with a bellfounder. In subsequent years, the wardens carried out this task themselves. The accounts indicate that, as the project continued and as the wardens proved themselves capable and, possibly, attracted more experienced candidates, they tended to delegate less. In 1513–14, for example, a warden took charge of engaging carters, but a decade earlier recruitment had been delegated to a mason.

ii) Architectural Units

Churchwardens can also be found running the construction of smaller units, often within more wide-scale rebuilding work that was under the charge of another body – usually fabric warden(s), a gentry patron or other authority.[57] These largely concerned items that appear regularly as part of the wardens' maintenance responsibilities (especially the roof, windows and bells) or a set of tasks or responsibilities (often the woodwork or transport). The threat of rebuilding costs, as well as some professional embarrassment, probably ensured conscientious maintenance. Churchwardens engaged in other, middling-scale projects often associated with wider rebuilding work on the church house, charnel house,[58] battlements,[59] pews,[60] tombs,[61]

---

[56] J. F. D. Shrewsbury, *A History of Bubonic Plague in the British Isles* (Cambridge, 2005), 159.
[57] Fabric wardens are the subject of Chapter 4.
[58] Thomas Bruce Dilks, ed., *Bridgwater Borough Archives, 1377–1399* (Yeovil, 1938), 188–90.
[59] Robert Reynes, *The Commonplace Book of Robert Reynes of Acle*, ed. Cameron Louis (New York, 1980), 174–75; Pegge and Nichols, *Illustrations of the Manners and Expences of Antient Times in England, in the Fifteenth, Sixteenth, and Seventeenth Centuries*, 156.
[60] J. E Foster, *Churchwardens' Accounts of St. Mary the Great, Cambridge, from 1504 to 1635* (Cambridge, 1905).
[61] Littlehales, *London City Church*, 225.

paving,[62] pulpits,[63] clocks[64] and wall paintings.[65] These were, however, not necessarily much less expensive or demanding than 'full' architectural projects: the contract for St Bene't's roof in Cambridge shows not only how structurally complex such work could be but also the highly technical and elaborate contractual arrangements they required.[66] New bells could cost as much as a new chapel, while the screen at St Mary the Great, Cambridge, was significantly more expensive than many architectural projects.[67] Repair work could also be demanding – rebuilding part of the church at Glastonbury, Somerset, after the fall of a pinnacle, including the making of new seats and other expenses, cost over £33, according to an undated set of accounts of c. 1465.[68] There is some evidence of delegation – a man is paid to ride to Witham Friary to buy stone, for example, and much of the work at the quarry may have been organised by the craftsman John Deverell – but the wardens were involved in every aspect of the work.

The patronage of units within larger projects is harder to distinguish within the accounts since building expenses were often not entered separately. In 1530–31, John Muckelowe and William Hadley, the churchwardens at Halesowen, Worcestershire, contracted ('bargeyne') with Edward Nichols 'and his fellow ... for the making of the aisle' and made a down payment ('in earnest').[69] Over the next three years the new wardens, John Hadley and William Wall (replaced in the final year by William Green), can only have been responsible for a proportion of the total work on the aisle, however. They repeatedly paid for the transport of timber in 1531–33, a period which ends with 'the making of the indenture of covenants betwixt the parish and the carpenters' (entered a second time as 'betwixt the carpenters & us'), and then for the purchase, transport and laying of lead, clay, sand and nails for the roof in 1533–34. At the end of 1534, £7 was 'paid to the carpenters for their last payment' and an ale was held by Hadley 'at the raising ("Reryng") of the church roof'.[70] The most plausible explanation is that the wardens were

---

[62] Robert Dymond, 'The History of the Parish of St Petrock, Exeter', *Reps. and Trans. Devon Assoc.*, no. 14 (1882): 402–92.
[63] Cotton, *St Andrew, Canterbury, CWAs*, 35.   [64] Ibid., 44.
[65] Hussey, *Testamenta Cantiana (East)*, 202. The churchwardens at Heybridge paid 6s 8d for three images: ERO D/P 44/5/1 f. 3r.
[66] CCCC 06/B/1; Robert Willis, *The Architectural History of the University of Cambridge, and of the Colleges of Cambridge and Eton*, ed. John Willis Clark, vol. 1 (Cambridge, 1886), 282–83.
[67] Foster, *St Mary the Great, Cambridge, CWAs*; Sandars, *Great Saint Mary*, 63–67.
[68] W. E. Daniel, 'Churchwardens' Accounts, St John Glastonbury', *N&Q for Somerset and Dorset* 4 (1895): 235–37.
[69] Somers, *Halesowen CWAs*, 60.   [70] Ibid., 64–65.

responsible for the roof alone, stockpiled timber while the aisle walls were being erected in 1531–33 and finally contracted with carpenters and plumbers to build it in 1533–34, once the walls were up. They may have damaged a wall and window in the process, for a small load of stone was bought and a mason paid, and they also paid for liming the walls ('ridding of the church with lime').[71] Other authorities within the parish, absent from the churchwardens' accounts, must have handled the erection of the aisle's stonework by Nichols, and it is tempting to wonder if William Hadley or Muckelowe took over its construction after contracting for it.

Similarly, at All Hallows, London Wall, the churchwardens noted those who had 'given money towards the building of the new aisle' and another gift 'towards the building of the church' in 1528–29.[72] But the wardens' accounts include no record of payment for stone, glass, lime or sand, while they expended large sums on scaffolding and timber, and made a contract for the guttering. Some gifts were recorded as being specifically for the carpenter or timber. It is likely that the wardens were responsible for only the roofing or general woodwork. The work was nevertheless extensive enough to require some delegation: the wardens paid for advice from a bailiff and a woodman in choosing scaffold polls (the bailiff receiving three times as much); the accounts for a play were kept in a separate 'gathering book', perhaps with its own wardens; a collection was run within the parish by two men; and another, outside the parish (at 'diverse churches'), by five local grandees who kept their own account book. The wardens paid out large sums to three parishioners – 40s, 40s and 20s to Master Anker, John Wobe and Ralph Appleby, who was one of the collectors, respectively. These men may have been covering some of the expenses and were being paid back, but it is possible that they were running the work to which the wardens were contributing.

Although churchwardens' accounts regularly note them making contracts with workmen (or 'bargains', 'bonds', 'agreements', 'indentures' or other similar phrases), the text of only one contract explicitly between churchwardens and a workman survives. The building of a new angel roof at St Bene't, Cambridge, was contracted out by Thomas Byrd and Thomas Wrangyll, alias Richardson, who were churchwardens in 1452, presumably for a newly constructed clerestory.[73] The wardens contracted out the work in full, but the degree of detail, the range of vocabulary, and the specifications for the roof are remarkable.

[71] Ibid., 66. [72] LMA P69/ALH5/B/003/MS05090/001; Welch, *Allhallows CWAs*, 56–59.
[73] CCCC 06/B/1; Willis, *Cambridge*, 1:282–83.

Case Studies

The breadth and depth of principal beams, end beams, braces, ridgepiece, spars, and pendants is given in inches, along with details of the cornice, battlements, crest and casement. The wardens, or the body they represented, must have had a clear idea of what they wanted, presumably developed in negotiation with the carpenter, but the contract includes no mention of payment, timing or transport – nor of who had run work on the clerestory.[74]

The distinction between financing and organisation can be found again in this context. Wardens could run discrete projects funded by other parish stores. Accounts for the rebuilding of the aisle roofs at St Mary-at-Hill, London, in 1526 were kept in a separate account book ('lytell qware').[75] It is in a different, messier hand from that of the regular accounts, probably kept by a warden himself rather than copied by a scribe. The accounts are sophisticated nevertheless, with headings and neat tabulations of the amounts of lead being transferred to and from the plumber. The total spent by the wardens was more than £50, funded from 'Porth's chest', of which almost half the funds came from two parishioners, Hillton and Husecam, and the rest was owed to the church.[76] Both the chest and Hillton also had their own accounts. The significance of the use of separate accounts must not be overlooked: it is possible, even likely, that other examples of churchwarden-run projects (and, of course, those run by other bodies) were kept in separate account books, now lost, but the total was not entered into the regular accounts, as they were at St Mary-at-Hill.

Churchwardens could also take on responsibility for making contracts and discharging the contractees' responsibilities as representatives for another body that would pay the contractor. When Richard Darnell left £100 to the building of five new arches in East Bergholt, Suffolk, in the 1530s, the work was run by a churchwarden but financed by Darnell's son Jakes, who took over the work when the warden died.[77] The chancery case that followed hinged on who was liable for the funds. At Morebath in Devon, the wardens Thomas Borrage and William Leddon entered the text of a contract for a new high cross, totalling

---

[74] Cf. records of two later contracts that were probably made by churchwardens but date from after the Reformation. At Milverton, Somerset, in 1556–58, where a churchwarden, William Lancaster, was a defendant against the mason William Pople; and at St Philip and St James, Bristol, in 1544–47, where the wardens James Faucet, James Pylte and Thomas Barren negotiated with the former abbot of Tewkesbury to fulfil a contract for rebuilding the chancel. TNA: PRO C 1/1460/85; C 1/1107/14; cf. PROB 11/88/396.

[75] LMA P69/MRY/B/005/MS01239/001/002, ff. 527–34. It was subsequently bound with the churchwardens' accounts.

[76] Littlehales, *London City Church*, 334–38. [77] French, *People*, 93–94.

£7, into their accounts in 1535.[78] The contractor, William Popyll, was to 'find all manner of stuff' except for the beam and wall plates which were to be provided and transported by the wardens ('it must we find... we to bring it in place').[79] The wardens worked with two parish stores to fund the work, contributing only relatively small sums – indeed they were probably unable to afford it otherwise. Their income typically came to £3–£4, and the greater part went on repair work. The existence of other bodies with their own sources of income, which were not included in the accounts, may explain how the wardens were able to afford the work.[80]

One of the most common units paid for by the churchwardens was the bells. The wardens at Tavistock, Devon, purchased bells and a timber frame in 1423–24.[81] The bells were 'for the new belltower' so the wardens were probably contributing one unit in a larger rebuilding project.[82] This large project was probably outside their competence but they took over the less demanding responsibility of constructing a new vestry in 1470–71. The purchase of new bells at Bishop's Stortford, Hertfordshire, was handled by the churchwardens, John Jenyns and John Sadde, in 1492–93, when money was paid both for the making of an 'indenture and bond' for founding the bells and on their delivery.[83] Here the work was contracted out, but the wardens still had to ride personally to Bury St Edmunds to pay the bellfounder on an almost annual basis.

However, work on the steeple at Leverton, Lincolnshire, in 1498 was run directly by the churchwardens, Christian Pickle and Robert Taylor, who purchased stone, lime, lead and timber, organised quarrying and transport, and paid the craftsmen.[84] Less than £10 was recorded in expenditure (and £9 in income), so the work was probably not 'to build the steeple' but was perhaps for raising it and making a bell loft for purchases of bells in 1495, 1503 and 1512.[85] The wardens visited the quarry in Swineshead Fen, about 12 miles away, travelling back through Boston, which lies roughly halfway between the two. They charged for expenses incurred while buying lead at Boston (about six miles away) and lime at Freiston (four miles). Such practices were probably common but this is one of few examples when the wardens can be found visiting

---

[78] John Erskine Binney, *The Accounts of the Wardens of the Parish of Morebath, Devon. 1520–1573.* (Exeter, 1904), 70; Duffy, *Morebath*, 78–79.
[79] Binney, *Morebath CWAs*, 70. [80] See Introduction, section e, pp. 45–46.
[81] R. N. Worth, *Calendar of the Tavistock Parish Records* (Plymouth, 1887), 7.
[82] '*per novis campanis*'.
[83] Stephen G. Doree, *The Early Churchwardens' Accounts of Bishops Stortford, 1431–1558* (Hitchin, 1994), 44–50; J. L. Glasscock, ed., *The Records of St. Michael's Parish Church, Bishop's Stortford* (London, 1882), 20–22.
[84] LA Leverton Par/7/1 ff. 3r–6v; Peacock, 'Leverton CWAs', 338–40.
[85] Gasquet, *Parish Life*, 35.

different sites explicitly to find all the materials required for the project. An exceptional example can be found at St Lawrence, Reading, where the wardens purchased a licence to employ a mason, Chayney, who was at Hampton Court in 1520 and rode to fetch him (a distance of almost fifty miles) and pay him for a new font.[86] His reputation must have been significant to have merited the expense, and the decision to employ him indicates the discernment of the contractees.[87]

The other major building project, again not strictly architectural, for which churchwardens were often responsible, was the rood screen and loft.[88] This appears in contracts, accounts and wills, as, for example, in 1488, when John Fane left five marks to the rood loft at Tunbridge, Kent, 'on condition that the churchwardens build it within two years'.[89] For the construction of the rood loft at Yatton, Somerset, in 1446–57, the wardens were closely involved not only in overseeing the logistics of the work but in its planning and commissioning too.[90] In 1446–47, they paid expenses for men riding to five different locations, in one case to look at another church's loft and in the others probably to source materials. In at least one case it was the warden, John Hullman, who travelled to Selwood to buy timber. They also paid two men for advice.[91] The next year, the decision was made and they paid the carpenter, John Crosse, more than £5 in part-payment. A decade later they recorded that the whole payment made to him was more than £31, although only £19 is recorded in their accounts. The wardens were closely involved in Crosse's work: paying for paints, oils, timber and glue, as well as for drink 'to make him well willed'.[92] There are fewer examples where the entire work was contracted out, but at St Andrew Hubbard, London, the wardens, William Childerley and Robert Wilkins, organised the purchase of a new rood loft (as well as pews and a platform in the steeple) in 1521–23 by the carpenter James Nedam.[93] This was undoubtedly contractual since no payments for timber or board were made, but a sum was paid as deposit ('in earnest'), the usual practice for building contracts, and Nedam received numerous instalments. He broke the terms of the contract,

[86] Kerry, *St Lawrence, Reading*, 14; Charles Coates, *The History and Antiquities of Reading* (London, 1802), 218–19.
[87] Gabriel Byng, 'The "Dynamic of Design": "Source" Buildings and Contract Making in the Later Middle Ages', *Architectural History* 59, 2016: 123–48.
[88] Duffy, 'Parish, Piety, and Patronage', 136; *French, People*, 158.
[89] Nicolas, *Testamenta Vetusta*, 1826, 2:392.
[90] SRO D/P/yat 4/1/1; Hobhouse, *Church-Wardens' Accounts*, 82–100.
[91] Churchwardens also took advice on other parts of the fabric, as when a woodcarver looked at the benches of Nettlecombe, Somerset, in 1544: French, *People*, 163.
[92] Hobhouse, *Church-Wardens' Accounts*, 88.
[93] LMA P69/AND3/b/003/MS01279/001, ff. 114–7; Burgess, 'Implications', 111–14; Burgess, *The Church Records of St Andrew Hubbard, Eastcheap, c. 1450–c. 1570*.

however, and was replaced. At St Andrew, Canterbury, the wardens contracted out the building of a new rood screen (as well as a pulpit, bell frames and paving work), probably to Richard Birch, in c. 1506–10. Birch received more than £13 'in part payment of a more sum' in 1507–08, £11 in 1509–10, and smaller payments in 1504–07. The wardens were nevertheless still involved in the work: as at Yatton, they travelled to 'view' another in Thanet ('Tenet') in Kent.[94]

There are numerous other examples of work on screens, showing a similar combination of part-contracting and logistical management. In 1525–26, at Ashburton, Devon, the four churchwardens paid the carpenter, Peter Kerver, £16 for the rood loft, but also spent more than £5 on materials, labour, transport and the rent of a house to make it in.[95] At Lydd, Kent, in 1522–26 the wardens travelled to the quarry, arranged for the transport of stone and sand, paid the mason in instalments, purchased scaffolding, and organised board, food and drink for the craftsmen.[96] The wardens at Tintinhull, Somerset, William Golight and John Brown, paid Thomas Dayfote 40s for building the rood loft 'by agreement', that is by contract, in 1451–52, but they were also involved in the work, buying materials and transport, and paying for labour in removing the old one and inserting the new.[97] Golight was paid for bringing Dayfote to raise the loft ('*solarium*'), and Brown for fetching a man, possibly John Brayne, who led the construction, and his servant John Davy. The wardens paid for painting the rood loft seven years later.[98] Lastly, at St Mary-at-Hill, London, the wardens followed a similar approach to building work when setting up the rood, using a separate heading in the accounts of 1496–98. This included making a contract ('endent'), and buying materials and paying wages.[99]

iii) Ad Hoc Contributions

Perhaps common, but often well hidden from the historian, were ad hoc contributions by the wardens to projects run by other bodies, donated both from underspends and from fundraising drives. Evidence of these exists in nearly every surviving fabric account.[100] At Bodmin, Cornwall, the warden, William Mason, donated 10s 'of part of [the] arrears [that is, the excess] of [the] account of the wardenship' c. 1469, while the

---

[94] Cotton, *St Andrew, Canterbury, CWAs*, 31–46.   [95] Hanham, *Ashburton CWAs*, 76.
[96] Arthur Finn, ed., *Records of Lydd*, trans. Arthur Hussey and M. M. Hardy (Ashford, 1911), 337–45.
[97] '*Ex conventione*'. SRO D/P/tin/4/1/1 pp. 21–3 (formerly numbered at p. 49–51); extracts in Hobhouse, *Church-Wardens' Accounts*, 185.
[98] Ibid., 175–207.
[99] LMA P69/MRY/B/005/MS01239/001/001, ff. 142r–153r; Littlehales, *London City Church*, 224–29.
[100] See Chapter 1, section b.i, pp. 52–54.

churchwardens, David Witfen and Martin Hogge, gave over 39s in c. 1470, and a gift 'of the arrears of the Wardens' parcel' is also mentioned separately.[101] At North Petherwin, Cornwall, the churchwardens paid for the travel of a mason to a project run by the masters, who in turn paid for various liturgical items and topped up the wardens' payments for the bede roll when they ran out of money.[102] More substantial gifts were made by the wardens to the tower at Hedon, Yorkshire, possibly in fulfilment of an agreement to provide a regular income: more than £65 one year, more than £48 the next and more than £11 a decade later.[103] At Bolney, Sussex, the churchwardens donated small sums to the new tower, usually from parochial fundraising drives such as ales or collections, which they presumably ran on behalf of the building campaign.[104]

Evidence also appears in churchwardens' accounts. Sometimes help took the form of straightforward donations. At St Mary-at-Hill, London, in 1499–1500, the wardens contributed over £26 to the new steeple.[105] In other places the churchwardens paid for some tasks directly. There is evidence of substantial building work in the wardens' accounts at St Michael, Bath, from the 1360s to the 1370s: (for example, 3s 1d was spent 'to transport stones to the church works', while the archdeacon gave 2s and John Gregory lent 10s).[106] However, even if the works were the extension of the nave, rather than repair, it must have been largely funded and run by external authorities or 'off the books'. The sums running through the wardens' hands during this period were small: never more than £7 in income or £3 in expenditure on building work. At St Lawrence, Reading, the wardens raised more than £21 in 1518, although apparently only for repairs, but the accounts also refer to a screen 'in the new chapel' and they paid a carpenter more than £7 for work and for his men's board. Two years later, they covered the rood loft and, in the next year, new arches were built and glass was placed in the new choir windows.[107] Whether the other tasks this implies (a new chapel and windows and the remainder of the screen) were carried out in separate accounts or by another authority is obscure.

---

[101] Wilkinson, *Bodmin Church*, 3, 11, 33.
[102] Johns, Mattingly, and Thorpe, *North Petherwin*, 26, 37.   [103] Boyle, *Hedon*, Note x.
[104] Dale, 'Bolney CWAs'; Byng, 'Bolney', 107.
[105] LMA P69/MRY/B/005/MS01239/001/001, f. 181; Burgess, 'Lessons', 325; Littlehales, *London City Church*, 239.
[106] '*in cariagio petrarum ad opus ecclesie*'. Charles Buchanan Pearson, 'The Churchwardens Accounts of the Church & Parish of S. Michael without the North Gate, Bath, 1349–1575', *Journal of Somerset Archaeology and Natural History Society* 23, 24, 25 (1879, 1880 1878); Charles Buchanan Pearson, 'Some Account of Ancient Churchwarden Accounts of St. Michael's, Bath', *Transactions of the Royal Historical Society* 7 (1878): 309–29.
[107] Kerry, *St Lawrence, Reading*, 14; Coates, *Reading*, 218–19.

Organising Construction I: The Churchwardens

Even less clear is the example of Walberswick, Suffolk.[108] Building work on the tower was contracted in 1426 (probably finished by 1450), apparently as part of plans to replace an earlier chapel, pulled down in 1473.[109] No construction was recorded in the surviving churchwardens' accounts, however, until the 1470s.[110] There was a bequest for building the nave in 1470, and in 1471 an unusual entry by the churchwardens recorded the sum of the church's capital at more than £23, suggesting that they had been saving and were taking stock ahead. Indeed, in 1472, almost £18 was spent on stone, along with its carriage, working and a cart, but for the next seventeen years only occasional purchases of materials, transportation and labour are recorded in the accounts. In some years nothing was purchased, nor anyone paid, for building work. In 1496, the battlements and windows were still under construction; the next year the ceiling was painted, but thirty-two tons of stone was also purchased; and in 1512 testators were still giving for work in the chancel, and the north aisle was only just completed.[111] The porch was built in 1483 and painted and glazed three years later. The wardens seem to have been cooperating with another body, although the nature of their involvement is mysterious. Pounds argues that the wardens were responsible for fixtures and fittings, but they purchased an unusually large amount of stone if so.[112] A gift of 40s to the making of a new aisle in 1474 did appear in the churchwardens' accounts, but other bequests are missing – sent, perhaps, to other authorities.[113] The only clue is the contract for the tower, made by a contracting committee of four senior parishioners, indicating the managerial structure that oversaw building work.

Ken Farnhill has argued that one of the best-known churchwarden-led projects also belongs to this category: the building of the new tower at Swaffham, Norfolk, from 1507 to c. 1516.[114] Swaffham is unusual in having a second documentary source against which the churchwardens' accounts can be compared: the 'Black Book' kept by the long-serving rector John Botwright from 1454. In the bede roll it records numerous large gifts to the steeple, totalling over £200, that are not found in the churchwardens' accounts. 'Incorrect' totals also suggest that the large sums recorded in the accounts (£35–£45 each year) were not the only sums being raised for the tower. Farnhill argues that part of the work may

---

[108] Lewis, *Walberswick CWAs*. [109] Salzman, *Building in England*, 499–500.
[110] According to Thomas Gardner, *An Historical Account* of Dunwich (London, 1754), 152.
[111] Middleton-Stewart, *Inward Purity and Outward Splendour*, 108.
[112] Pounds, *English Parish*, 404.
[113] Middleton-Stewart, *Inward Purity and Outward Splendour*, 93.
[114] NRO PD 52/71, f. 9 onwards; Farnhill, *Guilds*, 109–10, 115; Heslop, 'Swaffham', 259–61.

Organisation

have been run by another authority which received the bede roll donations. However, the churchwardens' accounts post-date the bede roll gifts, so it may be that the latter were added to a separate 'deposit account' from where they were spent by the churchwardens, who saw no need to show their origin.

D) ORGANISATION

i) Choosing the Overseers

From these examples, it is clear that churchwardens could and did run building work. Nevertheless, as Burgess has argued, and as will be demonstrated in the following chapter, many parishes chose alternative managerial structures. In fact, there were important limitations on the churchwardens' capacity to run major architectural projects. Some of these were practical: the wardens' income was typically small and difficult to increase, while the office's ordinary responsibilities were already onerous and time-consuming.[115] The annual or biennial changeover of wardens in many parishes meant that they could offer little continuity during a prolonged campaign, making it difficult for new wardens to assess progress, instruct the mason, monitor changes in design or maintain relationships with suppliers.[116] Others were cultural: as Burgess has shown, the office could be relatively junior in larger parishes and those occupying it may have lacked experience in office, authority and even age (although exceptions will be cited shortly), not to mention the personal wealth to cover some initial outlays themselves. Their remit was set by both rule and local custom, and, in many places, it may not have been flexible enough to include building work. Although they may have been *en route* to more senior positions, construction was often too important, expensive, complex or even privileged to be entrusted to the churchwardens. It might be better run by dedicated wardens without other communal responsibilities or by a larger and more stable group of senior parishioners with their own resources.

Why then did some parishes choose to run their building projects, or indeed any other important task, through the churchwardens? There were several possible advantages: most prosaically, the institution offered a well-established, convenient and reliable communal fund whose structures and authority were already widely accepted, bypassing any need to set up and run a new committee. It had probably already proved itself

---

[115] See Chapter 1, section c.i, pp. 65–66.
[116] A changeover of wardens caused problems at Tavistock, Devon: I. S Leadam, ed., *Select Cases in the Court of Requests: A. D. 1497–1569* (London, 1898), 19.

capable of organising numerous types of ad hoc parochial projects, or even if it had not, new practices could be introduced to improve its performance. The office had developed, probably over decades, to ensure that money was well spent, necessary tasks were completed efficiently and the parish had sufficient oversight of its work, chiefly through audit and election.[117] In some parishes, the wardens were probably in charge of much of the community's expendable income, and the fundraising techniques they employed were generally accepted. Importantly, they also had experience of handling maintenance work, which required the commissioning, instructing and payment of craftsmen and labourers, and the negotiating of contracts. Even if the position of churchwarden was not an elite one in every parish, its holders probably already had some of the experience and status necessary to run building work. Wardens would need familiarity with handling funds and keeping accounts, with sufficient literacy, often in Latin and English, to check the scribe's work, and enough free time to carry out the role. They were nearly always male heads of household, often in taxation rolls at relatively high assessments, or had experience as executors, witnesses, jurors or senior guildsmen.[118] Some were craftsmen themselves and had worked on the church fabric.[119] In many parishes the wardens were required to use their own wealth to finance their work, and poorer parishioners might be let off service.[120] Examples noted in this chapter include Thomas Colyns in St Mary-at-Hill, London, Thomas Taylor and William Beverley at Louth, Lincolnshire, and Roger Pyrk at Saffron Walden, Essex, who was still owed £3 in 1468, two years after running work on the porch.[121] 'Ralph Harris Churchwarden' (d. 1509), is carved into the screen at Norton Fitzwarren in Somerset – whether Harris ran the work in that capacity or provided private funds, it is evidently the case that the position was of some significance locally.[122]

Parishes proved capable of organising their wardens in a variety of sophisticated ways to ensure good management and the responsible use of communal income and property, the keeping of accounts for visitations and audit, the unfailing celebration of a multitude of obits and chantries, and the maintenance of the church fabric.[123] Churchwardens were

---

[117] Introduction, section b, pp. 22–23.
[118] E.g. Clive Burgess, 'London Parishioners in Times of Change: St Andrew Hubbard, Eastcheap, c. 1450–1570', *The Journal of Ecclesiastical History* 53, no. 1 (2002): 45; DeWindt and DeWindt, *Ramsey*, 28, 40; Doree, *Bishops Stortford CWAs*, xiii; Carnwarth, 'Thame', 186–87.
[119] E.g. at Ashburton, Devon: Hanham, *Ashburton CWAs*, 24, 29.
[120] Peter Northeast, *Boxford Churchwardens' Accounts 1530–1561* (Woodbridge, 1982), xii; J. F. Williams, *The Early Churchwarden's Accounts of Hampshire* (Winchester, 1913), xiii; Duffy, *Morebath*, 12.
[121] ERO D/DBy Q18, f. 76.   [122] Vallance, *Screens*, 64.   [123] Burgess, 'Lessons', 9 n. 31.

Organisation

typically appointed in pairs, often serving an overlapping tenure of two years, with the junior member promoted after a year, ensuring continuity and the sharing of good practice.[124] Larger parishes would take on further wardens and sidesmen as necessary, dividing responsibilities between them,[125] or were divided into administrative districts for collections and ales.[126] In some places, the wardens met twice during the year to evaluate their work.[127] They used paper accounts to record day-to-day expenses and retained bills and receipts to verify their transactions.[128] These were compiled annually into neat summaries that were examined, orally or in writing, by the *auditores*, whose names, marks and corrections survive on some accounts.[129] The accounting procedure was important and established enough at several churches, for example, at St Botolph, Aldersgate, London, and Chagford, Devon, that the same marginal headings were repeated even if there were no cost to be entered beneath them.[130]

Nevertheless, churchwardens were not invariably chosen to carry out building work, so it remains to be seen what motivated the parishes that used them. It is suggestive at least that the examples tend to share one or more of the following characteristics: typically long-serving churchwardens of relatively high social status, wealth, age or experience in office, of unusually high number (up to four wardens or more, rather than the usual two), with a relatively large average income, or with experience of taking a leading role in parish affairs. They were probably, in other words, 'strong' wardens, as defined earlier in this chapter – dominated by elite men within the parish. In many examples the office of churchwarden was probably of relatively higher status and so attracted senior candidates, creating a virtuous circle that made them natural choices to lead, or even initiate, a building project. The small sample under consideration here means that such conclusions cannot be easily generalised, and it is important to note how locally variable these conditions were, even among the market towns that dominate this chapter. In parishes with well-established, long-serving and powerful ('strong') churchwardens – at Louth for example – they could run both smaller projects (windows, rood loft or roof) and larger (steeples, aisles and towers). In parishes where the wardens were a more junior ('weak') body, the parish, or its leadership, could choose between them and other authorities to run work. At Saffron

---

[124] Swayne, *Sarum, CWAs*, x–xi; Hanham, *Ashburton CWAs*, xviii; C. C. Webb, ed., *The Churchwardens' Accounts of St Michael, Spurriergate, York, 1518–1548* (York, 1997), 11.
[125] E.g. St Andrew Hubbard in 1521–22: Burgess, 'Lessons', 317; or at Pilton, Somerset: Hobhouse, *Church-Wardens' Accounts*, 49.
[126] Hobhouse, *Church-Wardens' Accounts*, 78.   [127] Webb, *St Michael, Spurriergate, CWAs*, 5.
[128] Littlehales, *London City Church*, xiv.   [129] Doree, *Bishops Stortford CWAs*, xvi.
[130] Cox, *Churchwardens' Accounts*, 32; Osborne, *Chagford CWAs*, 5.

Walden, Essex, for example, the wardens took charge of various smaller projects during the mid-fifteenth century but, when the large new nave was built after 1485, the work was given to a separate committee involving the churchwardens as well as at least one more senior parishioner.[131] The reverse process could occur too, however. At Bridgwater, Somerset, a fabric warden had been appointed to run construction on the spire in the 1360s, but significant building work on new chapels in the fifteenth century was overseen by the churchwardens – an acknowledgement, perhaps, of their growing power by the town's civic government.[132] The choice was clearly dependent on both the nature of the work and the capacity of the wardens, which was itself temporally variable.

It is possible to show in some of the cases considered above that wardens in charge of construction tended to be drawn from the higher ranks of parish society. In urban areas, this included experience in local government, guild administration or other positions of responsibility. It also meant, of course, personal wealth. Louth provides a particularly clear example, where the wardens included 'gentlemen', merchants, constables, yeomen, guild aldermen and a lord's steward, many of whom donated to the work. One, John Chapman, gave £20, while others – Thomas Taylor and William Beverley – probably used their own funds to pay for work (in 1501–02) and were paid back the next year.[133] They may also have been older: several died during the period of construction (Thomas Taylor, John Chapman, William Johnson, Thomas Argram, Thomas Messenger and Simon Lincoln). Two, Chapman and Beverley, were executors for the vicar. Carnwarth has noted the high calibre of churchwardens at Thame, Oxfordshire: working as pledges, jurors, affeerors and tax collectors.[134] During construction the wardens were Thomas Bunce and John Manyturn (d. 1452). Bunce appears in several collections for the work; Manyturn gave a candlestick, received sums in several wills and gave to several collections.[135] The wills of the Swaffham, Norfolk, churchwardens, John Oxburgh and John Newell, show them to be wealthy farmers and guild members.[136] Their replacements included Aubrey Grygges, a gentleman.[137] At Eye, Suffolk, only Anyell left sufficient evidence for his high status to be demonstrated: he had five meadows and several market

---

[131] ERO D/DBy Q18.
[132] SRO D/B/bw 23a; cf D/B/bw 41 and 20a; Dilks, *Bridgwater Borough Archives, 1200–1377*, 159–61.
[133] Dudding, *Louth CWAs*, 39.   [134] Carnwarth, 'Thame', 184.
[135] William Patterson Ellis and Herbert Edward Salter, *Liber Albus Civitatis Oxoniensis* (Oxford, 1909); Ellis, 'Thame CWAs', 1902, 26.
[136] Their wills survive: NRO ANF Liber 5 (Sparhawk) ff. 143, 167; ANFLiber 6 (Batman) f. 84.
[137] *Calendar of Inquisitions Post Mortem and Other Analogous Documents Preserved in the Public Record Office: Henry VII*, vol. 1 (London, 1898), 442; Basil Cozens-Hardy, *Calendar of Such of the Frere Mss. as Relate to the Hundred of Holt* (Norwich, 1931), 56.

Organisation

stalls, and left money to the making of the church belfry in 1479.[138] At Great Dunmow, Essex, a warden gave two-and-a-half times as much as the second highest donor to the new steeple.[139]

Occasionally it is possible to map out the career of a warden in local office (whether municipal, manorial or parochial) or the guilds, even in rural parishes, as, for example, with Edward Bull, the churchwarden with responsibility for the building work at Croscombe, Somerset, in 1506. He had served as receiver of stock for the Young Men's Guild (1477–78), presenter for the Fullers' Guild (1480–85), joint receiver of stock for the Fullers (1485–88), and finally their sole receiver of stock (1488–1501). He had even served as churchwarden, in 1493–94. Similarly, William Childerley at St Andrew Hubbard, London, had served as collector and on several occasions as churchwarden before taking over control of the new rood loft. He left almost £30 of goods in his will, including 10s to the battlements of the church.[140] It is not possible to show that wardens in these parishes were of uniformly higher standing than those of parishes where the wardens did not run building work, but the foregoing summary suggests that social status, experience and wealth were important considerations.[141]

There were often organisational, as well as social, reasons for using churchwardens in these parishes. Most obviously, at Dunmow, Louth, Eye and Ashburton, there were four churchwardens, rather than the usual two, to run the work.[142] There were three wardens at Saffron Walden during a period of intensive building work in 1439–44, dropping to two once work was over.[143] Three wardens also contracted for the work at St Philip and St James, Bristol.[144] There were four at Thame too, although here they operated as two pairs, representing New and Old Thame, and were responsible for different sides of the church: only two were (explicitly) involved in the new aisle.[145] These larger groups of wardens indicate how demanding the office had become and the extra capacity parishes were willing to create so that wardens could carry out work competently. Importantly, at Walsall, Great Dunmow and possibly

---

[138] SkRO(IB) EE2/E/3/i. He, Fisk and Harvey appear regularly in deeds: FB 161/L1/1-2; HD 1538/151/11; EE2/M1/1-2; EE2/E/3/b; HD 1538/216/5; EE2/E/3/f ; EE2/M1/1/18.
[139] ERO D/P 11/5/1 f. 2r.
[140] His fellow warden, Robert Wilkins, was executor to Childerley's wife's will, and left substantial amounts of property. Burgess, *The Church Records of St Andrew Hubbard, Eastcheap, c. 1450–c. 1570*, 81, 221–22.
[141] In a survey of several parishes Kümin found that the richest and poorest taxpayers served the least often: Kümin, *Shaping*, 33–38; French, *People*, 85.
[142] Cf. Kümin, *Shaping*, 30.   [143] ERO D/DBy Q18 ff. 1–22.   [144] TNA: PRO C 1/1107/14.
[145] Carnwarth, 'Thame', 182.

Swaffham, an additional warden was probably appointed in order to handle building work.

In some of these examples, when accounts survive over many years, it can be shown that the wardenship was regularly occupied for long periods. At Croscombe, Edward Bull, who oversaw the building work, was unique but not exceptional in serving for twenty-five years. William Branch served as churchwarden for much of 1478–1507 (including for the first year of building work), and John Carter served frequently from 1485 to 1513.[146] Given his age and experience, it is likely that Bull was not merely a functionary for a higher body but was personally leading the work – indeed, French has described Croscombe as having a 'parish oligarchy'.[147] However, long tenure also meant, of course, that many wealthy families would not hold office, and it is reasonable to recognise in a figure such as Edward Bull both personal initiative and skill and acknowledgement by contemporaries of his competence – or an unwillingness to serve themselves. At St Peter Westcheap and Thame the wardens also typically served for multiple years. This may be interpreted in two ways – either the positions were of greater importance and so could attract skilled and respected candidates (as well as responsibility for building work), or the authority and experience that these men accumulated over long tenures made them natural choices to run building work. In other words, their length of time in office could be either indicative or constitutive of the reasons why they also managed construction.

Churchwardens' accounts rarely run for sufficiently long periods for us to be able to establish parochial custom for building projects. However, at Saffron Walden the accounts run from 1439 to c. 1490 and include numerous discrete projects, each presumably cementing a tradition of churchwarden oversight. This included the roof screen, loft and beam (1444–46); the west tower (c. 1441–45); the north chapel turrets (1458–60); the churchyard cross (1459–60); a large, gilded and painted tabernacle (1459–64); work on the St Nicholas Chapel (c. 1465–66); the south porch (1466–72); and the south aisle roof (c. 1490).[148] Building work was so regular that the wardens built a permanent lodge in the churchyard for the craftsmen. Even when the parish began a larger project, rebuilding the entire nave after 1485, and it was handed to a

---

[146] The role of guilds in providing training for those who would hold civic office has been shown elsewhere. Charles Phythian-Adams, *Desolation of a City: Coventry and the Urban Crisis of the Late Middle Ages* (Cambridge, 1979), 118–25.

[147] French contrasts this with a rotational system, a 'family honor' that might be closer to entrenched privilege than the technocratic leadership of Croscombe: French, *People*, 79–81.

[148] ERO D/DBy Q18; Byng, 'Saffron Walden', 337.

Organisation

fabric committee to run, the churchwardens still travelled to Cambridge to contract for the work and sat on the committee themselves.[149]

It has already been argued that the preponderance of examples from small towns is representative of documentary survival rates only, but urban churchwardens may have had advantages in the running of major projects.[150] Strikingly, a much larger proportion of urban contracts than rural ones identified some contractees as churchwardens (27 and 5 per cent, respectively), albeit this is based on a small and unrepresentative sample.[151] Some urban parishes had built up substantial estates, largely from bequests, which were administered by the churchwardens.[152] Not only did this increase their income considerably (and improve its predictability and reliability), but it also required wardens able to manage an extensive portfolio and invest for profit. Urban churchwardens could pass a longer apprenticeship in guilds or municipal government before taking office,[153] while the prospect of yet higher civic office provided an incentive for them to show their organisational ability to the parish.[154] Another result may have been to change the culture of urban fundraising: French argues that property income removed parishioners from an active role in financing parish activities making it harder for sums to be raised through ales or collections.[155] However, the conclusions of the previous chapter are consistent with Kümin and Burgess who argue that urban parishes could call on further resources from 'living' parishioners when required, as for church construction.[156] Nevertheless, urban parishes were by no means invariably richer or better run than rural ones, and able men in Croscombe, Leverton and Morebath all proved capable of both organising work and raising funds from new and established sources. Importantly, the next chapter will show how almost all the examples of building work carried out by officials other than the churchwardens are also from urban areas (Bodmin, Bridgwater, Bristol, London, Hedon,

---

[149] Francis Woodman, *The Architectural History of King's College Chapel* (London, 1986), 198; Richard Griffin Braybrooke, *The History of Audley End* (London, 1836), 180–230; Harvey, *English Mediaeval Architects*, 64.
[150] Introduction, section e, pp. 45–46.
[151] This includes contracts for semi-architectural projects such as rood lofts and two examples from the late 1530s and 1540s.
[152] E.g. Clive Burgess, 'Strategies for Eternity', in *Religious Beliefs and Ecclesiastical Careers*, ed. Christopher Harper-Bill (Woodbridge, 1991), 23; Drew, *Early Parochial Organisation*, 23 n. 84; French, 'Parochial Fund-Raising', 120; Webb, *St Michael, Spurriergate, CWAs*, 1: 5; Pearson, 'St Michael, Bath, CWAs', 1; Doree, *Bishops Stortford CWAs*, xii.
[153] E.g. Doree, *Bishops Stortford CWAs*, xiii.
[154] Clive Burgess, 'Time and Place: The Late Medieval English Parish in Perspective', in *The Parish in Late Medieval England: Proceedings of the 2002 Harlaxton Symposium*, ed. Clive Burgess and Eamon Duffy (Donington, 2006), 15.
[155] French, 'Parochial Fund-Raising', 123; Burgess, 'Shaping', 258.
[156] Burgess and Kümin, 'Penitential Bequests', 621.

Organising Construction I: The Churchwardens

Saffron Walden and Totnes). The institutional life of both urban and larger rural parishes was broad and flexible enough that the churchwardens were only one of several managerial structures available to the parochial leaders.

ii) During Construction

Many churchwardens adapted their practices once building work began, but in most cases it is remarkable how much administrative continuity there was, given the complex and expensive demands of construction. As we have seen, several, but not all, adopted special temporary accounting procedures: a dedicated subsection, or even running subtotals of the cost of work. Others ran construction through separate accounts. Most, nonetheless, mixed building work in the accounts with their other obligations, and many managerial changes were presumably not recorded in the accounts. As we have seen, the delegation of certain tasks or decisions, particularly when they required expertise, is recorded in some accounts, but this must have been common during large-scale, complex building projects. Most deputies presumably either did not charge for their services or their records were subsumed into another payment. It is also likely that some took on junior managerial posts during construction, as at Walsall or Great Dunmow – but, again, without requiring notice in the accounts. At Kilmersdon in Somerset, for example, one parishioner, Thomas Richmonde, promised Richard Jamys, the warden running building work on a new aisle, that he 'would be a helper' to him.[157] Only at Louth is responsibility for the choice of master mason recorded as delegated, in this case to a local mason, although presumably his choice had to be ratified. But this was surely not an exceptional arrangement.[158]

Once building work had commenced, at least one warden tended to stay in office for its duration, ensuring continuity in management and the retention of an official with the requisite expertise. At St Peter, Westcheap, John Astett stayed in office for the period of construction, and it is likely he was installed for that purpose since he replaced two long-serving officers.[159] Similarly, at Walsall, Thomas Fletcher stayed in office during construction and his co-warden changed only once.[160] At Thame, however, both the parish's churchwardens stayed in office throughout construction and for at least five years afterwards, although wardens here tended in any case to serve long tenures during this period.

[157] TNA: PRO C 1/1014/48–49; French, *People*, 73.
[158] See also Merton, Adderbury and York: Knoop and Jones, *Mediaeval Mason*, 34.
[159] LMA P69/PET4/B/006/001, f. 27–33.
[160] WLHC 276/62* pages 3–37; Mander, 'All Saints, Walsall, CWAs'.

Organisation

An entry in 1448 indicates that they did ceremonially give up their positions each year, even if they were immediately reappointed.[161] For building work, however, parishes could break convention. At Bishop's Stortford in Hertfordshire, the names of the wardens survive for only two years during the purchase of the bells (1493–94 and 1494–95), but in both the wardens were John Jenyns and John Sadde, unlike the parish's standard arrangement whereby the wardens served overlapping tenures, each of two years.[162] This was not a universal approach, however: at Louth, the churchwardens rarely served for more than a year (although with exceptions in Thomas Taylor, Richard Beverley and John Spencer), and continuity in oversight must have been provided through civic or parochial government.[163] The value of continuity in management is shown in the accounts: those at Louth changed little over the fifteen years that the project ran, despite its exceptional ambition, while, at Ludlow, having at least one warden serve throughout construction allowed them to adapt and improve their accounting procedures.[164]

Occasionally the accounts show that the long-serving officer took on responsibility for the building work, while the other (or others) carried out the regular duties. Thomas Savage at Great Dunmow is a particularly clear example, acting, probably, as a sort of project manager.[165] At St Andrew Hubbard, London, in 1521–22, the junior warden, William Childerley, ran work on the rood loft (as well as the steeple and pews), while the senior warden took charge of their usual responsibilities. The accounts make the division clear, separating the two wardens' accounts and noting, for example, 'money paid for the steeple by William Childerley'.[166] Similarly, for the building work on the spire of Leverton in 1498, the warden Robert Taylor took on most of the managerial and logistical duties: he fetched lime, paid a deposit for lead and paid the plumber.[167] There are further examples in Astett at St Peter, Westcheap, and Edward Bull at Croscombe. Others can be shown to have taken a personal role in the work. At Morebath, Thomas Borrage contracted for the rood loft and personally carried the beam to the church after

---

[161] OHC PAR273/4/F1/1 f. 12. The format of the accounts changed to add a lengthy Latin introduction in a good clerical hand.

[162] Doree, *Bishops Stortford CWAs*, 44–50; Glasscock, *Bishop's Stortford*, 20–22.

[163] Dudding, *Louth CWAs*, xv.

[164] There are minor changes in neatness or handwriting. The lack of improvement cannot be explained as being due to the better quality of the accounts at the project's inception: the accounts are often oddly laid out, and they do not use standardised wording or proper wage lists. After construction had finished, the wardens tried a non-tabulated version which was less easy to read, see LA Louth St James Par/7/1 p. 325.

[165] ERO 11/5/1 f. 2r.   [166] LMA P69/AND3/B/003/MS01279/001, f. 113v.

[167] LA Leverton Par/7/1 ff. 3r–6v; Peacock, 'Leverton CWAs', 338–40.

Organising Construction I: The Churchwardens

giving up his position.[168] John Hadley, churchwarden of Halesowen, Worcestershire, stayed in office for three years during the building of the aisle roof (1531–34) and held an ale to celebrate its installation ('reryng').[169] At Louth, however, all four wardens appeared to have been involved in the tower's execution and fulfilled their usual tasks as well, but one probably acted as lead warden (for example, in 1504–05: 'Thomas Taylor and his fellow churchwardens').[170] The importance of individual wardens who took personal responsibility for overseeing building work can be seen at Swaffham.[171] The building of the new tower, begun in 1507, was carried out under John Oxburgh and John Newell, who had been wardens since 1504 and would remain in place until their deaths in 1511 and 1516 respectively.[172] Oxburgh was probably the overall manager, often receiving donations personally.[173] On his death, he was replaced by Walter Payne, but without Oxburgh's personal leadership the arrangement was found wanting and the parish took the unusual step of appointing a third warden, Aubrey Grygges, in 1512.

Did the experience of running parochial building projects stimulate organisational innovation and the rise of the churchwarden system, or vice versa, or were the developments were unconnected?[174] Kümin notes the large number of churchwardens' accounts which begin with a major project underway, and it is plausible that some were kept precisely because they contained records of building work.[175] At St Mary-at-Hill, Burgess argues that sophisticated and efficient administrative structures were generated by the need to manage several chantries and a property portfolio.[176] He does, however, suggest that the construction of an aisle from 1487 'prompted a reform of parish record keeping', when accounts became more regular and one warden began a written account of the 'obligations and assets' of the church, and the churchwardenship was reorganised into junior and senior officers.[177] This chapter has surveyed numerous instances where account keeping was improved and adapted during building work but no certain examples where it started for the same reason. In many or most cases, the structure of the accounts was already well established, and building work fits more or less awkwardly alongside existing responsibilities. Most examples are taken from the mid-fifteenth century or later, by which time most

---

[168] Binney, *Morebath CWAs*, 70, 78; cf. Duffy, *Morebath*, 192.
[169] Somers, Halesowen CWAs, 60–67.   [170] Dudding, Louth CWAs, 74–85.
[171] NRO PD 52/71, f. 9 onwards; Heslop, 'Swaffham', 259–61.
[172] Their wills survive: NRO ANF Liber 5 (Sparhawk) ff. 143, 167; ANF Liber 6 (Batman) f. 84.
[173] NRO PD 52/71, f. 10v.   [174] Dymond, *Bassingbourn CWAs*, xxiv.
[175] Several additional examples have also been surveyed above. Kümin, *Shaping*, 83–84; cf. Doree, *Bishops Stortford CWAs*, xvii.
[176] Burgess, 'Shaping', 252.   [177] Ibid., 253–54.

Organisation

parishes had had churchwardens for well over a century. An accounting system which included audited written records was necessary to safeguard complex and varied communal funds and to present at visitations, regardless of the existence of major building projects.

iii) Audit, Accounting and Oversight

When 'weaker' churchwardens had control of a building project, there is good reason to believe that their independence was restricted by the parish, which was probably expressed formally by the assembly, the masters, the municipality or the auditors, and informally by their peers. Churchwardens' accounts regularly state that their 'election' and the auditing of their accounts took place before the 'whole parish' or with its 'consent', 'assent' or 'counsel'.[178] Ad hoc meetings could also be arranged: the purchaser of a major cross at Tavistock, Devon, claimed that the item was displayed, with notice, on a series of holydays.[179] However, attendance at such meetings could be highly limited and exclusive, and senior bodies can often be found directing building work.[180] At Bridgwater, Somerset, for example, the construction of the Holy Trinity chapel was overseen by the churchwardens but partially funded by the common treasury. The municipal authorities clearly retained decision-making powers over the work's management: for example, they instructed the wardens when to make the mason's final payment, perhaps having approved the work.[181] In some parishes churchwardens were selected by other office holders, as at St Mary the Great, Cambridge, or another senior body, as at Prescot, Lancashire.[182] Another group with oversight of the churchwardens' activities in some parishes were the auditors, usually small groups of wealthy men, often with experience of holding local office, who executed their office at or before the assembly.[183] The accounting procedure in many places emphasised to wardens that they were being lent the parish's funds, which they then 'owed' back to the parish and from which 'debt' agreed expenditure alone could be deducted. The process of the audit may have emphasised the wardens' subordination: at Croscombe, the wardens 'bring in a bill of their cost[s] done the year past' to be approved alongside the guild stocks and, at Yatton, the wardens similarly 'brought in the accounts'.[184] In some parishes, the churchwardens had to

---

[178] Kümin, 'European Perspective', 27. [179] Leadam, *Select Cases*, 18.
[180] See Chapter 4, section d.i, pp. 205–06.
[181] Dilks, *Bridgwater Borough Archives, 1400–1445*, 49.
[182] Foster, *St Mary the Great, Cambridge, CWAs*; F. A. Bailey, ed., *The Churchwardens' Accounts of Prescot, 1523–1607*, vol. 104 (Preston, 1953); DeWindt and DeWindt, *Ramsey*, 109; J. A. Raftis, *A Small Town in Late Medieval England: Godmanchester, 1278–1400* (Toronto, 1982), 442.
[183] Duffy, *Morebath*, 23; French, *People*, 48.
[184] SRO D/P/yat 4/1/1; Hobhouse, *Church-Wardens' Accounts*, 80.

give a bond and sureties.[185] As in elections, the assembly may have had little more than the opportunity to ratify decisions made by a senior body.[186]

Occasionally, the limitations imposed on the churchwardens' discretion were expressed in writing. For example, in 1504 the vestry at St Michael, Cornhill, agreed, among other things, that no churchwarden was to incur an expense of more than 10s without authorisation.[187] When wardens acted without approval, they could be punished and their decisions overturned: at Yatton they paid for an image of St Christopher in 1467–68 'without leave of the parish', and the wardens were compelled to have it repainted and to reimburse the church the sum of 20s.[188] The priest probably had a role as overseer and arbiter: at Leverton, in 1531, the parishioners spent a bequest intended for a cope on the purchase of a bell, which the priest determined to be 'against good conscience' and ordered 'amends making'.[189] He also commanded the parishioners to gather to assess the churchwardens' accounts and 'at their instance' he named two new wardens. These cases do, however, indicate that wardens acted with a degree of independence – sometimes too much so. When the churchwardens at Walden or Bishop's Stortford, Hertfordshire, rode to make contracts in Cambridge or Bury St Edmunds respectively, we can assume they departed with instructions but also with the right to negotiate with the mason or bell founder within certain parameters.[190]

It was through the churchwardens that parochial building projects may have met another, higher, form of oversight: that operated by the archdeacon, who would inspect accounts and demand action to remedy deficiencies.[191] Attempting to match archidiaconal visitations with building work is fraught with difficulties, however. In the diocese of Ely, a period of regular visitations under Ralph de Fodringhey and the drawing up of inventories in c. 1278–1316, for example, does overlap with a period of intensive church construction, but visitations were so regular and their reports so imprecise that it is difficult to identify building work that took place as a result. The records do regularly note poor repair but rarely demand full-scale rebuilding work, although a new roof, window

---

[185] Swayne, *Sarum, CWAs*, xi.
[186] DeWindt and DeWindt, *Ramsey*, 39; Carnwarth, 'Thame', 182.
[187] William Henry Overall, *The Accounts of the Churchwardens of the Parish of St. Michael, Cornhill, in the City of London, from 1456 to 1608* (London, 1883); see the similar examples at All Saints, Bristol (1488), and St Stephen, Bristol (1524): Burgess, 'Benefactions of Mortality', 80–81. In 1551–52, the wardens at St Botolph, Aldersgate, needed the permission of six 'honest and elderly neighbours' to spend more than 20s.
[188] SRO D/P/yat 4/1/1 f. 86; French, *People*, 73, 201.
[189] LA Leverton Par/7/1 f. 26v; Peacock, 'Leverton CWAs', 352.
[190] Doree, *Bishops Stortford CWAs*, 44–50; Byng, 'Saffron Walden', 334.
[191] Powicke and Cheney, *C&S*, 1964, 2:1008.

Organisation

or stonework may have been necessary. It was common, however, to commute visitations or delegate them to juniors, reducing the active role archdeacons could have had in church building.[192] Indeed, there is reason to suppose that there was some parochial hostility to ecclesiastical oversight: parishioners in Madley, Herefordshire, for example, fought the dean and chapter of the cathedral for control of money being collected for a project to promote a shrine to the Virgin in 1318.[193] Perhaps the decision to pass control of building work to bodies other than the churchwardens was taken partly to avoid inspection by the archdeacon.[194] More significant, potentially, was the need to gain episcopal approval for rebuilding work, consecration, and exceptional agreements to allow the erection of a chapel or the merger of parishes.[195]

A useful case study of the relations between churchwardens and a local urban elite (both as a social group and an official body, the masters) for major projects can be found for the new rood loft at St Mary the Great, Cambridge.[196] The project was contracted out to John Nunne and Roger Bell on 30 June 1520 by the two wardens and four other named men, all of whom were members of the 'eight masters' (with the exception of the junior warden who would join the following year), 'with other more parishioners', for the substantial sum of £92 6s 8d.[197] The carpenters were to receive £52 6s 8d at the sealing of the contract and instalments of £20 on 24 June 1521 and at completion on 20 April 1522 'at such time as the said John Nunne and Roger have clearly and wholly finished all the premises'.[198] Indeed, the wardens' accounts record the paying of £20 in two instalments in 1522 (no accounts survive for 1521, when the penultimate £20 was to be paid). As the work was entirely contracted out, little information survives in the accounts. However, they do record £32 6s 8d (across three entries) spent 'in party of payment' to Nunne and Bell in 1518, two years before the contract was signed, and the holding of a weekly collection in 1519 (recorded on a separate roll). Presumably the wardens commissioned the work in 1518, paid a large deposit of more than £32 and agreed to three instalments of £20. However, they probably proved unable to raise the necessary funds to pay the first instalment

---

[192] Robert E. Rodes, *Ecclesiastical Administration in Medieval England* (Notre Dame, 1977), 103.
[193] My thanks to Dr Ian Forrest for this reference: HCA 715.
[194] Examples of resistance to visitations can be found in: French, *People*, 35.
[195] E.g. at Broadhempston, Devon, c. 1400: F. C. Hingeston-Randolph, *The Register of Edmund Stafford (A. D. 1395–1419)* (London, 1886), 39.
[196] Cf. Chapter 4, section d.ii, pp. 210–11.
[197] This phrase was probably standardised: it also appears in the churchwardens' inventory of 1518. Foster, *St Mary the Great, Cambridge*, CWAs, 36–48; Sandars, *Great Saint Mary*, 63–67; cf. Duffy, 'Parish, Piety, and Patronage', 140.
[198] Sandars, *Great Saint Mary*, 63–67.

of £20 (required in 1519 or 1520), despite the special weekly collection in 1519. They had to bring in the parish elite for direct help – men like Robert Goodhale, who left £10 in 1521. Four parishioners stepped forward to pay the overdue instalment and vouch for the remaining £40 in 1520, but either they or the carpenters insisted on a contract being drafted to provide legal recourse should a similar shortfall happen again. The wardens began to receive bequests for the work, and the final two payments of £20 were found, partly with the help of the wealthiest parishioners.

E) CONCLUSION

Churchwardens were not invariably responsible for church building, and with good reason. Their sources of income were typically small, difficult to increase and all but entirely consumed by their regular duties, which were onerous and time-consuming. Custom often limited their responsibilities to repair work (for which small, regular sources of income were well suited), and, if their experience and social status did mark them out for office, in some parishes they were not yet of the seniority required for the organisation of a major building campaign. Nevertheless, in parishes with 'strong' wardens, the office could be held in high enough regard, and occupied by wardens who were sufficiently senior (as evinced by age, status, wealth, office holding and other, unknown, variables) or in control of so much of the community's expendable wealth – that it was desirable for them to run building work. The involvement of some wealthier parishioners in church maintenance, as churchwardens, probably a social privilege as well as a financial burden, may have stimulated their interest in and association with church construction, if only to control the expenditure to which their money was put. Poor maintenance created the need for new building work and some may have taken on responsibility for preventing the former to avoid the latter. Although perhaps directed by different institutions, urban and rural parishes were both able to look to the churchwardens to run building work. It was local variation in institutional politics, parochial precedent and the authority of the wardens that were the most important determinants of organisational approach. Often, the wardens must have presented the most convenient option: an adaptable, efficient and generally accepted organisational structure that had been honed for decades.

Wardens in charge of building work tended to serve in unusually large numbers and to divide tasks between them, with one taking the leading role in construction and serving for its duration. Occasionally an additional warden or project manager was appointed for this purpose and

Conclusion

could keep his own accounts. Although churchwardens could run the whole of a major campaign, often they took charge of only a part of the work, whether defined by task or material (such as transport or timber) or by architectural unit. If the latter, they were commonly responsible for features customarily associated with the wardens' liturgical and maintenance duties, particularly the roof, screen or bells. Their work was probably closely overseen by the masters, assembly or municipality, thereby reducing the wardens' discretion. However, many of the senior or wealthy men who can be found running work as 'strong' churchwardens are probably better understood as members of the upper ranks rather than their subjects. Parishes with 'weak' wardens were probably more likely to run the work through other bodies, at least if they were available and the work was sufficiently important.

Chapter 4

ORGANISING CONSTRUCTION II
Contracting Committees and Fabric Wardens

A) INTRODUCTION

When the wealthy London parish of St Mary-at-Hill decided to embellish its church with new battlements in 1512–13, its leaders gave the management of the work not to the churchwardens but to two senior parishioners, John Allthorpe and Stephen Sanderson. They promised 'to take charge and keep reckoning', under the oversight of the alderman and with the help of the parson and an assistant.[1] Here, the churchwardens had an exceptionally high income and a large property portfolio, but the parish leadership still believed a dedicated administration would be better able to handle the work, and they set up a hierarchical structure integrated with both parochial and municipal government. Other parishes would come to similar conclusions, giving oversight either to temporary committees or other permanent institutions, including guilds and civic bodies.

As at St Mary-at-Hill, churchwardens' accounts provide the most numerous guides even to projects that they were not running, but occasionally other accounts, contracts and inscriptions shed light on the committees that oversaw decision-making, contracted for the work or ran the building site on a day-to-day basis. Temporary bodies rarely merited naming and so, in this book, the anachronistic terms 'fabric committee', 'contracting committee' and 'fabric wardens' will be used respectively. The workings of this specialised administrative machinery can show not only the practice of parochial government beyond the well-known powers of the churchwardens but also the institutional manifestation of local differences in power and authority. The membership, organisation and discretionary powers of fabric committees are of particular importance for setting church construction in its contemporary social and economic context, revealing the powers held by the parish masters, a group that

[1] LMA P69/MRY/B/005/MS01239/001/002, ff. 328–40; Littlehales, *London City Church*, 284.

in some cases ran work directly, made up the committees that took decisions about contracting or appointed wardens on the parish's behalf. Church construction offers a rare glimpse of these powerful bodies in action as they negotiated with the wider community and the institutions of parochial and municipal government.

B) CONTRACTING COMMITTEES

i) *Making Contracts*

Despite the proliferation of examples of part-contracting in churchwardens' accounts, surveyed in the previous chapter, surviving contracts for parochial building work were commonly made by groups of two to six contractees who were not named as current office holders (except in the case of the roof at St Bene't's, Cambridge; Table I.4).[2] Rather, their place on taxation records and activities as witnesses, pledges or former office holders in guilds, parishes or local government indicate the contractees' membership of senior local groups. A useful parallel may be drawn with vestry subcommittees of the sixteenth and seventeenth centuries, where small groups of parishioners drawn from the senior membership of select vestries (already a limited subsection of the parish), as defined by wealth, status, age, office holding and length of tenure or residency, ran discrete projects with the authority of the vestry.[3] One such subcommittee, for example, was appointed to 'oversee' the widening of the chancel at St Bartholomew-Exchange, London, in 1642 and was composed of seven parishioners drawn from the leading members of the vestry.[4]

Around half of contracts for parochial work are from villages, offering a better range of examples than fabric and churchwardens' accounts, and including both small places (Hornby, Yorkshire, and Thornham Parva, Suffolk) and relatively large ones (Fotheringhay, Northamptonshire, and Wyberton, Lincolnshire).[5] Urban areas are still overrepresented, but, in addition to many small or medium-sized towns such as Wycombe and Wolverhampton, there are an equal number of large ones: Bristol, Bury St Edmunds, Cambridge, London and York. In these places, contracting committees drew upon highly developed civic administrations. However, it would require little greater imagination, or organisational expertise, to create or adapt a managerial structure for a building project in a rural parish than it would to introduce churchwardens or a guild

---

[2] See Chapter 3, section c.ii, pp. 152–53.   [3] Kissack, 'Vestry', 12–26; Burgess, 'Lessons', 331.
[4] Edwin Freshfield, The *Vestry Minute Books of the Parish of St. Bartholomew Exchange in the City of London: 1567–1767* (London, 1890), xii.
[5] Cf. Introduction, section e, p. 46.

administration. Contracting committees were probably similar in operation, and even membership, to those used for other communal arrangements: raising tax, holding property, collecting communal amercements, agreeing by-laws, running pastures, waste and public works, organising rent strikes and raising troop levies.[6] Their internal operation is largely hidden from the historian. Their discussions have been lost and may have been confidential,[7] but they probably held regular meetings to make decisions and agree plans,[8] and may have used majoritarian decision-making.[9] The membership of other committees often had a representational character, usually chosen by district or by different parts of the tenantry.[10]

The contractees named in medieval building contracts were probably not a legal fiction: someone, able to act in the name of the parish, would need to decide upon the plans, anticipate costs, find contractors, carry out negotiations, instruct the mason(s) and stamp their seal.[11] Officers would then need to be chosen who would ensure that the terms of the contract were carried out, run quality control, assess progress, pay the masons, purchase materials or organise transport, and keep accounts. Even when 'the parish' is the only body named as contractee (as for Dunster, Somerset, 1442), 'the Gentlemen Wardens Yeomen and Commons of the town and parish' (Wolverhampton, 1476), or 'the township' (Cottesbrooke, Northamptonshire, 1533), it would still require certain parishioners to meet, instruct, assess and pay the contractor, decide the requirements for building work and agree to plans.[12] At the shared church of Dunster, although 'the parish' was the only contractee, the contract

---

[6] Schofield, 'England', 39–40; Dyer, 'Taxation and Communities'; Dyer, 'Village Community', 409–13.

[7] DeWindt and DeWindt, *Ramsey*, 101–02.

[8] R. B. Dobson, *The Peasants' Revolt of 1381* (London, 1970), 78; John F. Nichols, 'An Early Fourteenth Century Petition from the Tenants of Bocking to Their Manorial Lord', *The Economic History Review* 2, no. 2 (1 January 1930): 305.

[9] Joan Wake, 'Communitas Villae', *The English Historical Review* 37, no. 147 (1 July 1922): 407; Britnell, 'Tenant Farming and Farmers', 211; Warren Ortman Ault, *Open-Field Husbandry and the Village Community* (Philadelphia, 1965); Warren Ortman Ault, *Open-Field Farming in Medieval England* (London, 1972).

[10] Anne Reiber DeWindt, 'Local Government in a Small Town: A Medieval Leet Jury and Its Constituents', *Albion: A Quarterly Journal Concerned with British Studies* 23, no. 4 (1 December 1991): 627–54; Wake, 'Communitas Villae'.

[11] Cf. the practice in Renaissance Italy where artists usually worked for an identifiable individual (or small group) even when the project was for a large confraternity or monastery; or the practice in major monastic or cathedral building projects when work was put under the control of an individual member of the chapter, often the sacrist: Baxandall, *Painting and Experience*, 5; Vroom, *Cathedral Building*, 51–53.

[12] Salzman, *Building in England*, 514–15, 600; R. M. Serjeantson and H. I. Longden, 'The Parish Churches and Religious Houses of Northamptonshire: Their Dedications, Altars, Images and Lights', *Archaeological Journal* 70 (1913): 302.

ends: 'Into the which witness I put thereto my seals I give and I write at Dunster', indicating that the author had a role in negotiating the terms, as symbolised by the use of his seal.[13] Fabric accounts give some impression of this direct personal engagement with contracting masons, since sums are paid for travelling to meet them, negotiating a price and paying a deposit (usually, 'in earnest'). At Bolney, Sussex, for example, the patron engaged in 'bargaining' with the mason, agreed a price, paid a small sum as deposit and celebrated the agreement with an ale.[14] The only example I have found where such a committee was named is at Wycombe, Buckinghamshire, in 1508–09, where the contracting committee was entitled the 'wardens and rulers of the new works'.[15] They presumably oversaw the work as well as contracting it out. Contracts were often made with the contractees' personal seals, a legally and personally important gesture to signify the resolution of negotiations and the cementing of the agreement by the small number of men (contracting committees appear to have been exclusively male) involved in negotiations. This often required the masons to borrow seals from other men, while the contractees could use 'the community seal' if they had one. It has even been suggested that some parish seals were made in connection with building work.[16]

ii) Membership

Although it is impossible to determine a 'threshold of inclusion' for joining a contracting committee, some of the criteria for membership can be posited. Many will be shown to have been senior members of local society, holding office, engaging in the local land market, appearing regularly as witnesses or being assessed highly for taxation. In rural areas, their number occasionally included the manorial lord or another member of the gentry, or the parson (Table I.4). The social composition of the committees was varied, however, and not always drawn from the pinnacle of local society. A distinction should be made between those consisting of members of the parish leadership or masters (no surviving example is made explicitly by the masters acting as a body) and those deputising on their behalf. Even if the

---

[13] Bettey, *Church & Community*, 40; French, *People*, 47; Katherine L. French, 'Competing for Space: Medieval Religious Conflict in the Monastic-Parochial Church at Dunster', *Journal of Medieval and Early Modern Studies* 27 (1997): 215–44; Frederick Hancock, *Dunster Church and Priory: Their History and Architectural Features* (Taunton, 1905); H. C. Maxwell Lyte, 'Dunster and Its Lords', *The Archaeological Journal* 38 (1881): 217.
[14] Dale, 'Bolney CWAs'; Byng, 'Bolney'.
[15] TNA: PRO E 210/985; Salzman, *Building in England*, 557–59.
[16] Elizabeth New, 'Signs of Community or Marks of the Exclusive? Parish and Guild Seals in Later Medieval England', in *The Parish in Late Medieval England*, ed. Clive Burgess and Eamon Duffy (Donington, 2006), 125.

Organising Construction II

Figure 4.1   Arlingham tower (© Roger Smith)

work was too important or taxing for the churchwardens, this is not to say that the leadership wanted to run it personally or necessarily had sufficient legal, constructional or administrative expertise. The heuristic rule that medieval people looked on office holding as a burden no doubt applied here too.[17] Authors have noted that the churchwardens were often drawn from a broad range of relatively wealthier parishioners, sometimes omitting the very wealthiest, and this is true of many contracting committees too, although a direct comparison is rarely possible.[18]

The unusually large quantity of parishioners, nineteen, named in the contract for the tower at Arlingham, Gloucestershire, of 1372, 'and all the parishioners', allows for a uniquely useful examination of the social status of named contractees (Figure 4.1).[19] The list was headed by the lord of the manor and vicar. Of the other seventeen, all but one appear as witnesses to deeds concerning property in the parish dating from 1346 to 1400 (Table 4.1).[20] Importantly, the order in which the names are listed on the

[17] E.g. Dobson, 'Urban Decline', 278.   [18] See discussion in French, *People*, 85–89.
[19] *'et omnes parochianos'*. BCM/A/1/11/39; Salzman, *Building in England*, 445.
[20] In BCM/A/1/11.

Table 4.1 *Arlingham, Gloucestershire, members of the 1372 contracting committee*

Contractee	Appearances as a witness in property deeds (1346–1400)
John de Yate	18
Roger vicar	0
William de Erlyngham	0
Robertum de Middleton	11
Walter Hutt	11
John de Thornhulle	1
John Heyward	22
William Scheef	11
Walter Jakemones	19
Walter Frer	8
John Bulgaston	6
Radulf Wych	1
Richard Bulgaston	2
Richard Kokkes	7
Hugh atte Wode	2
Walter Symondeshale	5
John Forster	0
Walter Hykemones	1
John Cordy	1

Sources: Property deeds in the Berkeley Castle Muniments Room (BCM/A/1/11).

contract mirrors the frequency with which they appear as witnesses: those in the top half act on average ten times each; those in the bottom, three times. Walter Jakemones and John Heyward, who witnessed sixteen and eighteen grants respectively, are in the top nine, while John Forster, who never acted as witness, is near the bottom, as are Walter Hykemones, Radulf Wych and John Cordy, who appear only once. Even these men probably belonged to senior families – other members of the Cordy and Wych families often acted as witnesses – and were perhaps relatively young at the time. Two, John Thornhull and Walter Frere, were future proctors of the church.[21] Those who appear often as witnesses but are not on the contract had probably died by 1372. Richard Styward, for example, last appears as a witness in 1372, and his wife was widowed by 1377.[22] Walter Wyth, lord of Barrow, last appears in 1360; John Janes, in the 1340s; while the Westmoncote family is too complicated to determine when individual members had died. This suggests that all, or almost all,

---

[21] BCM/A/1/11/36.   [22] BCM/A/1/11/91; BCM/A/1/11/49.

the leading families in the parish are listed on the tower contract, roughly in order of their status. In this they followed the form of later vestries, where the order in which names were signed in the minute book reflected their seniority.[23] It is implausible that they could all have been involved in drawing up the contract, let alone in running the work. That these men were named may reflect the sense in which the tower was to be a parochial project, an initiative dominated by the leading parishioners, who understood themselves to be sanctioning the agreement on behalf of, or even as, the parish. Perhaps they would provide all, or the lion's share of, the financing.

Unlike Arlingham, most parochial building contracts name only two to six contractees. Indeed, the rarity with which more than six are included indicates the maximum convenient number that could be involved in the process or even a convention for the ideal size of a subcommittee (Table I.4). Only four committees also included gentry contractees, but there is reason to believe that these are better characterised as corporate rather than gentry-led projects.[24] The contract for the new rood loft and other timberworks at Stratton, Cornwall, in 1531, for example, was made by seven parishioners headed by the successful and active knight, Sir John Chamond, formerly warden of the High Cross guild, and Richard Carlygham, clerk, similar to the arrangement of names on the Arlingham contract.[25] Here, the men explicitly claimed to be acting 'in the name for and in the behalf of all the parish'. At Great Sherston, Wiltshire, 1511, John Tomsson 'gent.' was included in the list of contractees for a church house, alongside three others 'with all the whole parish of the town'.[26] The contractees for the chancel of Surfleet, Lincolnshire, in 1418 were probably the rector, Adlard Welby, and John Sutton, who sued in 1429, as the work had not been done 'well and sufficiently' by the agreed date.[27] John would have been a young man in 1418 (he died in 1459–60).[28] He was described as 'gentleman of Surfleet' in 1432.[29] Great St Mary, Cambridge, where the text of the contract made by members of the 'eight masters' including the churchwardens was, unusually, entered into the churchwardens' accounts, has already been discussed.[30]

---

[23] Kissack, 'Vestry', 27. [24] See Chapter 5, section b.i, pp. 215–21.
[25] Catherine Cleveland, *The Battle Abbey Roll*, vol. 1 (London, 1889), 255; Whiting, *Reformation*, 220; Vallance, *Screens*, 65; Richard William Goulding, *Records of the Charity Known as Blanchminster's Charity* (Louth, 1898), 91–94.
[26] W. Symonds, 'Five Ancient Deeds at Sherston Magna', *Wiltshire Notes and Queries* 6 (October 1908): 448–50; Salzman, *Building in England*, 561–62.
[27] Maurice Willmore Barley, *Lincolnshire and the Fens* (Wakefield, 1972), 61; Alfred Welby, 'Chancel of Surfleet Church Re-Built 1420', *Lincolnshire N&Q* 17 (1922): 110–11; Salzman, *Building in England*, 496–97; Harvey, *English Mediaeval Architects*, 80.
[28] LA BNLW/1/1/55/17. [29] TNA: PRO C 1/8/23. [30] Chapter 3, section d.iii, pp. 171–72.

Most common are those contracts made by several unrelated people, probably acting as a subcommittee of the parish assembly or the masters, as at Great Sherston and Stratton. It is possible, but unlikely, that they were in fact acting as private patrons of building work. At Helmingham, Suffolk, John Couper the elder, John Couper the younger, Robert Couper the elder and William May contracted for a substantial tower in 1487–88.[31] Neither family appears to be at the apex of village society, however: the Smiths, Talmages, Bottes, Joces, Wythes and others, some of whom are named as knights, esquires or gentlemen, appear more often or higher up the list of witnesses in surviving deeds. It is likely that the Coupers and Mays were indeed acting as a contracting subcommittee on behalf of a joint project financed by the lord of the manor and the churchwardens, as will be argued in the next chapter.[32] At Walberswick, also in Suffolk, Thomas Bangor, Thomas Wolfard, William Ambrynghale and Thomas Pellyng contracted for the new tower in 1425.[33] Given the size of the commission and the number of contractees, it is almost cetain that they were acting as a contracting subcommittee. Judith Middleton-Stewart describes them as 'parish elders'.[34] Another project with several unrelated contractees is the steeple of Thornham Parva, Suffolk, in 1485–86, under Roger Baldry, Harry Vale and Thomas Grene.[35]

The smallest 'committees', if one may still term them that, tended to be of two apparently unrelated people who were probably fabric wardens, or even churchwardens, appointed by the contracting committee or parish leadership to run building work on their behalf. The accounts of two such pairs of wardens will be considered shortly. The battlements in Orby, Lincolnshire, for example, were contracted by Richard Ballard and John Heryng in 1529.[36] It has been suggested that they were churchwardens, and it is possible they were making a private contract, but they would have been a suitable choice as fabric wardens and it is curious that their title was omitted if they were churchwardens.[37] Richard would request to be buried in the church in his will of 1537 (proved the following year), to which he also left considerable sums of money, including for repair

---

[31] BLO Tanner MS 138, f. 87; Salzman, *Building in England*, 547–49. Members of the family appear regularly as witnesses to deeds for one another.
[32] Chapter 5, section b.iii, pp. 226–28.
[33] BL Add. Ch. 17634; Salzman, *Building in England*, 499–500; Lewis, *Walberswick CWAs*, vii.
[34] Middleton-Stewart, *Inward Purity and Outward Splendour*, 96. Bangor left 20s to the tower in 1432.
[35] TNA: PRO C 1/76/30; cf. SkRO(IB) HD 1538/111/4.
[36] TNA: PRO C 1/613/10; see also Roger Robinson and Philip Proctor, who contracted for the building of Wyberton church and tower, in Lincolnshire, in 1419: TNA: PRO C 1/7/104; William Henry St. John Hope, 'The New Building of Wyberton Church, Lincolnshire in 1419–20', *Lincolnshire N&Q* 14 (1917): 225–37; Salzman, *Building in England*, 495–96, 575.
[37] Hope, 'Wyberton', 230–31.

work.[38] John was one of his executors. Members of the Heryng family held land in several nearby parishes in Lincolnshire, including Ingoldmells, the church of which was to provide a model for the new battlements at Orby.[39]

It was common for urban contractees to have experience of municipal office. Some of the earliest evidence for the role of contracting committees in parochial building work is from a contract for a row of houses in York in 1335, made by three men, Richard Thorp, Nicholas Appleby and William Shireborn 'and the rest of the parishioners'.[40] The named contractees were all from the upper ranks of urban government. Appleby was a merchant and one of the town's MPs that year.[41] Shireborn was bailiff of York, related to a future mayor, and regularly witnessed grants and quitclaims, including one to Appleby.[42] Appleby and Thorp had among the highest taxation assessments in the city.[43] It suggests, at least, that, of two Richard Thorps entered as freemen of the city, he was the fisherman and not the chapman.[44] A Walter Shireborn had the second highest assessment. The contract was witnessed by the mayor and William Shireborn's colleagues as bailiffs of York, John de Bristol and John Caperoun.

Almost two centuries later, those involved in the drawing up of a contract in Wycombe, Buckinghamshire, 1508–09, were again closely related to the civic hierarchy of the parish. The contract was made by Thomas Pymme, Richard Byrch, Nicholas Devon, George Petyfer, John Bracebridge and Thomas Baven.[45] Pymme was either the mayor of Wycombe (d. after 1508) or his son, apposer of the foreign receipts

---

[38] TNA: PRO PROB 11/26/217. My thanks to Paul Ballard for his assistance with the family's history. William Farrer and J. Brownbill, eds., *VCH Lancashire*, vol. 3 (London, 1907), 3, 78–85, n. 61.

[39] LA BNLW/1/1/5/32; INV/13/105; INV/3/53; INV/9/12; Lincoln Consistory Court Wills 1543–45, 184.

[40] 'ac inter ceteros parochianos'. Salzman, *Building in England*, 430; cf. Philip Short, 'The Fourteenth-Century Rows of York', *Archaeological Journal* 137 (1979): 86–136.

[41] R. H. Scaife, 'Civic Officials of York and Parliamentary Representatives' (York City Library, n. d.), Y920; D. M. Smith, *A Guide to the Archives of the Company of Merchant Adventurers of York* (York, 1990), 65, 85; Appleby's son leased a tenement near the church for £72 in 1391–2: Maud Sellers, ed., *York Memorandum Book*, vol. 2 (Durham, 1912), 35; Maud Sellers, ed., *The York Mercers and Merchant Adventurers, 1356–1917* (Durham, 1918), 107 n. 1.

[42] Scaife, 'Civic Officials of York and Parliamentary Representatives', Y920; Francis Collins, ed., *Register of the Freemen of the City of York, 1272–1759*, vol. 1 (Durham, 1897), 32, 21; Francis Drake, *Eboracum* (London, 1736), 361; Smith, *Merchant Adventurers*, 66, 84, 89–90.

[43] P. M. Stell and A. Hawkyard, 'The Lay Subsidy of 1334 for York', *York Historian* 13 (1996): 8.

[44] Collins, *Register of the Freemen of York*, 1:19, 26; there was still a Sir Thomas Thorpe in the parish in 1388: Sellers, *York Memorandum Book*, 2:21.

[45] TNA: PRO E 210/985; Salzman, *Building in England*, 557–59; W. H. St. John Hope, 'Notes on the Architectural History of the Parish Church of High Wycombe', *Records of Buckinghamshire* ix (1909): 13.

of the exchequer from 1516.[46] Petyfer (who owned a fulling mill as well as several other properties) and Byrch were MPs and mayors for Wycombe.[47] A Petyfer stood surety for Byrch, and Pymme and John Petyfer had nearby properties.[48] Bracebridge was mayor in 1539–40, and a descendant was MP and mayor later in the century. Baven and Devon are named as burgesses only, but the names of many other MPs for Wycombe are lost, so it is possible that they held this position.[49] In 1524, Birch, Bracebridge and Petyfer were assessed at some of the highest values in the town, but Devon was not, and the only Bavens are found at very low assessments.[50] The choice of a mason from Surrey may have been Pymme's – he held land in Fernhurst, not far from Chertsey.[51] In both York and Wycombe, the work was undoubtedly parochial but membership of the contracting committees can be explained partly, if not wholly, by municipal hierarchies.

iii) Responsibilities

Only 9 per cent of contracts for parochial building projects contracted out the entirety of the work (Table I.4); a large majority reserved duties for the contractees, usually including the purchase of some or all of the transport, materials and equipment. Sometimes these were listed in detail: at Wycombe, in 1509, the contractees were to purchase materials, scaffolding, equipment and transport; while at Walberswick, in 1425, the contractees were to find and transport the materials, and pay for 'all manner [of] thing[s] that [are] needed to staging and winding and shovels and all manner [of] vessel that is needful to the steeple' as well as provide a lodge for working, eating, drinking and sleeping.[52] Often they were obliged to bring the materials to the building site. At Great Sherston, in 1511, they were to quarry the stone, bring it to within twenty feet of the building work and clear the site, at Helmingham, they agreed to transport the materials to the churchyard in 1487–88, and at Arlingham in 1372, they were to place them 'in a convenient place' within forty feet of the

---

[46] Leslie Joseph Ashford, *The History of the Borough of High Wycombe from Its Origins to 1880* (London, 1960), 83; R. W. Greaves, *The First Ledger Book of High Wycombe* (Welwyn Garden City, 1956), 49, 55–56, 67–70, 76.

[47] Greaves, *High Wycombe*, 61, 63, 72, 77, 88, 98; M. K. Dale, 'Pettifer, George (by 1489-1558/59), of Chipping Wycombe, Bucks', in The House of Commons 1509-1558, ed. S. T. Bindoff (London, 1982); M. K. Dale, 'Birch, Richard (by 1489-1527 or Later), of Chipping Wycombe, Bucks', in The House of Commons 1509-1558, ed. S. T. Bindoff (London, 1982).

[48] Greaves, High Wycombe, 49.   [49] Ibid., 86.

[50] Albert Charles Chibnall and A. Vere Woodman, *Subsidy Roll for the County of Buckingham, Anno 1524* (Aylesbury, 1950), 28–29.

[51] WSRO SAS-BA/17.   [52] Salzman, *Building in England*, 499–500, 557–59.

works. They were also to purchase fuel and lodgings for the mason and his men, and hay for a horse.[53] In 1442, at Dunster, not only were they to bring the materials to the churchyard but also to help the contractor to move the crane, equipment and heavy stones and provide him with a place to put his tools.[54] This was true of smaller-scale work, such as on rood screens, too.[55]

These duties would require time and effort, and were most sensibly executed by a few dedicated officers. The contracting committee could delegate the work to the churchwardens, as was shown in the previous chapter, or to dedicated fabric wardens, as will be discussed in the next section, but it is possible that they could also run the work themselves. Indeed, having personally met and agreed with the mason as to the responsibilities of each party, no one else would have as good an understanding of the proposals. The contracting committee may have been incentivised to run the work itself by the need to avoid financial penalties. Contractees often bound themselves, their executors and heirs to pay the mason, although it is probable, of course, that they were carrying out their duties on behalf of the parish, which would foot the bill. At Helmingham, in 1487–88, for example, the four contractees would have to pay the contractor 'according after the time of their letting and loss' if they were delayed in their work 'through the fault' of the contractees in failing to provide materials or equipment after due warning.[56] Similarly, at Wycombe, if the contractor 'lack or be hindered' in provision of materials, despite giving 'reasonable warning', then they were to receive their wages in addition to the contracted sum.[57] The contracts rarely indicate which authority would finance the work or execute the organisational duties taken on by the committee, even for important activities like paying the contractor or transporting materials. In most contracts, when responsibilities are reserved, it is written that the contractees 'shall find' the materials.[58] However, this is hardly conclusive: it is evidently not the case that the duke of York personally 'shall find' the materials for Fotheringhay, Northamptonshire, as the contract claims.[59]

When the contracting committee had a large membership – almost twenty named parishioners at Arlingham, or possibly all the male property owners in the parish as at Dunster, Wolverhampton, or Great Sherston – appointing fabric wardens would be unavoidable. The same might be true if the committee was particularly grand and wished to pass on the quotidian work to others. Although it is plausible that small

---

[53] '*in loco apto*'. Ibid., 445, 547–49, 561. [54] Ibid., 514–15.
[55] Goulding, *Blanchminster's Charity*, 91.
[56] BLO Tanner MS 138, f. 87; Salzman, *Building in England*, 547–49.
[57] TNA: PRO E 210/985; Salzman, *Building in England*, 557–59.
[58] E.g. at Arlingham: Ibid., 445. [59] Ibid., 505–9.

Fabric Wardens

contracting committees took on organisational tasks directly, there are very few instances where this can be shown to have taken place, as perhaps for the screen of St Mary the Great, Cambridge, considered above, or at All Saints, Bristol. There, eight parishioners, many previous or future churchwardens, but none currently in office, are mentioned in the churchwardens' accounts as being involved in the raising of funds and choosing oaks for rebuilding after a fire in 1464, although no direct reference is made to a committee.[60] I have found no extant examples of fabric accounts run by a body that was also explicitly a contracting committee, but those of a committee carrying out an expensive, albeit non-architectural, parochial project do survive. The purchase of a new cross at Bethersden, Kent, for almost £16 in 1508–09, was run by a committee of four leading parishioners, including two quondam churchwardens, who kept their own accounts.[61] There are entries in the accounts for drawing up a contract, indicating that the four also formed a contracting committee (although, as the contract does not survive, this must be speculative), but they must have reserved several responsibilities and run aspects of the work directly: they made two trips to London, for example, and organised the transport of the cross to the village. Being part of a committee brought with it financial, as well as organisational, burdens. Although most of the funding came from a combination of bequests and donations from the parishioners, a shortfall of £2 was made up by the committee. This was paid back to them out of the 'church goods' and by the 'parish', which was probably represented by the churchwardens alongside whose accounts these were found.

c) FABRIC WARDENS

i) Identity and Appointment

Instituting fabric wardens was sensible: they provided a dedicated organisational structure without other responsibilities, accountable both for the project's execution and for the compilation of accounts for audit. Numerous types of sources suggest that fabric wardens were regularly used for parish church construction. When a testator required that their executors execute a construction project, some were, presumably, to act as fabric wardens, albeit for an individual not a parish.[62] Testators

---

[60] Burgess, 'Lessons', 461.
[61] Francis Robert Mercer, ed., *Churchwardens' Accounts at Betrysden: 1515–1573* (Ashford, 1928), 1–2, xiii.
[62] The nave of Winchester Cathedral is a particularly explicit example, where Wykeham's executors were to find lime, sand and quarries, and pay the contractors. See Nichols, *Collection*, 339, 766.

Figure 4.2   The east end of Long Melford, with an inscription to John Clopton
(© Gabriel Byng)

sometimes named individuals who may have acted as fabric wardens: Richard Turnour wished to fulfil a grant he had made for a new steeple to 'Mr Parke of London, merchant, and Mr Lamb of Leeds, and others of the parish' of Sutton Valence, Kent, in 1528. Since Parke and Lamb were not masons, it is likely that they were fabric wardens or representatives of a contracting committee.[63] An inscription at Long Melford, Suffolk, is explicit about this, reading: 'John Clopton, of whose goods this chapel is embattled by his executors'.[64] Several other inscriptions there list the names of donors followed by a phrase such as 'of whose goods the said Katherine, John Clopton, Master Williamm Qwaytis and John Smith, did these six arches new repair', making a clear distinction between patronage and management (Figure 4.2).[65] Two other committees of three or four people are named: Giles Dent (the parson), John Clopton, Jon Smith and

[63] Hussey, *Testamenta Cantiana (East)*, 333.
[64] However, the names that follow the inscription, Robert Smith and Roger Smith, were not among his executors. Perhaps they were employed as fabric wardens. Clopton (d. 1497) left 100 marks to 'garnishing' the chapel, which he describes as 'new made' in his will of 1494 and is dated in the inscription to 1496. William Harvey, *The Visitation of Suffolke*, ed. Joseph Jackson Howard, vol. 1 (Lowestoft, 1866), 34–40.
[65] For a survey of the inscriptions see: Woodman, 'Writing on the Wall', 186–88. Note that two of those used here are now lost.

Fabric Wardens

Roger Smith 'with the help of the well-disposed men of this town'; and John Clopton, Master Robert Cutler and Thomas Ellis. In the latter case, Cutler and Ellis were executors and Clopton supervisor of the patron's will. It is likely that Clopton, Cutler, Ellis, Qwaytis, the Smiths and the 'well-disposed men' acted at different times as members of a fabric committee or as fabric wardens. Clopton, whose relatives and acquaintances would be depicted in the church's windows, was apparently a long-term member and probably led the effort. The presence of the priest on the committee is unusual, although paralleled by the occasional presence of priests among the names of contractees. Katherine, wife and presumably executrix of Roger Moryell, is a rare example of a female fabric warden.[66] She was in an unusually advantageous position, as a wealthy widow with her hand on the purse strings and a clear mandate from her husband's will.[67] Quite why the efforts of the wardens of Long Melford were recorded in this way is difficult to recover, but the exceptional ambition of the project and the large numbers involved in its management and financing is suggestive.

In villages and in many urban parishes, fabric wardens might be appointed by the parish assembly or the masters, but, when municipal authorities ran projects, they would take over the appointment process. Details of the appointment of fabric wardens for the building of Totnes tower in Devon survive in the Mayor's Court proceedings (Figure 4.3).[68] In January 1449, the court appointed six wardens ('*procuratores*', often translated 'factors'), a 'receiver of the pence' to run the Sunday collection for the work (who, in later years, was one of the wardens) and a master mason, Roger Growden.[69] The managerial structures used for the project are shown relatively clearly. In October of the same year two men were appointed as 'overseers of the workmen of the belfry and of quarrymen', apparently separate from the wardens and presumably as permanent employees of the works.[70] The wardens may have been divided into two supervisors and four superintendents.[71] As no further information survives regarding accounting procedure, it is reasonable to surmise that the receiver was accountant for the work, acting independently from the superintendents and submitting his records to the mayor's court for audit. The mayor, John Burhed, took on the task of constructing a new quay for unloading barges. The appointment

---

[66] See Chapter 5, section b.i, pp. 220–21.   [67] See discussion of women and building in p. 95.
[68] 'Totnes', 282; Hugh Robert Watkin, *The History of Totnes Priory & Medieval Town* (Torquay, 1914), I: 395–425; Percy Russell, *The Good Town of Totnes* (Exeter, 1964), 34–42; Julian M Luxford, *The Art and Architecture of English Benedictine Monasteries, 1300–1540: A Patronage History* (Woodbridge, 2005), 196.
[69] Watkin, *Totnes*, 395.   [70] Ibid., 400.   [71] As in January 1451. Ibid., 421.

Figure 4.3   Totnes tower (© John Ward)

process for the wardens is not recorded, although officers seem to have been chosen biannually at the January and October meetings of the court (and in the April session in 1449). Almost half served only one term, but in 1450 the number of wardens was reduced to four, and the same wardens were then reappointed throughout 1451 with two additional members, forming a stable core that had been absent in 1449 (Table 4.2). Only one served throughout the period: William Rowe, Burhed's neighbour, who would become a long-serving mayor from 1452, apparently having proved himself on the tower project. Other wardens fulfilled more junior positions in the town as receivers, boundary wardens, tax assessors, chapel wardens and fisheries wardens, while two were fined for rejecting the role of provost. Some apparently did not hold office. Although highly developed, the arrangements at Totnes were comparable to other non-ecclesiastical municipal building works when they were not let out to contract. In Norwich, an assembly appointed a committee of twenty-four men in 1407 to recruit builders and organise fundraising for the new guildhall.[72] However, they subsequently placed the two chamberlains in charge (1408–15), or at least chose to run the work through their accounts – indeed, they accounted for much of the maintenance work required by the town. Another committee ran a local levy in 1408. However, the building of major works in Beverley, Yorkshire, from the fourteenth century onwards, including the Bar, was overseen by the twelve keepers ('*custodes*') of the town, the council that ran town affairs, who appear to have run the work directly since the building expenses appear in their accounts.[73] Other municipalities contracted out whole projects.[74]

A useful comparison can be made with the appointment of fabric wardens by the parish, if perhaps supervised by municipal government, at St Mary-at-Hill, London. An appendix to the churchwardens' accounts of 1499–1500 notes sums given to a former warden and auditor, Thomas Colyns, to pay him and his colleague Harry Edmond back for their expenditure on the new steeple, which came to a total of more than £69 with the work still continuing. Colyns adds a memorandum himself, describing not only the accounts he kept but also the £11 he paid out personally.[75] The payment

---

[72] Richard Howlett, 'A Fabric Roll of Norwich Guildhall', *Norfolk Archaeology* XV, no. 2 (1903): 174–89; the size of this committee might relate to the council traditionally appointed to oversee communal affairs: Philippa Maddern, 'Order and Disorder', in *Medieval Norwich*, ed. Carole Rawcliffe and Richard Wilson (London, 2006), 192; Ian Dunn and Helen Sutermeister, *The Norwich Guildhall* (Norwich, 1977); Ernest A. Kent, *Norwich Guildhall: The Fabric and the Ancient Stained Glass* (Norwich, 1928).

[73] Knoop and Jones, *Mediaeval Mason*, 40; the most remarkable of these is the Bar (a gate) of 1409: Arthur Francis Leach, *The Building of Beverley Bar* (s.l., 1900); George Poulson, *Beverlac: Or, The Antiquities and History of the Town of Beverley*, vol. 1 (London, 1829), 118–72; for context on the keepers, see R. B. Dobson, 'The Risings in York, Beverley, and Scarborough, 1380–1381', in *The English Rising of 1381*, ed. R. H. Hilton and T. H. Aston (Cambridge, 1987), 125–26.

[74] Knoop and Jones, *Mediaeval Mason*, 40–42.

[75] LMA P69/MRY/B/005/MS01239/001/001, f. 181; Littlehales, *London City Church*, 239; Burgess, 'Lessons', 326; the fabric warden for the rebuilding of a house owned by St Ewen, Bristol, was owed almost £2 for over a decade: Masters and Ralph, *St Ewen, Bristol, CWAs*, 11–24.

Table 4.2 Wardens of the building of Totnes tower (1449–52)

Procuratores	Jan 1449	April 1449	Oct 1449	Jan 1450	Oct 1450	Jan 1451	Oct 1451	Receiver	Boundaries warden	Fisheries warden	Tax assessor	Mayor	Chapel warden
John Symon	x	x											
William Rowe	x	x		x	x	x	x					x	
Geoffrey Veale	x							x					
Robert William	x												
Robert Kent	x	x				x							
Thomas Brydwode	x	x											
John Bastard	x												
Stephen Bykelord		x											x
Geoffrey Martin		x							x				
John Hokemore				x	x	x	x			x			
Roger Symon				x	x	x	x	x			x		
Nicholas Cohew				x	x	x	x						
Henry Norris						x	x						
Richard Kent							x						
Overseers													
William Tydy			x										
John Hakewill			x										
Receivers													
John Hokemore				x	x	x	x						

Source: Hugh Watkin, *The History of Totnes Priory & Medieval Town*, vol. 1, (Torquay, 1914).

took place in the presence of the mayor, the parson and at least four other parishioners, but it was the churchwarden, William Smart, who handed Colyns the money. Two years later, Colyns was paid, again by the churchwardens, for travel to Maidstone to 'bind Mawnde the mason in to perform his covenants' and a contract for the windows was made. A separate entry that year records expenditure 'to have' a grant to the 'building of the south aisle' from the main patron 'with Mister Alderman and diverse of the parish', sent apparently to persuade the donor.[76]

Even more explicitly, in 1512–13, the churchwardens noted that John Allthorpe and Stephen Sanderson have promised to take charge and keep reckoning to pay all such workmen as shall make the battlements of our church ... as shall be thought best & determined by Mr Alderman and the parishioners and Mr Parson is to assist them with his good diligence and wisdom ... and Thomas Monders is chosen by the said parish to wait upon the said Stephen and Allthorpe in their absence and at their commandment for the furtherance of the same work.[77]

Here project management and account keeping were combined in the hands of two officers, and an assistant or understudy named. Whether the priest would usefully contribute his skills and advice, or was named to acknowledge his status within the church, is conjecture. The only information regarding their appointment is the phrase after Monders' name, 'by the said parish', and given it appears in the churchwardens' accounts and the priest was evidently involved, a parish assembly or meeting can be assumed. However, some oversight by the civic government, 'Mr Alderman', was evidently to take place. Although Colyns and Allthorpe and Sanderson kept accounts, these have not survived.

Accounts at Saffron Walden, Essex, give a small amount of information about the structure, but not the appointment, of a fabric committee for the new nave.[78] In 1485, the accounts of the collectors for the rood light, now bound into the churchwardens' accounts, recorded that they 'delivered [their money] to William Middleton and John Nicholls to Thomas Spurgeon, receivers for the new work of the south aisle'.[79] It is likely that the 'receivers' were part of a committee of fabric wardens, probably in charge of fundraising, as at Totnes. Spurgeon and Nicholls were churchwardens in 1485–86 and so perhaps took on fundraising as a natural extension of their regular duties. The men were members of large local

---

[76] LMA P69/MRY/B/005/MS01239/001/001, f. 202r; Littlehales, *London City Church*, 244.
[77] LMA P69/MRY/B/005/MS01239/001/002, ff. 328–40; Ibid., 284.
[78] Harvey, *English Mediaeval Architects*, 59, 316.   [79] ERO D/DBy Q18, f. 140.

families that appeared regularly in property deeds and had already worked as receivers or run collections.[80] The three were, respectively, a yeoman, a draper and a dyer. Middleton, as might be expected, was probably in charge of the work and seems to have been the most senior of the group – he had served a long term as churchwarden from 1481 to 1484 before graduating to the fabric committee. Although the fabric accounts of Middleton, Nicholls and Spurgeon have disappeared, several other examples survive.

ii) Fabric Accounts: The Wardens

We have already met the small number of surviving accounts kept by fabric wardens:[81] at North Petherwin, now in Cornwall (1505–07 and 1518–24),[82] Bodmin, Cornwall (1469–72),[83] St Augustine, Hedon, East Yorkshire (1428–38),[84] and Bridgwater, Somerset (1366–67).[85] Another set is extant for the building of a church house by the parishioners of St Ewen, Bristol, in c. 1493, while the Berry Chapel in Bodmin will be discussed shortly.[86] In the urban case studies it is possible to suggest whether the town or the parish initiated the work, that is, whether the Totnes or St Mary-at-Hill model was followed. At Hedon, the churchwardens were sworn in before the mayor and bailiffs, who, alongside the burgesses, would also examine and pass their accounts.[87] Accordingly, since there was no autonomous parochial structure, the fabric wardens were also presumably appointed directly or indirectly by the mayor and bailiffs. Perhaps significantly, the town's government had recently been strengthened.[88] Similarly, at Bodmin, an indenture made twenty years after the building work suggests that the churchwardens were audited ('debetyd and assigned') before the mayor and that the parish stock was held by the general receivers.[89] In Bridgwater, the

---

[80] ERO D/ACR1 f. 38; TNA: PRO PROB 11/18/272; PROB 11/37/451; PROB 11/42B/699.
[81] Chapter 1, section b.i, pp. 52–53.
[82] CRO P167/5/1 mm. 42–44, 73, and mm. 35–7, 48; Johns, Mattingly, and Thorpe, *North Petherwin*, Appendices 2 and 3.
[83] CRO BBOD/244; Wilkinson, 'Bodmin Church', 1875.
[84] Boyle, *Hedon*, Note x; Ainslie, *Hedon*, 7.
[85] SRO D/B/bw 23a; Dilks, *Bridgwater Borough Archives, 1200–1377*, 159–64.
[86] Masters and Ralph, *St Ewen, Bristol, CWAs*, 11–24.   [87] Boyle, *Hedon*, 89.
[88] Martin Weinbaum, *British Borough Charters 1307–1660* (2010), xl, xxv.
[89] J. Wallis, *The Bodmin Register* (Bodmin, 1827), 289–90; somewhat later, in the 1550s, the churchwardens' accounts note 'moneys delyvered them before hand, by the grete receyvers, towards the reparacon on the Church', ibid. 291. For the powers of the guild merchant from the late fourteenth century see ibid. 150–52.

guild merchant was closely involved with work on the church in the late fourteenth century (although, as already noted, the churchwardens may have grown in relative importance in the early fifteenth century): in 1373–74, the common receiver's accounts included expenditure on repairs of the tower and roof, as well as recording a direct payment to the churchwardens.[90] Lastly, in all these places, as this section will show, fabric wardens were closely linked to the civic hierarchy of the town. To generalise cautiously, therefore, when a town was identified with a single parish, the administration of the latter was often under the leadership of the former, which would initiate major projects such as church construction and decide on their administration. In large towns with multiple parishes to each ward, like London, and villages without a civic government, like North Petherwin, leadership fell to parochial authorities, such as the masters (or, perhaps, to 'strong' wardens, as at Croscombe).[91] In city parishes, it is likely that there was nevertheless some oversight by civic authorities, as at St Mary-at-Hill. The examples of Kilmersdon and St Margaret, Westminster, will be discussed shortly and are consistent with these conclusions. A possible exception can be found in the small stannary town of Chagford in Devon, which was run by the 'eight men' (and which 'elected' a fabric committee of eight 'for the repairing of the High Cross' in 1500).[92] However, there is no evidence that the town ever had a civic government and its administration may have been closer to that of a large village.[93]

In the urban examples, fabric accounts were kept by men who had held important offices in parochial and civic society. The St Ewen fabric wardens, John Smith and Thomas Apowell, served singly and did not have an official title – the accounts are headed 'for such business as he had in building of the new church house'.[94] 'Master' Apowell served as churchwarden on four occasions from 1474 to 1493, and Smith served in 1494–96. Both men had other positions of responsibility: receiving money for the parish, acting as auditors when accounts were lost in 1495–96 and making decisions about rents in 1497. Apowell also served as bailiff in 1486.[95] For him the work clearly came at the summit of a long career

---

[90] Dilks, *Bridgwater Borough Archives, 1200–1377*, 221–22; French describes this as a 'new roof': French, *People*, 148; the burgesses had established a guild merchant with considerable autonomy under two stewards and a bailiff in the later thirteenth century: R. W. Dunning and C. R. Elrington, eds., *A History of the County of Somerset*, vol. 6 (London, 1992), 223–28; Weinbaum, *Borough Charters*, 102.
[91] Cf. Archer, *Pursuit of Stability*, 83; Pounds, *English Parish*, 145.
[92] Osborne, *Chagford CWAs*, 26.
[93] Jane Hayter-Hames, *A History of Chagford* (London, 1981); W. G. Hoskins, *Devon* (London, 1954).
[94] Masters and Ralph, *St Ewen, Bristol, CWAs*, 11, 16.
[95] William Barrett, *The History and Antiquities of the City of Bristol* (Bristol, 1789), 681.

Organising Construction II

Figure 4.4   Bodmin, Cornwall, from the southwest (© Tim Jenkinson)

through the parochial and civic hierarchy. Smith's eligibility is more obscure, although he was evidently part of the leading group of parishioners. Apowell was also wealthy: he, his wife and daughter all purchased pews, he gave 20s to a collection for vestments in 1473–74 and his wife donated linen to veil an image in 1475–76. At Bodmin the wardens' title is never given (except once as 'receiver of the billing'), it is noted only that the accounts were kept 'for the church fabric' (Figure 4.4).[96] There were two fabric wardens over the course of construction, each working alone: Thomas Jerman (?October 1469–October 1471), a member of the Guild of St Eloy;[97] and Thomas Lucomb (October 1471–June 1472), who served as mayor of the town on four occasions (three before the building work and one afterwards) and served as a tax collector.[98] They also contributed significant sums personally. Jerman lent almost £8, while Lucomb lent almost £7, glazed the gable window and had his arms carved in the ceiling.[99] The single set of accounts at Bridgwater was kept by

[96] '*pro fabrica Ecclesie*'. Wilkinson, 'Bodmin Church', 32, 29.
[97] CRO ART/2/5/7; Wilkinson, 'Bodmin Church', 38.
[98] CRO BTRU/18; CRO AR/1/812; Wallis, *Bodmin Register*, 277.
[99] Wilkinson, *Bodmin Church*, 1874, 35, 24, 31.

Fabric Wardens

Figure 4.5   Bridgwater tower and spire (© Graham Shaw)

William Tanner, 'receiver' (*'receptor'*).[100] Tanner was the town's MP a few years later in 1371, appeared regularly as a witness to deeds in the 1360s and borrowed money from the church (Figure 4.5).[101]

[100] SRO D/B/bw 23a; Dilks, *Bridgwater Borough Archives, 1200–1377*, 159–64.   [101] Ibid., 209.

Organising Construction II

Figure 4.6 Hedon from the southwest (© Keltek Trust)

At Hedon, the wardens worked in pairs, following the format of most churchwardens, and were explicitly named as 'wardens of the fabric of the new belltower' (Figure 4.6).[102] The names of five survive: John Thorkleby and William West (1428–30), followed by Robert Baty and John Ellerton (1434–35), and John Ellerton and William Chapman (1437–38). Baty probably gave up the position to become a bailiff. The wardens had graduated through local government and the churchwardenship. Baty and Ellerton had already served together as churchwardens in 1428–30, and as bailiffs in 1422–23 and 1444–45;[103] and Chapman and Ellerton had worked as chamberlains.[104] The town ran collections street by street (as did Bodmin), and Chapman had worked as a collector in 1428–29.

The selection of the wardens at Bodmin, Bridgwater and Hedon is relatively opaque. At Bodmin, the position was probably chosen annually in October, but reappointment was possible (Jerman served at least two

---

[102] '*custodem fabrice nove campanilis*'. Boyle, *Hedon*, note X.
[103] ERYA DDHE/19/1, pp. 192, 199; Baty and Ellerton appeared regularly as witness to deeds.
[104] ERYA DDHE/19/1, pp. 250, 245; DDCC/45/20 and 29.

years), as was replacement (in Jerman's case by Lucomb). The extra set of accounts prepared by Jerman, summarising his income over the course of his tenure, and his replacement by a more senior peer, suggest that his management may have been found wanting by the parish authorities. At Bridgwater, the accounts are for a single accounting year, which suggests an annual appointment in the manner of the churchwardens.[105] At Hedon, indeed, the wardens were appointed annually and changed regularly, as no man served for the entire period of construction, but the accounts are too fragmentary to determine their typical term of office: Thorkleby and West for at least two consecutive years; Ellerton possibly for four years; and Baty and Chapman perhaps just for one each. If others had served as wardens in 1430–34 and 1435–37, as is likely, then the ranks of collectors, bailiffs, churchwardens and chamberlains in the town would have provided a pool of experienced volunteers. William Rihill, for example, was collector (1428–30), procurator of a chantry (1429–30) and bailiff (1431). Continuity in oversight may have rested with the town's government or a subcommittee since wardens moved between different local offices and the fabric wardenship, rarely occupying the latter for more than a couple of years.

The first set of fabric accounts at North Petherwin is different from the other surviving examples (Figure 4.7).[106] Rather than appointing fabric wardens, work on the south aisle and porch in 1505–07 was run directly by the masters, 'the eight men'. There are no expenses related to non-building projects, however, and so it is unlikely that these were the masters' regular accounts. Instead, they set up a separate fabric account but its management is not revealed and the eight men are not named. Their role may have been to coordinate a project that was funded by twelve parochial guilds and stores. The accounts can be contrasted, for example, with those of 'the four men' of Chagford, who ran occasional works on the church and its furnishings through their regular accounts, but which were otherwise concerned with collecting and disbursing sums to the churchwardens and stores.[107] No single body is named as the keeper of a separate set of accounts for work carried out on the north 'amlatory', or chancel chapel, and rood loft at North Petherwin in 1518–24 but payments are noted as being made 'by the hands of' fifteen different men, many of whom received payments in 1505–07. They included many of the wealthiest men in the parish, John Talcarn, Henry Seccomb, William Good and John Perte, and others assessed for the Lay Subsidies on middling sums, but few of the poorest.[108]

---

[105] SRO D/B/bw 23a.
[106] CRO P167/5/1 mm. 42–44, 73, and mm. 35–37, 48; Johns, Mattingly, and Thorpe, *North Petherwin*, appendices 2 and 3.
[107] E.g. a new shrine costing about £4 in 1536: Osborne, *Chagford CWAs*, 130.
[108] T. L. Stoate, ed., *Devon Lay Subsidy Rolls, 1524–7* (Bristol, 1979), 139.

Figure 4.7 North Petherwin, showing the south aisle and porch (© Roy Reed)

Fabric Wardens

It is not possible to reconstruct a managerial structure, but there is some indication that fabric wardens served in pairs, including Talcarn and Seccomb, while other payers appear singly, some much more regularly than others. Many entries are initialled, presumably as part of the auditing procedure. The rood loft would cost a substantial £58 in total.

iii) Fabric Accounts: Account Keeping

The accounts provide surprisingly sharp contrasts. At Bridgwater and Hedon, they followed a similar practice to those of guild or churchwardens. In the latter parish, they begin with an introduction naming the wardens and the date, followed by an account of arrears (always none), receipts and expenses for stone, 'necessary expenses' and wages. Over the course of construction, the format of the accounts changes little. Indeed, the procedure is so well established that the same subheadings are used even when there is nothing to record. The wardens kept paper accounts (*parcellae*) which were checked against the annual accounts at audit.[109] The collectors also kept 'indentures', possibly records between themselves and the wardens or the donors of how much each had donated.[110] It is no surprise to discover that some of those running the work were former churchwardens, and it is plausible that the system was deliberately borrowed. The structure of the accounts at Bridgwater is very similar, albeit less extensive, since the work was largely contracted out and sources of income were less varied. As with the town's churchwardens' accounts, groups of income or expenditure are entered in paragraphs (not tabulated), with subheadings in the left-hand margin and totals in a larger script below.[111] The audits of both fabric and churchwardens' accounts were probably run by the town authorities at the same time – at Hedon, for example, it was at Michaelmas, from when the accounts are dated and a festival often used, including by churchwardens, as the start of the accounting year.

The Bodmin records include several different documents related to the building work. Although evidently copied out and rationalised for audit or commemoration (numerous references are made to the original bills and receipts), they do not follow the format of other fabric, or churchwardens', accounts. Unlike Hedon, they show the personal imprint of the wardens, suggesting they could act with considerable autonomy. Jerman's accounts

---

[109] See two entries in 1429–30: '[...]*tempus compoti prout patet per parcellas huius compoti super hunc compotum*[...]'; '*prout patet per parcellas super hujus compotum ostensas et examinatas*'.
[110] The collectors would not have made contracts with the craftsmen.
[111] Cf. the 1385/86 churchwardens accounts, in a better hand than the fabric accounts: SRO D/B/bw 20a.

(written in the first-person singular in English with occasional Latin), from 1469 to Michaelmas 1471, are divided between income and expenditure, and grouped under relevant subsections, so that guild donations, sales and payments for wax and oblations are noted separately, while major pieces of task work are divided from repeat payments.[112] Jerman tended to use different terminology for different types of income: 'item of' for donations and '*de*' for guilds. His accounts were probably a neat copy, in a good clerical hand, of two separate annual accounts: references are made to sums received 'this year'; a memorandum notes gifts given after Michaelmas 1470, halfway through Jerman's office; and a subtitle in the expenses is for Easter 1471 (half way through his second year of office). Gifts from the same guilds appear twice in the receipts, presumably recording annual donations, and the names of churchwardens change (William Mason early in the accounts; David Witfen and Martin Hogge later). The reason for this re-compilation of two accounts may have been commemorative, as is suggested by the addition of formal Latin headings and a Latin title page, or, as suggested above, to give a summary of his time in office in the face of criticism.

Lucomb's accounts (in Latin) from October 1471 to June 1472, which are headed 'Last Year', are shorter and more formal, with two lists of income and expenditure and no subheadings.[113] They are followed, under the heading 'Next Year', by an undated 'memorandum of the accounts' by Lucomb and Jerman (still in Latin), although presumably compiled by the former.[114] The other Bodmin documents are more diverse in nature. The next set of accounts, by Jerman, summarises various families of income for 1469 through Michaelmas 1471, from sales, wax, gifts, guilds, the 'five stewards', collections and levies (in English and in the first person singular).[115] This document has the appearance of a summary of the monies taken during Jerman's time in office, prepared from the full accounts, again perhaps to commemorate the contributions of the guilds or in response to concerns over his management: it ends with the total received, the total spent and the reckoning of the sum clear (about £2). There follows a series of memoranda (in Latin) recording the debts of guilds and individuals and the current ownership of various donations or moneys owed, apparently to check the fulfilment of pledges as part of an audit or stocktaking following or preceding a major wave of work.[116]

---

[112] CRO BBOD/244 ff. 1–17, with a Latin title page at f. 22.
[113] '*Ulti[m]o a[nn]o*'; CRO BBOD/244 f. 18.
[114] '*P[roxim]o A[nn]o*' (added later); '*m[emoran]d[um] de comp[oto]*'; CRO BBOD/244 f. 19.
[115] CRO BBOD/244 ff. 20.
[116] The folio numbering here is confused (the memoranda continue over six folios but are out of order): CRO BBOD/244 ff. 23–27.

Fabric Wardens

iv) Guild Fabric Wardens: The Berry Chapel Tower

When guilds took charge of work directly, they faced a choice much like that of the parish – to run new building work through their ordinary accounts or to set up a separate account with dedicated wardens. The former required less organisational change but threatened to overwhelm the wardens; the latter was probably the most practical. A set of fragmentary fabric accounts run by a guild survives for the tower of Berry Chapel in Bodmin, Cornwall, which encompasses work on the south aisle, paintings and other furnishings (Figure 4.8).[117] The chapel seems to have had considerable independence: it was both architecturally distinct (it sits on a hill above the parish church) and long established with burial and baptism rights. Indeed, J. H. Adams argues that it was the former parish church.[118] It is, however, by no means the only example of an independent chapel run or built by a guild.[119] The management of the fabric wardens cannot easily be recovered (little evidence of auditing or oversight survives), but it is revealing that the guild's wardens provided only a minority of the financing, which otherwise relied on private donations and other guilds. There were three guilds associated with the chapel, so some form of cooperative organisation can probably be assumed, with fabric wardens employed to coordinate their contributions. Constructing the tower was evidently sufficiently taxing, or politically complex, to demand its own managerial structures.

The Berry accounts give an example of institutional problem solving that sheds light on the parochial projects already discussed. The earliest accounts begin in September 1501 and were run by John Cok, receiver of the pence (*'receptor denariorum'*) of the Holy Rood Guild. This arrangement was unsatisfactory, however, and by the next set of accounts, a second warden, Richard Kuch, had been appointed to take over running the work while Cok handled the income. Receivers continued to serve in pairs, appointed annually, although many served for longer periods, for the remainder of construction. The fabric wardens included several former and future mayors (John White and Thomas Philips), and others were members of leading local families (Cok and Hugh Rush).[120] In

---

[117] CRO B/BOD/314/1/1–14.
[118] J. H. Adams, 'The Berry Tower', *Devon and Cornwall N&Q* 28 (1959–61): 243–46; J. H. Adams, 'The Berry Tower', *Devon and Cornwall N&Q* 29 (1962–64): 125 and 186; J. Maclean, *Parochial and Family History of the Parish and Borough of Bodmin, in the County of Cornwall* (London, 1870), 99–101; Mattingly, 'Guilds of Cornwall', 299; Nicholas Orme, *The Saints of Cornwall* (Oxford, 2000), 98; Karen Jankulak, *The Medieval Cult of St Petroc* (Woodbridge, 2000), 57.
[119] Bainbridge, *Gilds*, 127–29; Rosser, *Solidarity*, 51; Swanson, *Church and Society*, 280.
[120] Cok's father of the same name features in the parish church fabric accounts in connection with the guild of St Anianus; CRO BBOD/244 f. 24.

Figure 4.8   Berry chapel tower (© Tim Jenkinson)

1505–06 work on the south aisle was nearing completion, and the fabric of the tower and battlements was finished in August 1510, under the master mason Harry Steman. Major work continued in furnishing and glazing over the next four years under the same managerial structures.

Fabric Wardens

v) Organisation, Delegation and Contracting

The decision to use single wardens at Bodmin and Bridgwater is curious: a major building project was demanding in time and expertise, and a second warden would help reduce the likelihood of mistake or corruption, an adaptation made by the Berry fabric wardens. Indeed, as mentioned above, there is a 'memorandum of the accounts' in Bodmin headed by both wardens. There is some sign of delegation, of which Bodmin offers the most detailed evidence. Here, the churchwardens raised and donated money; senior guild officers occasionally sold materials or donated sums; and others carried out organisational tasks. During Jerman's tenure as warden, Lucomb received money from the churchwardens for the work, while Thomas Bere, who worked with the churchwardens, housed the carpenters and made a journey to fetch lime. Richard Trote was paid for riding to find a carver and 'to labour to have the timber home', and a relative, Bartholomew, who was mayor, collected money from those who were not members of a guild, worked with Jerman in St Eloy's Guild and gave half a window.[121] John Bare took a letter to carpenters in Devon, while the Hancocks, particularly the two Johns (one a mason 'and his fellows', the other a smith, and both members of St Eloy's Guild), donated sums, handled part-payments and regularly worked on site. Having a dedicated managerial structure did not, in other words, change the necessity of finding others to help run such a substantial project.

The warden absolved himself of several tasks by contracting out units of various sizes: under Jerman, Richard Richowe 'and his fellows' were paid £28 for the pillars, more than £17 for the north and south walls, and almost £14 for the porch and pillars; Samuel Carpenter received almost £10 for task work and £7 for work on the roof 'as it appears by [an] account between the said Sam and me', and William Carpenter received a part-payment of £3 for task work.[122] Samuel received £14 for task work under Lucomb, while Jerman and Lucomb's joint account includes £15 to William in part-payment. In total, some two-fifths of total recorded expenditure went on contractual work. Six windows were glazed by parishioners, apparently paying for the work directly. However, much of the work was run by Jerman or Lucomb: both their accounts, but particularly Jerman's, record detailed expenditure on many small tasks, involving transport, materials and labour (individual sums could be as low as 1d, as, for example, for the purchase of a single nail or a day's work).

As we have seen, the fabric wardens at Hedon managed the minutiae of building work, but much of the fundraising effort was delegated to

---

[121] Wilkinson, 'Bodmin Church', 21. [122] Ibid., 27.

the churchwardens. They were also able to call on a large band of volunteers from local government, most notably for the collections that were run street by street by pairs of collectors, often serving for several years. William Tanner at Bridgwater had comparatively less to do. There was little fundraising outside the imposition of a levy, which was run by a legion of collectors across the town and neighbouring villages, and much of the work (nine-tenths of its recorded cost) was contracted out, largely to one Nicholas Waleys, leaving only a few tasks for Tanner to oversee himself, usually involving timber or quarrying, which suggests that the provision of materials had been retained as a responsibility by the contractees. Nevertheless, these tasks were not inconsiderable and clearly required time and travel. There is mention of other men who helped by fetching the mason from Bristol, litigating and carrying letters, but otherwise Tanner seems to have taken sole responsibility.

D) AUTHORITY AND AUTONOMY

i) *The Committee and the Parish*

That the named contractees were personally responsible for choosing, meeting and instructing the contractor does not imply that their work was entirely divorced from the approval of others in the parish. The creation, selection process and regulation of fabric wardens is obscure, but there is some indication that a broader section of the parish would be asked to ratify their appointment, decisions or expenditure. The addition of phrases such as 'with all the whole parish' (Great Sherston, Wiltshire, 1511), or 'and all the parishioners' (Arlingham, Gloucestershire, 1372) suggests that legally the contractee was the parish and the named contractees understood themselves to be acting as its representatives.[123] Sometimes the contractees would name themselves as 'the parish' (Dunster, Somerset, 1442), 'town and parish' (Wolverhampton, 1476), or 'the township' (Cottesbrooke, Northamptonshire, 1533).[124] Of corporate contracts (that is, ones not led single-handedly by gentry, clergy or an institution), over half use a phrase of this kind. Strikingly the ratio is considerably higher in towns (three-quarters) than in villages (a third), which could suggest either that urban projects really were more communal in spirit, finance or management or that rural leaders did not feel as great a need to demonstrate the communal nature of their projects

---

[123] '*et omnes parochianos*'; Salzman, *Building in England*, 561, 445.
[124] Ibid., 514–15, 600; Serjeantson and Longden, 'The Parish Churches and Religious Houses of Northamptonshire', 302.

as urban ones.¹²⁵ The documentary record suggests the former is unlikely.¹²⁶ There is no correlation between the use of these phrases, or of the size of the contracting committee, and the population or wealth of the town or village (as measured in taxation returns).¹²⁷ Otherwise there are few noticeable differences between urban and rural contracting committees. Large towns and villages tended to have slightly smaller committees but only by a small margin.¹²⁸

Even in contracts which did not claim to be communally sanctioned, the contractees must have acted with some form of legal or popular mandate, whether expressed formally or implicitly, especially if communal funds were going to be raised.¹²⁹ Most convenient would be to use the annual parish assemblies, which often elected the churchwardens and audited their accounts. However, even if the assembly admitted a broader range of parishioners than the masters, its membership was far from universal. Little certain information survives regarding attendance, let alone authority or influence, but it is likely to have been limited to male householders or a subset of them, perhaps varying according to the importance of the meeting.¹³⁰ It has already been noted that in many sources 'the parish' or 'township' might represent this group alone.¹³¹ More reflective of reality perhaps are similar, but less universal, claims about the contractees: 'and with the other parishioners'¹³² (York, 1335) or 'and other more parishioners' (Cambridge, 1520), when the contractees acted with, perhaps as representatives of, a larger number of parishioners, which nevertheless fell short of the entire parish.¹³³ Being a 'named' parishioner was recognised as a distinctive mark by contemporaries: at Arlingham, Gloucestershire, the contract notes those 'named as well as those unnamed'.¹³⁴

---

¹²⁵ The absolute figures are: two-thirds in large towns; four-fifths in small towns; two-sevenths in villages.
¹²⁶ At least as regards to finance and management: Chapter 1, section b.iii, pp. 74–75; Chapter 4, section c.i, pp. 187–92.
¹²⁷ The Spearman's rank correlation for number of contractees and total assessment in 1524 is 0.1; population, 0.01; mean assessment, 0.05.
¹²⁸ Means of 3 in large towns; 5.7 in small towns; 2.8 in villages (with Arlingham omitted as an outlier). Again, the small sample size probably creates misleading averages.
¹²⁹ The claim at St Philip and St James, Bristol, in 1544–47, to act 'in the name of all the parishioners' implies the contractees' representative character without indicating a ratification process: TNA: PRO C 1/1107/14. See Chapter 1, section c.vii, pp. 92–94 in this volume. Cf. Burgess, 'Lessons', 323.
¹³⁰ Kümin, 'Looking beyond', 90; Burgess, 'Shaping', 262–67; Kümin, *Shaping*, 95–96; French, *People*, 74; cf. Steve Hindle, 'A Sense of Place? Becoming and Belonging in the Rural Parish 1550–1650', in *Communities in Early Modern England*, ed. Alexandra Shepard and Phil Withington (Manchester, 2000), 109s.
¹³¹ Introduction, section b, p. 23.   ¹³² '*ac interceteros parochianos*'.
¹³³ Salzman, *Building in England*, 430, 466; Sandars, *Great Saint Mary*, 66; in Edinburgh, in 1387, the contractees for chapels at St Giles were defined as the 'worthy men and noble [the lord of Nether Liberton and the Provost of Edinburgh] and the community of that ilk ("ylke")': William Maitland, *The History of Edinburgh* (Edinburgh, 1753), 270.
¹³⁴ '*tam non nominatos quam nominatos*'. Salzman, *Building in England*, 445.

Even if the assembly was consulted, its powers may have been limited, at most, to approving the existence, membership, discretionary powers or the outlines of the architectural plans of the contracting committee. At St Mary the Great, Cambridge, something of this dynamic can be judged from the contract for the rood loft, where the contractees were 'named by the assent and consent of all the parishioners of the said parish', a formula similar to those used to describe communal agreements, or the appointment of churchwardens, in some parishes.[135] The contractees were probably able to use a substantial amount of discretion, however: the contract was signed on 30 June, almost three months after the annual meeting on 9 April, suggesting a period of negotiation handled by the contractees without necessarily referring their decisions back to the parish. Critically, the parishioners gave their assent to the naming of the contractees and not, apparently, to the contract itself. At Stratton, Cornwall, the wording of the contract also indicates that the contractees were acting as representatives of, but not necessarily in consultation with, the parish: 'in the name for and in the behalf of all the parish'.[136]

Design and cost were only two of the agreements that project managers would have to make. Most sensitive of all would be the arrangement of communal financial agreements.[137] When organising a levy for the building of Totnes steeple in 1452, the mayor, vicar and fabric wardens went 'round the vill to examine the parishioners how much each voluntarily wishes to give'.[138] For building work at Bodmin, Cornwall, similarly, a grant 'was agreed throughout the town'.[139] The parish could also be active in assessing the activities of its wardens. In the 1490s, at St Ewen, there was doubt about the 40s that the fabric warden Thomas Apowell claimed to have spent on timber, and he was granted a year to prove that the purchase had taken place and that he should be reimbursed.[140] Ales, parties and entertainments may have been used as tools of persuasion during funding drives.[141] At Bredon, Worcestershire, villagers were treated to a wassail for helping to carry logs for building work in 1395–96.[142] French argues that collections were linked to entertainments to minimise local resistance, using characters such as Robin Hood to persuade parishioners to donate.[143] We saw earlier how a play at All Hallows, London Wall, was held in the first year of building work and

---

[135] Sandars, *Great Saint Mary*, 66; cf. Cox, *Churchwardens' Accounts*, 14, 137.
[136] Goulding, *Blanchminster's Charity*, 91.   [137] Chapter 1, section c.iv, pp. 77–79.
[138] Watkin, *Totnes*, 425.
[139] CRO BBOD/244 f. 20; Wilkinson, *Bodmin Church*, 1874, 32–33.
[140] Masters and Ralph, *St Ewen, Bristol, CWAs*, 23–24.   [141] Chapter 1, section c.ii, pp. 66–69.
[142] Dyer, *Lords and Peasants*, 362.   [143] French, 'Parochial Fund-Raising', 126–27.

raised a substantial sum of money.[144] At St Andrew, Plymouth, large sums of 'dancing money' were paid 'for the steeple' by at least five parishioners in 1499–1500.[145] An inscription in the tower gallery at Cawston, Norfolk, ends: 'Be merry and glad what good ale this work made' – a cautionary instruction or celebratory valediction?

That parochial elites did try win popular assent but could fail to do so, and that junior parishioners could take legal recourse should this occur, is demonstrated by a case at the Court of Requests concerning a major parochial purchase at Tavistock in Devon. This was not building work but it was comparable in cost, if not in complexity, to construction. In 1519, John Amadas, a wealthy local, petitioned the court for money he claimed he was owed after buying a silver cross (possibly from a relative) for more than £62. According to one former warden, John Williams, the decision had been agreed by four parishioners and 'the more part & most substantial men'. His successor, John Goodstoke, argued, however, that the agreement must have been made by 'persons to the number of six or eight & not by the whole inhabitants & rulers of the said parish' and that therefore they did not have 'the whole power or authority that to do without the assent of the whole parish and not by the agreement of the whole inhabitants'. Williams replied that Amadas had displayed the cross at 'diverse holydays' and Amadas added that the vicar and warden had advertised the decision to both the parish and the substantial men, and eventually 'the whole parishioners' had agreed the purchase.[146] Clearly, in this parish at least, the elite did require the consent of 'the parish' (whoever that was understood to be) and could face stiff opposition, even from the churchwardens, if it was felt that too few had been consulted. Nevertheless, Amadas was able to argue that the final decision of a few substantial men was adequate to represent an agreement by the parish if they had allowed for some wider consultation. Tavistock would appear to be a counterexample to the generalisation that civic rather than parochial government directed major church projects in small towns.[147] However, Williams does not seem to identify the 'most substantial men' with the masters (they are a vague group of wealthy men rather than a governing

---

[144] Chapter 1, section c.iii, pp. 62–63; Welch, *Allhallows CWAs*, 57.
[145] John M. Wasson, *Records of Early English Drama. Devon* (Toronto, 1986), 214; Katie Normington, *Gender and Medieval Drama* (Woodbridge, 2004), 49–50.
[146] Leadam, *Select Cases*, 17–29; Kümin, *Shaping*, 237; French, *People*, 74–76; Duffy, *Morebath*, 22; G. H. Radford, 'Tavistock Abbey', *Reports and Transactions of the Devonshire Association* 46 (1914): 130; Edward Hasted, *Hasted's History of Kent*, ed. Henry Holman Drake (London, 1886), 251; Anita Hewerdine, *The Yeomen of the Guard and the Early Tudors: The Formation of a Royal Bodyguard* (London, 2012), 144–45; T. L. Stoate, ed., *Devon Lay Subsidy Rolls, 1524–7* (Bristol, 1979), 152; T. L. Stoate, ed., *Devon Lay Subsidy Rolls 1543–5* (Almondsbury, 1986), 137.
[147] Tavistock had a population of approximately 1,400 in 1524. Sheail, *Distribution of Wealth*, 2:62.

institution) and Goodstoke even claimed that 'the rulers', perhaps meaning the municipal government, had not been adequately consulted. The problem, in other words, was not that Amadas' cross was purchased by the masters but that it was carried out by an exclusive group without either popular or civic sanction.

Another case study from an urban parish suggests how 'popular' sanction of parochial leadership in architectural projects was structured through engagement with different tiers of influential parishioners. An indenture of May 1402 between the abbot of Peterborough and the parishioners for the demolition of the old parish church and the building of a new one was made by twenty-four men, including the clerk and a bailiff, who were acting on behalf of the other parishioners.[148] However, when the parishioners came to appoint a clerk, Thomas Pykwell, to apply for permission from the bishop, a larger number was involved – some forty-seven named men and many others from the congregation.[149] Oddly, the forty-seven included only sixteen of the twenty-four men who made the indenture with the abbot. The flow of responsibility is difficult to reconstruct but the impression is nevertheless hierarchical – Pykwell leading the effort alongside an elite of twenty-three, their legitimacy given partially through selection by a larger group of forty-seven important male parishioners, who in turn were part of a yet larger subset of parishioners who were present at the selection meeting. Twenty-four was a standard number used in local government, as, for example, in later vestries.[150] The importance of popular authority was recognised by the permanent vicar of the parish when he approved the nomination of Pykwell.[151] Two further examples show similar committees of senior parishioners leading building work: first, at St Thomas, Salisbury, twelve parishioners 'elected' for the purpose, petitioned the rector of the church to rebuild the chancel after a collapse in 1448, committing the parish to reconstruct one side of the new work and take on its repair.[152] Members of two of the twelve families also reconstructed the chancel chapels.[153] Lastly, there is a very early rural example, from Glapwell in Derbyshire, where fifteen leading parishioners gave land for roofing and, if necessary,

---

[148] *'vice sua ac vice nomine et mandato ceterorum parochianorum et incolarum predicte communitatem sive universitatem ville et parochie'*: W. T Mellows, ed., *Peterborough Local Administration* (Kettering, 1939), 219–22.

[149] *'et alii quamplures in multitudine copiosa ad divinam congregati communitatem sive universitatem dicte parochie'*: Ibid., 222–23.

[150] Cox, *Churchwardens' Accounts*, 13.

[151] Mellows, *Peterborough Local Administration*, 223–24.

[152] Haskins, 'St Thomas, Salisbury', 3–4; Brown, *Popular Piety*, 111.

[153] Elizabeth Crittall, ed., *VCH Wiltshire*, vol. 6 (London, 1962), 144–55.

Authority and Autonomy

the complete rebuilding of the chancel in c. 1250, provided that the canons of Darley Abbey carried out repair work in the future.[154]

Perhaps more important was the informal authority, grounded on trust, experience and deference, that the members of these committees inspired.[155] It was shown earlier that in parishes with a wealthier economic elite, financing was concentrated in their hands, and they were presumably able to act with considerable autonomy.[156] In less polarised parishes, where fundraising was more widely spread, the 'elite' would need to win a higher degree of popular support, which may not have been made any easier by being less economically distinct. Larger rural and urban parishes had more complex governmental structures that determined seniority or eligibility for office, providing a relatively independent source of authority for those appointed to run the work – although, as noted earlier, the authority, or at least the quality, of civic government could be contested.[157] Smaller parishes could put less faith in the functioning of local bureaucracy to select and monitor fabric wardens. Members of fabric committees were probably well known to their wealthier neighbours and those who had demonstrated that they had the necessary ability and character and a proven record in office may have been trusted to carry out the work as peers and friends.[158]

ii) The Committee and the Masters

It was argued earlier that in parishes where parochial administration was not dominated by civic government, as in large villages and cities, the impetus for a building project originated in the parish leadership.[159] In the Somerset village of Kilmersdon, for example, 'a convocation was had among the good men of the said parish for the enlargement of their said parish church', namely the building of a new aisle, in 1538–44.[160] Similarly at St Margaret, Westminster, decisions regarding construction in c. 1487–1523 were taken by 'the assent of the worshipful of the parish' or 'the assent of diverse of the honest men of the town'.[161] This may also have been the case at the small village of Helmingham in Suffolk, in the

---

[154] Reginald R. Darlington, *The Glapwell Charters* (Derby, 1959), 140–41.
[155] Cf. the relatively high status of many of the churchwardens who ran building work: Chapter 3, section d.i, p. 160.
[156] Chapter 1, section c.iii, pp. 74–75.
[157] Introduction, section b, pp. 22–24; Burgess, 'Shaping', 260–61.
[158] DeWindt and DeWindt, *Ramsey*, 100.   [159] Chapter 4, section c.ii, pp. 192–93.
[160] Although here they chose to run the work through the churchwardens. TNA PRO C1/1014/48–49; French, *People*, 73; the village, together with Ashwick and Luckington, had a population of c. 200 in 1524–25 and an average individual payment of about 3s: Sheail, *Distribution of Wealth*, 2:299.
[161] Rosser, *Medieval Westminster*, 264.

1480s, which will be discussed in the following chapter.[162] The relationship between contractees and masters is hard to unravel, but it is likely, by parallel with later vestries, that in some places the former acted as a subcommittee with the masters' approval or mandate, and possibly a similar membership and a good deal of oversight.

The contract for the new rood loft at St Mary the Great, Cambridge, in 1520, discussed in the previous chapter, sheds light on the relationship between contractees and the elite body that ran the parish.[163] Uniquely the contractees included both the churchwardens and four other named men, 'with other more parishioners', who were all closely linked to the parochial hierarchy.[164] All but one were quondam members of the 'eight masters'. In 1520, the eight included three of the named contractees (Richard Clerk, Robert Hobbs and Dr William Butts). The fourth, Henry Hallehed, was a master in 1518 and 1521. The masters had chosen the churchwardens who appeared as contractees and would run the work: Peter Cheke ('gentleman' and another master) and his junior Robert Smith (not a master until 1521).[165] The appointment of this subcommittee probably demonstrates the close control that the elite maintained over the contracting process. All of them had worked their way through the parish hierarchy: Hallehed, Hobbs and Smith had been members of the eight since at least 1516, and all had held a number of other parochial offices including churchwarden, auditor and money collector.[166] The unusual combination of masters and wardens acting as contractees is probably explained by both the seniority of the wardens and the circumstances of the contract's creation.[167]

When fabric wardens were appointed, the relationship between them and the committee overseeing the work, or with the parish leadership or municipality more generally, is largely obscure. The model might be like that of churchwardens, bound by local custom, regulation and informal controls to obey the will of the parish assembly, or at least its most important members.

---

[162] Chapter 5, section b.iii, pp. 226–27. Sheail, *Distribution of Wealth*, 2:324.
[163] Chapter 3, section d.iii, pp. 171–72.
[164] Foster, *St Mary the Great, Cambridge, CWAs*; Sandars, *Great Saint Mary*, 63–67.
[165] Robert Masters, *The History of the College of Corpus Christi and the B. Virgin Mary (Commonly Called Bene't)* (Cambridge, 1753), 57.
[166] Hallehed had collected money in 1514. Hallehed, Butts and Clerk were witnesses in 1518, when Clerk was beadle and Smith churchwarden. Butts, Hallehed, Hobbs and Clerk had been auditors in 1520, and Cheke, Clerk and Butts in 1518. C. T. Martin, 'Butts, Sir William', in *Oxford Dictionary of National Biography* (Oxford, 2004); J. E. Clarke and J. E Foster, 'History of a Site in Senate House Yard with Some Notes on the Occupiers', *Proceedings of the Cambridge Antiquarian Society* 13 (1909): 129; J. M. Anderson, *The Honorable Burden of Public Office: English Humanists and Tudor Politics in the Sixteenth Century* (New York, 2010), 15–16; David McKitterick, *A History of Cambridge University Press: Printing and the Book Trade in Cambridge, 1534–1698*, vol. 1 (Cambridge, 1992), 22.
[167] Chapter 3, section d.iii, pp 171–72. A similar arrangement probably took place at Saffron Walden in 1485: Byng, 'Saffron Walden', 334–35.

Authority and Autonomy

This is indicated at St Mary-at-Hill, in 1512–13, when the wardens, Allthorpe and Sanderson, were to act in accordance with the decisions of 'Mr Alderman and the parishioners' although they were also 'to take the charge' of building the battlements.[168] Indeed, they had proved themselves in several offices, including those of churchwarden and auditor, as well as being elder members of the community and personally wealthy.[169] The mayor's court at Totnes took a relatively interventionist position, despite the large number and occasionally high status of the wardens, handing down instructions to organise quarrying and provide equipment, while the receiver was to 'render his account of receipts and expenditure at any law court of the mayor'.[170] In April 1449, the wardens were instructed to make foundations and knock down the porch; the following January they were to inspect four recently completed towers in the vicinity and a year later to quarry stone, transport it and begin the body of the work. They were even instructed not to leave the stones in the river because they would be eroded. Sadly, the court proceedings are missing from 1453–64, the period during which work was finished.

Elections, contracts and audits also helped enforce centralised control. Wardens were temporary and could be replaced, either if their performance was unsatisfactory, as perhaps at Bodmin, or at annual or biannual elections, as at Hedon and Totnes.[171] Some tasks could be delegated 'upwards' to more senior parishioners. However, the seniority of many wardens, particularly Thomas Lucomb at Bodmin and William Rowe at Totnes, indicates a higher degree of independence than the churchwardens. Rather than delegating tedious tasks to more junior parishioners such as churchwardens, parish leaders may have manifested their control by appointing peers and friends, closely identified with the plans, to run the work. The dynamic of the Totnes court is unknown: decisions may have been initiated by the wardens and sanctioned by the mayor, for example. Most contracts were distinctly vague as to the details of the work, leaving it unclear as to who was to take responsibility for choosing designs, materials and labourers but creating space for the project managers to determine decisions themselves. Indeed, instances where the wardens' independence was limited naturally required documentation and so evidence is more likely to survive – their scope for individual action would rarely have been entered in the documentary record.

---

[168] LMA P69/MRY/B/005/MS01239/001/001, f. 181; Littlehales, *London City Church*, 284.
[169] Allthorpe was an auditor in 1508–09, when he added a memorandum to the accounts himself, in 1509–10, and with Sanderson in 1513–14. Allthorpe was churchwarden in 1501–03, and Sanderson in 1505–07 and 1516–17. Sanderson paid 13s 4d for burial in the chapel in 1523–24.
[170] Rea, 'Totnes', 282; Watkin, *Totnes*, 395–425.   [171] Chapter 4, section c.ii, pp. 177–80.

E) CONCLUSION

The previous chapter demonstrated that churchwardens did not invariably head parish church building projects, while those who did left little documentary evidence behind. Although positive evidence is slight, two sets of sources indicate who these bodies might have been. The first is building contracts, often made by groups of two to six unrelated contractees drawn from the middling and upper echelons of the parish, who negotiated designs, costs and deadlines. These contracting committees often retained significant responsibilities and would need to delegate them to the churchwardens or to appoint fabric wardens. The latter would provide dedicated oversight of the work and be answerable to the masters or the assembly, or both, formally at the time of the audit and, probably, informally throughout construction. The accounts of several such wardens survive, along with evidence of other lost examples. Some were run much like churchwardens' accounts, and many of their keepers had probably graduated from that position, or from guilds or municipal government, where they had built up sufficient seniority and experience to earn the trust of their peers and learn the skills required to manage building work. Others show a more personal influence. It may be doubted whether the organisational structures employed in building work were always as sophisticated as those laid out in this chapter. In smaller villages without highly developed parochial or civic government, particularly before the highly specialised parish administration of the long fifteenth century, it was perhaps less common to find written contracts, contracting committees and fabric wardens – evidence for this is, of course, difficult to come by.[172]

The institutions initiating and overseeing these projects can be identified with some certainty. In small sized towns with a single parish, civic authorities tended to direct parochial administration and, with it, work on the church building. Large villages and large towns or cities with many parishes had to develop distinct parochial governments, often including formal institutions such as the masters, who would choose the managerial structure of new building projects and often appoint fabric committees from their own number. These arrangements could be highly exclusive, and local hierarchies of wealth and power expressed themselves in the limited involvement of most parishioners, particularly women and poorer groups, in overseeing building work. Contracts and audits served to cement the control of the wealthier groups over fabric committees. Given their prominent role in financing the work, this is hardly surprising.[173] If fabric wardens were able

[172] Introduction, section e, pp. 45–46. [173] See Chapter 1, section c.vii, pp. 92–95.

Conclusion

to act with considerable independence, probably often greater than that of the churchwardens, it was due to the high social status of the men who occupied those positions. Nevertheless, these enterprises often claimed their authority from the wider community: thus, the whole parish was occasionally named as contractee, even if this was logistically impossible; or the contractors claimed to be acting 'on behalf of' the parish, while plans and accounts may have been approved at the parish assembly. Evidence of consultation survives in several sources, indicating that, even if the elite initiated and controlled much or all of the building process, they did seek some degree of popular approval while doing so, albeit often from limited subsets of the parish. Together with churchwardens, temporary fabric committees comprise the main parochial mechanisms for running building projects, and are quite different from the third and final situation: building work run by the manorial lord or advowson holder.

Chapter 5

ORGANISING CONSTRUCTION III
Aristocracy, Clergy and Institutions

A) INTRODUCTION

Parishes, guilds and municipalities were not, of course, the only bodies that ran parish church construction. Individual families and institutions also carried out building work, from substantial farmers and parish gentry to great lords and institutions. They were responsible for some of the best-known parochial architectural commissions, from wholesale rebuildings on a large scale to chapels, windows and screens.[1] However, if documents relating to projects run by fabric committees or churchwardens are rare, then those concerning projects controlled by a single patron, most often a manorial lord or advowson owner, are elusive indeed. Inevitably, it is large and enduring institutions, such as cathedral chapters and priories or Oxbridge colleges, that furnish the most examples, but where possible, this chapter will focus on the gentry because of their significance in the history of parish church building. These examples can occasionally be contrasted with surviving information on noble patronage.

As in the previous chapter, contracts and accounts offer the most important information. They provide clues not only for the level of involvement that wealthy families and institutions could have in building projects but also for the organisational and financial structures they adopted. Contracts and accounts also allow for some judgement of their managerial priorities and their search for efficient, honest and reliable governance. Occasionally the form, although rarely the tenor, of cooperation between lords and tenants is revealed, as different functions and financial responsibilities were negotiated between them. Taken with the findings of the previous chapter, this shows the different social axes along which the organisation of church building fell – community and local leadership, tenants and lords, church and laity. Exclusion, conflict and

---

[1] See Chapter 2.

Aristocratic Projects

force are, of course, difficult to find in accounts that record only cooperation but their traces are still, sometimes, visible.

B) ARISTOCRATIC PROJECTS

i) *Aristocratic Contractees*

The aristocracy were rarely members of contracting committees and, where exceptions survive, there is reason for doubting their active involvement. We have already encountered the contract of 1372 for the tower at Arlingham, Gloucestershire, in which every major household is included, and the list is topped by the lord of the manor and the vicar, and the contract for the tower of Helmingham will be discussed shortly.[2] Typically, the most senior social position named on a contracting committee was 'gentleman', as at Surfleet, Lincolnshire, in 1420; Wycombe, Buckinghamshire, in 1509; Great Sherston, Wiltshire, in 1511; and St Mary the Great, Cambridge, in 1520.[3] The aristocracy appear most commonly as the sole contractees for private building projects on parish churches: at Southchurch, Essex, in 1293, Etchingham, East Sussex, in 1363, St Dunstan, London, in 1381, Hornby, Yorkshire, in 1410, Catterick, Yorkshire, in 1412, St Mary-on-the-Hill, Chester, in 1433, Fotheringhay, Northamptonshire, in 1434, Broxbourne, Hertfordshire, in 1476, and Biddenham, Bedfordshire, in 1522.[4] Although many were gentry, these nine form a usefully broad cross-section from nobility such as the duke of York or Lord Cobham to a former Lord Mayor of London, and from villages to major cities, with a telling dearth in the middle decades of the fifteenth century.[5] Roughly the same proportion of surviving urban and rural parish building contracts have aristocratic contractees (40 and 37 per cent, respectively). The contracts usually reveal little as to how the work was run and only suggest who would pay for it, but they do demonstrate that, like the examples surveyed in the previous chapter, responsibilities were typically retained and would need to be executed directly or delegated.

When the work was commissioned by a lord of many manors, personal interest in design and financing may be assumed, but it is most unlikely that he personally executed the tasks that were not contracted out. Just

---

[2] See Chapter 4, section b.ii, pp. 178–80. BCM/A/1/11/39; 445.
[3] Salzman, *Building in England*, 496, 557–59, 561, 466–67; an interesting example outside of England can be found at Edinburgh in 1387, when the lord of Nether Liberton and the town's provost are the only contractees named, the others are 'the community of that ilk' Richard Fawcett, *Scottish Medieval Churches: Architecture & Furnishings* (Stroud, 2002), 333; Richard Fawcett, *The Architecture of the Scottish Medieval Church, 1100–1560* (New Haven, 2011), 214.
[4] Citations will be given when each church is treated in turn.
[5] Introduction, section d, pp. 39–45.

like a contracting committee, he could delegate to an existing official or appoint a fabric warden with the requisite expertise and time to oversee the work on his behalf. Such a strategy was employed by William Troutbeck, lord of four manors and of significant other lands by the time of his death, when he contracted for the south chancel chapel at St Mary-on-the-Hill, Chester, in 1433.[6] The language would seem to suggest direct involvement: William will pay the mason, Thomas Betes, and provide materials, scaffolding, a windlass and 'such manner [of] necessaries'.[7] Both parties appended their seals to the contract. However, in this case the work was to be under 'the oversight' of John Asser, Master Mason of the counties of Chester and Flint with North Wales, c. 1433–46. Troutbeck was probably able to commission Asser's help through his posts as chamberlain of Chester (1412–39) and chancellor of the duchy of Lancaster (1423–39).[8] Possibly Asser's position was too senior to serve as fabric warden; the contract gives him oversight of making the chapel 'and all things that belong thereto, honestly', suggesting he provided quality control rather than logistical support.[9]

When Richard, duke of York, rebuilt the parochial nave of Fotheringhay College, Northamptonshire, in 1434 (Figure 5.1), he deputed the work to William Wolston and Thomas Pecham ('*commissarii*').[10] Wolston was lord of Wollaston, some twenty miles south of Fotheringhay, which he inherited in 1430,[11] and he owned a large fee in Elton, Huntingdonshire, about a mile east (c. 1429–47).[12] He was not only local, but he would also act as an agent of the duke's on several occasions over the next few years: in 1436 he received a payment at the exchequer of more than £8,000,[13] was rewarded

---

[6] John Parsons Earwaker, *The History of the Church and Parish of St. Mary-on-the-Hill, Chester* (London, 1898); F. H. Crossley, *Cheshire* (London, 1949), 175; F. H. Crossley, *Journal of the Chester and North Wales Architectural, Archaeological, and Historic Society*, 34, no. 2 (1940), 158; George Ormerod, *The History of the County Palatine and City of Chester*, 2nd ed., vol. 1 (London, 1882), 87–88; Harvey, *English Mediaeval Architects*, 9; John Harvey, 'The Architects of English Parish Churches', *The Archaeological Journal* CV (1948): 20; W. H. Rylands, '[No Title]', *Ars Quatuor Coronatorum* VI (1893): 188.

[7] Salzman, *Building England*, 503.

[8] Dorothy J. Clayton, *The Administration of the County Palatine of Chester: 1442–1485* (Manchester, 1990), 163.

[9] Salzman, *Building England*, 503.

[10] William Dugdale, *Monasticon Anglicanum*, vol. 6, part 1 (London, 1830), 1414; John Henry Parker, *Some Remarks upon the Church of Fotheringhay* (Oxford, 1841); H. K. Bonney, *Historic Notices in Reference to Fotheringhay* (Oundle, 1821), 41; A. Hamilton Thompson, 'The Statutes of the College of St Mary and All Saints, Fotheringhay', *The Archaeological Journal* 75 (1918): 246–47.

[11] L. F. Salzman, ed., *VCH Northamptonshire*, vol. 4 (London, 1937), 57–62; *Inquisitions and Assessments Relating to Feudal Aids, Northampton to Somerset*, vol. IV (London, 1906), 45, 52; cf. *Calendar of the Close Rolls of Henry VI, 1422–1429*, vol. 1 (London, 1933), 203.

[12] William Page, Granville Proby, and S. Inskipp Ladds, eds., *VCH Huntingdonshire*, vol. 3 (London, 1936), 154–66.

[13] TNA: PRO E403/724; Frederick Devon, ed., *Issues of the Exchequer: Being a Collection of Payments Made out of His Majesty's Revenue, from King Henry III to King Henry VI Inclusive* (London, 1837), 429.

Aristocratic Projects

Figure 5.1 Fotheringhay nave and tower (© Jonathan Ward)

with land that year[14] and was in the duke's retinue in 1441.[15] Previously to the building work, in 1419, he had been a royal tax collector for Northamptonshire.[16] Whether Wolston had already worked for the duke by 1434, or if he was taken on specifically for this job, is unknown, but he was both conveniently situated and evidently proved himself competent. Wolston may already have had a link with the college: his successor and probable son-in-law, and his descendants, were buried there.[17] As for Pecham, he was made master of Fotheringhay in 1434.[18] Comparisons with non-parochial work can be made, as for the building of Kirby Muxloe Castle (1480–84), where the fabric officer was Roger Bowlott, Lord Hasting's local agent, who kept the accounts with an assistant.[19] The contractees at Fotheringhay reserved a large number of responsibilities: they

[14] TNA: PRO CP 25/1/292/68, no. 186; Emanuel Green, *Pedes Finium, Commonly Called Feet of Fines, for the County of Somerset, Henry IV to Henry VI* (London, 1906), no. 186.
[15] Percy H. Reaney and Marc Fitch, *Feet of Fines for Essex 1423–1547*, vol. IV, Essex Archaeological Society at the Museum in the Castle (Colchester: Leopard's Head Press, 1899), 23; TNA: PRO E101/53/33; P. A. Johnson, *Duke Richard of York, 1411–1460*, Oxford Historical Monographs (Oxford: Clarendon Press, 1988), 241.
[16] *Calendar of the Fine Rolls: Henry V, 1413–1422*, vol. 14 (London, 1934), 299.
[17] TNA: PRO PROB 11/29/411.
[18] A. Hamilton Thompson, *Visitations of Religious Houses in the Diocese of Lincoln*, vol. 1 (London, 1915), 101; Serjeantson and Adkins, *VCH Northamptonshire*, 2:170–77.
[19] Knoop and Jones, *Mediaeval Mason*, 42–43.

were to provide materials, equipment and transport (and 'all manner of stuff'), appoint labourers (subject to approval by the mason), determine the number of men to be employed at any point and pay £300 in instalments (mostly by the foot).[20] It is likely that Wolston supervised these responsibilities, although neither who 'shall be ordained to have the governance and oversight of the said work' nor who was to be 'clerk of the work' was defined. It is possible that Wolston and Pecham further deputed the work to a college or manorial official. The new nave was certainly substantial enough to require a larger staff to manage it than Wolston, or Pecham, alone. There is no evidence of the duke's involvement, other than his providing the funding, but the exceptional detail given in the contract might display a desire to centralise control over decision-making in a project that would otherwise be handled by a deputy.

Such delegation was no doubt common, but no other contract demonstrates it. In 1381, John, Lord Cobham, commissioned designs from Henry Yevele for the south aisle, porch and buttresses of St Dunstan near to his London house.[21] The contractor, Nicholas Typerton, was only to dig the foundations for the work, but the entire project was contracted out, with Typerton providing materials, transport and 'all things which pertain to the said work'.[22] He was to be paid five marks at the start of work, followed by four further installations of the same amount 'from time to time'.[23] There is no information as to who was to pay Typerton or to assess whether the work was 'good and sufficient', but it is implausible that such tasks were to be carried out by Cobham himself, who was also building Cobham College, Chrishall, Rochester Bridge and Cooling Castle, probably also to designs by Yevele.[24] Nevertheless, it was Cobham who set his seal to the contract. An unnamed officer, probably connected with Cobham's London residence, would presumably be left in charge as fabric warden. Similarly Sir John Say, the royal officer and lord of twenty-two manors by the time of his death,[25] contracted out the building of the south chancel chapel of Broxbourne, Hertfordshire, in 1476.[26] He certainly had a personal interest in the work: he wished to be

---

[20] Salzman, *Building in England*, 505–09.
[21] BL Harl. Ch. 48. E. 43; Rosamund Allen, 'Cobham, John, Third Baron Cobham of Cobham (c.1320–1408)', in *Oxford Dictionary of National Biography* (Oxford, 2004); Thomas Boyles Murray, *Chronicles of a City Church, an Account of the Parish Church of St. Dunstan in the East* (London, 1859), 10–11; John Harvey, *Henry Yevele C. 1320–1400: The Life of an English Architect* (London, 1944), 39; Salzman, *Building in England*, 462–63; Christopher Hussey, 'Cobham, Kent', *Country Life* 95 (4 February 1944): 200–203.
[22] 'toutz choses q' apertent al dit ouerayne'.   [23] 'de temps en temps'.
[24] 'bon et suffisaunt'; Saul, *Death, Art, and Memory*, 234–35, 48–49.
[25] J. L. Kirby, 'Say, Sir John (D. 1478)', in *Oxford Dictionary of National Biography* (Oxford, 2004).
[26] TNA: PRO E 210/2638; Salzman, *Building in England*, 537–38.

buried there beside Elizabeth, his late first wife (their brasses there survive), and he took advice from a marbler as to the height of the tomb.[27] It is unlikely that he would personally have seen to the provision of materials, scaffolding and transport in order that the mason 'be not let of his workmanship at no time'. However, no overseer, warden or architect is mentioned. Examples of institutions that ran work through a bailiff, steward or other official will be given shortly, and it is plausible that nobles may have done similarly.

When the contractee was a local figure, however, personal involvement was not only convenient and reliable but also cheap. For the parish gentry, there were fewer officials to choose from; fewer still, given that their choice would need to be honest, available and competent – and affordable.[28] Many gentry themselves probably had the necessary skill-set from running their household and lands. Some, including wives or widows, were versed in technical aspects of construction: in 1444, Agnes Paston disputed about the number, length, breadth and thickness of the chapel joists at Paston Hall in Norfolk, giving Stansted Church as an example.[29] There are several examples of local lords contracting for work and retaining responsibility for transport or materials. John Conyers married into the lordship of Hornby, where he contracted for a new south aisle in 1410.[30] For this, he was to provide a fother of lead and its carriage. The language suggests that John himself would pay the mason (unusually, 'at times and days to the foresaid Richard [the mason, finds] agreeable') and organise the materials. Indeed, without a large manorial staff to choose officials from, and with a vested interest in reducing costs, monitoring progress and providing local patronage, it may have been unnecessary to appoint anyone else to carry out these duties. The responsibilities taken by the gentry could be significantly more onerous, however. Two years later and twelve miles to the southwest, at Catterick, Yorkshire, Katherine Burgh and her son William, whose grandfather had married into the manor of Brough, contracted with the same mason for a new church.[31] William's burial in the north aisle with his father and son is recorded on the reverse of the contract. The Burghs agreed to provide carriage, materials and scaffolding 'at their own cost'.[32] The earliest

---

[27] TNA: PRO C 140/67/43; TNA: PRO PROB 11/6/459.
[28] Cf. Chapter 2, section d. pp. 122–27; Carpenter, *Locality and Polity*, Chapter 5; P. W. Fleming, 'Charity Faith and the Gentry of Kent', in *Property and Politics: Essays in Later Medieval English History*, ed. Tony Pollard (Gloucester, 1984), 36–58.
[29] Norman Davis, *Paston Letters and Papers of the Fifteenth Century* (Oxford, 2005), 27, cf. 246.
[30] H. B. McCall, *Richmondshire Churches* (London, 1910), 62; Salzman, *Building in England*, 482–83.
[31] William Page, ed., *VCH Yorkshire North Riding*, vol. 1 (London, 1914), 301–13; Salzman, *Building in England*, 487–90; James Raine, *Catterick Church* (London, 1834), 22.
[32] Salzman, *Building in England*, 487–90.

example among these gentry contracts is also one of the most onerous: in 1293, at the Essex village of Southchurch, Sir Peter de Southchurch was to provide the materials and transport them to the place where the chapel was to be built in the churchyard.[33] He was also to make a watercourse. The family was wealthy, with some 900 acres of land, but it is plausible that Peter took over some of these responsibilities himself.[34] The building was either never constructed or has been destroyed.

One unavoidable cause of delegation was death. Many testators, both within and outside the aristocracy, asked their executors to carry out or finish building work, a heavy burden to add to the administrative costs of executing a will.[35] In 1527, John Rooper asked for the windows at St John's Hospital, Canterbury, to be designed 'with such imagery or pictures as I shall show to my executors'[36] and, in 1508, Benett Webbys, mayor of and MP for Sandwich, allowed for as much money as was required to finish work he had begun on the churchyard walls there, limited only 'by the discretion of my executors'.[37] Sir Nicholas Norpice asked that his chantry chapel in Hawkhurst, Kent, where he was chaplain, be finished 'according unto such covenants and bargains as is between Edmond Robert and Russell' in 1513.[38] Robert was the executor of the will, probably a 'clerk of the choir', and may already have been acting as fabric warden.[39] Some details of such a contract in the Reformation period, made between the four executors of Jacot Coffyn and the mason Robert Terell, survive for a 'ambulatory gild or chapell' at Heanton Punchardon, in Devon, in 1538–44, which forms the north aisle.[40] Many testators requested that their wife starts or completes work, presumably with money from the estate, and such provisions probably offered the majority of opportunities for laywomen to run building work.[41] Sir Thomas Danvers, a member of parliament and lord of

---

[33] CCA-DCc-ChAnt/S/38, Byng, *Southchurch*, 138–39.
[34] William Pollitt, *Southchurch and Its Past* (Southend, 1949), 23–25.
[35] See the lengths that the testators went to in commissioning a tomb for Sir John Dallingridge from 1416, eight years after his death: Nigel Saul, Jonathan Mackman, and Christopher Whittick, 'Grave Stuff: Litigation with a London Tomb-Maker in 1421', *Historical Research* 84, no. 226 (1 November 2011): 572–85.
[36] Nicolas, *Testamenta Vetusta*, 1826, 2:629.   [37] Ibid., 2:492.
[38] Hussey, *Testamenta Cantiana (East)*, 156. This is probably the north chapel.
[39] W. J. Lightfoot, 'Notes from the Records of Hawkhurst Church', *Archaeologia Cantiana* 5 (1863): 79.
[40] TNA: PRO C 1/1074/18. Richard Coffin (d. 1523), lord of Alwington and sheriff of Devon, is buried in the chancel.
[41] Kathryn Kelsey Staples, *Daughters of London: Inheriting Opportunity in the Late Middle Ages* (Leiden, 2011), 18; Caroline Barron, *Medieval London Widows, 1300–1500* (London, 2003), 65; note that others desired arrangements such as 'at the discrescion of Margaret my wyff & of the church master', as in the will of Thomas Anderson in Coningsby, Lincolnshire, 1530: C. W. Foster, *Lincoln Wills: 1530–1532*, vol. 3 (London, 1930), 4.

Aristocratic Projects

Waterstoke in Oxfordshire, asked in 1502 that the chancel be finished as he had 'begun and as my wife know my mind'.[42] Even more explicitly, John Wyke, who married into the manor of Yeovilton, ordered the building of the south aisle at Nynehead, Somerset, in 1410 'according to the supervision and direction of my wife', who was also his executor, but left just £10 for it.[43] The rest was presumably to come from his wife's inheritance, unless the parishioners were expected to make up the shortfall.[44]

Few single-handed contracts survive from wealthy men outside the aristocracy. Their poor survival rate may be due to the higher proportion of oral contracts used by such people. In Croscombe, Somerset, for example, Richard Maudeley, a 'clothman' used an oral contract to hire a carpenter, Robert Kerver, to build a new rood loft, but Kerver subsequently failed to carry out the work and a case was brought to chancery.[45] A late example also survives for an 'ambulatory' at Exbourne, Devon, by a wealthy local, Richard Downe.[46] However, one written contract does survive: John Edwards, a mercer, paid for a roof at the now lost St-John-atte-Hill, Bury St Edmunds, in 1439.[47] Edwards was to make ready the walls of the chapel 'to receive it'; otherwise the carpenter, John Heywood, was to construct the roof at his own cost. The level of detail in the dimensions of the roof (principals and rafters are defined in inches) shows that Edwards understood well what he was requesting. Perhaps he had experience as a churchwarden, or Heywood or another carpenter advised him. It suggests anyway that Edwards would be personally involved in the execution of the work. That members of the gentry and wealthy locals could run building work themselves, as is indicated by the contracts surveyed in this section, can be shown with the only surviving set of private fabric accounts, those for the new tower of Bolney in Sussex.

ii) The Bolney Accounts

If they did choose to run building work directly, wise lords, like fabric wardens, would keep accounts to monitor expenditure, assess progress

---

[42] Danvers had a papal licence to have a portable altar; J. R. H Weaver, ed., *Some Oxfordshire Wills, 1393–1510* (Oxford, 1958), 75; Francis Nottidge Macnamara, *Memorials of the Danvers Family* (London, 1895), 165, 223; M. D. Lobel, ed., *VCH Oxfordshire*, vol. 7 (London, 1962), 220–30. Cf. the will of his wife, Sybil.
[43] '*secundum visum et ordinacionem uxoris mee*'.
[44] TNA: PROB 11/2A/361; Weaver, *Somerset Wills*, 1:43. He also held half the manor of Lillesdon.
[45] French, *People*, 54; Hobhouse, *Church-Wardens' Accounts*, 56–57.
[46] In 1558–79. TNA: PRO C 3/138/92; Stoate, *Lay Subsidy*, 1986, 106.
[47] BL Add. MS 14848, f. 304; G. M. Hill, 'The Antiquities of Bury St Edmund', *Journal of the British Archaeological Association* 21 (1865): 118; Salzman, *Building in England*, 512–13.

and assure other contributors to the work that their money was being well spent. Even a poverty-stricken parishioner in London kept accounts (a 'bill of parcelles') for work on his house in 1527.[48] The only surviving private fabric accounts for parochial work are for the construction of a new church tower in the Sussex village of Bolney, in 1536–37 (Figures 5.2 and 5.3).[49] Their author was the lord of the manor, John Bolney. Unlike most surviving accounts, including the Bolney churchwardens' accounts, which are usually fair copies made for the annual audit, John's are the rough, weekly, working accounts. He appears to have kept them himself, using the first-person singular, writing 'I, John Bolney' or 'for my part, John Bolney'. Occasionally the legibility of his writing deteriorates so much that it is unlikely that a clerk was responsible and doubtful that they could be examined at audit. Nevertheless, the accounts were signed off on one occasion: by John Smith, Richard Felder, 'Flusstger' and 'the fryer'.[50] The auditors were probably all local men and presumably chosen because they were of some standing: Smith may have been churchwarden, and 'Flusstger' is probably George Fluster who was paid for 'driving of the steeple', and was assessed at more than £2 in 1524.[51] The identity of the friar is lost, but mendicant houses at Lewes, Shoreham and Arundel were not far away.[52] Given that most of the men were signing off the accounts of their lord, whose account book was often poorly kept, it may be doubted quite how independent their judgement really was.

John Bolney was from a long-established minor gentry family in the parish. They had possessed the parish's only manor since the thirteenth century, although not the church's advowson, which was included in a prebend at Chichester Cathedral. Several of John's ancestors had attended Winchester College, New College, Oxford, or the Inner Temple and may have become lawyers or administrators. John had inherited the manor at age fifteen when his father, Richard, died in 1500, and John was buried at Bolney in November 1557.[53] When he began building work John was fifty-one years old and was making a concerted effort to improve his family's standing, adding a crest to their arms and carrying out

---

[48] Littlehales, *London City Church*, 342.
[49] WSRO Par 252/9/1; Dale, 'Bolney CWAs'; Byng, 'Bolney'; Knoop and Jones could find no examples before the Elizabethan age: Knoop and Jones, *Mediaeval Mason*, 43.
[50] A Richard Fylder was buried in the parish in 1558: Edward Huth, ed., *The Parish Registers of Bolney, Sussex: 1541–1812* (London, 1912), 5, 64.
[51] Cornwall, *Lay Subsidy*, 89.
[52] William Page, ed., *VCH Sussex*, vol. 2 (London, 1973), 97, 93–94.
[53] For the history and identification of John Bolney, see Byng, 'Bolney', 107–09; cf. Marie Clough, *The Book of Bartholomew Bolney* (Lewes, 1964), xxxiii; L. F. Salzman, ed., *VCH Sussex*, vol. 7 (London, 1940), 136–40.

Figure 5.2   The west doorway of Bolney (© Gabriel Byng)

Organising Construction III

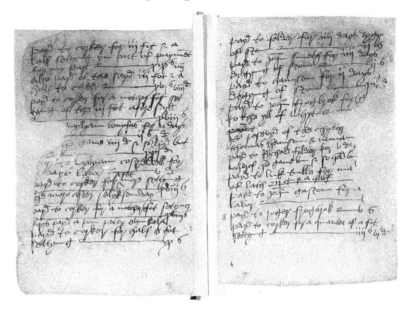

Figure 5.3 Bolney fabric accounts, Par 252-9-1 #09 ff. 5v–6r (© Sussex Record Office)

building work on his house, Blasse Place.[54] He sold a small amount of land in West Firle in 1530 and 1532, possibly to fund the tower.[55]

The accounts demonstrate the demanding involvement required of project managers and show Bolney sharing responsibilities with the parish and churchwardens. Most importantly, he divided financial and organisational responsibility with 'the parish', which 'covenanted' with a carpenter while Bolney oversaw the stonework. He even shared some tasks concerning the masonry with senior parishioners, including the churchwardens, who paid masons directly and ran ales and collections for the work, handing the profits to Bolney.[56] A churchwarden also arranged lodgings for two masons. Another parishioner visited the Isle of Wight for reasons unknown, but perhaps to purchase stone. Cooperation between parish and lord in organising the work may have been encouraged by the creation of opportunities for employment and good works. The stone was sourced locally and extracted directly, while of twenty-seven workers were named in the accounts, eleven share their surname with taxpayers in the 1524–25

---

[54] Robert Garraway Rice, *Transcripts of Sussex Wills*, ed. Walter Hindes Godfrey, vol. 1 (Lewes, 1935), 164.
[55] Clough, *Bartholomew Bolney*, xxvii. [56] See Chapter 2, section c, pp. 121–22.

224

Aristocratic Projects

lay subsidy returns for Wyndham, which included Bolney, and twenty-four can be found in nearby vills.[57] Twenty parishioners with surnames like those of workmen in Bolney's accounts appear in the parish registers, which began in 1541.[58] Those workers not included in the subsidy rolls or parish register were probably too poor to be recorded in the former, or were dead by the time of the latter. Although the master carpenter, Roger Frogbrok, was local, Bolney chose a master mason from Southover, Thomas Puckle,[59] who worked on other important commissions in Sussex in the 1530s: at the Cluniac Priory in Southover[60] and at Camber Castle.[61] Puckle sent two of his craftsmen, John Corker and William Holmes, to oversee the work.[62]

The relationship between Bolney, his building work and other governing bodies within the parish, particularly the churchwardens, is not explicit in the accounts. It is not recorded, for example, why the churchwardens donated to the work nor whether the auditors were parish masters. Bolney noted that 'the parish' had contracted for timberwork but he gives no information as to who had acted in its name – whether churchwardens or a contracting committee. Nevertheless, the auditors constituted a form of independent oversight by local leaders of a gentry-led project and it is possible that the audit was a condition for financial and organisational support. There is no evidence that Bolney himself was directly involved in the official management of the parish. Taxation records and collections for the clerk's wages show that the churchwardens, entirely typically, were drawn from the middling ranks of the village.[63] Their relationship to the building work is also obscure. On two occasions Bolney notes transactions of interest to the churchwardens alone and unrelated to the building work. One records money that 'William Langford and Thomas Garland hath delivered in to the hands of the parishioners', and the other notes a sum held by the wardens 'which they gathered for the hognel time'.[64] The first uses a formula familiar from parish audits, while the second would appear to be a simple record of fact, but its purpose is unclear. Possibly these were memoranda, used to calculate what contribution Bolney could expect from the wardens (the Hognel warden would, indeed, donate a considerable sum to the work). He also recorded a set of purchases apparently unconnected to the building work and which in most parishes would have been made by the churchwardens: a cord for the Lent cloth, tapers, wax and visitation

---

[57] Cornwall, *Lay Subsidy*, 89–90. [58] Huth, *Bolney*.
[59] ESRO PAR 413/12/1 f. 13v; Cornwall, *Lay Subsidy*, 96; R. F. Hunnisett, *Sussex Coroners' Inquests, 1485–1558* (Lewes, 1985), para. 76.
[60] Colin E. Brent, *Pre-Georgian Lewes c. 890–1714* (Lewes, 2004), 284.
[61] Harvey, *English Mediaeval Architects*, 8.
[62] Howard Colvin, ed., *The History of the King's Works*, vol. 4 (London, 1963), 423, n. 1.
[63] Cornwall, *Lay Subsidy*, 89–90; cf. Rice, *Sussex Wills*, 1:163.
[64] Dale, 'Bolney CWAs', 248, 247.

payments. Bolney may have been helping to defray the wardens' usual expenses during a period of intensive fundraising for the tower. More plausibly, however, the purchases were related to the consecration of the tower, which took place during Lent.

The impression given by the accounts is not only of a high level of collaboration in a 'gentry' building project, involving a large number of parishioners and parochial bodies, but also of cooperation that was so varied that it could touch almost every aspect of the project. Bolney may have been chief donor and project manager but he shared both responsibilities with other parishioners. Most significantly the parish handled the contracting for the timberwork itself and four men even signed off his accounts. Even if this was a rubber-stamping exercise it suggests that the parish was able to act with some autonomy and to demand accountability from its lord. Without these unique surviving accounts, the tower would appear to be an act of single-handed patronage: the arms of John Bolney alone were inscribed into the fabric of the building.

iii) The Contracts at Helmingham and Biddenham

Just two contracts provide good evidence for the nature of cooperation between the gentry and the parish: those of Biddenham and Helmingham. The latter, for the tower of the church of St Mary in 1488, is more obscure and will be dealt with first (Figure 5.4). The four men that made up the contracting committee were noted in the previous chapter.[65] They were to 'pay or do to be paid' to the mason 10s per foot for a sixty-foot tower – an implausibly modest total of just £30 for a large and finely crafted building.[66] However, the contract also requests that the mason 'discharge' the contractees of £300, 'the which sum [he] is accorded and agreed to receive as he does his work', from five other parishioners – John Tollemache and Elizabeth his wife, Edmund Joyce, John Wyllie the elder and William Holm. The most plausible explanation is that the total cost of the tower was to be £300, with the £30 paid either in addition to that sum or to be subtracted from it. Salzman's suggestion that the group of five may have been employing the mason to build other parts of the church is possible but would not explain why the cost but not the specification for these additions is included in the contract, nor why the tower was so inexpensive.[67] No other contract uses this arrangement.

---

[65] Chapter 4, section b.ii, p. 181.
[66] This is probably the source of Roundell's claim that the tower was built by Lionel Tollemache, John's heir, for £30, sometime before 1512: Charles Roundell, 'Tollemaches of Helmingham', *Suffolk Institute of Archaeology Proceedings* xii (1904): 100–101.
[67] Salzman, *Building in England*, 549 n. 1.

Figure 5.4 Helmingham tower (© Gabriel Byng)

Organising Construction III

The leading role of Tollemache is suggested by the inscription around the doorway, destroyed by Dowsing, which probably read: 'pray for the soul of John Tollemache'.[68] John had married Elizabeth, his second wife and widow of William Joyce, lord of Helmingham, in 1487, so the new tower may have been intended either to mark their union or to emphasise or justify the arrival of the new lord. John and Elizabeth moved to the Joyces' house, Creke Hall, after their marriage, which John's son would rebuild as Helmingham Hall in the 1510s.[69] The font and parapet, dated 1543, were also given by the Tollemaches. However, the contract makes it clear that John was neither the sole funder nor, necessarily, involved in contracting for, or oversight of, the work. For financing, he would apparently rely on two other senior parishioners (Wyllie and Holm) as well as his brother-in-law, Edmund.[70] However, an additional note on the dorse of the contract records that the mason was to use expensive black flint and freestone on the exterior alone 'for the most avail and best to be saved for the profit of the township of Helmingham', suggesting that some funds at least had come from communal collections.[71] Indeed, money had been left towards the bells by one parishioner in 1461, which indicates a long period of stockpiling funds.[72] It is likely, therefore, that parish funds were to be funnelled through Holm and Wyllie, the only members of the group of five who were not relatives of the Tollemaches – it may even be that they were churchwardens. The four members of the contracting committee were thus to oversee the contracting, and possibly the construction, of the church, as deputies of a project co-financed by the manorial lord and the parish. The latter had probably insisted on their representation on the contracting committee. Why else would a manorial lord consent to having four men lead the contracting process on his behalf? As we have seen, many others were quite content to do it themselves. Like Bolney, John Tollemache would be recorded in the fabric of the work and he probably donated considerable sums to the tower, but his role in the contracting process at least was considerably less than Bolney's.

A very different model of cooperation again is provided by the contract for the north aisle at Biddenham, Bedfordshire, in 1522 (Figure 5.5).[73] The contract is between Sir William Butler (d. 1534), a member of the Grocers'

---

[68] James Bettley and Nikolaus Pevsner, *Suffolk: East* (New Haven, 2015), 271–77.
[69] For the history of the family see Edward Devereux Hamilton Tollemache, *The Tollemaches of Helmingham and Ham* (Ipswich, 1949), 32–33.
[70] John's eldest son Lionel (who built the tower's parapet) would marry Edmund's daughter, securing the family's position as lords of the manor.
[71] Salzman, *Building in England*, 547–49.   [72] Tollemache, *Tollemaches*, 33.
[73] TNA: PRO E41/318; an extended treatment can be found in Byng, 'Biddenham'.

Figure 5.5   Biddenham north aisle (© Gabriel Byng)

Company, who had risen through the ranks from Alderman of Cheap Ward and Sheriff (1507), to Auditor (1514–15) and Mayor of London (1515–16),[74] and John Laverok (d. 1533), a mason from St Albans, and Thomas Somde, a member of the Stock Fishmongers' Company and possibly the link between Butler and Laverok.[75] The Butlers had been resident in Biddenham since the early fourteenth century but Sir William's father had married into a gentry family and inherited further property in the parish.[76] The family would subsequently acquire the manor in 1540, after the dissolution of Denny Abbey.[77] Sir William probably built the aisle both to accommodate the chantry he founded in his will and to provide a family burial aisle. His son would indeed be buried there, although his grandson and great-granddaughter were not.[78]

Butler and Somde are the only named contractees, and only Butler and his executors are bound for the cost of the work, a total of £26. However, the contract also includes extensive agreements about the role that the

---

[74] TNA: PRO PROB 11/25/123; BLA Trevor-Wingfield Collection.   [75] HALS 2AR225.
[76] Page, *VCH Bedfordshire*, 1912, 3:36–40; Frederic Augustus Blaydes, *The Visitations of Bedfordshire* (London, 1884), 6.
[77] R. H. Brodie and James Gairdner, eds., *Letters and Papers, Foreign and Domestic, of the Reign of Henry VIII*, vol. 15 (London, 1896), 166, 179.
[78] TNA: PRO PROB 11/37/155.

parish was to play in the project. Sir William 'promises and grants' that the stone will be carried from the quarry to a place chosen by Laverok, 'and for the workmanship of the same [to be] at the cost, charge and expense of the parishioners and other the inhabitants of the said parish'. The contract continues: 'that the old wall now standing . . . shall be taken down at the cost and charge and expense of the said parishioners'.[79] It is likely, in this context, that 'at the cost, charge and expense' indicated an organisational as much as a financial responsibility – that the parishioners were to see that any and all arrangements necessary were made. This was made more explicit later in the contract when a third clause required that the parishioners 'find or cause to be found and ready to be laid and carried . . . rough stone, lime, sand, timber and other things necessary for mason's work'.[80] A fourth requirement indicates another way in which the parishioners were to be involved, contributing not only to the financing and logistics of the aisle but to its design also. The height of the aisle was to be determined 'by the discretion of the said John Laverok and other [of] the discreet parishioners of the said parish'.[81] This may have represented a check by the parishioners on Sir William's project, in order to ensure that the new work should be in keeping with the old, or, more plausibly, the recognition by Sir William that knowledgeable parishioners possessed skills that he did not and would ensure that Laverok did not make the roof too low in order to cut costs.

The contract suggests a highly involved patron who has managed to defray the financial and organisational burden of his project by passing some, very costly, elements of it on to other parishioners. Although their involvement was to be varied and onerous, it would also be limited and they do not appear as co-contractees, as is the case at Helmingham. There is no indication that 'the parishioners' or their representatives were present at the contract's drafting. The overriding impression is that Sir William and Lavarok, and probably Somde, were the only ones present at the drafting and led the design and commissioning process. In this case, Sir William had presumably already agreed with the parishioners that they would take on some tedious and expensive tasks in a project that was undoubtedly his. They would benefit from an enlarged church but it would be his chantry and burial aisle. Indeed, the requirement that a 'discreet parishioner' would judge the height of the aisle suggests the tight limit that would be placed on their involvement in the development of its design and the kind of senior parishioner with whom Sir William was willing to do business. It is not implausible that some coercion was involved, given the expense of the tasks taken on by the parishioners

---

[79] Byng, 'Biddenham', 262–63.   [80] Ibid.   [81] Ibid.

and their absence from the writing of the contract. There is also no indication as to who 'the parishioners' were or who had been entitled to make the agreement on their behalf. Would the whole of the parish be involved, under the leadership of a few men who had negotiated with Sir William? Or were 'the parishioners' best understood as 'the masters' or male householders?

The contract is a rough draft over three folios, with many corrections and annotations, made part-way through the negotiations that would lead to a neatly copied indenture (the form of most surviving contracts), and it suggests that the negotiating procedure involving Sir William, Laverok and the parishioners was complex. The changes are mixed in type but most were undoubtedly meant to clarify the text or correct grammatical errors. However, some more significant alterations occur: for example, a note adds 'timber for scaffold and other things' to rough stone, lime and sand in a list of materials that the parishioners were to pay for.[82] The most substantial addition was the entry for the roof, given in a marginal annotation to the text. This allows the drafting process to be reconstructed: the text was written out in full, presumably on the basis of preliminary discussions, and formed the starting point for further negotiations between Butler and the parishioners, during which responsibility for the roof and timber were agreed. This process could have taken place over some time, even days, allowing Sir William to meet the parishioners and persuade them to take on the scaffolding timber; that is, if they were not present at the meeting with Laverok. Once all the parties had agreed to the changes, they were added to the draft as notes. At some point the wording of the contract was also examined in detail, perhaps with the help of a clerk or other literate parishioner, and ambiguities or grammatical errors rectified on the paper version. Lastly the draft would be copied out twice, cut in two and sealed.

c) CLERICAL AND INSTITUTIONAL PROJECTS

i) *The Clergy*

Secular lords and gentry were not the only people to run building work. Only two examples survive of priests sitting on contracting committees: at Arlingham, Gloucestershire, where every man of consequence in the village seems to have been included, and probably at Surfleet, Lincolnshire, where a priest took legal action along with a parishioner over unfinished work. It is possible that the priest was named as a plaintiff solely because his status was useful to his fellow plaintiff. However,

---

[82] Ibid.

architectural contracts by rectors do survive, as for example for a new chancel ceiling, reredos and altar, with a window and doors, described by Salzman as an 'enclosed chapel', at Tempsford, Bedfordshire, in 1512.[83] The living was a rectory throughout the middle ages, worth almost £29, minus £4 for the pension of the prior of St Neots.[84] The entire work was contracted out and it was agreed that the carpenter 'shall find all manner [of] stuff and workmanship thereto ... So that [the contractee] shall be at no manner [of] cost nor charge [for any] other [manner] of stuff nor of workmanship'. The incumbent did not always contract out the entire work, however. The vicar at Hackington, John Rowe, was the sole contractee for a new rood in 1519.[85] It was to be paid for 'at the proper costs and charges of the said Michael [Boneversall, the carpenter]', who was to provide the materials, but John would pay for transport. The total cost was £17 plus 20s a foot, a substantial sum given that the vicarage was valued at only £6 in the *Valor Ecclesiasticus*. Rowe would have needed to use his private wealth and, indeed, he left a substantial obit in the parish.[86] It is plausible that Rowe oversaw the transport himself but the contract is not explicit. Wills indicate other ways in which clergy could cooperate with the laity; as when the rector of Yeovil, Somerset, Robert Samborne (d. 1382), left most of his goods to fund the completion of the church's rebuilding. This does seem to have taken place, despite his history of disputes with the town.[87] The total quantity of clergy contracts is modest but they are represented in a far greater proportion of rural than urban examples (25 and 7 per cent, respectively), pointing perhaps to the strength and independence of civic institutions in urban parishes, although the sample size is small and probably unrepresentative.

No equivalent to the Bolney accounts survives for a priest but this could be due to evidential losses over time. The personal accounts of a few parsons survive, and suggest that they would have been just as capable of running fabric accounts as churchwardens or lords like John Bolney.[88] Nevertheless, the documentary record of the role of clergy in cooperative parochial building work is relatively small – they feature only intermittently in fabric wardens' or churchwardens' accounts (except occasionally as auditors, working with or as a master of the parish, or even writing the accounts themselves).[89] Their achievement, as Burgess points out, was

---

[83] Salzman, *Building in England*, 563–64.
[84] J. Caley and J. Hunter, eds., *Valor Ecclesiasticus*, vol. 4 (London, 1821), 198; William Page, ed., *VCH Bedfordshire*, vol. 2 (London, 1908), 251–55.
[85] Aymer Vallance, 'R.N., with an Appendix on the Rood Screen', *Archaeologia Cantiana* 44 (1932): 267–68.
[86] A. Hussey, *Kent Obit and Lamp Rents* (Ashford, 1936), 57.   [87] French, *People*, 153–54.
[88] Heath, *Medieval Clerical Accounts*.   [89] Chapter 2, section e, pp. 127–29.

Clerical and Institutional Projects

partly in creating an environment in which donations to church building, or acting as fabric wardens, were understood to be good works.[90] However, as literate, relatively wealthy and high status members of the parish, their help could be practical too. Their experience in running maintenance on the chancel was no doubt useful, and donations to repair work were occasionally made to them.[91] No doubt good accounting by wardens, particularly in rural parishes, often depended on the priest.[92]

Unlike parish gentry, rectors were legally obliged to carry out repair work on the chancel, but few legal agreements, including diocesan statutes, licences for appropriation and institutions of vicarages, encompass new building rather than maintenance.[93] The exception may have been cases of ruin or destruction. Richard Poore's statutes for Salisbury of 1217–19 charge the rector to 'make good the defects of the church' only when it 'is falling down or ruinous'.[94] At St Erth, Cornwall, for example, it was agreed that if 'the chancel should happen to fall into ruins without any blame to the vicar ... then the rebuilding shall fall on the Dean and Chapter [the rector] and the vicar proportionately'.[95] Such demands were enforced by visitations, as at Horton in 1280 where 'the chancel is completely destroyed' and was to be rebuilt.[96] None give any indication of the management of projects, however, and these examples suggest that chancel building was not customarily an obligation of the rectory.

ii) Stewards and Bailiffs

When the manorial lord or the owner of the church was an institution, construction and repair work would need to be delegated either to a temporary warden, as by Lord Cobham and the duke of York, or to a dedicated official. If the institution owned the manor, the obvious choice was the bailiff. The organisation of a large building site would complement the bailiff's duties in overseeing the lands and buildings, collecting fines and rents, and managing the profits and expenses of the manor and farm. He was resident, had an incentive to execute his responsibilities well and was already a trusted employee, avoiding the need to appoint a new officer. One of the most spectacular examples of building work carried out by a bailiff is

---

[90] Burgess, 'Time and Place', 18–19.
[91] E.g. at Brookland, Kent: Hussey, *Testamenta Cantiana (East)*, 38. [92] Duffy, *Morebath*, 19.
[93] Introduction, section b, pp. 22–23. Giles Constable, *Monastic Tithes: From Their Origins to the Twelfth Century* (Cambridge, 1964), 43–44.
[94] Powicke and Cheney, *C&S*, 1964, 1:82 c. 68.
[95] F. C. Hingeston-Randolph, *The Register of John de Grandisson, Bishop of Exeter (1327–1369)*, vol. 2 (London, 1894), 607.
[96] 'cancellum ... funditas est prostratum', F. N. Davis, *The Register of John Pecham, Archbishop of Canterbury, 1279–1292*, vol. 1 (London, 1969), 129.

Organising Construction III

Figure 5.6   Adderbury interior (© A. McRae Thomson)

the new chancel at Adderbury, Oxfordshire (1408–18), run by John Berewyk ('*firmarius*'), who leased the manor's revenues in return for a fixed rent (Figure 5.6). The work was funded by New College, Oxford, which owned the church. The licence for appropriation had passed responsibility for chancel repair work to the college in 1381.[97] Costs were met out of the bailiff's rent, with the remainder going to the college as usual, although there were some small gifts from locals, including free labour from the vicar. This created a simple financial model. Even the magnificent chancel at Adderbury required only 56 per cent of the manorial receipts over the whole period of construction of 1408–19, although occasionally expenditure exceeded Berewyk's rent and the college was forced to pay him sums directly.

The accounting system Berewyk employed was similar to, but more sophisticated than, many of the accounts examined in previous chapters. He kept a section of the accounts entitled 'The New Building' from 1408 and, when building work proper began in 1412–13, he subdivided it into three parts: stone, stores, and implements; wages; and other costs, usually

---

[97] Hobson, *Adderbury*, 82–83; Nicholas Allen, *An English Parish Church: Its History: The Church of St. Mary the Virgin, Adderbury, Oxfordshire* (Adderbury, 2011), chap. 4.

with at least one further section for costs apart from the building work.[98] When work started on the glass in 1415, for example, the glaziers were also entered beneath a separate heading. Nevertheless, entries unconnected with building work often made their way into these sections, just as entries connected with it are found under 'other costs'. In arranging his accounts, the bailiff was, however, merely adapting his usual system, as the nature of the building work changed and new demands were made. He begins with receipts, divided into subsections, each with their total, and overall income, followed by expenses, organised similarly, and the final sum he owes to the college. The range of technical vocabulary and the accuracy of the arithmetic all tend to be good, while the quality of the Latin (with English substitutions for technical vocabulary only) and spelling is better than that of many churchwardens accounts.

Several major units, the east window and roof, were contracted out, but the bailiff was otherwise closely involved in purchasing materials, financing quarrying, transport and equipment and paying wages, drink and board. There are further indications that the bailiff ran the work directly on the site. He kept the weekly paper accounts (sadly lost), which were presented to the college at time of audit to certify his expenditure. He paid two masons, Reed and Saltcombe, for advice and to make journeys to quarries or to Oxford and used a large range of technical terminology. Hobson argues that Berewyk himself compiled the accounts, with help from a college official who calculated the totals due and chose to accept or reject individual entries.[99] However, other officials do appear in the accounts, receiving payment in connection with running the work in 1412–16. William Mownter, a member of the college and vicar of nearby Radclive, was occasionally resident at Adderbury in 1412–13 and 1413–14, and was involved in sourcing and purchasing materials, even keeping his own paper accounts. He may have been the '*contrarotulator operis*' (noted in 1414–15), an officer often appointed for auditing projects on major churches. He started receiving a wage in 1413–14 and the next year, he was repaid for masons' wages. The vicar, John Love, also handled several payments and kept accounts, and was paid for his work as 'supervisor of the works'.[100] John Monk, vicar of Adderbury before 1415, seems to have taken over the role in 1416–17. The timing of the arrival of Mownter points towards the reason for his appointment: building work began in full in 1412–13, absorbing almost the entire year's rent, after four years of stockpiling materials. By 1416–17 building work was reduced and the following year it was finished.

---

[98] '*Novum Edificium*'. [99] Hobson, *Adderbury*, 56.
[100] '*pro suis laboribus diversis habitis circa supervisum operis*', ibid., 16.

Did the college send Mownter to run the building site and make decisions over design and detail, to share the organisational burden with Berewyk, or to run financial oversight? Importantly, Mownter was resident for only relatively short periods (amounting to fifteen to sixteen weeks), while the 'supervisors' changed regularly and were paid relatively small sums (usually 20s a year), indicating that their duties were brief or minor and were perhaps mostly concerned with the production of 'papers' to show at audit. They were probably intended to share the bailiff's managerial and administrative load while affirming his honesty and compliance with the college's wishes, rather than to act as project managers. The college would rely on this oversight to protect its financial interests. It had other means, in addition to delegating to Mownter and other officials, of ensuring that the design was to its liking, of which contracting may have been essential: when the carpenter contracted for the roof, he had to travel to Oxford to sign it. Besides, the college had reason to trust Berewyk: he had already served as bailiff for the manor, had sums allowed him 'for his services and goodwill' and had supervised repair work on the rectory.[101]

The strategies used to keep strong central oversight over building work on a parish church are in evidence again at Hardley, Norfolk, where the Great Hospital, Norwich, rebuilt the chancel in 1456–63. The building accounts here were entered into the manorial steward's accounts. The Hospital contracted out the construction of the roof to a carpenter, John Peper, but seems to have used their regular mason, John Everard, to design the chancel.[102] The sums for which the steward was answerable were small: Francis Woodman suggests no more than £5 per annum, even though manorial receipts were considerable. The steward may have shared the financial burdens (and so perhaps the organisational ones too) with another body. Woodman suggests additional payments to Everard may have come from either the church's wardens or the Hospital's main account, and to this could be added the labourers' wages, which do not appear in the accounts. A contrasting example survives for the building of the new chancel at Harmondsworth, Middlesex, by Winchester College in the 1390s. Winchester had acquired the manor and church as part of Wykeham's endowment for the college in 1391.[103] In this case it was John Gussych, the clerk of the College's Warden, who was sent to

---

[101] Hobson, *Adderbury*, 75.
[102] Francis Woodman, 'Hardley, Norfolk, and the Rebuilding of Its Chancel', in *Studies in Medieval Art and Architecture Presented to Peter Lasko*, ed. David Buckton and T. A. Heslop (Stroud, 1994), 203–10.
[103] The manor was leased out in parcels under a single bailiff. Thomas Frederick Kirby, *Annals of Winchester College* (London, 1892), 147–49; T. F. T. Baker, J. S. Cockburn, and R. B. Pugh, eds., *VCH Middlesex*, vol. 4 (London, 1971), 7–10.

Clerical and Institutional Projects

oversee the work of masons and carpenters at the church in 1394–95. From 1394, the college kept special accounts for works in Winchester and on the college's manors, for reimbursement by Wykeham, as well as taking on some expenses itself through the household and bursar's accounts – including £70 on Harmondsworth chancel in 1403–04.[104]

iii) Fabric Officers

Of course, the owner of a church might not own a manor in the parish, in which case a different official would need to be chosen to carry out building work. The financing of the building of St Mary the Great, Cambridge, for example, was headed by the proctors, the university's financial officers, and the vice-chancellor, although building expenses also appear in the churchwardens' accounts. A table 'from the records of the proctors' gives annual sums collected from 1478 (when a historian writing shortly afterwards notes that the first stone was laid) to 1519 (when the nave was finished) – a total of over £550.[105] A list of gifts totalling more than £500 was kept by William Stockdale (vice-chancellor in 1493–98) in 1493 'and on certain years which followed', coming to some £1,350 in total.[106] The work was overseen by senior fellows acting as fabric wardens ('*aediles*' or '*operis prepositi*') – although quite what responsibilities came under their unusual title is unclear. Nine served in total, usually for several years. Historians of the church rarely, however, include the sums raised by the churchwardens – in the surviving accounts these are quite modest but, revealingly, none come from the proctors. In 1513, for example, the wardens received and spent almost £17, and expenditure consisted entirely of collections, gifts and sales.[107] The work that year was on the porch and vestry, and included a sufficient quantity of wages and materials to suggest that they were not sharing the work. In 1515, considerable sums were spent hanging bells and a contract with a plumber was fulfilled the following year. It is impossible to tell with any great certainty how responsibilities were divided between university and parish.

---

[104] The bursars took over the accounts from the Warden in 1398; Bridget Cherry and Nikolaus Pevsner, *London 3: North West* (1991), 325; John Harvey, 'The Buildings of Winchester College', in *Winchester College: Sixth-Centenary Essays*, ed. Roger Custance (Oxford, 1982), 82; Kirby, *Winchester College*, 152, 137–38.

[105] '*ex procuratorum commentariis*'; John Lamb, ed., *A Collection of Letters, Statutes, and Other Documents from the Ms. Library of Corp. Christ. Coll.* (London, 1838), 7–8; Christopher Nugent Lawrence Brooke, 'Urban Church and University Church: Great St Mary's from Its Origin to 1523', in *Great St Mary's Cambridge's University Church*, ed. John Binns and Peter Meadows (Cambridge, 2000), 19–20.

[106] '*et certis annis tunc sequentibus*'; Sandars, *Great Saint Mary*, 13–14.

[107] Foster, *St Mary the Great, Cambridge, CWAs*, 17–31; Thomas Fuller, *The History of the University of Cambridge*, ed. Marmaduke Prickett and Thomas Wright (Cambridge, 1840), 194.

Organising Construction III

Figure 5.7 Merton College Chapel, Oxford (© Gabriel Byng)

A more detailed example is St John the Baptist, Oxford, where the advowson was owned by Merton College, which began rebuilding the church completely in c. 1287, as both parish church and college chapel (Figure 5.7).[108] Responsibility was given to a college officer, Walter Cuddington (c. 1260–1313). Unlike the manorial stewards and bailiffs surveyed in the previous section, his office seems to have been created in order to oversee the building work carried out in the college: from 1286 to 1311 he organised work on the chapel, sacristy and north and east wings of Mob Quad, as well as smaller tasks on the gardens, kitchen and houses. His office was not named and he never held a pre-existing college position. His accounts are simply entitled 'for the necessary expenses of the house'.[109] No senior mason or other official, such as a clerk of the works, appears with enough regularity to suggest they had a role in organising the work. On several occasions, however, Cuddington paid for advice from a Brother Thomas, possibly a monk recently involved in

---

[108] G. H. Martin and J. R. L. Highfield, *A History of Merton College, Oxford* (Oxford, 1997), 39; Tim Ayers, *The Medieval Stained Glass of Merton College, Oxford*, vol. 1 (Oxford, 2013), 5.

[109] '*ad expensis necessarias domus*'; J. R. L Highfield, ed., *The Early Rolls of Merton College, Oxford* (Oxford, 1964), 294–315.

building work.[110] He may, nevertheless, have been relatively senior: he was kin of Walter de Merton, and probably related to two other Cuddingtons who were respectively bursar and dean (1288–90) and bursar and chaplain (1282, 1285).[111] He would later take holy orders.[112] The use of a permanent officer is testament to the large-scale works taking place at Merton during this period. Later building projects at the universities would be organised under fabric committees: one at Oxford appointed two fabric wardens ('masters of Arts') to arrange the purchase of materials and hire of workmen in 1447.[113]

Building work first featured in Cuddington's accounts in 1286–87, when he appears to have been stockpiling funds, but the greater part of the building work on the new church is not recorded until the accounts for January–July 1291, when £90 was spent. Cuddington used subheadings in 1289–90 but in the extensive accounts for 1291 items were grouped by the day or week, probably because there were simply too many entries to combine like with like at audit. A large number of workmen were employed and totals for wages are given on either a daily (membrane 2 for March) or weekly basis (membranes 1, 3 and 5 for January–February and April–July), paid on Saturdays, following, presumably, the working accounts used to produce the surviving neat copies. Occasionally so much was spent in a week that midweek totals are noted (for example, on 30 April, 9–10 May, 6 and 12–13 June), typically on the dorse of the roll. In this sense the entries reflect Cuddington's regular, daily role in the building work – and probably his struggle to keep up. In 1293, more than £116 was spent, but Cuddington seems to have mastered the operation better by then and expenditure is grouped in weeks, without exception, each beginning with the Saturday of account and ending with the total. The reason is to be found, perhaps, in the two men who received their pay under the heading '*custus lathomorum*' the next year, perhaps running the building site on Cuddington's behalf and allowing him to concentrate on financial oversight.

Much less demanding than assigning an official to the work was contracting it out altogether, as for the new chancel at Sandon, Hertfordshire, rebuilt by the dean and chapter of St Paul's, London, in 1348.[114] The chapter owned both the advowson and the parish's main manor, which it often leased to a canon, but it did not explicitly

---

[110] Ibid., 304. [111] MCR 3620.
[112] H. E. Salter and Mary D. Lobel, eds., *VCH Oxfordshire*, vol. 3 (London, 1954), 95–106, n. 22.
[113] Not a parish church project. Salzman, *Building in England*, 7.
[114] LMA MS 25122/1264; *Royal Commission on Historical Manuscripts*, vol. IX (London, 1883), 39; Salzman, *Building in England*, 437–38; Harvey, *Perpendicular*, 61; Harvey, *English Mediaeval Architects*, 254.

entrust oversight or control of the work to the lessee, bailiff or any other official.[115] It is likely that the chapter paid the mason directly, although perhaps with income from the manor, which was part of the '*communa*', money divided between all the officers of the cathedral rather than a single prebend. As at Adderbury, significant oversight was to come directly from the chapter. The business of organising the contract was handled by two canons, Alan Hothom (d. 1352) and John Barnet (d. 1373), neither apparently connected to the parish. Hothom was a major canon and pluralist rector, appointed to prebendaries at the cathedral almost twenty years earlier, and was personally wealthy.[116] Barnet was probably the junior of the two, in both years (Hothom had taken orders in 1316) and status (he would acquire the rectory of East Dereham almost twenty-five years after Hothom), and was recently appointed prebendary of Chamberlainwood and rector of Westwell, Kent.[117] The reason for the choice of either man is obscure: it may simply have been convenient since neither held a demanding cathedral office but one was experienced, senior and trusted, and the other junior but able. However, Hothom may have been practised in commissioning building work. He had held the prebendaries of Dinder (1331–33), and Compton Donden (1329), both in Somerset, which have Decorated work in their chancels.[118] He was also rector of Shere, Surrey (c. 1317–20), with its early fourteenth-century chancel.[119]

The contract is largely free of stylistic criteria (for example, no other building or plan is referred to) but, as befits a project overseen from a distance, is both precise and relatively detailed. It describes the dimensions of the new chancel, its materials (Barnack stone ('*de Bernaco*') for the buttresses and the remainder 'of good white stone'),[120] windows (a three-light one in the east wall and two two-light ones in the north and south

---

[115] William Page, ed., *VCH Hertfordshire*, vol. 3 (London, 1912), 270–76.

[116] Reginald R. Sharpe, ed., *Calendar of Letter-Books Preserved among the Archives of the Corporation of the City of London at the Guildhall*, vol. 1 (London, 1899), 660–61; William Dugdale, *The History of St. Pauls Cathedral in London, from Its Foundation Untill These Times* (London, 1658), 117; *Calendar of the Manuscripts of the Dean & Chapter of Wells*, vol. 2 (London, 1914), no. 303.

[117] He would go on to become bishop of Ely: W. M. Ormrod, 'Barnet, John (D. 1373)', in *Oxford Dictionary of National Biography* (Oxford, 2004); Francis Joseph Baigent, *The Registers of John de Sandale and Rigaud de Asserio, Bishops of Winchester (A.D. 1316–1323)* (London, 1897), 433–34; William Henry Bliss and Charles Johnson, *Calendar of Entries in the Papal Registers Relating to Great Britain and Ireland: 1342–62*, vol. 3 (London, 1897), 202–5.

[118] He also held Sneating, Essex (destroyed 1833); *Calendar of the Patent Rolls Preserved in the Public Record Office: Edward III 1330–34*, vol. 2 (London, 1893), 178; Thomas Scott Holmes, ed., *The Register of Ralph of Shrewsbury, Bishop of Bath and Wells, 1329–1363* (London, 1896), 515, cf. 647–8, 654–5.

[119] Baigent, *The Registers of John de Sandale and Rigaud de Asserio, Bishops of Winchester (A.D. 1316–1323)*, 433–34; and Dereham: Blomefield, *Norfolk*, 1808, 10:204–18.

[120] '*de bona alba petra*'. Salzman, *Building in England*, 437.

Clerical and Institutional Projects

walls), buttresses (angle and north and south ones), door and foundations. The craftsman, Thomas Rikelyng, was to be paid 20 marks ('*per particulas prout circa construccionem*') and have the material of the old chancel. No sureties were named, although his heirs and executors were bound, and no time limit given. Who was to pay him, to assess the quality and progress of the work (and whether the terms of the contract were fulfilled 'in the said form'), and to make any further decisions regarding design or execution, is unknown.[121] Possibly, as at Adderbury, these would be overseen by a manorial officer, with occasional visits by Hothom or Barnet to check financial accountability. Overall control could be maintained in London through audit and the writing of contracts, although, unlike at Adderbury, this contract was made in Sandon, not in London, indicating that Hothom and Barnet had visited and surveyed the site. Unlike Adderbury too, very little was reserved for the cathedral officers to carry out (there is no mention of transport and the contractor is to provide materials), although other contracts (for the roof or glass) must have been lost.

The cathedral contracted for building work again in 1413, for a new choir roof in Halstead, Essex.[122] On this occasion the contractee was the dean and chapter, with no indication of who it was who had agreed terms with the carpenter, John Taverner. This had become the standard form for the cathedral's building contracts since the work at Sandon. The work was entirely contracted out, requiring that Taverner 'will find or cause to be found all and every kind of stone and board and also manual work and any other art and work of carpentry'.[123] Nevertheless, the contract is of some length and shows familiarity with the church, and others nearby, and with the requirements of good roofing. It demands seasoned oak ('*de corde quercino bene siccato et indurato*') for a roof in the manner of a 'Chare roof', with thirty couples of rafters and ceiled with 'English board', in the style of Romford chancel. It is suggested that the chancel walls should be raised three feet, depending on the advice of masons. Like Hothom and Barnet, whoever made the contract must have visited the church and probably also Romford, and been well informed as to roof technology, even if he (or they) was advised by Taverner or another craftsman. This must have taken place prior to and separately from the sealing of the contract, which took place in London. Romford, a chapel of Hornchurch, is some thirty miles closer to London than Halstead but the cathedral owned neither the church nor any land there. The

---

[121] '*in forma predicta*'. Ibid.   [122] Salzman, *Building in England*, 490–91.
[123] '*inveniet vel inveniri faciet totum et omnimodum mearemium et bord ac opus manuale et quicquid aliud artem et opus carpenterie*'. Ibid.

recommendation of Romford was, nevertheless, probably made by the contractees: it was recently built on a new site (consecrated in 1410), probably by Robert Chichele, the illustrious and wealthy London merchant, MP and mayor.[124] Chichele's brother, Henry, the future archbishop of Canterbury, then bishop of St David's, had consecrated the building. He was already an important figure in the royal service and had spent much of his career in London, but he had also been a fellow of New College, Oxford, which owned Hornchurch.[125] The chapter, in other words, drew upon its social network in choosing the design of the church, even as it divested itself of most organisational responsibility.

D) CONFLICT AND COOPERATION

The parish church provided a venue for both cooperation and conflict between lords and tenants. Church building by a lord, or his bailiff, sits on this fault line: necessitating collaboration and providing mutual benefits even as it demonstrated how inequalities in power and wealth allowed, even required, parishioners to perform different roles and activities within the parish. Construction tended to reveal but also to complicate the play of largesse and deference, and resistance, that characterised medieval life. It has already been argued that financial cooperation was necessary for much 'gentry' building work to take place.[126] At Bolney, Helmingham and Biddenham manorial lords worked alongside parish authorities on their own projects: raising funds, running the building site and contracting for work. There is reason to think that such cooperation was largely on the lord's terms – it was their contribution alone that would be recorded in the fabric of the building and they are conspicuous by their absence in most surviving contracts and fabric accounts kept by the parish. Nevertheless, the examples are varied, from hands-on project managers like John Bolney, to the Tollemaches, who appear to have provided funding without sitting on the contracting committee themselves – a sign, presumably, of self-assertion, and tough negotiating, by the parish. The dynamic was not necessarily that of a manorial lord persuading and

---

[124] Carole Rawcliffe, 'Chichele, Robert (d. 1439), of London', in *The History of Parliament: The House of Commons 1386–1421*, ed. J. S. Roskell, L. Clark, and C. Rawcliffe (Woodbridge, 1993); H. F. Westlake, *Hornchurch Priory: A Kalendar of Documents in the Possession of the Warden and Fellows of New College, Oxford* (London, 1923), no. 6; ERO T/P 195/2, Havering Liberty, f. 81; W. R. Powell, ed. *VCH Essex*, vol. 7 (London, 1978), 82–91; Philip Morant, *The History and Antiquities of the County of Essex*, vol. 1 (London, 1768), 58.

[125] Jeremy Catto, 'Chichele, Henry (c. 1362–1443)', in *Oxford Dictionary of National Biography* (Oxford, 2004).

[126] Chapter 2, section d, pp. 122–27.

coercing his tenants into contributions to 'his' project.[127] Quite the reverse appears to have taken place at Wimborne, Dorset, in 1448–49, where the churchwardens spent large sums sending out parishioners to see Sir John Herryng, paying for cakes and wine, and showing him the site of the new tower. The process culminated in the drawing-up of an indenture, although his actual contribution is unknown.[128] Here at least it was the parishioners who sought out the extra financial muscle of the gentry, even if Herryng drove a hard bargain. Even the nobility could be persuaded: John Leland reported that at Winchcombe in Gloucestershire, c. 1454–74, the parishioners had to ask Ralph Boteler, Lord Sudeley, for the final sums to finish the nave.[129] This does suggest a profound difference between gentry-led projects, as at Bolney or Biddenham, and parish-led ones, as at Wimborne, even if both depended on extensive cooperation between lord and tenants. At the least, building work showed the dedication of many gentry families to their parish churches.[130]

Regardless of financing, church construction could not be a unilateral venture: it was the parishioners' church that would be turned into a building site, and their assent would be necessary, if only not to disrupt the work deliberately.[131] It was the parish too which would have to fund the increased cost of repair work for any new addition. Villagers were certainly ready to use violence in obstructing some manorial ventures, but only rarely and in extreme cases, it seems, for parish church construction.[132] Litigation connected with building work typically concerned the failure of parishioners to honour their commitments to corporate endeavours rather than anything more obstructive.[133] Indeed, many parishioners stood to gain from building work financed by a lord: labourers at Bolney and Hardley were mostly local, allowing the patron to exercise patronage and provide employment in his own community, at the same time as he emphasised his own wealth and authority. At Fotheringhay, when York's commissioners retained the right to appoint labourers, they probably did so in order to choose trustworthy local men

---

[127] Although it was at Ketteringham, Norfolk, in 1608: Richmond, 'Gentry and Religion', 133, n. 30.
[128] Brown, *Popular Piety*, 117.
[129] John Leland, *The Itinerary of John Leland in or about the Years 1535–1543*, ed. Lucy Toulmin Smith, vol. 2 (London, 1908), 55.
[130] Introduction, section a, pp. 6–7.
[131] See the opposition given by 'rebels', both in non-payment and obstruction, to the rebuilding of belfries in Lincolnshire parishes: Owen, *Church and Society*, 113–14.
[132] Pounds, *English Parish*, 407; Kristi Bain, 'Community Conflict and Collective Memory in the Late Medieval Parish Church', *Martin Marty Center-Religion and Culture Web Forum*, 2014.
[133] Two Cambridgeshire examples: CUL, EDC 7/13/6.

whom they wished to promote or knew to be reliable.[134] The patron might also strengthen local infrastructure – roads, watercourses or docks, as at Totnes.[135] Above all, of course, all stood to benefit from improvements to the church.

Cooperation could work in other, non-financial, ways too: the local gentry might provide the connections to master masons even if they could not provide the financing, for example.[136] At Hardley, the Hospital may have provided its retained mason while the church contributed other sums.[137] Wills of wealthy patrons regularly insisted upon cooperation with the parish, or at least a representative body, in a way that contracts and accounts could not. In 1424–25, Roger Flore asked that the mason he hired to make Oakham steeple vault fulfil his 'covenant' but also that 'my neighbours' should say if they were willing to contribute, one having already done so.[138] John Baker (d. 1464) desired an aisle to be made 'with the advice of the parishioners' at Folkestone, while John Philipp (d. 1477) contributed to a new floor in the tower of Warehorne, Kent, only 'if the parishioners will it to be done'.[139] Some wills are clear that the body to be consulted is the parish's leadership – the masters or a more informal group. When Alice Chester replaced the rood loft at All Saints, Bristol, 1483, she did it 'according to the parish entente ... taking to her counsel the worshipful of the parish with other[s] having best understanding and sights in carving'.[140] William Stevenson left money for two lights 'by the advice ("vyce") of the parson and the church masters' at Roughton, Lincolnshire, in 1521.[141] Katherine Harston asked that a new banner at St Mary Coslany, Norwich, be painted with scenes 'devised by my executors with the assent of the most honest of the said parish' in 1534.[142] Lastly, Richard Ballard left money for repairing the church in 1538 'when as the vicar of Orbye and three of the best of the town shall think most necessary'.[143] However much arms and inscriptions might suggest an act of singlehanded patronage, the decision to build a new unit, as well as its financing and organisation, would have to be negotiated and agreed with the lay authorities of the parish.

---

[134] Salzman, *Building in England*, 505–9.   [135] Chapter 4, section c.i, pp. 187–89.
[136] Byng, 'Patrons and Their Commissions', 241.   [137] Woodman, 'Hardley'.
[138] Frederick James Furnivall, ed., *The Fifty Earliest English Wills in the Court of Probate* (London, 1882), 59.
[139] Nicolas, *Testamenta Vetusta*, 1826, 1:306; Hussey, *Testamenta Cantiana (East)*, 352.
[140] Clive Burgess, *The Pre-Reformation Records of All Saints', Bristol*, vol. I (Bristol, 1995), 16.
[141] This could refer to the churchwardens. C. W. Foster, *Lincoln Wills: 1271–1526*, vol. I (London, 1914), 89.
[142] Duffy, 'The Parish, Piety and Patronage: The Evidence of Rood-Screens', 150.
[143] TNA: PRO PROB 11/26/217.

Conclusion

E) CONCLUSION

There is little reason to believe that John Bolney was an exception: manorial lord, architectural patron and active project manager. Wealthy families contributed directly to parochial funds, of course, but, if they wished to initiate a major new project that was to take their arms, name or tomb, the most convenient strategy was to manage it personally. For the parish gentry, who were closely identified with their church and might be active in its religious life, as well as for a few other wealthy yeomen or merchants, it was easier, cheaper and more reliable or even enjoyable to oversee work themselves.

Nevertheless, accounts, contracts and wills show that their projects were marked by a high degree of collaboration with parish authorities, from financing and decision making, to contracting and organisation. Indeed, it would have to be – not only did most gentry patrons probably require funding from other sources and organisational help from craftsmen and local officials, but they also had to ensure that their project received local support for both its successful execution and long-term maintenance. Some gentry patrons were not as involved as Bolney, however. John Tollemache may have provided much of the income at Helmingham but he did not actively commission the work – even though his name alone would be recorded in an inscription. Rectors, both residential and otherwise, could and did take their duty of repair seriously, however often some parishes might need to petition bishops or attend court to compel contributions, and this could stretch to include a substantial chancel rebuilding project, as at Adderbury.

The simplest managerial and financial structures for large secular, collegiate or monastic estates to use would be to run building work as part of manorial business, under the bailiff, with the work entered in his regular accounts and funded by manorial income. The institution could decide designs, instruct masons and maintain control through the use of contracts and audits and by appointing occasional overseers to visit the site for a few weeks at a time. For institutions that built churches without a manor in the parish, another officer would have to be found or, if the church was of exceptional size or part of more widespread work, a new position created to oversee the work. Nobles, and probably institutions and wealthy gentry, could deputise to a trustworthy local agent. Now that we have laid out the different methods of running church construction under communal officers, fabric wardens and families or institutions, it is possible to determine the strategies each employed for executing their duties.

Chapter 6

APPROACHES TO BUILDING WORK

A) INTRODUCTION

Historians of parish church building, indeed of much Gothic construction, have often assumed that its execution was short-termist, slow and haphazard. This has characterised accounts of both finance and expenditure, with patrons passively collecting money as and when it came in and spending it immediately with little forward planning. Even scholars who have admired the record-keeping of churchwardens have not tended to show them as actively running the income for building projects in order to meet their own priorities and requirements. Part of the reason is the difficulty of finding standards of success. Failure – that is, work that is not finished on time, on budget or to the patrons' wishes – is not a good indication of bad management for not all events can be foreseen or overcome, but nor is completion. It is difficult to find fatal examples of foolhardiness, irrationality or imprudence since churches were built in a relatively forgiving, if unstable, climate. Parishes are enduring institutions: a shortage of money, a fraudulent contractor, a sudden change in prices, a violent storm – all or most could be solved with more time to raise funds, find workmen and continue the work.

The more revealing question is whether decision-makers sought out and implemented managerial and financial strategies that could be reasonably believed to be sufficient for the patrons to achieve their ambitions in the context of an unpredictable and unreliable future. The challenge for the historian is that the appropriateness of many practices cannot be judged without a contextual understanding that is rarely possible: high debt could be an indication of excellent or of very poor organisation, for example, while many important organisational tasks incurred no expenditure and are thus invisible in the historical record. Anecdotal evidence for poor management is perhaps the most revealing, and will be discussed, but sources are rare outside major secular or ecclesiastical projects – and

'Simple Economy'

even here it tends to show either fraudulence or the adaptation of administrative systems when problems arose.[1] However, some managerial and financial approaches can be isolated in contracts and accounts. Indeed, the officers who were the subjects of Chapters 3–4 were chosen, partly, for their organisational skill and experience. Parochial leaders, including lords, recognised that building work demanded able managers, usually involving numerous people and groups in a strict hierarchy, and they also knew where they were to be found. These men, drawn from the upper ranks of parish life and with experience of organising communal projects, holding office and paying for repair work, should have been capable project managers – it was, after all, often their own money that they were spending.[2]

B) 'SIMPLE ECONOMY'

John James describes the funding of church construction as a 'simple economy'. He argues that 'the Middle Ages did not have the sophisticated funding techniques of later centuries. Money could only be spent when it came in, and when it ran out work had to stop. As the amount donated varied from year to year, the quantity of work varied with it.'[3] Versions of this economic model, not always so extremely expressed, have been adopted by other historians, often with the assumption that parish church building was even more haphazard than that of great churches. Richard Morris describes fundraising as a 'slow and fitful process', noting the unpredictability of income and the absence of loans to cover unexpected shortfalls,[4] and Reginald Dudding imagines parish church building carrying on 'with scanty labour and scantier means'.[5] A guide to the church at Hedon, Yorkshire, one of the more sophisticated examples of project management considered in Chapter 4, describes building work as taking place 'as and when funds and man-power permitted'.[6] For James, this explained the entire constructional process of Chartres, where teams of masons appeared on site and worked for short periods while their income lasted, their changes to the design absorbed into the whole. Historians of masons in England have often reached related conclusions: Heather Swanson, for example, concludes that 'when funds dried up the masons

---

[1] Knoop and Jones, *Mediaeval Mason*, 31–33. Knoop and Jones are admirably circumspect on the quality of management, p. 29.
[2] See Chapter 1, section c.vii, pp. 92–95.
[3] John James, *The Contractors of Chartres*, vol. 1 (Dooralong, 1979), 13; cf. Pierre du Colombier, *Les Chantiers Des Cathedrales* (Paris, 1953), 14, 24–25.
[4] Morris, *Landscape*, 283, 356.   [5] Dudding, *Louth CWAs*, xviii.   [6] Ainslie, *Hedon*, 7.

Approaches to Building Work

moved on'.⁷ This thesis finds support from those art historians who emphasise that craftsmen 'worked as and when they could' or who doubt that patrons or architects conceived of a completed project at its inception.⁸ Anthropologists have even used James' conclusions to explore how coherent designs were produced by shifting groups of people.⁹ These arguments once had their corollary in economic historians who argued that farmers approached their husbandry in an irrational fashion.¹⁰ In these examples medieval patrons are painted as the passive victims of changes in income, spending their money when they had it, and often incapable of or unwilling to plan the funding for an entire project at its outset or to estimate its cost and duration.

The most recent and most eloquent adaptation of this thesis is by Marvin Trachtenberg. He argues that, since income was 'thin and erratic', medieval builders relied on time – that is, future income – to finish projects for which they did not currently have sufficient capital. Alternatively, they chose on occasion to reduce the scale of the project instead.¹¹ Patrons were a 'trans-generational community' who deliberately chose to build slowly, even when they could do otherwise, in order to realise vast buildings and emphasise the historic identity of the community. Pamela Graves has advanced a similar argument about the seigniorial patronage of English parish churches, where lords built slowly over generations to emphasise 'inheritance and legitimacy'.¹² Even the organisational structures used to run church building have been used as evidence of this relaxed approach to financing. Trachtenberg argues that permanent fabric funds demonstrated that patrons had no intention of finishing work quickly, but rather of maintaining a semi-permanent state of construction. There are two important responses to this claim, however: first, that such funds were set up partly to handle the constant influx of gifts and regular income to the fabric of great churches, which

---

⁷ Swanson, *Medieval Artisans*, 90.
⁸ For example: Neil Stratford, 'Romanesque Sculpture in Burgundy: Reflections on Its Geography, on Patronage, on the Status of Sculpture, and on the Working Methods of Sculptors', in *Artistes, Artisans, et Production Artistique Au Moyen Age*, ed. X. Altet and I. Barral, vol. 3 (Paris, 1990), 236.
⁹ David Turnbull, 'The Ad Hoc Collective Work of Building Gothic Cathedrals with Templates, String, and Geometry', *Science, Technology, & Human Values* 18, no. 3 (1 July 1993): 315–40; David Turnbull, *Masons, Tricksters and Cartographers: Comparative Studies in the Sociology of Scientific and Indigenous Knowledge* (London, 2000), Chapter 2; Tim Ingold, *Making: Archaeology, Anthropology, Art and Architecture* (London, 2012).
¹⁰ See the discussion in David Stone, *Decision-Making in Medieval Agriculture* (Oxford, 2005), Chapter 1.
¹¹ Marvin Trachtenberg, *Building-in-Time from Giotto to Alberti and Modern Oblivion* (New Haven, 2010), 111–26; Morris makes a similar argument for parish churches in Morris, *Landscape*, 356.
¹² Graves, 'Social Space', 314.

continued even when no building work was in process; and second, that the demands of repair were constant. Although Trachtenberg refutes arguments of short-term, non-rational decision-making and of inflexibility and strategic simplicity on the part of medieval patrons, he nevertheless argues that there was little sense of urgency and that speed and scale were usually adapted to income, rather than vice versa.

Trachtenberg gives the example of the Siena *Duomo Novo*, where the master masons acknowledged that building work was too slow but accepted the income level as invariable, choosing instead to reduce the scale of their ambitions.[13] Some textual support can be found in medieval accounts of building work in English churches, as, for example, at Vale Royal in 1312, where the abbey claimed, in a petition for funding from the king, to be building 'year to year, according to their means'.[14] At Meaux, Abbot Thomas (1182–97) was described by the abbey's chronicler, writing in the 1390s, as building 'little by little as he was able'.[15] Gervase writes of building work at Canterbury in 1183: 'no work was done for want of funds'.[16] These examples are, however, suggestive at best: they indicate that managers adjusted expenditure not to exceed revenue and cannot show that income was not strategically managed. Unforeseeable falls in income or increases in cost were no doubt common given the unpredictable nature of both building work and agrarian revenues. Certainly, there were cases of construction by institutions so wealthy or with such apparently certain income or necessity for buildings that they did not plan adequately, as perhaps at Meaux or St Albans,[17] and of churches which were dependent on the largesse of a single patron and could build only while their generosity continued, as at Vale Royal and Westminster Abbey, but also, perhaps, at some parish churches too.[18] A break in construction could, however, indicate structural necessity, seasonal reductions in work or a deliberate change in design.[19] This chapter will argue that, far from being passively accepted, the inherent unpredictability of building work motivated the development of a number of devices to safeguard the completion of projects.

---

[13] Trachtenberg, *Building-in-Time*, 115.
[14] Howard Colvin, ed., *The History of the King's Works*, vol. 1 (London, 1963), 252.
[15] Thomas de Burton, *Chronica Monasterii de Melsa*, ed. Edward Augustus Bond, vol. 1 (London, 1866), 217, for details of the chronicle's authorship see xliv–xlv.
[16] Robert Willis, *The Architectural History of Canterbury Cathedral* (London, 1845).
[17] Thomas de Walsingham, *Gesta Abbatum Monasterii Sancti Albani*, ed. Henry T. Riley, vol. 1 (London, 1867), 218.
[18] J. M. Maddison, 'Architectural Development of Patrington Church', in *Medieval Art and Architecture in the East Riding of Yorkshire*, ed. Christopher Wilson (Norwich, 1989), 133–48; cf. Stewart Cruden, *Scottish Medieval Churches* (Edinburgh, 1986), 184.
[19] Robert Branner, 'Review', *The Art Bulletin* 37, no. 1 (1 March 1955): 62.

C) MANAGERIAL STRATEGIES

i) The 'Contract System'

The use of contracts in building projects has already been surveyed, but patterns in their development suggest that they demonstrate an important way in which patrons responded to a changing economic environment.[20] Their use for parochial building work appears to have increased significantly after the Black Death: prior to 1348, only one survives on a parish church, by the end of the century five more are extant, and in the first half of the fifteenth there are nine (Table I.4). This reflects a sharp increase in surviving building contracts for secular and large ecclesiastical buildings, which led Knoop and Jones to argue that this constituted the rise of a 'contract system' in the late fourteenth century. They argue it was caused by a scarcity of labour that required 'more economical methods of working'.[21] The association between contracting and a need for 'efficient and economical' building or periods of 'financial stringency' has been made by other historians.[22] That contracting did tend to reduce costs is also indicated by the subcontracting carried out by master masons, businessmen whose profits relied on reducing the cost of building work as far as possible.[23] It also allowed parishes to put work out to tender, encouraging contractors to underbid one another, a process which may be indicated by entries in churchwardens' accounts which note them riding to find masons and 'bargaining'.[24]

However, the need to seek 'more economical methods of working' was universal among medieval patrons and we have already encountered several very lavish projects built under contract. Indeed, as we have seen, parochial building contracts were fully developed in form by the late thirteenth century.[25] To explain why contracting became increasingly common in this period, especially at a parochial level, it is necessary to look not simply to a need for economy but to other changes in the economic environment, and particularly the sudden rise in wages and prices in the wake of the Black Death. This would have made predicting the cost of construction work extremely difficult, and patrons knew that dramatic rises in cost over the duration of a project risked bankrupting it.

---

[20] Introduction, section e, p. 46, and Chapter 4, section b.i, 175–77.
[21] Douglas Knoop and G. P. Jones, 'The Rise of the Mason Contractor', *Jnl. RIBA*, 43 (October 1936): 1061; Douglas Knoop and G. P. Jones, 'Some Notes on Three Early Documents Relating to Masons', *Ars Quatuor Coronatorum* XLIV (1931): 224.
[22] Christopher Wilson, 'A Mid-Fourteenth Century Contract for the Choir Roof of Glastonbury Abbey', *The Antiquaries Journal* 88 (2008): 218; Colvin, *King's Works*, 1963, 1:107.
[23] E.g. John Wastell at King's College chapel (1512): Woodman, *King's College Chapel*, 167.
[24] Jean Gimpel, *The Cathedral Builders*, trans. Carl F. Barnes (London, 1961), 120.
[25] Byng, 'Southchurch'.

Managerial Strategies

In an era when building wages could increase by a fifth or more in a decade, fixing the price ahead of the commencement of building work was prudent and allowed for better financial planning.[26] Contractors did not build inflation into their contracts, accepting, presumably, that this was one of the consequences of contracting out. Master Raymond at Lugo Cathedral in Spain was exceptional when he stipulated in his contract of 1129 that, if the value of the currency fell, he was to be paid in kind.[27] There is also qualitative evidence of contemporary fears, repeated in legislation and in cases before Justices of the Peace, that workers were increasingly breaking contract, working less hard and demanding greater leisure time after the Black Death.[28] Contractors, of course, had nothing to gain by working slowly and risked legal action should they fail to fulfil their part of the bargain. Contracts prevented contractors from holding their patrons hostage, demanding greater sums to finish the work: at Hackington, Kent, the contractee insisted that 'no more nor other sums to be thereof asked or demanded'.[29] Contracting transferred risk – of unexpected disruptions, increases in the cost of building materials and labour, fraud, unreliable workers and failures of material – to the contractor and away from the parish. This also encouraged contractors to work efficiently, use materials sparingly and secure better prices, something they were probably in a better position to do than their patrons.

To prove this thesis, however, it must be shown, first, that contracting was uncommon prior to the Black Death and, secondly, that it was prevalent after it. A major problem is that the poor survival rate of parochial contracts from the early fourteenth century is suggestive at best, especially given the common use of oral agreements, while even the twenty-six that survive after it do not demonstrate widespread practice. In this section we shall take these propositions in turn, beginning with the second. Although surviving contracts are small in number, we have already seen that in most cases the direct employment of labour in late medieval accounts took place alongside the contracting out of part of the work, from task work to entire buildings, just as nearly all contracts for 'whole' projects reserved some responsibilities for the contractees.[30] The

---

[26] Introduction, section c, pp. 26–32.
[27] Martin S. Briggs, *The Architect in History* (Oxford, 1927), 70; Colombier, *Les Chantiers Des Cathedrales*, 76.
[28] Hatcher, 'England in the Aftermath', 14; John Harvey, *Medieval Craftsmen* (London, 1975), 128; Salzman, *Building in England*, 55; Christopher Dyer, 'Work Ethics in the Fourteenth Century', in *The Problem of Labour in Fourteenth-Century England*, ed. James Bothwell, P. J. P. Goldberg, and W. M. Ormrod (Woodbridge, 2000), 21–42.
[29] Vallance, 'R.N.', 267–68. [30] See the many examples in Chapter 3, section b.iii, pp. 183–85.

same craftsman often received payment both as contractor and as wage-labourer. It is, in fact, more accurate to write of the rise of a 'part-contract system', since so few projects were contracted out in their entirety.[31] Moreover, oral contracts for architectural units were also employed into the fifteenth century, no doubt more regularly than surviving evidence suggests.[32] Also indicative of widespread contracting was the production of standardised contracts: William Kingsmill produced a specimen building contract in his *Formulare* of the early fifteenth century, of which several copies survive.[33]

The quantity and spread of surviving contracts suggest that a considerable number of places had workshops capable of taking on large part-contracts by the fifteenth century, improving efficiency and reducing costs (Table I.4). Skilled workshop masons with specialist tools could produce repeat designs with speed and accuracy, reducing transport costs and the employment of cutters on site, and working as easily in winter as in summer. Prefabricated elements could be shipped whole to the building site, where labourers and less skilled local masons would be required merely to insert the component into the stone framework with little further adjustment. At Hardley, Norfolk, the cut stone elements of the new chancel were made in Norwich in 1458–59 before being carted to the building site and reassembled quickly by local labourers under the supervision of a few of the mason's men two years later; the roof was also prefabricated offsite and transported there. Woodman argues that such professionalised craftsmen had permanent urban workshops with a staff of workmen and 'almost production line output'.[34] The master mason at Bolney, Sussex, who had a workshop in Lewes from which he ran several projects in the area, was able to construct the new church tower in nine months, using local labourers under the supervision of two of his men.[35] At Over, Cambridgeshire, blocks were marked with their height, presumably to simplify ashlar construction when the pre-cut stone was delivered to the building site. In this case the quality of the cutting was significantly better than that of the laying, indicating that different groups of masons were responsible for each.[36] Dealers and masons traded stone as a commodity,[37] while large building sites, including parish churches, made a profit by selling off excess stone at above purchase price.[38]

---

[31] Cf. Woodward, *Men at Work*, 35.
[32] E.g. at Louth: Dudding, *Louth CWAs*, 128–29; French, *People*, Chapter 2.
[33] BLO MS. Lat. misc. e. 103; BL Add. MS 17716 f. 70v; BL Royal MS. 12 B 24, f. 245.
[34] Woodman, 'Hardley', 204.   [35] Byng, 'Bolney', 106.
[36] Laurence Turner, 'The Masons' Marks in the Church of St Mary, Over, Cambridgeshire', *Proceedings of the Cambridge Antiquarian Society* 51 (1958): 67–77.
[37] Colvin, *King's Works*, 1963, 1:210.   [38] E.g. Foster, *St Mary the Great, Cambridge, CWAs*.

Managerial Strategies

Woodman argues that some large towns, like Norwich and Cambridge, became depots for stone shipped in large quantities to take advantage of economies of scale and then sold off in smaller quantities for profit.[39]

Many authors, however, have been sceptical that any but a few masons had the means to handle contract work. For example, T. H. Lloyd has argued that there is no evidence of any such permanent workshops in fifteenth-century Stratford-upon-Avon, Warwickshire, suggesting instead that builders were itinerant journeymen, who were paid directly and rarely worked in teams.[40] Similarly, Heather Swanson concluded that in late medieval York 'very few masons were in a position to act as independent contractors' although many lived and worked permanently in the city.[41] Knoop and Jones and L. R. Shelby reached similar conclusions.[42] The core of their evidence is that few craftsmen were wealthy enough to cover the cost of a large contract.[43] However, as previous chapters have suggested, contractors did not need substantial capital to carry out large projects: part-payment, part-contracting and credit from suppliers and subcontractors meant that the contractor would need to invest relatively little of his own money. Indeed, there are many examples where contractors almost certainly did not have capital equal to their projects: John Laverok, contractor at Biddenham, Bedfordshire, was to be paid £24 but disposed of a little more than £3 in his will.[44] At the other end of the scale, Roger Denys, who left £20 to his wife, was able to contract for a project of more than £120.[45] The contractor Thomas Aldrych presumably never invested £300 of his own money in the work at Helmingham, Suffolk, nor William Horwode the same sum at Fotheringhay, Northamptonshire, nor Richard Cracall more than £100 at Catterick in Yorkshire.[46] These are only parochial examples – even larger sums can be found in some secular work, as at Cowling Castle, which cost £460 in 1380.[47] Furthermore, even if some towns, like Stratford-upon-Avon, could not support permanent workshops, churches could use contractors from some distance: Roger Denys was a freeman of London but contracted for work in Lincolnshire at

---

[39] Woodman, 'Hardley', 209.
[40] T. H. Lloyd, *Some Aspects of the Building Industry in Medieval Stratford-upon-Avon* (Oxford, 1961), 8–9.
[41] Swanson, *York*, 9; cf. David Parsons, 'Stone', in *English Medieval Industries: Craftsmen, Techniques, Products*, ed. John Blair and Nigel Ramsay (London, 1991), 2; Salzman, *Building in England*, 48.
[42] Knoop and Jones, *Mediaeval Mason*, 102–3; Lon R. Shelby, 'The Role of the Master Mason in Mediaeval English Building', *Speculum* 39, no. 3 (July 1964): 399.
[43] Swanson, *Medieval Artisans*, 82–85.
[44] Of course, he may have invested the difference in land, but the small sum suggests he was not a wealthy man. HALS 2AR225.
[45] Harvey, *English Mediaeval Architects*, 80; Salzman, *Building in England*, 495–97.
[46] Salzman, *Building in England*, 547–49, 505–9, 487–90.
[47] Knoop and Jones, *Mediaeval Mason*, 42.

Approaches to Building Work

Table 6.1 *Contractor masons' hometowns*

Contractor	Resident/'of'	Project location	Approximate distance (miles)
Roger Denis	London	Wyberton	110
Roger Denis	London	Surfleet	100
Jonne	Scone	Edinburgh	45
Thomas Esshyng	Betchworth	Etchingham	40
John Laverok	St Albans	Biddenham	30
Richard	Newton	Hornby	30
Thomas Aldrych	North Lopham	Helmingham	20
William Chapman	Chertsey	Wycombe	20
Richard Cracall	Patrick Brompton	Hornby	17
Jon Marys	Stogursey	Dunster	15
Nicolas Wyshongre	Gloucester	Arlingham	12
Nicholas Toft	Reach	Cambridge	10
Adam Powle	Dunwich	Walberswick	6
Robert Terell	Fremington	Heanton Punchardon	6
Richard Horssale	Tetbury	Great Sherston	5
Richard Cracall	Patrick Brompton	Catterick	5
Richard Russel	Blythburgh	Walberswick	3
William Jackson	Bratoft	Orby	2
William Horwood	Fotheringhay	Fotheringhay	0
John Taverner	Halstead	Halstead	0

Source: John Sheail, *The Regional Distribution of Wealth in England as Indicated in the 1524/5 Lay Subsidy Returns*, edited by R. W. Hoyle, Vol. 2 (Kew, 1998).

Wyberton and Surfleet.[48] The exceptional distance might suggest he had moved permanently, but others can be found travelling thirty miles or more: John Laverok of St Albans contracted for the north aisle of Biddenham, Bedfordshire, and Thomas Esshyng of Betchworth, Surrey, contracted for windows at Etchingham, Sussex (Table 6.1). A mason who was at Hampton Court in 1520 travelled almost fifty miles to provide a new font for St Lawrence, Reading.[49] Perhaps more revealing, however, is how short the distance usually was between the project and the place where contractors lived or were 'of'; usually just a few miles, indicating that most projects did not have to look far for masons capable of acting as contractors. They can be found even in small villages, with populations of no more than a few hundred, including such places as Newton in Patrick Brompton, North Yorkshire, Bratoft, Lincolnshire, Betchworth, Surrey, Crakehall,

---

[48] Harvey, *Perpendicular*, 174; Salzman, *Building in England*, 495.
[49] Kerry, *St Lawrence, Reading*, 14; Coates, *Reading*, 218–19.

Managerial Strategies

Yorkshire, Reach, Cambridgeshire, Sampford Arundel, Somerset, and Stogursey, Somerset.

The proposition that contracting was rare before the Black Death is, however, more difficult to prove. The earliest surviving contract for parochial work in England dates from 1293. It is for a chapel in the churchyard at Southchurch in Essex and is very similar in form to fifteenth-century examples, suggesting that parochial contracting was already well developed in some places.[50] The earliest manifestation of part-contracting is probably to be found in the use of task work, rather than day rates, identified on major projects from the late twelfth century.[51] However, there is some evidence to suggest that masons were establishing permanent workshops and perhaps were therefore able to work as independent contractors, as early as the late twelfth century. Records of masons owning tenements begin at this time and increase from the early thirteenth century.[52] Some of these properties, found alongside smiths, parchment-makers or goldsmiths, may have been workshops.[53] John of Gloucester, later the king's mason, leased a shop in Gloucester by c. 1245, which suggests that an urban workshop was a logical stepping stone for an ambitious mason.[54] Masons were sufficiently well established to appear as witnesses from the late twelfth and early thirteenth century. Some appear in early fourteenth-century taxation lists.[55] Prefabricated units, presumably made in an urban workshop, quarry or major building site, can be found in continental churches as early as the twelfth century.[56] One of the earliest examples is in fact in England, namely the production of standardised ashlar blocks on a vast scale for the east end of Durham Cathedral in the 1090s.[57] Lloyd has related the professionalisation and specialisation of the building

---

[50] Byng, 'Southchurch Chapel'.
[51] Knoop and Jones, 'Mason Contractor'. Shelby has shown that James' argument that such contracting can be found in Chartres half a century before this is highly unlikely: Lon R. Shelby, 'The Contractors of Chartres', *Gesta* 20, no. 1 (1 January 1981): 173–78.
[52] E.g. in Dursely, Gloucestershire, before 1188: BCM/A/1/22/1.
[53] CCA-DCc-ChAnt/C/911; BCM/A/1/22/2; TNA E/326/2336.
[54] Harvey, *English Mediaeval Architects*, 114.
[55] E.g. in St Crux, York: Stell and Hawkyard, 'Lay Subsidy', 7.
[56] Vibeke Olson, 'The Significance of Sameness: An Overview of Standardization and Imitation in Medieval Art', *Visual Resources: An International Journal of Documentation* 20, no. 2–3 (2004): 161–78; Vibeke Olson, 'Colonnette Production and the Advent of the Gothic Aesthetic', *Gesta* 43, no. 1 (1 January 2004): 17–29; Janet Snyder, 'Standardisation and Innovation in Design', in *New Approaches to Medieval Architecture*, ed. Robert Odell Bork, William W. Clark, and Abby McGehee (Farnham, 2011); Stratford, 'Romanesque Sculpture'.
[57] J. Bony, 'The Stonework Planning of the First Durham Master', in *Medieval Architecture and Its Intellectual Context*, ed. E. C. Fernie and Paul Crossley (London, 1990), 24–26; Lon R. Shelby, 'Mediaeval Masons' Templates', *Journal of the Society of Architectural Historians* 30, no. 2 (1 May 1971): 140–54.

Approaches to Building Work

industry to increasing urbanisation from the eleventh century, spreading from town to country, a trend that was to intensify in the thirteenth century.[58] Indeed, it is likely that prefabrication of standardised units such as ashlar blocks, shafts, mullions and capitals was a logical innovation for quarry owners or commercial masons aiming to reduce costs and increase production for the rapidly growing thirteenth-century market.[59]

Nevertheless, all this evidence indicates only that some of the economic conditions for contracting had developed in some quarries and towns by the early thirteenth century, while specific units were being made to order on large-scale projects where demand was guaranteed. Apart from the few surviving examples, there is little positive evidence for the widespread use of building contracts for large-scale work. Even in the context of a sophisticated and increasingly commercialised building trade, it is likely that part-contracting was not as developed or as common as it would become during the later fourteenth century. The coincidence of unstable and rising building costs, increasing risk and complaints of poor performance in the later fourteenth century probably did help formalise and intensify earlier trends in an industry that had already developed permanent workshops, prefabrication techniques and commercial structures. Indeed, the contents of many contracts indicate that these considerations, namely controlling cost and ensuring completion, were foremost in the contractees' minds.

ii) *Legal Safeguards*

The contracts themselves, or at least those that survive, reveal the parish leadership's careful management and their concerns about rising prices, delayed building periods, incompletion and poor performance. It is probable that contractees took legal advice, probably from inexpensive part-time legal advisers rather than professional lawyers, as churchwardens did when preparing parochial litigation[60] or as peasants did when drafting indentures for property transactions at the manor court.[61] Several examples have already been given where the level of technical detail suggests that craftsmen were consulted (e.g. the roof of St Bene't's, Cambridge) and the contractees appear to have made trips to see other examples first and to have paid for consultation services (e.g. the rood screen at Yatton, Somerset).[62] Some show significant negotiating and editing during the drafting process, as at Biddenham, Bedfordshire, where

---

[58] Lloyd, *Some Aspects*, 3. [59] Parsons, 'Stone', 25. [60] Littlehales, *London City Church*, 296.
[61] Matthew Tompkins, '"Let"s Kill All the Lawyers': Did Fifteenth Century Peasants Employ Lawyers When They Conveyed Customary Land?', in *Identity and Insurgency in the Late Middle Ages*, ed. Linda Clark (Woodbridge, 2006), 73–87.
[62] Chapter 3, section c.ii, p. 155.

Managerial Strategies

edits and reconsiderations took place between the first and final drafts.[63] Copies were made for other workmen: at St Mary-at-Hill, London, a copy of the indenture for building the windows was made for 'Master Vartu', probably Robert Vertue, a mason who was paid 20s, perhaps for advice on the contract, since the actual contractor's name was Mawnde.[64]

The most common legal guarantee of completed work, in frequent use for all types of building contract and indeed across most types of medieval agreement, was the employment of sureties who were bound to fulfil the terms of the contract on the contractors' behalf should they fail to do so.[65] The London Regulations of 1356 required contractees to find four or six men of the same trade to act as sureties for the completion of the contract.[66] In this, the law was probably following existing practice. Sureties can be found in the earliest building contracts, such as those of St Michael in the Cornmarket, 1310, and St Paul's, London, 1312, where three sureties were provided, including, in the former, the church's rector.[67] Otherwise the number could vary: three at Helmingham, Suffolk, in 1488, and one at Tempsford, Bedfordshire, in 1512.[68] Larger numbers were used at Henley, Oxfordshire, at the end of the fourteenth century and for the quay at Conesford, Norfolk, in 1432.[69] For their part, contractees almost invariably bound their heirs and executors to pay any fees or fines outstanding.

Having recourse to a contractor's sureties would be a worst-case scenario. It was desirable to find other ways of compelling a wayward contractor to finish the work to the specified standard. Presumably to avoid having to go to court, some contracts offered bonuses for completion on time (10 marks and a gown at Catterick) and fines for overruns.[70] A contractor might agree to pay a certain amount on a certain day if the contract was not fulfilled: at Arlingham, Gloucestershire, the mason bound himself with 40s and agreed that he would go to prison and give up 'all his moveable goods and heritages', if the work was not finished on time.[71] Several contracts used a version of the modern guarantee, based on the judgement of third party masons (usually defined by their skill), acknowledging the limitations of the patrons' expertise, the challenges of

---

[63] Chapter 5, section b.iii, p. 231.
[64] LMA P69/MRY/B/005/MS01239/001/001, f. 201v; Littlehales, *London City Church*, 244; Harvey, *English Mediaeval Architects*, 306.
[65] Pollock and Maitland, *History of English Law*, 1:191; Henry, *Contracts*, 192.
[66] Knoop and Jones, *Mediaeval Mason*, 250.
[67] Salzman, *Building in England*, 418, 419, 426, 428. [68] Ibid., 547–49, 561, 563–64.
[69] Knoop and Jones, 'Mason Contractor', 1064.
[70] Barley, *Lincolnshire and the Fens*, 61; Salzman, *Building in England*, 496–97; Harvey, *English Mediaeval Architects*, 80.
[71] Salzman, *Building in England*, 445.

defining what they desired and the risk of poor workmanship. At Helmingham, the contract agreed that 'if any default be found in workmanship ... by any manner of workmen or workman or any other man of cunning within the space of twenty years ... that the said steeple be not made sufficiently in all things after the patron and form aforesaid, that then [the mason] shall make or do to be made again' the steeple at his own cost.[72] The duration of this guarantee must have been more in hope than reality, although it might indicate that the mason, Thomas Aldrych of North Lopham, Norfolk, a small village some twenty miles north of Helmingham, had a permanent workshop of some longevity. A similar guarantee was used at Wycombe, Buckinghamshire: 'if the said work be not substantially and sufficiently wrought and made in everything belonging to masons' work and that work so adjudged insufficient by sufficient masons', then the contractor would finish the work 'well and sufficiently' at his own cost in as short a time as possible.[73] The approval of other masons could be further integrated into the building process: at Fotheringhay, Northamptonshire, the mason was to lay out the foundations 'sufficiently as it ought to be by oversight of masters of the same craft'.[74] A related strategy was employed for the Stratton rood loft in Cornwall, where the contractees were to 'amend the same rood-loft and all other [of] the premises at all times as need shall require' for four years after its completion.[75] The assessment of third-party masons was common outside parish church construction too and used as early as c. 1230, in Battle, Sussex, when it was greed that the masons' work was 'to be put to the judgement of good and lawful masons'.[76]

Quality was to be firmly controlled during the building process, and the cutting of corners, especially in the provision of materials, was often included in contractual agreements. The principal was explained at Helmingham in a clause that required 'black flint stone and free stone to be laid on the steeple without as near as they may [be] for the most avail and best to be saved for the profit of the township'.[77] At Fotheringhay, the mason was to use rough stone for the foundations and inner walls, and ashlar for the outer walls, windowsills, pillars, capitals, mullions, battlements, clerestory and 'bench-table-stones'.[78] Similarly, at Great Sherston, Wiltshire, the doors, windows, plinth, chimney, hearth and stairs were to

---

[72] Ibid., 547–49; a similar agreement for a new bell in Weston, Norfolk, in 1528 threatened nonpayment if it was found 'defective by two or three credible persons of music'; John H. Baker, ed., *The Reports of Sir John Spelman*, vol. 94 (London, 1978), 260–61.
[73] TNA: PRO E 210/985; Salzman, *Building in England*, 557–59.
[74] Salzman, *Building in England*, 505–09.   [75] Goulding, *Blanchminster's Charity*, 91–94.
[76] ESRO amsg/AMS5592/56.
[77] BLO Tanner MS 138, f. 87; Salzman, *Building in England*, 547–49.
[78] Salzman, *Building in England*, 505–09.

Managerial Strategies

be freestone, the rest rough stone.[79] At Surfleet, Lincolnshire, the contractors were to use English glass.[80] The quality of materials, when provided by the contractor, was often laid down, particularly for wood, which must be seasoned or 'heart of oak' (as at St John-atte-Hill, Bury St Edmunds).[81] Patrons could sue successfully when poor materials were used, as Roger de Multon did at St Ives in 1317, when alder and willow were used instead of oak.[82]

Contractees were alert to particular types of fraud, a reflection, as we have seen, of contemporary concerns about indolent or corrupt workers.[83] Where the contractees were providing materials, as at Helmingham, they could insert a clause ordering the mason to neither 'break nor spoil no manner of stuff ... that shall be to them delivered'.[84] At Morebath, Devon, for the materials provided by the wardens for the new cross, the contractor was 'to spoil it to his costs & charge'.[85] At Fotheringhay, there was even a limit on the number of men to be employed, to be set by the contractees, and at Surfleet, a requirement that work not be delayed or prolonged unnecessarily.[86] Although building sites would have provided relatively easy targets for theft, as took place at Winchester and York cathedrals in 1371 and 1408 respectively, few are recorded from parish churches in either manor or church court rolls, suggesting both that project managers kept tight control over security and that locals recognised the work as for the common good.[87] Stone taken from church fabrics or manorial quarries and used in peasant houses could, of course, have been purchased rather than stolen – especially if it turned up in the houses of wealthy peasants who were probably involved in maintaining or even building the church.[88]

The contract did, of course, reflect the contractors' interests too: above all it protected them from costly changes of design, new or unclear

---

[79] Ibid., 561, 466; at Edinburgh the contractees insisted 1,200 ashlar stones were to be used at the masons' cost, 'as falls to that work'.
[80] Ibid., 496–97.
[81] Salzman, *Building in England*, 473–76, 502. Similar provisions were made for non-parochial works, as at Durham Cathedral, 1398 and 1402, and the new quay at Norwich, 1432. Ibid., 512–13, 473–76, 502.
[82] Charles Gross, ed., *Select Cases Concerning the Law Merchant, A.D. 1270–1638*, vol. 1, 1908, 103–04.
[83] A good example, but outside England, can be found in Edinburgh in 1387 where the 'masons [were to] do their craft till that work truly without fraud as true men ought to do': Salzman, *Building in England*, 55, 466.
[84] BLO Tanner MS 138, f. 87; Ibid., 547–49.   [85] Binney, *Morebath CWAs*, 70.
[86] Salzman, *Building in England*, 505–9, 496.
[87] Kirby, *Wykeham's Register*, 2:127–28; Virginia Davis, *William Wykeham* (London, 2007), 115; Jon Cannon, *Cathedral: The Great English Cathedrals and the World That Made Them, 600–1540* (London, 2007), 133; Salzman, *Building in England*, 55.
[88] Sally V. Smith, 'Towards a Social Archaeology of the Late Medieval English Peasantry: Power and Resistance at Wharram Percy', *Journal of Social Archaeology* 9, no. 3 (1 October 2009): 404–7.

Approaches to Building Work

requirements and delayed or non-payment by the patron. Common clauses demanded that the contractor be paid in 'good and legal money' and 'without any delay or failure' and typically on specific days. Sensitivity to the cost of transport, as well as to the corner-cutting of employers, can be found in demands that materials be delivered within a certain number of feet of the building site (forty at Arlingham; twenty at Great Sherston).[89] Patrons bound their heirs and executors to pay, in the event of their death, while the contract at Surfleet permitted the suspension of work in case of non-payment.[90] When there was no written contract, it would be harder to claim for unpaid costs, as was still the case in the early sixteenth century, with Robert Long's work at Steeple Ashton, Wiltshire, where the contractor Thomas Lovell's executrix claimed that £49 of £80 was still to be paid.[91] Changes in design were factored in to some contracts: at Wolverhampton in 1476, if the contractees decided the steeple need not be of the full height specified the mason would be paid proportionately less by the foot.

To demonstrate the almost invariable concern of contractees with cost, deadline and agreements over transport and materials, they may be contrasted with the minimal 'stylistic' criteria in most contracts. Notwithstanding the remarkably extensive design criteria in some counterexamples, typically for projects run at some distance, such as Fotheringhay, most detailed only the broadest outlines of the building's appearance, usually including its dimensions and the number of windows or doors. Very few mention drawings or models.[92] Revealingly, many contracts specifically left design decisions to 'the discretion of the masons' (as at Halstead, Essex); allowing for their expertise and the need for flexibility in design, in contrast to inflexible questions of cost and deadline.[93] Sufficiency reappears repeatedly as the standard to which building work would be held: the battlements were to be 'sufficiently performed', at Orby, Lincolnshire, while the masons were to build 'well and sufficiently', at St Dunstan, London, 'well and sufficient', at Halstead and 'sufficiently and surely' at Thornham Parva.[94] These join other vague clauses: most commonly, that work must be made 'well', 'skilfully' or 'substantially'. A few examples will demonstrate the breadth of vocabulary: 'well and skilful', at Arlingham; 'well make', 'truly and duly', at Fotheringhay; 'make perfect ... after his best manner', at Tempsford; 'in good proportion surely[,] workmanly and substantially wrought', at Hackington; 'well and

---

[89] '*bone et legalis monete*'; '*sine dilacione seu defectu aliquali*'.　[90] Salzman, *Building in England*, 496.
[91] TNA: PRO C 1/367/38; French, *People*, 54; another example is the new sedilia at Folsham, Norfolk, in 1507: Baker, *The Reports of Sir John Spelman*, 94:261.
[92] But see Dunster (1442) and Wolverhampton (1476): Salzman, *Building in England*, 514–15, 547–49.
[93] '*iuxta discretionem lathamorum*'.　[94] Salzman, *Building in England*, 575, 462–63, 490–91, 27.

Managerial Strategies

worked manly', at Biddenham; and 'surely, cleanly, and craftily wrought ... honestly and well carved', at St John-atte-Hill, Bury St Edmunds.[95] The imprecision of these requests compared to the invariably precise demands regarding financial arrangements indicates the function that most contracts were intended to fulfil and the concerns that drove their use: timely completion, overall cost (and payment schedules) and honest workmanship.[96] Design, in addition to being difficult to prosecute over and challenging to render into words, was a more flexible procedure that would continue to develop after the contract had been agreed.[97]

It might be wrong to assume that relatively vague terms referring to quality and style had no legal effect, however, or that contractees considered them to be insignificant. Contractors were sued for poor workmanship, as at Thornham Parva,[98] and guilds could require members to rebuild poorly made structures.[99] Even when independent masons were not brought in to judge the work, the contractor might be bound to fulfil the contract to the contractees' satisfaction: at Arlingham, 'for the good performance of each and every article aforesaid to the satisfaction of the said parishioners'.[100] Often no assessor was named and judgement of the work was presumably to be negotiated: 'to be made and finished in wise as it is afore devised and declared', at Fotheringhay; and 'all and singular covenants of [the mason's] part before rehearsed [to be] well and truly observed and kept in [the] manner beforesaid', at Helmingham.[101] However, contractees could come to rue using such ill-defined language: when the contractees at Surfleet, Lincolnshire, sued their contractor in 1429, because the new chancel had not been 'well and sufficiently' made according to the form of the contract, the latter replied that it was, albeit a year late.[102] When the case was heard again, the contractees were absent and were ordered to be attached. Indeed, many contracts went to exhaustive lengths to eradicate ambiguity about logistical or financial arrangements – repeating the names of each party on multiple occasions and anticipating practical problems: a party could be described as the 'workmen or workman or any other man of cunning' who would 'make or cause to be made' the work at their own 'cost, charge and expense'.[103]

---

[95] 'bene et artificialiter constructe', at Arlingham; 'bon et suffisaunt', at St Dunstan, London; 'bono et sufficienti', at Halstead; Ibid., 445, 505–9, 563–64, 512–13; Byng, 'Biddenham', 262–63.
[96] Cf. Malcolm Hislop, *Medieval Masons* (Princes Risborough, 2009), 12.
[97] Gabriel Byng, 'The Dynamic of Design: "Source" Buildings and Contract Making in the Late Middle Ages', *Architectural History* 59 (2016): 123–48.
[98] TNA: PRO C 1/76/30.   [99] Salzman, *Building in England*, 66–67.
[100] 'omnibus et singulis articulis in supradicto bene faciendis et implendis parochiani predicti', ibid., 563–64.
[101] Ibid., 505–9, 547–49.   [102] Welby, 'Surfleet Church'.
[103] See the examples collected in Salzman, *Building in England*, Appendix B.

Approaches to Building Work

iii) Timing

Changes in the prices of building wages and materials were surveyed in the Introduction but such national generalisations neglect local and regional patterns in the cost and convenience of construction. Intensive periods of building work across a wide area may be attributed to more than a general influx of wealth, local rivalry or inspiration. Although it may have rendered labourers, craftsmen and materials in high demand, and therefore more expensive, widespread or large-scale building work increased the exploitation of natural resources, the flow of labourers, craftsmen and materials to the area, the commercialisation of the building trade, training opportunities for craftsmen and improvements to local infrastructure. Large building projects, contractors or merchants could buy and transport materials in bulk, benefitting from economies of scale and the development of roads and routes.[104] Workshops producing finished building materials, such as nails, laths and pins, were profitable enough to be transformed into veritable production lines, as perhaps could the preparation of some raw materials: lime, timber or metals. Craftsmen were assured of regular employment and could afford to flock to an area, perhaps working on several buildings at once or even setting up semi-permanent workshops, competing for contracts in the surrounding area, building good reputations and extensive experience. In York under Richard II, more than an eighth of independent skilled men in the town were builders.[105] Templates, tools and equipment could be reused across several buildings. Such efficiencies can best be seen in wealthy trading towns in the later middle ages, as at Norwich or Bristol, but they could take place in rural areas too. Patrons who chose to build during or shortly after the construction of other stone buildings in the area may have been taking advantage of a favourable climate for employing experienced craftsmen, purchasing materials locally, and utilising equipment and expertise.

Building around the same time as, or immediately after, a major building project had similar effects. Large numbers of parish churches engaged in building work around the time of construction on nearby cathedrals or abbeys, as for example in and around Lincoln and Salisbury in the early thirteenth century; in Cambridgeshire and Ely in the 1320s and 1330s; or in Winchester during the Perpendicular period.[106] Many

---

[104] Jennifer Alexander, 'Building Stone from the East Midlands Quarries: Sources, Transportation and Usage', *Medieval Archaeology* 39 (1995): 107–35.

[105] Dyer, *Standards*, 101.

[106] Bradley and Pevsner, *Cambridgeshire*, 377–81; Michael Bullen et al., *Hampshire: Winchester and the North* (New Haven, 2010), 22–23; Nikolaus Pevsner and John Harris, *Lincolnshire*, 2nd ed. (London, 1989), 49–50.

were built by masons who had worked on the major sites and used transport routes, labourers and know-how developed for their construction. Major works could lead to investment in local infrastructure: the Ely sacrist paid to strengthen roads and bridges ahead of the rebuilding work, for example,[107] while a substantial proportion of the large expenditure on building work would have been spent locally on food, accommodation, equipment, transport and other costs, providing an injection into the local economy of many parishes.[108] It might be objected that major building projects absorbed much of the available local labour force and the productive capacity of local quarries and woodland, increasing prices for parish building projects.[109] However, before the mid-fourteenth century, the number of landless was probably sufficient to supply a large quantity of cheap, unskilled labour.[110] Craftsman were harder to find but plentiful work attracted masons into the area, while providing experience and training to locals probably helped churches to find builders. At Vale Royal, Cheshire, only 5–10 per cent of masons were from the area, but 85 per cent of labourers were local.[111] The irregularity of work on major building sites would have made a certain quantity of highly trained masons and labourers available to nearby parishes for much of the year, and in the periods following or between building campaigns.[112] The effect on local quarries may have been muted since distant, high quality quarries were more widely used and nearby resources were better exploited.[113] Any effect was, however, relative to the broader economic context. Indeed, quantitative correlation is less revealing than qualitative explanation: it has already been argued that, although Perpendicular work was carried out in greater quantities in parish churches than great churches, the broad contours of both were similar.[114]

A second objection to the thesis that great church construction stimulated parochial building work is that it was financed by taxing tenants, local parishioners and rectories, thereby reducing funds available for parish church construction. However, comparing fabric accounts, contracts and chronicles with taxable income shows that great institutions were usually able to

[107] Chapman, *Sacrist Rolls of Ely, Notes*, 1:23; pace Bercea, Ekelund, and Tollison, 'Entry-Deterring'.
[108] Owen, 'Economic Legacy'; Owen and Soltow, 'Public Works', 289; von Simson, *Gothic Cathedral*, 166–70.
[109] G. P. Jones, 'Building in Stone in Medieval Western Europe', in *The Cambridge Economic History of Europe*, 2nd ed., vol. 2 (Cambridge, 1987), 771.
[110] Introduction, section b, pp. 11–13.
[111] Douglas Knoop and G. P. Jones, 'The First Three Years of the Building of Vale Royal Abbey, 1278–1280', *Ars Quatuor Coronatorum* XLIV (1931): 5–47.
[112] Stanford, *Savoy*, 18.
[113] Anne Blanc and Jean-Pierre Gely, 'Stone from Medieval Churches Located to the South and East of Paris', in *Working with Limestone*, ed. Vibeke Olsen (Farnham, 2011), 69, 72.
[114] Introduction, section d, pp. 40–45.

encompass vast building projects within their ordinary revenue. The cost of building Ely, for example, was borne by the priory's regular income and formed only a slight burden on local parishes. The *Historia Eliensis* records the cost of the octagon as £2,400 over twenty years, an annual average of £120, but even this immense sum formed less than two-fifths of the sacrist's mean annual expenditure in the fourteen extant rolls from 1291 to 1359.[115] Rebuilding three bays of the choir for £2,034, an annual mean of £136 over fifteen years, came to only 7 per cent of the bishop's income, which was recorded at £2,000 a year in the 1291 *Taxatio* and again in 1337, and these are probably fiscal undervaluations.[116] For the building work, the sacrist's income was indeed augmented by collections, rectorial income churches across Cambridgeshire and offerings. However, the collections were diocese-wide and small, raising about £2–£4.[117] Ely was not exceptional in this regard: examples of modest collections can be found elsewhere too.[118] The churches had all been appropriated by the priory long before and offerings were made by pilgrims from across the country. In fact, none were new impositions but rather 'allotments from the general and special funds'.[119] The Lady Chapel's funding was organised by John of Wisbech 'with the alms of the faithful' but responsibility ultimately fell to Bishop Montacute, who 'contributed many large sums'.[120] It is likely that the total loss to parishes within the diocese was more than balanced both by investment in local infrastructure and the stimulation to the local economy of an influx of wage-earning labourers.[121]

D) FINANCIAL PLANNING

i) Budgets, Estimates and Plans

Even if medieval parishes were adept at using legal instruments to control costs and transfer risk, this does not represent fully-fledged financial planning. This would require accurate estimates of the duration of building work and its cost, and the effective marshalling of sufficient resources to ensure completion. The use of contracts and donations for a specific numbers of years from guilds, pledges or property all represent estimations of time and cost that were understood to be secure enough to have

---

[115] Chapman, *Sacrist Rolls of Ely, Notes*.
[116] Miller, *Ely*, 81; Chapman, *Sacrist Rolls of Ely, Notes*, 1:54.
[117] F. R. Chapman, ed., *Sacrist Rolls of Ely, Transcripts*, vol. 2 (Cambridge, 1908), 36; 51.
[118] Willis, *Canterbury Cathedral*, 117; Woodman, *Canterbury*, 151; Ute Engel, *Worcester Cathedral: An Architectural History* (2007), 182.
[119] Chapman, *Sacrist Rolls of Ely, Notes*, 1:25.
[120] Henry Wharton, *Anglia Sacra*, vol. 1 (London, 1691), 651.
[121] See the debate between 'optimists' and 'pessimists', Introduction, section a, pp. 8–9.

Financial Planning

legal force.[122] As we have seen, almost all contracts laid down total cost and time requirements for building work, although Dunster in Somerset allowed for three years 'and farther if it may be' in 1442.[123] Some contracts also laid down further criteria to ensure good progress was made throughout the work: at Arlingham, the mason was to add twelve feet a year over three years, based presumably on his experience of how quickly he could build.[124] At Catterick, North Yorkshire, the contractor was to build the choir in one year, the rest of the building in three and the parapets during a further year. Presumably here the reason was to allow divine service to resume as quickly as possible.[125] The success of the contracting system relied on these estimations being accurate: contractors would need to determine the cost of the work accurately so that they could turn a profit, and the duration to avoid prosecution, while patrons would only agree to a deal which represented good value.[126] When projects were not contracted out, their managers can be found using accounts to monitor expenditure. At Louth, Lincolnshire, a separate subtotal was added to the churchwardens' accounts recording the total spent on the steeple. Later, the accounts were used to review the process and a memorandum notes the total cost at more than £305.[127]

Contracts and accounts show that contractees usually paid in instalments, sometimes continuing for some time after the work had been completed. Payment schedules not only reduced the likelihood of fraud and incentivised efficient completion but also spread the burden of payments over a longer period, providing more time for fundraising. Payment was often discretionary, as at Wycombe, Buckinghamshire, 1509 ('according as the said work goes forward so the said Wardens and Rulers to pay him at their discretion'); Stratton, Cornwall, 1531 ('yearly by such portions thereof as the work goes forth and that a John Chowyll or any workman will judge'); or St Dunstan, London, in 1381 ('from time

---

[122] Branner, 'Review', 61; Robert Branner, 'Letters to the Editor', *The Art Bulletin* 37, no. 3 (1955): 236; Otto G. von Simson, 'Letters to the Editor', *The Art Bulletin* 37, no. 3 (1955): 235–36; Erwin Panofsky, ed., *Abbot Suger on the Abbey Church of St. Denis and Its Art Treasures* (Princeton, NJ, 1946), 102, 52.

[123] Salzman, *Building in England*, 514–15, 547–49; Vallance, 'R.N.', 267–68.

[124] Salzman, *Building in England*, 563–64.   [125] Ibid. 487–90.

[126] That financing should be based on estimates for which the contractor was responsible was a Vitruvian principle, which he illustrated with the example of Ephesus, where the master builder was liable if the cost of building work exceeded his estimate by over a quarter. Vitruvius Pollio, *Ten Books on Architecture*, ed. Thomas Noble Howe, trans. Ingrid D. Rowland (Cambridge, 1999), Book X, Introduction.

[127] Although the accounts recorded the total at £288 2s. Robert Slater Bayley, *Notitiæ Ludæ, or Notices of Louth* (London, 1834), 146; T. Espin, *A Short Account of Louth Church* (London, 1807), 12.

Approaches to Building Work

to time').[128] The advantage here was the contractees', who could effectively choose how much and when to pay, thereby incentivising quick completion, although perhaps these requirements were supplemented with oral agreements as to the measurement of progress. Other contracts determined the instalments according to proportions of work completed. In 1476, at Broxbourne, Hertfordshire, three equal payments were to be made at the beginning of the project, at the start of the setting of the walls and at completion.[129] More common were payments per foot, as at Arlingham in 1372, Dunster in 1442, Helmingham in 1488 or Stratton.[130] These strategies could be combined: at Fotheringhay, in 1434, the contractor was to be paid 100s per foot, but almost £7 after finishing the foundations and 300s once the steeple was as high as the nave. At Dunster there was a limit on the amount which would be paid before the actual erection of the building began.[131] At Arlingham, the mason would receive a bushel of wheat and £10 4s a year in four instalments of different quantities, which worked out at 17s a foot. These were probably to be paid at every foot ('like as he does his work', at Dunster; 'at every journey [i.e. course] as he works after the foot', at Helmingham).[132] It is plausible that these complex arrangements were the fruit of arduous and disputatious compromises. Even more advantageous to the craftsman was when payment was fixed to specific days. At Great Sherston, in 1511, payment was to be made in five instalments on set days.[133] At Hackington the payments were in three annual instalments but the final one was to be paid once the work was completed.[134] Similarly, at Morebath, payment was on quarter days and the final one 'when it is done [and] he perform[s] his promise[s]'.[135] In 1413, for the new roof at Halstead, Essex, the carpenter received 40s at Christmas and at the Exaltation of the Holy Cross, and the rest (almost £9) on completion.[136] At Steeple Ashton, Wiltshire, in 1504–15, payment was 'at certain days between them agreed'.[137] These last examples, with regular payments on certain days, indicate substantial faith in the estimated time of completion but were presumably conditional on the work taking place according to the expected schedule. Differences in the payment schedules for building

---

[128] '*ensy de temps en temps*'; cf. Winchester Cathedral nave contractors: Nichols, *Collection*, 767; Salzman, *Building in England*, 557–59, 462–63; Goulding, *Blanchminster's Charity*, 91.
[129] TNA: PRO E 210/2638; Salzman, *Building in England*, 537–38.
[130] Ibid., 514–15, 445, 547–49; Goulding, *Blanchminster's Charity*, 91.
[131] Maxwell Lyte, 'Dunster and Its Lords', 217.
[132] TNA: PRO E 210/985; Salzman, *Building in England*, 557–59, 547–49; St. John Hope, 'High Wycombe', 13.
[133] Salzman, *Building in England*, 561.   [134] Vallance, 'R.N.', 267–68.
[135] Binney, *Morebath CWAs*, 70.   [136] Salzman, *Building in England*, 490–91.
[137] TNA: PRO C 1/367/38.

projects indicate differing analyses of the trustworthiness of each party, the likelihood of timely completion and the reliability of fundraising.

Wills and contracts show patrons demanding hasty completion. At Stratton, the carpenters were to work 'in all convenient haste & speed',[138] while at Tempsford, the contract decreed that the contractor 'shall take no other works in hand till this work be perfectly ended'.[139] Testators demanded that their projects should be swift: 'that the patrons of Harewood begin to build this church within the next year, and continue continuously, according to the power of the patrons, until it shall be fully rebuilt'.[140] In 1522, John Fox was entirely typical in giving the parishioners of St John the Evangelist, Lincoln, precisely a year to finish the roodscreen before his donation would be spent elsewhere.[141] Some time limits in contracts were probably the result of testamentary injunctions to begin or finish work within a certain period, before the bequest was to be put to other uses, or because episcopal permission for building work had been granted on condition of a quick finish.[142] Graves argues that the brevity of official tenure in urban authorities stimulated the authorities to attempt to complete building work as quickly as possible, to demonstrate its manager's 'authority in civic administration'.[143] It is likely that a fabric or churchwarden's performance in office would be judged against the progress made in building work. This may be contrasted with the idea that time was a useful building resource that could take the place of money: 'the mere prospect of this endless time-to-build ... would have tended to dissipate any inherent pressure to hurry'.[144] It can hardly have been desirable for buildings to spend years as building sites, aesthetically, functionally or financially. Buildings under construction decay faster than completed ones: half-finished walls let in water and cold, ice cracks stonework, unprotected mortar and timber decays, straw must be brought in to protect walls and the patience of the congregation is tested. Construction that continued over the course of a century or more, as for example at Saffron Walden, Essex, is often more accurately understood as a series of short-term projects each constructed quickly and to schedule.[145] There is nothing exceptional about projects at

---

[138] Goulding, *Blanchminster's Charity*, 91–92.   [139] Salzman, *Building in England*, 563–64.
[140] James Raine, ed., *Testamenta Eboracensia*, vol. 1 (London, 1836), 346.
[141] Foster, *Lincoln Wills*, 1914, 1:105.
[142] E.g. at Broadhempston, 1400–01: Hingeston-Randolph, *The Register of Edmund Stafford (A. D. 1395–1419)*, 39.
[143] Graves, 'Social Space', 314.   [144] Trachtenberg, *Building-in-Time*, 111.
[145] Byng, 'Saffron Walden'.

Approaches to Building Work

Bolney, Sussex, or Hardley, Norfolk, which were erected in a matter of months.[146]

As noted in the Introduction to this chapter, the fact that examples of mistakes are relatively rare is not especially revealing. However, it is telling that, in many, financial planning took place but proved inaccurate. Leland writes, without noting sources, that: 'The parishioners [of Winchcombe, Gloucestershire, c. 1454–74] had gathered £200 and began the body of the church; but that sum being not able to perform so costly a work, Ralph Boteler, Lord Sudeley, helped them and finished the work.'[147] If Leland's summary is correct, it indicates that an estimate was made, and substantial funds stockpiled, but that the cost of the work proved unexpectedly large. At Leverton, Lincolnshire, in 1526, Robert Brook was paid for seventeen alabasters for the rood loft by the widow of William Franks, but the total left proved to be sufficient only for sixteen, and a further sum had to be found for 'one other odd image to be set in the same place that every stage might be filled'.[148] There are similar examples from the later sixteenth century.[149] Even when the cost estimate was accurate, the assessment of future income could prove incorrect: there was frustration in Totnes at how slowly funds were raised for the building work.[150] The contractor at Heanton Punchardon, Devon, agreed to an eighty foot long chapel in 1538–44 before realising that an existing vestry limited the space by six feet.[151] Parishes could be caught out by their own credulity. In 1529, at Orby, Lincolnshire, the contractor was impressed by the crown and so unable to finish the battlements, but nevertheless took his advance.[152] It can probably be assumed that the conditions in most contracts were not inflexible, provided both parties agreed – those that ended up in court must demonstrate a rare case of complete breakdown in what was usually a mutually beneficial, if occasionally fraught, relationship.[153] However, even if patrons were well able to analyse cost, income and realistic building and payment schedules, we must now examine if and how they planned a steady income for the duration of the project.

---

[146] Trachtenberg, *Building-in-Time*, 112. [147] Leland, *Itinerary*, 1908, 2:55.
[148] LA Leverton Par/7/1 ff. 19v–20r; Peacock, 'Leverton CWAs', 349–50.
[149] Woodward, *Men at Work*, 36. [150] Graves, 'Social Space', 314; Russell, *Totnes*, 35.
[151] TNA: PRO C 1/1074/18.
[152] TNA C 1/613/10; Salzman, *Building in England*, 575; see also: Geoffrey the mason who stole vestments and books from St Leonard, Leicester, in 1298. My thanks to Dr Ian Forrest for this reference: Mary Bateson, *Records of the Borough of Leicester*, vol. 1 (London, 1899), 360.
[153] Cf. the flexible conditions attached to Italian Renaissance projects: Baxandall, *Painting and Experience*, 8–11.

Financial Planning

ii) Accumulating Capital and Pledges

A simple and effective way for parishes to ensure completion was to accumulate capital before commencing construction, a technique found in major church projects.[154] Trachtenberg argues that lengthy building projects with no set completion date were used to demonstrate a Christian renunciation of 'sensuous pleasures' in the present for the good of future descendants but, if that was the case, it may be set against a Biblical instruction that calls for funds to be accumulated ahead of building work, to ensure completion (Luke 14.28–30).[155] Planning and stockpiling for building projects may have started decades before the work began so that enough could be gathered. At Dunster, William Pynson left 40s for the building of the tower in 1419, but a contract was not drawn up until 1443.[156] Building work on Ludlow tower in Shropshire attracted bequests in 1453 but work began in c. 1469.[157] At Wimborne Minster, £40 had been accumulated in the years ahead of starting work in 1448.[158] This could be true of non-architectural projects too: the screen at Cawston was made in 1502 (according to the inscription) but a bequest was left to its building in 1460.[159] However, many parishes stockpiled for only a few years before starting work: at Walberswick, Suffolk, the churchwardens began saving in 1470, noted they had accumulated £23 in 1471, and started purchasing materials in 1472.[160] The same technique was also used by institutional officers like Walter Cuddington, who stockpiled large sums for around four years before beginning work on St John the Baptist, Oxford, in the 1280s.[161] Gentry patrons also adopted this approach: John Bolney sold land in 1530 and 1532 almost certainly to raise capital but did not start building until 1536.[162]

Stockpiling was common practice: archaeological discoveries indicate that wealthy peasants could own substantial amounts of coin, as much as £3 even in the thirteenth century, while peasants were able to raise large sums quickly for purchase, manumission, entry fines, marriages or

---

[154] It was also familiar enough for Alberti to recommend it; William W. Clark and Thomas G. Waldman, 'Money, Stone, Liturgy, and Planning at the Royal Abbey of Saint-Denis', in *New Approaches to Medieval Architecture*, ed. Robert Odell Bork, William W. Clark, and Abby McGehee (Farnham, 2011), 67; Dieter Kimpel and Robert Suckale, *Die Gotische Architektur in Frankreich, 1130–1270* (München, 1985), 223–25; De Re Aedificatoria, 11.2.

[155] Trachtenberg, *Building-in-Time*, 113; cf. Matthew Paris, *Chronicles of Matthew Paris: Monastic Life in the Thirteenth Century.*, ed. Richard Vaughan (Gloucester, 1986), 14–15.

[156] Paul Newman, *Somerset Villages* (London, 1986), 177.

[157] Of course, bequests could have been for repair work only and these examples must be hesitant at best: Jones, 'Ludlow CWAs', 244.

[158] Brown, *Popular Piety*, 119.   [159] Blomefield, *Norfolk*, 1807, 6:254–68.

[160] Lewis, *Walberswick CWAs*, 97.

[161] Martin and Highfield, *A History of Merton College, Oxford*, 39.

[162] Chapter 5, section b.ii, pp. 222–24.

Approaches to Building Work

amercements, whether from savings or loans.[163] The large net income of some members of the upper peasantry, both before and after the Black Death, has already been outlined.[164] Stockpiling cash could be dangerous, however: money collected for the repair of Eden bridge in Cumbria was 'concealed by unknown persons careless of their souls',[165] while the bishop had to order the priest of Northallerton, North Yorkshire, to hand over money collected for rebuilding the church to the perpetual vicar.[166] At Henley-on-Thames, Oxfordshire, in 1519, one of the 'goodmen' of the parish 'confessed' that a 25s bequest given to the rood loft was still in his children's possession.[167]

In fact, most parishes probably struggled to accumulate the entire capital for a major building project – coin was usually in too short supply, besides the risks of theft and inflation – but equivalent strategies could be followed instead. The vast majority of surviving annual accounts record a 'deficit', that is, the wardens spent less than their income, proving both the churchwardens' managerial acumen and, no doubt, the threat of censure.[168] The effect was to create a gradually increasing pot of capital in a 'deposit account', which would have made large, occasional, construction projects feasible.[169] As we have seen, this was probably the technique used for the building of a new chapel at Croscombe, Somerset – in 1506–07, at the start of the work, income was less than £5, and no obvious fundraising drive had begun, but the parish stock was £13. The following year it had fallen to under £4 after the mason had been paid £8.[170]

When a parish could not raise sufficient capital, it could build up pledges and develop reliable sources of future funding. Evidence for

---

[163] John Hatcher, *Rural Economy and Society in the Duchy of Cornwall, 1300–1500* (Cambridge, 1970), 255; Dyer, *Lords and Peasants*, 352; Marjorie Keniston McIntosh, *Autonomy and Community: The Royal Manor of Havering, 1200–1500* (Cambridge, 2002), 231; J. D. A. Thompson, *Inventory of British Coin Hoards, AD 600 – 1500* (London, 1956), 68, 108; Dyer, *Standards*, 178–79.

[164] Chapter 1, section c.vi, pp. 83–84, 88–89.

[165] My thanks to Dr Ian Forrest for this and the following reference: R. L. Storey, *The Register of Gilbert Welton, Bishop of Carlisle, 1353–1362* (Woodbridge, 1999), 107.

[166] Rosalind M. T. Hill, *The Register of William Melton, Archbishop of York, 1317–1340*, vol. 1 (York, 1977), 120–21.

[167] Frank E. Howard, 'Screens and Rood-Lofts in the Parish Churches of Oxfordshire', *Archaeological Journal* 67 (1910): 156.

[168] There are many examples, including: Doree, *Bishops Stortford CWAs*, xv; Hanham, *Ashburton CWAs*, viii. Note the caution as to using churchwardens' accounts for quantitative analysis in Introduction, section e, pp. 46–47.

[169] Kümin, *Shaping*, 89.

[170] Chapter 1, section b.ii, pp. 60–61. It is difficult to trace the stock through the accounts, especially between 1502 and 1506, but it seems this accumulation had continued for some time – in 1501–02 it was almost £17; in 1500–01 it was over £10; in 1499–1500 it was almost £13, and so on, going back to 1474–75. Hobhouse, *Church-Wardens' Accounts*, 29.

Financial Planning

accumulating pledges, often termed 'grants', 'proffers' or 'promises', before commencing building work can be found in many bequests. Some wills mention pledges made in life: John Donett asked his testators to fulfil 'the full contentation [sic] and payment of that sum of money thereto by me granted' to the building work,[171] another donated sums 'to the edifying of a new steeple ... according to a grant made by me'.[172] Testators often left money to building projects on condition that further sums were donated or that work began within a certain time period.[173] John Browne, a wealthy yeoman, for example, asked that his bequest for a new ceiling over the rood loft at West Malling, Kent, in 1488, 'be not paid until the time that the said new ceiling be in hand to be made and so to be concluded and finished'.[174] In 1534, Richard Clemens left £10 for gilding the rood loft 'at such times as the parishioners ... go forward' with it and Thomas Drake left money to the rood screen at Bunwell, Norfolk, in 1533 'if the parishioners ... go forward with it and set it up'.[175] Wills usually provide conditions naming the alternative to which the money was to be put should an insufficient quantity be realised or the deadline expire.

The most extensive, explicit, use of pledges was at Swaffham, Norfolk, where, in 1507–10, most of the gifts for the steeple are described as 'for his proffer to the steeple in party of payment of a more sum' or 'in full payment of his proffer to the steeple'.[176] The Black Book of Swaffham listed pledges that were recorded on paper ('bills' or 'parcels'): 'these parcels of profferings to the steeple and bills are ... due to be yet gathered by the old or else by the new church reeves' in 1457.[177] The fabric accounts at Bodmin include several folios recording sums owed ('*qui sunt a retro*') or promised ('*habent plegium*'), and sums paid in part by guilds and individuals.[178] Pledging had a wider social significance, occasionally visible in the accounts: parishioners might agree to match one another's pledges, for example,[179] while at Louth a section of the 1501–02 accounts is headed 'gifts given when the first stone was set of the brooch by diverse men', perhaps the realisation of pledges.[180] Some such pledges were not for a specific sum of money but for the cost of an architectural unit, such as an arch or window, a sponsorship that, as we have seen, was occasionally inscribed into the fabric.[181] Many such pledges did not simply represent good intentions, they had legal force and were almost as secure as direct donations. When pledges were not honoured, churchwardens

---

[171] Hussey, *Testamenta Cantiana (East)*, 310.   [172] Ibid., 333.   [173] E.g. ibid., 204.
[174] Duncan, *Testamenta Cantiana (West)*, 51–52.   [175] Duffy, 'Parish, Piety, and Patronage', 139.
[176] NRO PD 52/71.   [177] Williams, 'The Black Book of Swaffham', 251–53.
[178] CRO BBOD/244 ff. 23–27.   [179] Littlehales, *London City Church*, 158.
[180] LA Louth St James Par/7/1, p. 24; Dudding, *Louth CWAs*, 19, 61.
[181] Chapter 1, section c.v, pp. 81–82.

Approaches to Building Work

could sue: in Cambridgeshire, two villagers in Swaffham Prior were prosecuted for refusing to honour their commitments to the church fabric in 1451.[182] In Kilmersdon, Thomas Richmonde promised the churchwarden, Richard Jamys, he would pay over £6 to the building of a new aisle but later refused, and the warden took the case to court in 1538–42.[183] The churchwardens' accounts of 1516 at Leverton were copied on to the reverse of an unusual document, dated 1498. It records an agreement by two parishioners to pay 10s to the 'church work' in three equal instalments over three years and, in case of default, the churchwardens were to take a piece of land. Committing this modest promise to writing, and retaining it not only for the three years but for another eighteen, indicates the force such promises had.[184]

Finding regular and reliable sources of future income was obviously desirable for long-term projects but difficult. Most common were the fruits of a regular collection but a variety of other sources were used.[185] Three parishioners gave a messuage and shop to St Nicholas Cole Abbey, a London parish church, for work in 1397.[186] At Lewisham, then in Kent, half a house and garden were given 'to the building of the new steeple' in 1487, although possibly for sale not rent.[187] It may have been the need for large short-term injections of capital which led Richard Wombstrong to sell, rather than rent, his house in the parish of St Nicholas, Bristol, for 30 marks for making a chapel in an early example of c. 1200.[188] Rental income was not the only source of regular funding. In 1280 John Peckham granted the income of the benefice at Horton – worth more than £6 in 1291 – to the parishioners to aid with the cost of rebuilding.[189] At All Saints, Oxford, the vicarage, which included chancel maintenance, was given to the churchwardens.[190] As at Leverton, already noted, pledges could be of steady payment over time – more manageable for the donors and more reliable for the project managers. At Ramsey six men pledged to make quarterly payments of between 12d and 4s towards the new rood loft in the 1520s.[191] Testators often left a regular payment to building work: John St Nicholas, for example, left five marks a year for five years for the building of a chapel in Ash, Kent, in 1462.[192] To this list of reliable future sources of income may be added gifts of debt repayments.[193]

---

[182] CUL EDC 7/13/6. [183] TNA: PRO C 1/1014/48–49; French, *People*, 73.
[184] LA Leverton Par/7/1 f. 55v. [185] Chapter 1, section c.iii, pp. 69–75.
[186] Stow, *Survey of London*, 2.3. [187] Duncan, *Testamenta Cantiana (West)*, 47.
[188] J. F Nicholls and John Taylor, *Bristol Past and Present*, vol. 2 (Bristol, 1881), 158.
[189] Davis, *Pecham Register*, 1:129.
[190] Andrew Clark, ed., *Lincoln Diocese Documents, 1450–1544* (London, 1914), 208, 233, 238.
[191] DeWindt and DeWindt, *Ramsey*, 33 n. 38.
[192] Nicolas, *Testamenta Vetusta*, 1826, 2:292–93.
[193] E.g. Robert Soley at Wingham: Hussey, *Testamenta Cantiana (East)*, 368.

Financial Planning

Conditional bequests, pledges and the expected income from other sources such as rent were added to a hypothetical fund which would materialise only once it reached a sufficiently high quantity for completion to be assured. Deciding when accumulated capital, pledges and loans were sufficient to commence work, on the basis of the estimated sum required for completion, depended on the leadership's confidence in those sources. Waiting until the complete sum was stockpiled was probably usually unnecessary since income would continue, and probably increase, during construction, once parishioners could see the fruits of their generosity.[194] At Louth, for example, as Swaby argues, 'the wardens seem to have begun the work on the strength of £10 borrowed from St Mary's Gild'.[195] Here, however, the wardens' substantial regular income sufficed for a large proportion of the cost of the work and, besides, they may have regretted not stockpiling sufficient capital since they were forced to borrow heavily. The purchase of bells at Bishop's Stortford, Hertfordshire, in 1492–93 provides a good case study. Stockpiling began two years earlier, when a subsection of the accounts is dedicated to sums raised for the bells, and would continue until at least two years afterwards, when sums were still being collected for the bells and part-payments made to the bellfounder.[196] The latter's total payment was to be £42, of which only £24 is recorded in the accounts. The remainder was presumably raised in 1495–97, for which the accounts are lost, and after the parishioners could see what their money was being spent on. Here, as was probably the case in most large projects, stockpiling and part-payment were combined with another strategy to defray the cost of the work across several years: borrowed money.

iii) Borrowed Money

As was shown in an earlier chapter, large loans from lay parishioners, guilds and the church stock often appeared in churchwardens' accounts during building work, when exceptional measures were called upon for funding.[197] They were not uncommonly written off in later bequests. At Louth, Lincolnshire, the churchwardens regularly owed more than £50 to guilds and individual parishioners while building the steeple, a debt largely run up in order to pay for stone at the start of the project. It formed more than a sixth of the tower's total cost and the wardens rarely had capital ('arrears') of more than 50s, but this seems to have caused little

---

[194] Vroom, *Cathedral Building*, 156–58.
[195] John Swaby, *A History of Louth* (London, 1951), 99.
[196] Doree, *Bishops Stortford CWAs*, 44–50.
[197] Chapter 1, section b.iii, pp. 62–63; Swayne, *Sarum, CWAs*, xvi.

concern – the churchwardens even purchased a new organ for more than £13 during building work. The parish secured one loan against their best chalice and seem to have agreed to a loan of stone from the master mason.[198] There are many other examples, from both fabric wardens' and churchwardens' accounts. At Bridgwater, Somerset, the construction of a new chapel before 1415 and steeple repairs in 1429 were partly financed by loans from the guild merchant.[199] The wardens at Eye in Suffolk owed large sums for lead and flint in 1470.[200] The building of a house at St Ewen, Bristol, in 1493 was not paid off until 1504.[201] At St Mary-at-Hill, London, the wardens borrowed almost £29, more than half the total cost, from a parish chest, to pay for the roofs of the aisles in 1526.[202] A section of the churchwardens' accounts at All Hallows, London Wall, was given over to various loans, made by eight parishioners, many of whom also made donations, and coming to more than £11, a third of their total income in 1528–29.[203] Lastly, when a pinnacle fell from the tower in c. 1465 in Glastonbury, the churchwardens were able to spend over £33 despite having an income of less than £6.[204] Exactly how they afforded this is unclear but, unless the balance from previous years was exceptionally high, it must have been through credit, perhaps in the form of a delayed repayment to the wardens. Borrowing for construction work was a technique used by the gentry too: William Trussell borrowed large sums of money in the 1330s (several hundreds of pounds, compared to an annual income of less than £200) around the time he founded the college of Shottesbrooke, Berkshire, and rebuilt the church.[205] There is, however, little evidence of loans to building projects from manorial lords or advowson holders, although this would be a practical way in which ecclesiastical institutions and the gentry could help their tenants and/or fellow parishioners.

That churchwardens had the confidence to borrow so heavily (and the absence of obvious defaults indicates that they did so wisely) should not be surprising. In addition to borrowing in a private capacity, some were familiar with using credit as part of a deliberate investment policy and, of course, they did sometimes run up debts as part of day-to-day bookkeeping, although any overspend seldom continued for long.[206] There were

---

[198] LA Louth St James Par/7/1; Dudding, *Louth CWAs*, xiv, xviii.
[199] SRO D/B/bw 41, 16a; Dilks, *Bridgwater Borough Archives, 1400–1445*, 49, 103.
[200] *Royal Commission on Historical Manuscripts*, 1885, X:531.
[201] Masters and Ralph, *St Ewen, Bristol, CWAs*, xvii.
[202] LMA P69/MRY/B/005/MS01239/001/001, f. 536v; Littlehales, *London City Church*, 334.
[203] Welch, *Allhallows CWAs*, 56–59.   [204] Daniel, 'Glastonbury CWAs', 235–37.
[205] Saul, 'Shottesbrooke', 271.
[206] There are many examples, including: Doree, *Bishops Stortford CWAs*, xv; Hanham, *Ashburton CWAs*, viii.

Financial Planning

numerous advantages to borrowing money for building work. Credit provided large sums of capital early in construction, when materials had to be purchased and deposits paid, smoothed over temporary shortfalls in income and spread the cost of building work over a longer period that continued after completion. Construction required uneven and often unpredictable expenditure which could be evened out by borrowing, allowing unusually high costs one year to be paid off in more economical ones. Delayed payment was probably the most common form of credit employed by fabric wardens, not least in the form of part-payments, used in the majority of large contracts.[207] As was shown in the previous section, at Bishop's Stortford payments to the bell-founder continued for at least two years after the bells were installed. At Saffron Walden, Essex, 10s was paid to a quarry owner 'in remittance of 16s 4d owed to him by the wardens of the church for many years past'[208] and at Lydd, Kent, 5s 4d was paid for 'old debt' to the mason in 1524.[209] It was familiar enough for Chaucer's friar to complain that 'we owen fourty pound for stones'.[210] In some cases there was also a significant lag in the payment of wages.[211] Since church building was an expensive endeavour consisting of many small transactions, it lent itself to the accumulation of short-term credit 'periodically settled in large denomination coin' with contractors, subcontractors and suppliers – the prevalence of sums in both income and expenditure divisible by the value of a gold noble or angel was noted in the Introduction.[212] As suggested above, this may have promoted the use of builder-contractors able to purchase in bulk and given a degree of immunity from silver shortages.[213]

Informal loans, largely hidden from fabric accounts, were probably common. We have met several examples of wealthy parishioners taking responsibility for covering large initial payments, which the parish would then return over a longer period of time, when it had raised the money through the usual means.[214] At St Mary-at-Hill, London, a wealthy parishioner who was running a major project spent £11 of his own money.[215] Although individual sums of this magnitude would have to

---

[207] Briggs, *Credit and Village Society*, 53–56; for an example see Lewis, *Walberswick CWAs*, 35.
[208] ERO D/DBy Q18, f. 97.   [209] Finn, *Records of Lydd*, 342.
[210] Geoffrey Chaucer, *The Riverside Chaucer*, ed. Larry Dean Benson, 3rd ed. (Oxford, 2008), 134.
[211] Alford and Smith, 'A Reply', 159; Alford and Smith expound on the uneven nature of late payments in B. W. E. Alford and M. Q Smith, 'The Economic Effects of Cathedral Building in Medieval England: A Further Comment', *Explorations in Entrepreneurial History* 6 (Spring/Summer 1969): 329–30; see also: Woodward, *Men at Work*, 39.
[212] Mayhew, 'Population', 253.   [213] Chapter 6, section c.i, pp. 250–51.
[214] Craig, 'Co-Operation and Initiatives', 365.
[215] LMA P69/MRY/B/005/MS01239/001/001, f. 181r; Littlehales, *London City Church*, 239; Burgess, 'Lessons', 326.

be loaned by the wealthiest parishioners, peasant lenders were not exclusively drawn from affluent families and, when sums were raised from numerous creditors, it may have provided an opportunity for middling parishioners to support church construction.[216] Larger sums could be loaned by the rector – the Dean and Chapter of Salisbury lent 12 marks to the building of the tower of St Thomas, Salisbury, in 1404.[217] The parish was a low risk debtor and such loans may have been understood as good works as well as a public show of wealth and generosity. The degree to which credit could make up for reductions in money supply or falling communal income must not be overstated, however: credit probably fell in availability at exactly those times.[218]

E) CONCLUSION

There was little that was 'simple' in the economics of building a parish church. The rise of the contractor-mason, probably with a permanent workshop and a modest staff, allowed for efficiencies in the production of designs, standardisation and the spread of 'part-contracting'. Although contracting transferred risk from patron to contractor, particularly desirable during the era of soaring wages and material prices in the decades after the Black Death, the former still needed to be careful to ensure their projects were completed on time and to budget. Contracts were invariably concerned with fixing duration and cost, as well as limiting fraud and laying out guarantees of completion and payment. Design details, flexible and difficult to describe, were considered to be of secondary relevance to contract making and were usually arranged separately, often after the contract had been sealed and even once work had commenced. Contractors (and suppliers) were typically paid in staggered amounts, both because few parishes could manage to pay for the entirety of a project in one go and in order to incentivise completion. Contracting committees tended to keep control of substantial aspects of construction, especially the provision of materials and transport, perhaps because few contractors could afford to fund these or because patrons thought they could secure better prices.

Timing probably also guided decision-making – parishes were more likely to build when prices were advantageous, as for example, when the area was flooded with craftsmen and materials during a major building project nearby. Parishes developed several techniques to ensure financing

---

[216] Briggs, *Credit and Village Society*, 143–44; Edward Britton, *The Community of the Vill: A Study in the History of the Family and Village Life in Fourteenth-Century England* (Toronto, 1977), 111.
[217] Haskins, 'St Thomas, Salisbury', 3.   [218] Mayhew, 'Population', 254.

Conclusion

was reliable, efficient and evenly spread over time. Project managers stockpiled both money and pledges (which were not realised until work commenced) cultivated reliable streams of future income and judiciously borrowed money when required and in order to allow greater time for fundraising. They made difficult decisions about the likelihood of future income streams and when to commence construction, based on estimations of total cost and duration. The men who funded and ran building work were strategic, cautious and economising: evidence of failures suggests the causes were most likely to be inaccurate, rather than incomplete, financial planning, unscrupulous contractors or unexpected costs. Ultimately, of course, work could be paused or slowed until funds became available again.

CONCLUSION

How was it that, in late medieval England, which was so often beset by severe economic and social pressures, it was possible to carry out so much building work on so many parish churches? The answer must come in several parts: efficient and well-planned managerial and financial strategies take their place next to the concentration of wealth in the hands of a few peasants and townsfolk, as well as members of the aristocracy and institutions, who were willing to work collaboratively to patronise construction. The development of a part-contracting system was critical in a time of increased risk but so too was a belief in the necessity of good works for the passage of the soul through purgatory and a desire among wealthier parishioners to be associated with architectural patronage, not least as it helped define their social position in an age of rapid social change and geographic mobility. Changes in the distribution of land and real wages must be set against the rising price of labour and materials. Explanation should not make the achievement seem less remarkable. By the turn of the fourteenth century, when only small numbers of the upper peasantry were left in many parishes and countless lived perilously close to starvation, the large quantity of church construction which took place required enormous commitment and cooperation from a very few households, whether from piety, competition or social expectation. Similarly, by the fifteenth century, even if many parts of the population had become individually wealthier, the dramatic increase in the cost of construction and the challenges of recession and a contracting money supply created new obstacles for project managers.

The most important limitation on the capacity of the parish to build was its social structure, as it mediated communal wealth. Throughout the medieval period a large proportion of the parish could afford to donate little or nothing, rarely even their own labour, so financial and organisational responsibility depended upon the size, wealth and ability of wealthier parishioners. Even after the later fourteenth century, church building was

Conclusion

an activity run and financed, when possible, by wealthier groups, albeit ones that had often grown significantly since the early fourteenth century, acting corporately but not communally. In parishes with wealthier elites, it was expected that they would monopolise the financial effort, which was evidenced not only in the absence or limited size of collections in these places but also by the relative insignificance of levies and communal fundraising activities such as ales and plays. To many eyes, the church's fabric must have appeared a testament to the wealth, generosity, piety or domination of a relatively small number of their neighbours – associations they no doubt welcomed and even fostered with the use of inscriptions and subscription lists.

This takes on a distinctive significance given the remarkable social and economic changes that took place during the long fifteenth century. New opportunities for land and employment created greater expendable income for many, and, at the same time, parish activities increased and diversified, drawing in a wider range of social groups, including (some) women and the young. Church construction was not unaffected – a greater proportion of the parish could donate than ever before, not least through guilds – but, where possible, it remained a privilege and a burden shouldered largely by the relatively wealthy. It was the less demanding, less exclusive activities that would experience the greatest change – attendance at ales, the organisation of festivals and membership of fraternities – not church building, an ancient preserve of the wealthy. Church fabrics demonstrated the importance of economic and social differentiation as much as communal action. This is not to say that church building undermined community cohesiveness; it may well have done the reverse by proving in stone and mortar the beneficial consequences of having a wealthy elite, as well as demonstrating their piety and generosity. It does, however, point to the dangers of taking 'the parish', 'the parishioners' or 'the community' as an historical agent in architectural patronage, when sources do not reveal who was excluded.[1] A sentence such as 'the community extended its nave' or 'the parish enlarged its ... chapel' can hide wholly unequal forms of participation.[2] The building may have been part of local 'communal identity', but its significance for any individual must have varied greatly according to their social and economic position within the parish.

Even among those who gave, there was considerable variation in the nature and extent of donations and of executive control, distinctions

---

[1] Cf. French, *People*, 20–27; Duffy, *Stripping*, 334–37; Christine Carpenter, 'Gentry and Community in Medieval England', The Journal of British Studies 33, no. 4 (October 1994): 340–80.
[2] French, *People*, 152.

occasionally visible in inscriptions and iconography as well as in accounts, contracts and wills. It would be oversimplifying to claim that church construction was wholly dominated by the elite (fabric wardens and churchwardens, for example, were not always quite at the pinnacle of local society, while subscribers to collections could number in their hundreds), but eligibility for memorialisation in the fabric itself or a role on a contracting committee was highly restricted. In small towns, new parochial projects were often directed by civic authorities, which were dominated by the wealthiest townsfolk; in some, perhaps many, large towns and villages projects were led by a similar group in parochial government, the masters. Nevertheless, consultation was vital – the elite's projects could go ahead only if they had the support, or at least the consent, of the community. Possibly attaining this was not difficult: the architecture of the village's communal buildings was used and enjoyed by all. If it was felt necessary the wealthy could try to persuade their juniors with bread and circuses, that is ales and plays, and many no doubt also listened – the advice of local craftsmen, legal advisers or guild wardens could be very useful.

Although the gentry are not often found on fabric or contracting committees, they did contribute directly to the common pot. Nevertheless, when they led their own building projects, they could run them personally, ensuring close control of the project and reducing management costs. Contracts and accounts indicate collaboration was probably common for gentry-led projects – relatively few families were wealthy enough for it to be otherwise – even if the archaeological record tends to obscure such cooperation. Joint enterprises between lords and parishioners could take many different forms: some common approaches, aside from direct donations from one group to the other, were dividing the project into walls and roof, stone and timber, or labour and materials. The extent to which responsibility for design was shared varied, presumably in accordance with the relative sums each group was contributing. In this way, parish church building could become an important site of cooperation, backed, perhaps, by coercion or persuasion as well as mutual advantage, between members of the village elite and their lord. It was only the wealthiest institutions and lords who could afford to finance work from their regular income alone. To do so they often set up a simple financial model, running the work through the officials who managed these manorial revenues directly. When bailiffs or stewards were not available, a position could be created to oversee the work, or a local representative appointed, if one was available. This is not to imply that great lords and institutions did not take great interest in the work or seek to control its development: contracts, auditing and regular visits to check on progress and financial accountability were all used to keep a close eye on the project.

Conclusion

Throughout it all, costs had to be kept down, plans made, contracts negotiated, accounts kept, payments administered, workmen monitored and deadlines met. The range of skills and degree of experience required were substantial, while failure was public and costly. Responsibility for oversight could be given to the churchwardens, when they were suitably 'strong', that is experienced, powerful or long-serving, or to fabric wardens, appointed by the parish assembly or masters, or by local government. Which of these was most common is of less significance than the fact that parishes deliberated about, implemented and improved managerial systems to ensure effective oversight, continuity and efficiency on the building site. Whoever ran the work was probably under the supervision of the parish hierarchy and its auditors, and delegated when appropriate, particularly to parishioners with specialist knowledge – as, for example, when the village mason chose the project architect. That they employed legal controls and financial planning with considerable success is far from surprising given the experience they had in local office, whether as jurors, bailiffs or guild officials, and their responsibility for providing the sums they were spending. The motivation of those who took on the onerous responsibility of managing and paying for parochial building projects is beyond the remit of this book. Nevertheless, it is remarkable how many parishioners were willing to donate their personal wealth to collective building work, giving enough together to construct England's 11,000 medieval churches.

BIBLIOGRAPHY

MANUSCRIPTS

Berkeley Castle Muniments

BCM/A/1/11

British Library, London

Add. Ch. 17634
Add. MS 14848
Add. MS 17716
Add. MS 5861
Harl. Ch. 48 E. 43
Royal MS 12 B 24

Bedfordshire and Luton Archives and Records Service, Bedford

Trevor-Wingfield Collection *Introduction: History of the Butler Family*

Bodleian Library, Oxford

Lat. MS misc. e. 103
Tanner MS 138

Cambridgeshire Archives, Cambridge

P11/5/1

Cambridge University Library

EDC 7/13/6
Palmer MS A55

Canterbury Cathedral archives

DCc-ChAnt/M/356
DCc-ChAnt/M/366
DCc-ChAnt/S/38

Bibliography

Corpus Christ College Cambridge archives

   CCCC06/B/1

Cornwall Record Office, Truro

   AR/1/812
   BBOD/314/1/1–14
   BBOD/244
   BTRU/18
   P167/5/1

Essex Record Office, Chelmsford

   D/ACR1
   D/DBy Q18
   D/P 192/5/2
   D/P 44/5/1

East Riding Yorkshire Archives and Local Studies, Beverley

   DDHE/19/1

East Sussex Record Office, Brighton

   amsg/AMS5592/56

Hertfordshire Archives and Local Studies, Hertford

   2AR225

Hereford Cathedral Archives

   715

Lincolnshire Archives, Lincoln

   BNLW/1/1/5/32
   BNLW/1/1/55/17
   INV/13/105
   INV/3/53
   Louth St James Par/7/1
   Leverton Par/7/1

London Metropolitan Archives

   P69/ALH5/B/003/MS05090/001
   P69/AND3/B/003/MS01279/001
   P69/MRY/B/005/MS01239/001/001
   P69/PET4/B/006/001

London School of Economics archive

   Beveridge Price History W9

Bibliography

Norfolk Record Office, Norwich

PD 52/71

Oxfordshire History Centre, Oxford

PAR273/4/F1/1

Suffolk Record Office (Ipswich Branch)

EE2/E/3/i

Somerset Record Office, Taunton

D/B/bw
D/P/tin/4/1/1
D/P/yat 4/1/1

Trinity College Archives, Cambridge

Michaelhouse 206

The National Archives, Kew

PRO C 1/1014/48–49
PRO C 1/367/38
PRO C 1/613/10
PRO C 1/7/104
PRO C 140/67/43
PRO C 142/102/2
PRO C 241/275/36
PRO CP 25/1/292/68, no. 186
PRO E 150/1064/2
PRO E 210/2638
PRO E 210/985
PRO E 403/724
PRO PROB 11/17/436
PRO PROB 11/18/272
PRO PROB 11/20/152
PRO PROB 11/25/123
PRO PROB 11/27/560
PRO PROB 11/29/411
PRO PROB 11/3/484
PRO PROB 11/37/155
PRO PROB 11/37/451
PRO PROB 11/42B/699
PRO PROB 11/5/2
PRO PROB 11/5/210
PRO PROB 11/6/459
PRO PROB 11/88/396
PRO C 1/1074/18
PRO C 1/1107/14

Bibliography

PRO C 1/1460/85
PRO C 1/76/30
PRO C 3/138/92
PRO E 41/318
PROB 11/13/90
PROB 11/25
PROB 11/26/217

Walsall Local History Centre

276/62*

West Sussex Record Office, Chichester

Par 252/9/1
SAS-BA/17

PRIMARY SOURCES

Astle, Thomas, Samuel Ayscough, and John Caley, eds. *Taxatio Ecclesiastica Angliae Et Walliae*. London, 1802.
Atchley, E. G. C. F. 'Some Documents Relating to the Parish Church of All Saints, Bristol'. *Archaeological Journal* 58 (1901): 147–81.
Baigent, Francis Joseph. *The Registers of John de Sandale and Rigaud de Asserio, Bishops of Winchester (A.D. 1316–1323)*. London, 1897.
Bailey, F. A., ed. *The Churchwardens' Accounts of Prescot, 1523–1607*. Vol. 104. Preston, 1953.
Bateson, Mary. *Records of the Borough of Leicester*. Vol. 1. London, 1899.
Binney, John Erskine. *The Accounts of the Wardens of the Parish of Morebath, Devon. 1520–1573*. Exeter, 1904.
Brewer, J. S., ed. *Letters and Papers, Foreign and Domestic, of the Reign of Henry VIII*. Vol. 3 (2). London, 1867.
Brodie, R. H., and James Gairdner, eds. *Letters and Papers, Foreign and Domestic, of the Reign of Henry VIII*. Vol. 15. London, 1896.
Brown, William, ed. *The Register of Henry of Newark, Lord Archbishop of York, 1286–1296*. Vol. 2. Durham, 1913.
Burgess, Clive. *The Church Records of St Andrew Hubbard, Eastcheap, c. 1450–c. 1570*. London, 1999.
  The Pre-Reformation Records of All Saints', Vol. 1. Bristol, 1995.
Burton, Thomas de. *Chronica Monasterii de Melsa*. Edited by Edward Augustus Bond. Vol. 1. London, 1866.
Calendar of Inquisitions Post Mortem and Other Analogous Documents Preserved in the Public Record Office: Henry VII. Vol. 1. London, 1898.
Calendar of the Close Rolls of Henry VI, 1422–1429. Vol. 1. London, 1933.
Calendar of the Fine Rolls: Henry V, 1413–1422. Vol. 14. London, 1934.
Calendar of the Manuscripts of the Dean & Chapter of Wells. Vol. 2. London, 1914.

Bibliography

Calendar of the Patent Rolls Preserved in the Public Record Office: Edward III 1330–34. Vol. 2. London, 1893.

Caley, J., and J. Hunter, eds. *Valor Ecclesiasticus.* Vol. 4. London, 1821.

Cattermole, P., 'A 14th-Century Contract for Carpenter's Work at Ashwellthorpe Church', *Norfolk Archaeology* 40 (1989): 297–302.

Chapman, F. R., ed. *Sacrist Rolls of Ely, Notes.* Vol. 1. Cambridge, 1908.

———. ed. *Sacrist Rolls of Ely, Transcripts.* Vol. 2. Cambridge, 1908.

Chibnall, Albert Charles, and A. Vere Woodman. *Subsidy Roll for the County of Buckingham, Anno 1524.* Aylesbury, 1950.

Clark, Andrew, ed. *Lincoln Diocese Documents, 1450–1544.* London, 1914.

Clough, Marie. *The Book of Bartholomew Bolney.* Lewes, 1964.

Collins, Francis, ed. *Register of the Freemen of the City of York, 1272–1759.* Vol. 1. Durham, 1897.

Colvin, Howard, ed. *The History of the King's Works.* Vol. 4. London, 1963.

———. ed. *The History of the King's Works.* Vol. 1. London, 1963.

Cornwall, Julian C. K., ed. *The Lay Subsidy Rolls for the County of Sussex, 1524–25.* Lewes, 1957.

Cotton, Charles. *Churchwardens' Accounts of the Parish of St. Andrew, Canterbury.* London, 1916.

Cox, John Charles. *Churchwardens' Accounts from the Fourteenth Century to the Close of the Seventeenth Century.* London, 1913.

Cozens-Hardy, Basil. *Calendar of Such of the Frere Mss. as Relate to the Hundred of Holt.* Norwich, 1931.

Dale, Joseph. 'Extracts from Churchwardens' Accounts and Other Matters Belonging to the Parish of Bolney'. *Sussex Archaeological Collections* 6 (1853): 244–52.

Daniel, W. E. 'Churchwardens' Accounts, St John Glastonbury'. *N&Q for Somerset and Dorset* 4 (1895): 235–40.

Darlington, Reginald R. *The Glapwell Charters.* Derby, 1959.

Davis, F. N., ed. *Rotuli Hugonis De Welles, Episcopi Lincolniensis, A.D. MCCIX–MCCXXXV.* Vol. 2. London, 1907.

———. *The Register of John Pecham, Archbishop of Canterbury, 1279–1292.* Vol. 1. London, 1969.

Davis, Norman. *Paston Letters and Papers of the Fifteenth Century.* Oxford, 2005.

Deedes, Cecil, ed. *Registrum Johannis de Pontissara Episcopi Wyntoniensis, A. D. MCCLXXXII–MCCCIV.* London, 1916.

Devon, Frederick, ed. *Issues of the Exchequer: Being a Collection of Payments Made out of His Majesty's Revenue, from King Henry III to King Henry VI Inclusive.* London, 1837.

Dilks, Thomas Bruce, ed. *Bridgwater Borough Archives, 1200–1377.* Yeovil, 1933.

———. ed. *Bridgwater Borough Archives, 1377–1399.* Yeovil, 1938.

———. ed. *Bridgwater Borough Archives, 1400–1445.* Yeovil, 1945.

Doree, Stephen G. *The Early Churchwardens' Accounts of Bishops Stortford, 1431–1558.* Hitchin, 1994.

Drew, Charles. ed. *Lambeth Churchwardens' Accounts, 1504–1645, and Vestry Book, 1610.* London, 1940.

Bibliography

Dudding, Reginald C. *The First Churchwardens' Book of Louth, 1500–1524.* Oxford, 1941.
Duncan, L. L. *Testamenta Cantiana (West Kent).* London, 1906.
Dymond, D. P. *The Churchwardens' Book of Bassingbourn, Cambridgeshire 1496–c. 1540.* Cambridge, 2004.
Edwards, A. C. 'The Medieval Churchwardens' Accounts of St Mary's Church, Yatton'. *N&Q for Somerset and Dorset* 32 (September 1986): 536–46.
Ellis, William Patterson. 'The Churchwardens' Accounts of the Parish of St. Mary, Thame, Commencing in the Year 1442'. *Berkshire, Buckinghamshire and Oxfordshire Archaeological Journal* VII (1901): 113–19.
——— 'The Churchwardens' Accounts of the Parish of St. Mary, Thame, Commencing in the Year 1442'. *Berkshire, Buckinghamshire and Oxfordshire Archaeological Journal* VIII (1902): 24–30, 50–59, 71–77.
Ellis, William Patterson, and Herbert Edward Salter. *Liber Albus Civitatis Oxoniensis.* Oxford, 1909.
Feltoe, C. L., and Ellis H. Minns, eds. *Vetus Liber Archidiaconi Eliensis.* Cambridge, 1917.
Fenwick, Carolyn C., ed. *The Poll Taxes of 1377, 1379, and 1381: Bedfordshire-Leicestershire.* Vol. I. Oxford, 1998.
——— ed. *The Poll Taxes of 1377, 1379, and 1381: Lincolnshire-Westmoreland.* Vol. II. Oxford, 2000.
——— ed. *The Poll Taxes of 1377, 1379, and 1381: Wiltshire-Yorkshire.* Vol. III. Oxford, 2005.
Finn, Arthur, ed. *Records of Lydd.* Translated by Arthur Hussey and M. M. Hardy. Ashford, 1911.
Foster, C. W. *Lincoln Wills: 1271–1526.* Vol. 1. London, 1914.
——— *Lincoln Wills: 1530–1532.* Vol. 3. London, 1930.
Foster, J. E. *Churchwardens' Accounts of St. Mary the Great, Cambridge, from 1504 to 1635.* Cambridge, 1905.
Freshfield, Edwin. *The Vestry Minute Books of the Parish of St. Bartholomew Exchange in the City of London: 1567–1767.* London, 1890.
Furnivall, Frederick James, ed. *The Fifty Earliest English Wills in the Court of Probate.* London, 1882.
Geoffrey Chaucer. *The Riverside Chaucer*, ed. Larry Dean Benson, 3rd ed. (Oxford, 2008), 134.
Gillespie, Richard William. *Walsall Records: Translations of Ancient Documents in the Walsall Chartulary at the British Museum.* Walsall, 1914.
Glasscock, J. L., ed. *The Records of St. Michael's Parish Church, Bishop's Stortford.* London, 1882.
Glasscock, Robin E. *The Lay Subsidy of 1334.* London, 1975.
Goodman, A. W. *Winchester Diocese: Register of Henry Woodlock.* Vol. 1. London, 1941.
Goulding, Richard William. *Records of the Charity Known as Blanchminster's Charity.* Louth, 1898.
Greaves, R. W. *The First Ledger Book of High Wycombe.* Welwyn Garden City, 1956.
Green, Emanuel. *Pedes Finium, Commonly Called Feet of Fines, for the County of Somerset, Henry IV to Henry VI.* London, 1906.
Gross, Charles, ed. *Select Cases Concerning the Law Merchant, A.D. 1270–1638.* Vol. 1, 1908.

Bibliography

Hamilton Thompson, A. 'The Statutes of the College of St Mary and All Saints, Fotheringhay'. *The Archaeological Journal* 75 (1918): 241–309.

Visitations of Religious Houses in the Diocese of Lincoln. Vol. 1. London, 1915.

Hanham, Alison, ed. *Churchwardens' Accounts of Ashburton, 1479–1580.* Torquay, 1970.

Harvey, William. *The Visitation of Suffolke.* Edited by Joseph Jackson Howard. Vol. 1. Lowestoft, 1866.

Hervey, William. *The Visitations of Suffolk Made by Hervey, Clarenceux, 1561, Cooke, Clarenceux, 1577, and Raven, Richmond Herald, 1612.* Exeter, 1882.

Highfield, J. R. L., ed. *The Early Rolls of Merton College, Oxford.* Oxford, 1964.

Hill, Rosalind M. T. *The Register of William Melton, Archbishop of York, 1317–1340.* Vol. 1. York, 1977.

Hingeston-Randolph, F. C. *The Register of Edmund Stafford (A. D. 1395–1419).* London, 1886.

The Register of John de Grandisson, Bishop of Exeter (1327–1369). Vol. 2. London, 1894.

Hobhouse, Edmund, ed. *Calendar of the Register of John de Drokensford, Bishop of Bath and Wells (A.D. 1309–1329).* London, 1887.

Church-Wardens' Accounts of Croscombe, Pilton, Yatton, Tintinhull, Morebath, and St. Michael's, Bath: Ranging from A.D. 1349 to 1560. London, 1890.

Hobson, T. F. *Adderbury 'rectoria'.* Oxford, 1926.

Holinshed, Raphael. *Holinshed's Chronicles of England, Scotland, and Ireland: England.* London, 1808.

Holland, William. *Cratfield: A Transcript of the Accounts of the Parish, from A.D. 1490 to A.D. 1642.* Edited by John James Raven. London, 1896.

Holmes, Thomas Scott, ed. *The Register of Ralph of Shrewsbury, Bishop of Bath and Wells, 1329–1363.* London, 1896.

Howlett, Richard. 'A Fabric Roll of Norwich Guildhall'. *Norfolk Archaeology* XV, no. 2 (1903): 174–89.

Hunnisett, R. F. *Sussex Coroners' Inquests, 1485–1558.* Lewes, 1985.

Huth, Edward, ed. *The Parish Registers of Bolney, Sussex: 1541–1812.* London, 1912.

Jones, Llewellyn. 'Churchwardens' Accounts of the Town of Ludlow'. *Transactions Shropshire Archaeological Society*, 1 (1889): 235–84.

Jones, W. H. 'Terumber's Chantry at Trowbridge, with Deed of Endowment 1483'. *Wiltshire Archaeological and Natural History Society* 10 (1867): 240–52.

Kirby, T. F., ed. *Wykeham's Register.* Vol. 2. London, 1896.

Kite, Edward. 'Some Documents Relating to the Church of the B. V. Mary, Devizes, and Its Re-Founder, A.D. 1410–1458'. *Wiltshire Notes and Queries* 7 (1911): 193–202.

Lamb, John, ed. *A Collection of Letters, Statutes, and Other Documents from the Ms. Library of Corp. Christ. Coll.* London, 1838.

Layer, John, and William Cole. *Monumental Inscriptions and Coats of Arms from Cambridgeshire: Chiefly.* Edited by William Mortlock Palmer. Cambridge, 1932.

Leadam, I. S, ed. *Select Cases in the Court of Requests: A. D. 1497–1569.* London, 1898.

Leland, John. *The Itinerary of John Leland in or about the Years 1535–1543.* Edited by Lucy Toulmin Smith. Vol. 1. London, 1906.

Bibliography

The Itinerary of John Leland in or about the Years 1535–1543. Edited by Lucy Toulmin Smith. Vol. 2. London, 1908.
The Itinerary of John Leland in or about the Years 1535–1543. Edited by Lucy Toulmin Smith. Vol. 5. London, 1910.
'Leverington Parish Accounts'. *Fenland Notes and Queries* 7 (October 1909): 184–90.
Lewis, R. W. M. *Walberswick Churchwardens' Accounts, A.D. 1450–1499*. London, 1947.
Lightfoot, W. J. 'Notes from the Records of Hawkhurst Church'. *Archaeologia Cantiana* 5 (1863): 55–86.
Littlehales, Henry, ed. *The Medieval Records of a London City Church (St. Mary at Hill) A.D. 1420–1559*. London, 1904.
Majendie, L. A. 'Dunmow Parish Accounts'. *Transactions of the Essex Archaeological Society* 2 (1863): 229–37.
Mander, G. 'Churchwardens' Accounts, All Saints' Church, Walsall'. *Collections for a History of Staffordshire* 52 (1928): 175–267.
Masters, Betty R., and Elizabeth Ralph, eds. *The Church Book of St. Ewen's, Bristol 1454–1584*. Bristol, 1967.
Mercer, Francis Robert, ed. *Churchwardens' Accounts at Betrysden: 1515–1573*. Ashford, 1928.
Muskett, J. J. 'Lay Subsidies, Cambridgeshire, I Edward III (1327)'. *East Anglian N&Q*, 10–12 (August 1903).
Myers, A. R. *English Historical Documents 1327–1485*. London, 1996.
Nichols, J., ed. *A Collection of the Wills Now Known to Be Extant of the Kings and Queens of England*. London, 1780.
Nichols, John F. 'An Early Fourteenth Century Petition from the Tenants of Bocking to Their Manorial Lord'. *The Economic History Review* 2, no. 2 (1 January 1930): 300–07.
Nicolas, Nicholas Harris. *Testamenta Vetusta*. Vol. 1. London, 1826.
Testamenta Vetusta. Vol. 2. London, 1826.
Northeast, Peter. *Boxford Churchwardens' Accounts 1530–1561*. Woodbridge, 1982.
Northeast, Peter, and Heather Falvey. *Wills of the Archdeaconry of Sudbury, 1439–1474*. Edited by D. P. Dymond. Vol. 2. Woodbridge, 2010.
Olorenshaw, J. R. 'Some Early Soham Wills'. *Fenland N&Q* 4 (1900 1898): 246–50.
Osborne, Francis Mardon, ed. *The Church Wardens' Accounts of St. Michael's Church, Chagford 1480–1600*. Chagford, 1979.
Overall, William Henry. *The Accounts of the Churchwardens of the Parish of St. Michael, Cornhill, in the City of London, from 1456 to 1608*. London, 1883.
Palmer, W. M., and H. W. Saunders. *Documents Relating to Cambridgeshire Villages*. Vol. 1. Cambridge, 1926.
Paris, Matthew. *Chronicles of Matthew Paris: Monastic Life in the Thirteenth Century*. Edited by Richard Vaughan. Gloucester, 1986.
Payne, E. J. 'The Building of the Trinity Aisle, or North Transept, of Thame Church, Oxfordshire, A.D. 1442, et Seq'. *The Gentleman's Magazine* XVIII (June 1865): 176–89.
'The Churchwardens Accounts of the Church & Parish of S. Michael without the North Gate, Bath, 1349–1575'. *Journal of Somerset Archaeology and Natural History Society* 23, 24, 25 (1878, 1879, 1880), 1–100.

Bibliography

Peacock, Edward. 'Extracts from the Churchwardens' Accounts of the Parish of Leverton, in the County of Lincoln'. *Archaeologia* 41 (1867): 333–70.
Pearson, Charles Buchanan. 'Some Account of Ancient Churchwarden Accounts of St. Michael's, Bath'. *Transactions of the Royal Historical Society* 7 (1878): 309–29.
Powicke, F. M., and C. R. Cheney, eds. *Councils and Synods, 1205–1313.* Vol. 1. Oxford, 1964.
— eds. *Councils and Synods, 1205–1313.* Vol. 2. Oxford, 1964.
Raine, James. ed. *Testamenta Eboracensia.* Vol. 1. London, 1836.
— ed. *Testamenta Eboracensia.* Vol. 4. London, 1869.
Reaney, Percy H., and Marc Fitch. *Feet of Fines for Essex 1423–1547.* Vol. 4. Colchester, 1899.
Rice, Robert Garraway. *Transcripts of Sussex Wills.* Edited by Walter Hindes Godfrey. Vol. 1. Lewes, 1935.
Royal Commission on Historical Manuscripts. Vol. IX. London, 1883.
Royal Commission on Historical Manuscripts. Vol. X. London, 1885.
Rye, Walter. *Pedes Finium; or Fines, Relating to the County of Cambridge.* Cambridge, 1891.
Sellers, Maud, ed. *The York Mercers and Merchant Adventurers, 1356–1917.* Durham, 1918.
— ed. *York Memorandum Book.* Vol. 2. Durham, 1912.
Sharpe, Reginald R., ed. *Calendar of Letter-Books Preserved among the Archives of the Corporation of the City of London at the Guildhall.* Vol. 1. London, 1899.
Somers, Frank, ed. *Halesowen Churchwardens' Accounts (1487–1582).* London, 1952.
Stanford, Charlotte A. *The Building Accounts of the Savoy Hospital, London, 1512–1520.* Woodbridge, 2015.
Stell, P. M., and A. Hawkyard. 'The Lay Subsidy of 1334 for York'. *York Historian* 13 (1996): 2–14.
Stoate, T. L., ed. *Devon Lay Subsidy Rolls, 1524–7.* Bristol, 1979.
— ed. *Devon Lay Subsidy Rolls 1543–5.* Bristol, 1986.
Storey, R. L. *The Register of Gilbert Welton, Bishop of Carlisle, 1353–1362.* Woodbridge, 1999.
Swayne, Henry. *Churchwardens' Accounts of S. Edmund & S. Thomas, Sarum, 1443–1702.* Salisbury, 1896.
Symonds, W. 'Five Ancient Deeds at Sherston Magna'. *Wiltshire Notes and Queries* 6 (October 1908): 447–52.
Tropenell, Thomas. *The Tropenell Cartulary.* Edited by John Silvester Davies. Vol. 1. Devizes, 1908.
Wallis, J. *The Bodmin Register.* Bodmin, 1827.
Walsingham, Thomas de. *Gesta Abbatum Monasterii Sancti Albani.* Edited by Henry T. Riley. Vol. 1. London, 1867.
Weaver, Frederic William, ed. *Somerset Medieval Wills, XIVth and XVth Centuries.* Vol. 1. London, 1901.
Weaver, J. R. H., ed. *Some Oxfordshire Wills, 1393–1510.* Oxford, 1958.
Webb, C. C., ed. *The Churchwardens' Accounts of St Michael, Spurriergate, York, 1518–1548.* York, 1997.
Weinbaum, Martin,. ed. *British Borough Charters 1307–1660.* Digital edition. Cambridge, 2010.

Bibliography

Welch, Charles. *The Churchwardens' Accounts of the Parish of Allhallows, London Wall, in the City of London.* London, 1912.
Westlake, H. F. *Hornchurch Priory: A Kalendar of Documents in the Possession of the Warden and Fellows of New College, Oxford.* London, 1923.
The Parish Gilds of Mediæval England. London, 1919.
Wilkinson, J. J. *Receipts and Expenses in Building Bodmin Church, 1469–1472.* London, 1874.
'Receipts and Expenses in the Building of Bodmin Church, A.D. 1469 to 1472'. *Camden New Series* 14 (1875): 1–41.
Williams, J. F. 'The Black Book of Swaffham'. *Norfolk Archaeology* 23, no. 3 (1964): 243–53.
The Early Churchwarden's Accounts of Hampshire. Winchester, 1913.
Willis, Dorothy, ed. *Estate Book of Henry de Bray.* London, 1916.
Wilson, Christopher. 'A Mid-Fourteenth Century Contract for the Choir Roof of Glastonbury Abbey'. *The Antiquaries Journal* 88 (2008): 216–21.
Worth, R. N. *Calendar of the Tavistock Parish Records.* Plymouth, 1887.

SECONDARY SOURCES

Aberth, John. 'The Black Death in the Diocese of Ely: The Evidence of the Bishop's Register'. *Journal of Medieval History* 21, no. 3 (1995): 275–87.
Abou-El-Haj, Barbara. 'The Urban Setting for Late Medieval Church Building: Reims and Its Cathedral Between 1210 and 1240'. *Art History* 11, no. 1 (1 March 1988): 17–41.
Acheson, Eric. *A Gentry Community: Leicestershire in the Fifteenth Century, c. 1422–c. 1485.* New York, 1992.
Adams, J. H. 'The Berry Tower'. *Devon and Cornwall N&Q* 28 (1959–61): 243–46.
'The Berry Tower'. *Devon and Cornwall N&Q* 29 (1962–62): 125 and 186.
Ainslie, Edward and M. Herbert. *The Church of St. Augustine.* Hedon, 1926.
Alcock, Nat, and Dan Miles. *The Medieval Peasant House in Midland England.* Oxford, 2014.
Alexander, Jennifer. 'Building Stone from the East Midlands Quarries: Sources, Transportation and Usage'. *Medieval Archaeology* 39 (1995): 107–35.
Alford, B. W. E., and M. Q Smith. 'The Economic Effects of Cathedral Building in Medieval England: A Further Comment'. *Explorations in Entrepreneurial History* 6 (Spring/Summer 1969): 329–32.
'The Economic Effects of Cathedral Building in Medieval England: A Reply'. *Explorations in Entrepreneurial History* 6 (Winter 1969): 158–69.
Allan, Elizabeth. *Chepyng Walden: A Late Medieval Small Town, Saffron Walden 1438–1490.* Saffron Walden, 2015.
Allen, Martin. *Mints and Money in Medieval England.* Cambridge, 2012.
'Silver Production and the Money Supply in England and Wales, 1086-c. 1500'. *Economic History Review* 64 (2011): 114–31.
Allen, Nicholas. *An English Parish Church: Its History: The Church of St. Mary the Virgin, Adderbury, Oxfordshire.* Adderbury, 2011.
Allen, Robert C. *Enclosure and the Yeoman.* Oxford, 1992.

Bibliography

Allen, Rosamund. 'Cobham, John, Third Baron Cobham of Cobham (c.1320–1408)'. In *Oxford Dictionary of National Biography*. Oxford, 2004. http://dx.doi.org/10.1093/ref:odnb/5744.

An Inventory of the Historical Monuments in Essex: North West. Vol. 1. London, 1916.

An Inventory of the Historical Monuments in the City of Cambridge. Vol. 1. London, 1988.

Anderson, J. M. *The Honorable Burden of Public Office: English Humanists and Tudor Politics in the Sixteenth Century*. New York, 2010.

Archer, Ian W. *The Pursuit of Stability: Social Relations in Elizabethan London*. Cambridge, 1991.

Armi, C. Edson. *Masons and Sculptors in Romanesque Burgundy*. University Park, 1983.

Ashford, Leslie Joseph. *The History of the Borough of High Wycombe from Its Origins to 1880*. London, 1960.

Aston, Margaret. 'Iconoclasm at Rickmansworth, 1522: Troubles of Churchwardens'. *The Journal of Ecclesiastical History* 40, no. 4 (October 1989): 524–52.

Ault, Warren Ortman. 'Manor Court and Parish Church in Fifteenth-Century England: A Study of Village By-Laws'. *Speculum* 42, no. 1 (1 January 1967): 53–67.

Open-Field Farming in Medieval England. London, 1972.

Open-Field Husbandry and the Village Community. Philadelphia, 1965.

'The Village Church and the Village Community in Mediaeval England'. *Speculum* 45, no. 2 (1 April 1970): 197–215.

Ayers, Tim. *The Medieval Stained Glass of Merton College, Oxford*. Vol. 1. Oxford, 2013.

Bailey, Mark. *Medieval Suffolk: An Economic and Social History, 1200–1500*. Woodbridge, 2007.

'Self-Government in the Small Towns of Late Medieval England'. In *Commercial Activity, Markets and Entrepreneurs in the Middle Ages*, edited by Ben Dodds and C. D. Liddy, 1–24. Woodbridge, 2011.

'Sir John de Wingfield and the Foundation of Wingfield College'. In *Wingfield College and Its Patrons: Piety and Patronage in Medieval Suffolk*, edited by Peter Bloore and Edward A. Martin, 31–47. Woodbridge, 2015.

The Decline of Serfdom in Late Medieval England: From Bondage to Freedom. Woodbridge, 2014.

The English Manor, c. 1200–1500. Manchester, 2002.

Bainbridge, Virginia R. *Gilds in the Medieval Countryside: Social and Religious Change in Cambridgeshire, c.1350–1558*. Woodbridge, 1996.

Baker, Alan R. H. 'Evidence in the "Nonarum Inquisitiones" of Contracting Arable Lands in England during the Early Fourteenth Century'. *The Economic History Review*, 19, no. 3 (1966): 518–32.

Baker, John H. *An Introduction to English Legal History*. 4th ed. London, 2002.

The Men of Court 1440–1550. Vol. 1. London, 2012.

ed. *The Reports of Sir John Spelman*. Vol. 94. London, 1978.

Baker, T. F. T., J. S. Cockburn, and R. B. Pugh. eds. *VCH Middlesex*. Vol. 4. London, 1971.

Barley, Maurice Willmore. *Lincolnshire and the Fens*. Wakefield, 1972.

Barrett, William. *The History and Antiquities of the City of Bristol*. Bristol, 1789.

Bibliography

Barron, Caroline. *Medieval London Widows, 1300–1500.* London, 2003.
'The "Golden Age" of Women in Medieval London'. *Reading Medieval Studies* 15 (1969): 35–58.
Baxandall, Michael. *Painting and Experience in Fifteenth Century Italy.* 2nd ed. Oxford, 1988.
Bayley, Robert Slater. *Notitiæ Ludæ, or Notices of Louth.* London, 1834.
Benedictow, Ole Jørgen. *The Black Death, 1346–1353: The Complete History.* Woodbridge, 2004.
Bennett, Judith. 'Confronting Continuity'. *Journal of Women's History* 9, no. 3 (1997): 73–94.
'Medieval Women, Modern Women: Across the Great Divide'. In *Culture and History 1350–1600: Essays on English Communities, Identities, and Writing,* edited by David Aers, 147–75. Detroit, 1992.
Bennett, M. J. 'The Lancashire and Cheshire Clergy, 1379'. *Transactions of the Historical Society of Lancashire and Cheshire* 124 (1972): 1–30.
Bercea, Brighita, Robert B. Ekelund, and Robert D. Tollison. 'Cathedral Building as an Entry-Deterring Device'. *Kyklos* 58, no. 4 (2005): 453–65.
Beresford, Maurice. *New Towns of the Middle Ages: Town Plantation in England, Wales and Gascony.* London, 1967.
Bernard, G. W. *The King's Reformation: Henry VIII and the Remaking of the English Church.* New Haven, 2005.
Bernardi, Philippe. *Bâtir Au Moyen Age.* Paris, 2011.
Bettey, J. H. *Church & Community: The Parish Church in English Life.* Bradford-on-Avon, 1979.
The English Parish Church and the Local Community. London, 1985.
Bettley, James, and Nikolaus Pevsner. *Suffolk: East.* New Haven, 2015.
Biddick, Kathleen. 'Medieval English Peasants and Market Involvement'. *The Journal of Economic History* 45, no. 4 (1985): 823–31.
'Missing Links: Taxable Wealth, Markets, and Stratification among Medieval English Peasants'. *The Journal of Interdisciplinary History* 18, no. 2 (1 October 1987): 277–98.
Binski, Paul. *Gothic Wonder: Art, Artifice and the Decorated Style 1290–1350.* New Haven, 2014.
Blagg, Thomas M. *A Guide to the Antiquities of Newark and the Churches of Holme and Hawton.* Newark, 1906.
Blair, Lawrence. *English Church Ales.* Ann Arbor, 1940.
Blanc, Anne, and Jean-Pierre Gely. 'Stone from Medieval Churches Located to the South and East of Paris'. In *Working with Limestone,* edited by Vibeke Olsen, 59–74. Farnham, 2011.
Blanchard, Ian. *Mining, Metallurgy, and Minting in the Middle Ages: Continuing Afro-European Supremacy, 1250–1450.* Vol. 3. Stuttgart, 2005.
Blaydes, Frederic Augustus. *The Visitations of Bedfordshire.* London, 1884.
Bliss, William Henry, and Charles Johnson. *Calendar of Entries in the Papal Registers Relating to Great Britain and Ireland: 1342–62.* Vol. 3. London, 1897.
Blomefield, F. *An Essay towards a Topographical History of the County of Norfolk.* Vol. 1. London, 1807.
An Essay towards a Topographical History of the County of Norfolk. Vol. 2. London, 1807.

Bibliography

An Essay towards a Topographical History of the County of Norfolk. Vol. 6. London, 1807.
An Essay towards a Topographical History of the County of Norfolk. Vol. 8. London, 1808.
An Essay towards a Topographical History of the County of Norfolk. Vol. 10. London, 1808.
Bloxam, Matthew Holbeche. *The Principles of Gothic Ecclesiastical Architecture*. 10th ed. London, 1859.
Bolton, Jim. *Money in the Medieval English Economy 973–1489*. Manchester, 2012.
— 'The English Economy in the Early Thirteenth Century'. In *King John: New Interpretations*, edited by S. D. Church, 27–40. Woodbridge, 2003.
— 'The World Upside Down'. In *The Black Death in England*, edited by W. M. Ormrod and P. Lindley, 17–78. Stamford, 1996.
Bonney, H. K. *Historic Notices in Reference to Fotheringhay*. Oundle, 1821.
Bony, J. *The English Decorated Style: Gothic Architecture Transformed, 1250–1350*. Oxford, 1979.
— 'The Stonework Planning of the First Durham Master'. In *Medieval Architecture and Its Intellectual Context*, edited by E. C. Fernie and Paul Crossley, 19–34. London, 1990.
Booth, P. 'The Enforcement of the Ordinance and Statute of Labourers in Cheshire, 1349 to 1374'. *ARCHIVES*, no. 127 (2013): 1–16.
Bossy, John. 'The Mass as a Social Institution 1200–1700'. *Past & Present*, no. 100 (1 August 1983): 29–61.
Bowker, Margaret. *The Secular Clergy in the Diocese of Lincoln, 1495–1520*. Cambridge, 1968.
Boyle, J. R. *The Early History of the Town and Port of Hedon*. Hull, 1895.
Boys, William. *Collections for an History of Sandwich in Kent*. Canterbury, 1792.
Bradley, Simon, and Nikolaus Pevsner. *Cambridgeshire*. New Haven, 2014.
Brandon, Peter. *Sussex*. London, 2006.
Branner, Robert. 'Letters to the Editor'. *The Art Bulletin* 37, no. 3 (1955): 236–37.
— 'Review'. *The Art Bulletin* 37, no. 1 (1 March 1955): 61–65.
Braybrooke, Richard Griffin. *The History of Audley End*. London, 1836.
Brent, Colin E. *Pre-Georgian Lewes C. 890–1714*. Lewes, 2004.
Bridges, John. *The History and Antiquities of Northamptonshire*. Vol. 2. Oxford, 1791.
Briggs, Chris. 'Credit and the Peasant Household Economy in England before the Black Death: Evidence from a Cambridgeshire Manor'. In *The Medieval Household in Christian Europe, C. 850-c. 1550*, edited by C. Beattie, A. Maslakovic, and Sarah Rees Jones, 231–48. Turnhout, 2003.
— *Credit and Village Society in Fourteenth-Century England*. Oxford, 2009.
Briggs, Martin S. 'Building Construction'. In *A History of Technology*, edited by Charles Joseph Singer and Richard Raper, 2:397–448. Oxford, 1956.
— *The Architect in History*. Oxford, 1927.
Britnell, R. H. 'Boroughs, Markets and Trade in Northern England, 1000–1216'. In *Progress and Problems in Medieval England*, edited by Richard Britnell and John Hatcher, 46–67. Cambridge, 1996.
— *Britain and Ireland, 1050–1530: Economy and Society*. Oxford, 2004.

Bibliography

'Tenant Farming and Farmers: Eastern England'. In *AHEW*, edited by Edward Miller, 3:611–24. Cambridge, 1991.

The Commercialisation of English Society, 1000–1500. 2nd ed. Manchester, 1996.

'The English Economy and the Government, 1450–1550'. In *The End of the Middle Ages? England in the Fifteenth and Sixteenth Centuries*, edited by J. L. Watts, 89–116. Stroud, 1998.

'The Occupation of the Land'. In *AHEW*, edited by Edward Miller, 3:53–67. Cambridge, 1991.

'The Pastons and Their Norfolk'. *The Agricultural History Review* 36, no. 2 (1988): 132–44.

Britton, Edward. *The Community of the Vill: A Study in the History of the Family and Village Life in Fourteenth-Century England*. Toronto, 1977.

Britton, John. *The Beauties of Wiltshire*. Vol. 3. London, 1825.

Broadberry, S. N., Bruce M. S. Campbell, Alexander Klein, Bas van Leeuwen, and Mark Overton. *British Economic Growth, 1270–1870*. Cambridge, 2015.

Brooke, Christopher. 'Urban Church and University Church: Great St Mary's from Its Origin to 1523'. In *Great St Mary's Cambridge's University Church*, edited by John Binns and Peter Meadows, 7–24. Cambridge, 2000.

Brown, Andrew. *Church and Society in England, 1000–1500*. Basingstoke, 2003.

Popular Piety in Late Medieval England: The Diocese of Salisbury, 1250–1550. Oxford, 1995.

Buchanan, Alexandrina. 'Vestiges of Conversations? The Medieval Building Agreement and Architectural Language'. In *Language in Medieval Britain: Networks and Exchanges*, edited by Mary Carruthers, 7–32. Donington, 2015.

Bullen, Michael, John Crook, Rodney Hubbuck, and Nikolaus Pevsner. *Hampshire: Winchester and the North*. New Haven, 2010.

Burgess, Clive. '"A Fond Thing Vainly Invented": An Essay on Purgatory and Pious Motive in Late Medieval England'. In *Parish, Church and People: Local Studies in Lay Religion, 1350–1750*, edited by S. J. Wright, 56–84. London, 1988.

'London Parishioners in Times of Change: St Andrew Hubbard, Eastcheap, c. 1450–1570'. *The Journal of Ecclesiastical History* 53, no. 1 (2002): 38–63.

'Pre-Reformation Churchwardens' Accounts and Parish Government: Lessons from London and Bristol'. *The English Historical Review* 117, no. 471 (1 April 2002): 306–32.

'Shaping the Parish: St Mary at Hill, London, in the Fifteenth Century'. In *The Cloister and the World: Essays in Medieval History in Honour of Barbara Harvey*, edited by John Blair and Brian Golding, 254–69. Oxford, 1996.

'Strategies for Eternity'. In *Religious Beliefs and Ecclesiastical Careers*, edited by Christopher Harper-Bill, 1–33. Woodbridge, 1991.

'The Benefactions of Mortality: The Lay Response in the Later Medieval Urban Parish'. In *Studies in Clergy and Ministry in Late Medieval England*, edited by D. Smith, 65–87. York, 1991.

'The Broader Church? A Rejoinder to "Looking Beyond"'. *The English Historical Review* 119, no. 480 (1 February 2004): 100–16.

'The Churchwardens' Accounts of St Andrew Hubbard, Eastcheap, and Their Implications'. *London and Middlesex Archaeological Society Transactions* 50 (1999): 61–66.

'Time and Place: The Late Medieval English Parish in Perspective'. In *The Parish in Late Medieval England: Proceedings of the 2002 Harlaxton Symposium*, edited by Clive Burgess and Eamon Duffy, 1–28. Donington, 2006.

Burgess, Clive, and Beat Kümin. 'Penitential Bequests and Parish Regimes in Late Medieval England'. *The Journal of Ecclesiastical History* 44, no. 4 (1993): 610–30.

Byng, Gabriel. 'Patrons and Their Commissions: The Uses of Biography in Understanding the Construction of the Nave of Holy Trinity, Bottisham'. In *Writing the Lives of People and Things, AD 500–1700: A Multi-Disciplinary Future for Biography*, edited by R. F. W. Smith and G. L. Watson, 227–43. Farnham, 2016.

'The Chronology and Financing of the Perpendicular Work at Saffron Walden, Essex'. *Essex Archaeology and History*, 6 (2016): 329–43.

'The Construction of the Tower at Bolney Church'. *Sussex Archaeological Collections* 151 (2013): 101–13.

'The Contract for the North Aisle at St James, Biddenham'. *Antiquaries Journal* 95 (2015): 251–65.

'The "Dynamic of Design": "Source" Buildings and Contract Making in the Later Middle Ages'. *Architectural History* 59 (2016): 123–48.

'The Southchurch Chapel and the Earliest Building Contract in England'. *Journal of the British Archaeological Association* 168 (2015): 131–41.

Camm, Bede. 'Some Norfolk Rood Screens'. In *A Supplement to Blomefield's Norfolk*, edited by Christopher Hussey, 239–95. London, 1929.

Campbell, B. M. S. *English Seigniorial Agriculture, 1250–1450*. Cambridge, 2000.

Campbell, Bruce M. S. 'Population Pressure, Inheritance and the Land Market in a Fourteenth-Century Peasant Community'. In *Land, Kinship and Life-Cycle*, edited by R. M. Smith, 87–134. Cambridge, 1984.

'The Agrarian Problem in the Early Fourteenth Century'. *Past & Present* 188, no. 1 (1 August 2005): 3–70.

'The Complexity of Manorial Structure in Medieval Norfolk: A Case Study'. *Norfolk Archaeology* 39 (1986): 225–61.

The Great Transition. Cambridge, 2016.

'The Land'. In *A Social History of England, 1200–1500*, edited by Rosemary Horrox and W. M. Ormrod, 179–237. Cambridge, 2006.

Campbell, Bruce M. S., and Ken Bartley. *England on the Eve of the Black Death: An Atlas of Lay Lordship, Land and Wealth, 1300–49*. Manchester, 2006.

Cannon, Jon. *Cathedral: The Great English Cathedrals and the World That Made Them, 600–1540*. London, 2007.

Carnwath, Julia. 'The Churchwardens' Accounts of Thame'. In *Trade, Devotion and Governance*, edited by Dorothy J. Clayton, Richard G. Davies, and Peter McNiven, 177–97. Gloucester, 1994.

Carpenter, Christine. 'Gentry and Community in Medieval England'. *The Journal of British Studies* 33, no. 4 (October 1994): 340–80.

Locality and Polity: A Study of Warwickshire Landed Society, 1401–1499. Cambridge, 1992.

'Religion'. In *Gentry Culture in Late Medieval England*, edited by Raluca Radulescu and Alison Truelove, 134–50. Manchester, 2005.

Bibliography

'The Religion of the Gentry of Fifteenth-Century England'. In *England in the Fifteenth Century*, edited by D. Williams, 53–74. Woodbridge, 1987.
Catto, Jeremy. 'Chichele, Henry (c.1362–1443)'. In *Oxford Dictionary of National Biography*. Oxford, 2004. doi:10.1093/ref:odnb/5271.
Cavill, P. R. 'The Problem of Labour and the Parliament of 1495'. In *'Of Mice and Men': Image, Belief and Regulation in Late Medieval England*, edited by Linda Clark, 143–55. Woodbridge, 2005.
Chainey, Graham. 'The Lost Stained Glass of Cambridge'. *Proceedings of the Cambridge Antiquarian Society* LXXIX (1990): 70–81.
Chauncy, Sir Henry. *The Historical Antiquities of Hertforshire*. Bishops Stortford, 1826.
Cheney, C. R. *From Becket to Langton; English Church Government, 1170–1213*. Manchester, 1956.
Cherry, Bridget, and Nikolaus Pevsner. *London 3: North West*. New Haven, 1991.
Clanchy, M. T. *From Memory to Written Record: England 1066–1307*. London, 1979.
Clark, Elaine. 'Medieval Labor Law and English Local Courts'. *The American Journal of Legal History* 27, no. 4 (1983): 330–53.
Clark, Gregory. 'The Long March of History: Farm Wages, Population, and Economic Growth, England 1209–1869'. *Economic History Review* 60, no. 1 (2007): 97–135.
Clark, William W., and Thomas G. Waldman. 'Money, Stone, Liturgy, and Planning at the Royal Abbey of Saint-Denis'. In *New Approaches to Medieval Architecture*, edited by Robert Odell Bork, William W. Clark, and Abby McGehee, 63–75. Farnham, 2011.
Clarke, J. E., and J. E Foster. 'History of a Site in Senate House Yard with Some Notes on the Occupiers'. *Proceedings of the Cambridge Antiquarian Society* 13 (1909): 120–40.
Clay, William Keatinge. *A History of the Parish of Waterbeach in the County of Cambridge*. Cambridge, 1859.
Clayton, Dorothy J. *The Administration of the County Palatine of Chester: 1442–1485*. Manchester, 1990.
Cleveland, Catherine. *The Battle Abbey Roll*. Vol. 1. London, 1889.
Coates, Charles. *The History and Antiquities of Reading*. London, 1802.
Coldstream, N. *The Decorated Style: Architecture and Ornament, 1240–1360*. London, 1994.
Colombier, Pierre du. *Les Chantiers Des Cathedrales*. Paris, 1953.
Comber, John. *Sussex Genealogies – Horsham Centre*. Edited by William Bull and L. F. Salzman. Vol. 1. Cambridge, 1931.
Constable, Giles. *Monastic Tithes: From Their Origins to the Twelfth Century*. Cambridge, 1964.
Cook, G. H. *The English Mediaeval Parish Church*. London, 1954.
Coss, Peter R. *The Foundations of Gentry Life: The Multons of Frampton and Their World, 1270–1370*. Oxford, 2010.
   The Knight in Medieval England, 1000–1400. Stroud, 1993.
Cotton, Simon. 'Medieval Roodscreens in Norfolk: Their Construction and Painting Dates'. *Norfolk Archaeology* 40 (1987): 46–54.

'Perpendicular Churches'. In *Cambridgeshire Churches*, edited by Carola Hicks, 95–106. Stamford, 1997.
Coulson, Charles. 'Hierarchism in Conventual Crenellation: An Essay in the Sociology and Metaphysics of Medieval Fortification'. *Medieval Archaeology* 26 (1982): 69–100.
Coulton, G. G. *Art and the Reformation*. Oxford, 1928.
Five Centuries of Religion: Getting & Spending. Vol. 3. Cambridge, 1936.
Cox, J. C., and A. Harvey. *English Church Furniture*. London, 1907.
Cox, J. Charles, and Charles Bradley Ford. *The Parish Churches of England*. London, 1935.
Craig, J. S. 'Co-Operation and Initiatives: Elizabethan Churchwardens and the Parish Accounts of Mildenhall'. *Social History* 18, no. 3 (1993): 357–80.
Crittall, Elizabeth, ed. *VCH Wiltshire*. Vol. 6. London, 1962.
Crosby, J. H. *Ely Diocesan Remembrancer*. Cambridge, 1905.
Crossley, F. H. *Cheshire*. London, 1949.
Cruden, Stewart. *Scottish Medieval Churches*. Edinburgh, 1986.
Cutts, Edward Lewes. *Parish Priests and Their People in the Middle Ages in England*. London, 1898.
Dale, M. K. 'Pettifer, George (by 1489–1558/59), of Chipping Wycombe, Bucks'. In *The House of Commons 1509–1558*, edited by S. T. Bindoff. London, 1982.
Darby, H. C. *Medieval Cambridgeshire*. Cambridge, 1977.
The Medieval Fenland. Newton Abbot, 1974.
Dark, Sidney. *London*. London, 1924.
Davidson, Carol Foote. 'Written in Stone: Architecture, Liturgy, and the Laity in English Parish Churches, c. 1125–c. 1250'. PhD, University of London, Birkbeck College, 1998.
Davies, John Gordon. *The Secular Use of Church Buildings*. London, 1968.
Davis, James. *Medieval Market Morality: Life, Law and Ethics in the English Marketplace, 1200–1500*. Cambridge, 2011.
Davis, Virginia. *William Wykeham*. London, 2007.
Denton, J. H. 'The 1291 Valuation of the Churches of Ely Diocese'. *Proceedings of the Cambridge Antiquarian Society* XC (2001): 69–80.
'The Valuation of the Ecclesiastical Benefices of England and Wales in 1291–2'. *Historical Research* 66 (1993): 242–50.
'Towards a New Edition of the "Taxatio Ecclesiastice Angliae et Walliae Auctoritate P Nicholai IV circa AD 1291"'. *Bulletin of the John Rylands Library* 79, no. 1 (1997): 67–79.
DeWindt, Anne Reiber. 'Local Government in a Small Town: A Medieval Leet Jury and Its Constituents'. *Albion: A Quarterly Journal Concerned with British Studies* 23, no. 4 (1 December 1991): 627–54.
DeWindt, Anne Reiber, and Edwin Brezette DeWindt. *Ramsey: The Lives of an English Fenland Town, 1200–1600*. Washington, DC, 2006.
Dobson, R. B. *The Peasants' Revolt of 1381*. London, 1970.
'The Risings in York, Beverley, and Scarborough, 1380–1381'. In *The English Rising of 1381*, edited by R. H. Hilton and T. H. Aston, 112–42. Cambridge, 1987.
'Urban Decline in Late Medieval England'. In *The English Medieval Town: A Reader in English Urban History, 1200–1540*, edited by Richard Holt and Gervase Rosser, 1–22. London, 1990.

Bibliography

Drake, Francis. *Eboracum*. London, 1736.

Drew, Charles. *Early Parochial Organisation in England: The Origins of the Office of Churchwarden*. London, 1954.

Duffy, Eamon. 'The Disenchantment of Space: Salle Church and the Reformation'. In *Religion and the Early Modern State: Views from China, Russia, and the West*, edited by James D. Tracy and Marguerite Ragnow, 324–76. Cambridge, 2004.

—— 'The Parish, Piety, and Patronage in Late Medieval East Anglia: The Evidence of Rood Screens'. In *The Parish in English Life, 1400–1600*, edited by Katherine L French, Gary G. Gibbs, and Beat Kumin, 133–62. Manchester, 1997.

—— *The Stripping of the Altars: Traditional Religion in England, c. 1400–c.1580*. New Haven, 1992.

—— *The Voices of Morebath: Reformation and Rebellion in an English Village*. New Haven, 2001.

Dugdale, William. *Monasticon Anglicanum*. Vol. 6, part 1. London, 1830.

—— *The History of St. Pauls Cathedral in London, from Its Foundation Untill These Times*. London, 1658.

Dunn, Ian, and Helen Sutermeister. *The Norwich Guildhall*. Norwich, 1977.

Dunning, R. W., and C. R. Elrington, eds. *A History of the County of Somerset*. Vol. 6. London, 1992.

Durant, Gladys May. *Landscape with Churches*. London, 1965.

Dyer, Alan. *Decline and Growth in English Towns 1400–1640*. Cambridge, 1995.

—— 'Urban Decline in England, 1377–1525'. In *Towns in Decline AD 100–1600*, edited by T. R. Slater, 266–88. Aldershot, 2000.

Dyer, Christopher. *A Country Merchant, 1495–1520: Trading and Farming at the End of the Middle Ages*. Oxford, 2012.

—— 'A Golden Age Rediscovered: Labourers' Wages in the Fifteenth Century'. In *Money, Prices and Wages: Essays in Honour of Professor Nicholas Mayhew*, edited by M. Allen and D. Coffman, 180–95. 2014.

—— 'A Suffolk Farmer in the Fifteenth Century'. *The Agricultural History Review* 55, no. 1 (1 January 2007): 1–22.

—— *An Age of Transition? Economy and Society in England in the Later Middle Ages*. Oxford, 2005.

—— 'Changes in the Size of Peasant Holdings in Some West Midland Villages 1400–1540'. In *Land, Kinship and Life-Cycle*, edited by Richard M. Smith, 277–94. Cambridge, 1984.

—— 'How Urbanised Was Medieval England?' In *Peasants & Townsmen in Medieval Europe*, edited by Jean-Marie Duvosquel and Erik Thoen, 169–83. Gent, 1995.

—— *Lords and Peasants in a Changing Society: The Estates of the Bishopric of Worcester, 680–1540*. Cambridge, 1980.

—— *Making a Living in the Middle Ages: The People of Britain 850–1520*. New Haven, 2002.

—— 'Peasant Farming in Late Medieval England: Evidence from the Tithe Estimations by Worcester Cathedral Priory'. In *Peasants and Lords in the Medieval English Economy: Essays in Honour of Bruce M.S. Campbell*, edited by Maryanne Kowaleski, John Langdon, and Phillipp R. Schofield, 83–109. Turnhout, 2015.

Standards of Living in the Later Middle Ages: Social Change in England, c. 1200–1520. Cambridge, 1989.

'Taxation and Communities in Late Medieval England'. In *Progress and Problems in Medieval England*, edited by John Hatcher and R. H. Britnell, 168–90. Cambridge, 1996.

'Tenant Farming and Farmers. The West Midlands'. In *AHEW*, edited by Edward Miller, 3:636–47. Cambridge, 1991.

'The Agrarian Problem, 1440–1520'. In *Landlords and Tenants in Britain, 1440–1660: Tawney's Agrarian Problem Revisited*, edited by Jane Whittle, 23–30. Woodbridge, 2013.

'The Archaeology of Medieval Small Towns'. *Medieval Archaeology* 47, no. 1 (1 June 2003): 85–114.

'The English Medieval Village Community and Its Decline'. *Journal of British Studies* 33, no. 4 (1 October 1994): 407–29.

'The Hidden Trade of the Middle Ages'. In *Everyday Life in Medieval England*, edited by Christopher Dyer, 283–303. London, 1994.

'Work Ethics in the Fourteenth Century'. In *The Problem of Labour in Fourteenth-Century England*, edited by James Bothwell, P. J. P. Goldberg, and W. M. Ormrod, 21–42. Woodbridge, 2000.

Dymond, Robert. 'The History of the Parish of St Petrock, Exeter'. *Reps. and Trans. Devon Assoc.*, no. 14 (1882): 402–92.

Earwaker, John Parsons. *East Cheshire Past and Present*. Vol. I. London, 1877.

The History of the Church and Parish of St. Mary-on-the-Hill, Chester. London, 1898.

Eavis, Anna. 'The Church'. In *Fairford Parish Church: A Medieval Church and Its Stained Glass*, edited by Sarah Brown and Lindsay MacDonald, Revised, 30–48. Stroud, 2007.

Elrington, C. R., ed. *VCH Cambridgeshire*. Vol. 5. London, 1973.

Engel, Ute. *Worcester Cathedral: An Architectural History*. Chichester, 2007.

Espin, T. *A Short Account of Louth Church*. London, 1807.

Evelyn-White, C. H. *County Churches, Cambridgeshire and the Isle of Ely*. London, 1911.

Evelyn-White, C. H., and J. J. Muskett. *Cambridgeshire Church Goods: Inventories for the County and the Isle of Ely for Various Years, 1538–1556*. Norwich, 1943.

Everitt, A. M. 'Farm Labourers'. In *AHEW*, edited by J. Thirsk, Vol. 4:396–465. Cambridge, 1967.

Farmer, D. L. 'Prices and Wages'. In *AHEW*, edited by H. E. Hallam, Vol. 2: 716–817. Cambridge, 1988.

'Prices and Wages, 1350–1500'. In *AHEW*, edited by E. Miller, Vol. 3:431–525. Cambridge, 1991.

Farnhill, Ken. *Guilds and the Parish Community in Late Medieval East Anglia, c. 1470–1550*. Woodbridge, 2001.

Farrer, William, and J. Brownbill, eds. *VCH Lancashire*. Vol. 3. London, 1907.

Fawcett, Richard. *Scottish Medieval Churches: Architecture & Furnishings*. Stroud, 2002.

The Architecture of the Scottish Medieval Church, 1100–1560. New Haven, 2011.

Fentress, James, and Chris Wickham. *Social Memory*. Oxford, 1992.

Bibliography

Fleming, P. W. 'Charity Faith and the Gentry of Kent'. In *Property and Politics: Essays in Later Medieval English History*, edited by Tony Pollard, 36–58. Gloucester, 1984.

Ford, J. A. 'Art and Identity in the Parish Communities of Late Medieval Kent'. In *The Church and the Arts*, edited by Diana Wood, 225–39. Oxford, 1992.

Forrest, Ian. *The Detection of Heresy in Late Medieval England*. Oxford, 2005.

Foster, Andrew. 'Churchwardens' Accounts of Early Modern England and Wales'. In *The Parish in English Life, 1400–1600*, edited by Katherine L French, Gary G. Gibbs, and Beat Kumin, 74–93. Manchester, 1997.

French, Katherine L. 'Competing for Space: Medieval Religious Conflict in the Monastic-Parochial Church at Dunster'. *Journal of Medieval and Early Modern Studies* 27 (1997): 215–44.

——— 'Maidens' Lights and Wives' Stores: Women's Parish Guilds in Late Medieval England'. *The Sixteenth Century Journal* 29, no. 2 (1 July 1998): 399–425.

——— 'Margery Kempe and the Parish'. In *The Ties That Bind: Essays in Medieval British History in Honor of Barbara Hanawalt*, edited by Linda Elizabeth Mitchell, Katherine L. French, and Douglas Biggs, 159–74. Farnham, 2011.

——— 'Parochial Fund-Raising in Late Medieval Somerset'. In *The Parish in English Life*, edited by Katherine L. French, Gary G. Gibbs, and Beat Kumin, 115–32. Manchester, 1997.

——— *The Good Women of the Parish: Gender and Religion after the Black Death*. Philadelphia, 2008.

——— *The People of the Parish: Community Life in a Late Medieval English Diocese*. Philadelphia, 2001.

——— '"To Free Them from Binding": Women in the Late Medieval English Parish'. *The Journal of Interdisciplinary History* 27, no. 3 (1 January 1997): 387–412.

——— 'Women Churchwardens in Late Medieval England'. In *The Parish in Late Medieval England: Proceedings of the 2002 Harlaxton Symposium*, edited by Clive Burgess and Eamon Duffy, 302–21. Donington, 2006.

Friar, Stephen. *A Companion to the English Parish Church*. Stroud, 1996.

Fuller, Thomas. *The History of the University of Cambridge*. Edited by Marmaduke Prickett and Thomas Wright. Cambridge, 1840.

Gardner, Thomas. *An Historical Account of Dunwich*. London, 1754.

Gasquet, Francis Aidan. *Parish Life in Mediaeval England*. 3rd ed. London, 1909.

Gem, Richard. 'A Recession in English Architecture during the Early Eleventh Century and Its Impact on the Development of the Romanesque Style'. *Journal of the British Archaeological Association*, XXXVIII (1975): 28–49.

Gimpel, Jean. *The Cathedral Builders*. Translated by Carl F. Barnes. London, 1961.

Godfrey, C. J. 'Non-Residence of Parochial Clergy in the Fourteenth Century'. *Church Quarterly Review* CLXII (1961): 433–46.

——— 'Pluralists in the Province of Canterbury in 1366'. *The Journal of Ecclesiastical History* 11, no. 1 (April 1960): 23–40.

Goheen, R. B. 'Peasant Politics? Village Community and the Crown in Fifteenth-Century England'. *The American Historical Review* 96, no. 1 (1 February 1991): 42–62.

Good, Michael, ed. *A Compendium of Pevsner's Buildings of England on Compact Disc*. Oxford, 1995.

Graves, C. Pamela. 'Social Space in the English Medieval Parish Church'. *Economy and Society* 18, no. 3 (1989): 297–322.
Gray, H. L. 'Incomes from Land in England in 1436'. *The English Historical Review* 49, no. 196 (1 October 1934): 607–39.
Greenslade, M. W., ed. *VCH Staffordshire*. Vol. 17. London, 1976.
Gummer, Benedict. *The Scourging Angel: The Black Death in the British Isles*. London, 2009.
Hadwin, J. F. 'The Medieval Lay Subsidies and Economic History'. *The Economic History Review*, 36, no. 2 (1 May 1983): 200–17.
Haigh, Christopher. *Reformation and Resistance in Tudor Lancashire*. Cambridge, 1975.
Haines, Herbert. *A Manual of Monumental Brasses*. Vol. 1. Oxford, 1861.
Haines, R. M. 'Patronage and Appropriation in Ely Diocese: The Share of the Benedictines'. *Revue Bénédictine* 108 (1998): 298–314.
Hall, Spencer. 'Notices of Sepulchral Memorials at Etchingham, Sussex, and of the Church at That Place'. *The Archaeological Journal* 7 (1850): 265–73.
Halliday, Robert. 'The Churches of Ashley and Silverley'. *Proceedings of the Cambridge Antiquarian Society* LXXIII (1984): 29–44.
Hamilton Thompson, A. 'Pluralism in the Medieval Church'. *Association of Architectural Society Reports and Paper* 33 (1915): 35–73.
Hancock, Frederick. *Dunster Church and Priory: Their History and Architectural Features*. Taunton, 1905.
Harper-Bill, Christopher. 'A Late Medieval Visitation – the Diocese of Norwich in 1499'. *Proceedings of the Suffolk Institute of Archaeology and History* 34 (1977): 35–47.
— *The Pre-Reformation Church in England 1400–1530*. London, 1989.
Harriss, G. L. *Shaping the Nation: England, 1360–1461*. Oxford, 2005.
Hartridge, R. A. R. *A History of Vicarages in the Middle Ages*. Cambridge, 1930.
Harvey, Barbara F. 'The Population Trend in England between 1300 and 1348'. *Transactions of the Royal Historical Society*, 16 (1966): 23–42.
Harvey, John. *An Introduction to Tudor Architecture*. London, 1949.
— *English Mediaeval Architects: A Biographical Dictionary down to 1550*. Revised ed. Gloucester, 1987.
— *Henry Yevele c. 1320–1400: The Life of an English Architect*. London, 1944.
— *Medieval Craftsmen*. London, 1975.
— 'The Architects of English Parish Churches'. *The Archaeological Journal* CV (1948): 14–26.
— 'The Buildings of Winchester College'. In *Winchester College: Sixth-Centenary Essays*, edited by Roger Custance, 77–127. Oxford, 1982.
— *The Gothic World, 1100–1600: A Survey of Architecture and Art*. London, 1950.
— *The Perpendicular Style, 1330–1485*. London, 1978.
Haskins, C. 'The Church of St Thomas of Canterbury, Salisbury'. *The Wiltshire Archaeological and Natural History Magazine* 36 (1909): 1–12.
Hasted, Edward. *Hasted's History of Kent*. Edited by Henry Holman Drake. London, 1886.
— *The History and Topographical Survey of the County of Kent*. Vol. 5. Canterbury, 1798.
Hatcher, John. 'England in the Aftermath of the Black Death'. *Past & Present*, no. 144 (1994): 3–35.

'English Serfdom and Villeinage: Towards a Reassessment'. *Past & Present*, no. 90 (1 February 1981): 3–39.

Plague, Population, and the English Economy, 1348–1530. London, 1977.

Rural Economy and Society in the Duchy of Cornwall, 1300–1500. Cambridge, 1970.

'The Great Slump of the Mid-Fifteenth Century'. In *Progress and Problems in Medieval England: Essays in Honour of Edward Miller*, edited by Richard Britnell and John Hatcher, 237–72. Cambridge, 1996.

'Unreal Wages: Long-Run Living Standards and the "Golden Age" of the Fifteenth Century'. In *Commercial Activity, Markets and Entrepreneurs in the Middle Ages*, edited by Ben Dodds and C. D. Liddy, 1–24. Woodbridge, 2011.

Hatcher, John, and Mark Bailey. *Modelling the Middle Ages: The History and Theory of England's Economic Development*. Oxford, 2001.

Hay, George. 'The Late Medieval Development of the High Kirk of St Giles, Edinburgh'. *Proceedings of the Society of Antiquaries of Scotland* 107 (1976): 242–60.

Hayter-Hames, Jane. *A History of Chagford*. London, 1981.

Heard, Kate. 'Death and Representation in the Fifteenth Century: The Wilcote Chantry Chapel at North Leigh'. *Journal of the British Archaeological Association* 154, no. 1 (1 January 2001): 134–49.

Heath, Peter. *Medieval Clerical Accounts*. York, 1964.

The English Parish Clergy on the Eve of the Reformation. London, 1969.

'Urban Piety in the Later Middle Ages: The Evidence of Hull Wills'. In *The Church, Politics, and Patronage in the Fifteenth Century*, edited by Barrie Dobson, 209–34. Gloucester, 1984.

Henry, Robert L. *Contracts in the Local Courts of Medieval England*. London, 1926.

Heslop, T. A. 'Swaffham Parish Church'. In *Medieval East Anglia*, edited by Christopher Harper-Bill. Woodbridge, 2005.

Hesse, Mary. 'The Lay Subsidy of 1327'. In *An Atlas of Cambridgeshire and Huntingdonshire History*, edited by Tony Kirby and Susan Oosthuizen, 36. Cambridge, 2000.

Hewerdine, Anita. *The Yeomen of the Guard and the Early Tudors: The Formation of a Royal Bodyguard*. London, 2012.

Hill, G. M. 'The Antiquities of Bury St Edmund'. *Journal of the British Archaeological Association* 21 (1865): 104–40.

Hilton, R. H. *A Medieval Society: The West Midlands at the End of the Thirteenth Century*. Cambridge, 1966.

'Medieval Market Towns and Simple Commodity Production'. *Past & Present*, no. 109 (1985): 3–23.

'Small Town Society in England before the Black Death'. *Past & Present* 105, no. 1 (1 November 1984): 53–78.

Hindle, Steve. 'A Sense of Place? Becoming and Belonging in the Rural Parish 1550–1650'. In *Communities in Early Modern England*, edited by Alexandra Shepard and Phil Withington, 96–113. Manchester, 2000.

Hislop, Malcolm. *Medieval Masons*. Princes Risborough, 2009.

Hope, William and Henry St. John. 'The New Building of Wyberton Church, Lincolnshire in 1419–20'. *Lincolnshire N&Q* 14 (1917): 225–37.

Hoskins, W. G. *Devon*. London, 1954.
Howard, Frank E. 'Screens and Rood-Lofts in the Parish Churches of Oxfordshire'. *Archaeological Journal* 67 (1910): 314–47.
Hunter, J. R. 'Glass Industry'. In *Medieval Industry*, edited by D. W. Crossley. London, 1981: 143–50.
Hussey, A. *Kent Obit and Lamp Rents*. Ashford, 1936.
——— ed. *Testamenta Cantiana (East Kent)*. London, 1906.
Hussey, Christopher. 'Cobham, Kent'. *Country Life* 95 (4 February 1944): 200–03.
Hutton, Ronald. *The Rise and Fall of Merry England: The Ritual Year, 1400–1700*. Oxford, 1994.
Ingold, Tim. *Making: Archaeology, Anthropology, Art and Architecture*. London, 2012.
Inquisitions and Assessments Relating to Feudal Aids, Northampton to Somerset. Vol. IV. London, 1906.
Ives, E. 'Patronage At The Court Of Henry VIII: The Case Of Sir Ralph Egerton Of Ridley'. *Bulletin of the John Rylands Library* 52, no. 2 (1970): 346–74.
James, John. 'An Investigation into the Uneven Distribution of Early Gothic Churches in the Paris Basin, 1140–1240'. *The Art Bulletin* 66, no. 1 (March 1984): 15–46.
——— 'Funding the Early Gothic Churches of the Paris Basin'. *Parergon* 15 (1997): 41–82.
——— 'How Many Built All the Churches?' *AVISTA Forum Journal* 13, no. 2 (2003): 23–24.
——— 'Impact of Climate Change on Building Construction: AD 1050 to 1250'. *AVISTA Forum Journal* 20, no. 1/2 (Fall 2010): 43–49.
——— *The Contractors of Chartres*. Vol. 1. Dooralong, 1979.
——— *The Pioneers of the Gothic Movement: Interim Report*. Wyong, 1980.
——— *The Template-Makers of the Paris Basin: Toichological Techniques for Identifying the Pioneers of the Gothic Movement with an Examination of Art-Historical Methodology*. West Grinstead, 1989.
Jankulak, Karen. *The Medieval Cult of St Petroc*. Woodbridge, 2000.
Jenks, Stuart. 'The Lay Subsidies and the State of the English Economy (1275–1334)'. *Vierteljahrschrift Für Sozial- Und Wirtschaftsgeschichte* 85 (1998): 1–39.
Johns, Charles, J. Mattingly, and Carl Thorpe. *St Paternus' Church, North Petherwin: A Watching Brief Report*. Truro, 1996.
Johnson, P. A. *Duke Richard of York, 1411–1460*. Oxford, 1988.
Johnson, T. Thomas. 'Cathedral Building and the Medieval Economy'. *Explorations in Entrepreneurial History* 4 (1967): 191–211.
——— 'The Economic Effects of Cathedral Building in Medieval England: A Rejoinder'. *Explorations in Entrepreneurial History* 6 (Winter 1969): 170–74.
Johnston, Alexandra F. 'Parish Entertainments in Berkshire'. In *Pathways to Medieval Peasants*, edited by J. A. Raftis, 335–38. Toronto, 1981.
Jones, G. P. 'Building in Stone in Medieval Western Europe'. In *The Cambridge Economic History of Europe*, edited by M. M. Postan and E. Miller, 2nd ed., 2:768–74. Cambridge, 1987.
Kanzaka, Junichi. 'Villein Rents in Thirteenth-Century England: An Analysis of the Hundred Rolls of 1279–1280'. *The Economic History Review*, 55, no. 4 (1 November 2002): 593–618.
Keene, Derek. *Survey of Medieval Winchester*. Vol. 1. Oxford, 1985.

Bibliography

Kent, Ernest A. *Norwich Guildhall: The Fabric and the Ancient Stained Glass.* Norwich, 1928.
Kerry, Charles. *A History of the Municipal Church of St. Lawrence, Reading.* Reading, 1883.
Kershaw, Ian. 'The Great Famine and the Agrarian Crisis in England, 1315–1322'. In *Peasants, Knights and Heretics*, edited by R. H. Hilton, 85–132. Cambridge, 1976.
Kimpel, Dieter, and Robert Suckale. *Die Gotische Architektur in Frankreich, 1130–1270.* München, 1985.
King, H. W. 'Historical Evidence of the Date of Erection of Certain Church Towers and of Church Restoration in Essex'. *Transactions of the Essex Archaeological Society,* 1 (1878): 45–54, 116–27, 159–64.
Kirby, Thomas Frederick. *Annals of Winchester College.* London, 1892.
Kitsikopoulos, Harry. 'Standards of Living and Capital Formation in Pre-Plague England: A Peasant Budget Model'. *The Economic History Review*, 53, no. 2 (1 May 2000): 237–61.
Knoop, Douglas, and G. P. Jones. 'Some Notes on Three Early Documents Relating to Masons'. *Ars Quatuor Coronatorum* XLIV (1931): 223–35.
  'The First Three Years of the Building of Vale Royal Abbey, 1278–1280'. *Ars Quatuor Coronatorum* XLIV (1931): 5–47.
  'The Impressment of Masons in the Middle Ages'. *The Economic History Review* 8, no. 1 (November 1937): 57–67.
  The Mediaeval Mason. 3rd ed. Manchester, 1967.
  'The Rise of the Mason Contractor'. *Jnl. RIBA*, 43 (October 1936): 1061–71.
Knowles, David. *The Religious Orders in England.* Vol. 2. Cambridge, 1948.
Kosminsky, E. A. *Studies in the Agrarian History of England in the Thirteenth Century.* Oxford, 1956.
Kraus, Henry. *Gold Was the Mortar: The Economics of Cathedral Building.* London, 1979.
Kümin, Beat A. 'Late Medieval Churchwardens' Accounts and Parish Government: Looking beyond London and Bristol'. *The English Historical Review* 119, no. 480 (1 February 2004): 87–99.
  'The English Parish in a European Perspective'. In *The Parish in English Life*, edited by Katherine L. French, Gary G. Gibbs, and Beat Kümin, 15–32. Manchester, 1997.
  The Shaping of a Community: The Rise and Reformation of the English Parish, c. 1400–1560. Aldershot, 1996.
Lambert, Uvedale. 'Hognel Money and Hogglers'. *Surrey Archaeological Collections* 30 (1917): 54–60.
Lander, J. R. *Government and Community: England 1450–1509.* London, 1980.
Langdon, John. 'Horse Hauling: A Revolution in Vehicle Transport in Twelfth- and Thirteenth-Century England?' *Past & Present*, no. 103 (1 May 1984): 37–66.
  Horses, Oxen and Technological Innovation: The Use of Draught Animals in English Farming from 1066 to 1500. Cambridge, 1986.
Langdon, John, and James Masschaele. 'Commercial Activity and Population Growth in Medieval England'. *Past & Present* 190, no. 1 (2006): 35–81.
Langton, John. 'Late Medieval Gloucester: Some Data from a Rental of 1455'. *Transactions of the Institute of British Geographers*, 2 (1977): 259–77.

Leach, Arthur Francis. *The Building of Beverley Bar*. s.l., 1900.
Le Goff, Jacques. *The Birth of Purgatory*. London, 1984.
Lee, John S. *Cambridge and Its Economic Region, 1450–1560*. Hatfield, 2005.
Lillie, W. W. 'Medieval Paintings on the Screens of the Parish Churches of Mid and Southern England'. *Journal of the British Archaeological Association* 9 (1944): 33–47.
Litzenberger, Caroline. *The English Reformation and the Laity: Gloucestershire, 1540–1580*. Cambridge, 2002.
Lloyd, David, Margaret Clark, and Chris F. Potter. *St. Laurence's Church, Ludlow: The Parish Church and People, 1199–2009*. Little Logaston, 2010.
Lloyd, T. H. *Some Aspects of the Building Industry in Medieval Stratford-upon-Avon*. Oxford, 1961.
Lobel, M. D., ed. *VCH Oxfordshire*. Vol. 7. London, 1962.
Lopez, Robert S. 'Economie et Architecture Medievales, Cela Aurait Il Tue Ceci?' *Annales; Economies, Societes, Civilisations* 7 (1952): 433–38.
Lower, Mark Antony. *A Compendious History of Sussex*. Vol. 1. Lewes, 1870.
Luxford, Julian M. *The Art and Architecture of English Benedictine Monasteries, 1300–1540: A Patronage History*. Woodbridge, 2005.
Maclean, J. *Parochial and Family History of the Parish and Borough of Bodmin, in the County of Cornwall*. London, 1870.
Macnamara, Francis Nottidge. *Memorials of the Danvers Family*. London, 1895.
Maddern, Philippa. 'Order and Disorder'. In *Medieval Norwich*, edited by Carole Rawcliffe and Richard Wilson, 188–212. London, 2006.
Maddison, J. M. 'Architectural Development of Patrington Church'. In *Medieval Art and Architecture in the East Riding of Yorkshire*, edited by Christopher Wilson, 133–48. Norwich, 1989.
Maitland, Frederic William. 'History of a Cambridgeshire Manor'. In *Selected Historical Essays of F. W. Maitland*, edited by Helen M. Cam, 16–40. Cambridge, 1957.
Maitland, William. *The History of Edinburgh*. Edinburgh, 1753.
Manning, Charles Robertson. *A List of the Monumental Brasses Remaining in England*. London, 1846.
Manning, Owen, and William Bray. *The History and Antiquities of the County of Surrey*. Vol. I. London, 1804.
Marks, Richard. *Stained Glass in England During the Middle Ages*. London, 1993.
Marshall, Peter. *Religious Identities in Henry VIII's England*. Aldershot, 2013.
Martin, C. T. 'Butts, Sir William'. In *Oxford Dictionary of National Biography*. Oxford, 2004. http://dx.doi.org/10.1093/ref:odnb/4241.
Martin, G. H., and J. R. L. Highfield. *A History of Merton College, Oxford*. Oxford, 1997.
Mason, Emma. 'The Role of the English Parishioner, 1100–1500'. *The Journal of Ecclesiastical History* 27, no. 1 (1976): 17–29.
Masters, Robert. *The History of the College of Corpus Christi and the B. Virgin Mary (Commonly Called Bene't)*. Cambridge, 1753.
Mate, Mavis. 'Agrarian Economy after the Black Death: The Manors of Canterbury Cathedral Priory, 1348–91'. *The Economic History Review*, 37, no. 3 (1984): 341–54.

Bibliography

Mattingly, J. 'Medieval Parish Guilds of Cornwall'. *Journal of the Royal Institution of Cornwall* 10, no. 3 (1989): 290–329.
'Stories in Glass: Reconstructing the St Neot Pre-Reformation Glazing Scheme'. *Journal of the Royal Institution of Cornwall* 3 (2000): 9–55.
Maxwell Lyte, H. C. 'Dunster and Its Lords'. *The Archaeological Journal* 38 (1881): 62–79, 207.
Mayhew, N. 'Modelling Medieval Monetisation'. In *A Commercializing Economy: England 1086 to c.1300*, edited by R. H. Britnell and Bruce M. S. Campbell. Manchester, 1995: 65–76.
Mayhew, N. J. 'Population, Money Supply, and the Velocity of Circulation in England, 1300–1700'. *The Economic History Review*, 48, no. 2 (1 May 1995): 238–57.
McCall, H. B. *Richmondshire Churches*. London, 1910.
McClenaghan, Barbara. *The Springs of Lavenham: And the Suffolk Cloth Trade in the XV and XVI Centuries*. Ipswich, 1924.
McFarlane, K. B. *The Nobility of Later Medieval England: The Ford Lectures for 1953 and Related Studies*. Oxford, 1973.
McGibbon Smith, Erin. 'Court Rolls as Evidence for Village Society'. In *Town and Countryside in the Age of the Black Death: Essays in Honour of John Hatcher*, edited by Mark Bailey and S. H. Rigby, 245–76. Turnhout, 2012.
McHardy, A. K. 'Careers and Disappointments in the Late Medieval Church'. In *The Ministry: Clerical and Lay*, edited by W. J. Sheils and D. Wood, 111–30. Oxford, 1989.
'Ecclesiastics and Economics: Poor Priests, Prosperous Laymen and Proud Prelates in the Reign of Richard II'. *The Church and Wealth: Studies in Church History* 24 (1987): 129–37.
'Some Late-Medieval Eton College Wills'. *The Journal of Ecclesiastical History* 28, no. 4 (1977): 387–95.
McIntosh, Marjorie Keniston. *Autonomy and Community: The Royal Manor of Havering, 1200–1500*. Cambridge, 2002.
McKitterick, David. *A History of Cambridge University Press: Printing and the Book Trade in Cambridge, 1534–1698*. Vol. 1. Cambridge, 1992.
Mellows, W. T., ed. *Peterborough Local Administration*. Kettering, 1939.
Melo, Arnaldo, and Maria do Carmo Ribeiro. 'Construction Financing in Late Medieval Portuguese Towns'. In *Nuts & Bolts of Construction History*, edited by Robert Carvais, Andre Guillerme, Valerie Negre, and Joel Sakarovitch, Vol. 2, 305–12. Paris, 2012.
Middleton-Stewart, Judith. *Inward Purity and Outward Splendour: Death and Remembrance in the Deanery of Dunwich, Suffolk, 1370–1547*. Woodbridge, 2001.
Miller, Edward. *The Abbey & Bishopric of Ely*. Cambridge, 1951.
Moorman, J. R. H. *Church Life in England in the 13th Century*. Cambridge, 1945.
Morant, Philip. *The History and Antiquities of the County of Essex*. Vol. 1. London, 1768.
Morris, Richard. *Cathedrals and Abbeys of England and Wales: The Building Church, 600–1540*. London, 1979.
Churches in the Landscape. London, 1989.

'The Church in the Countryside: Two Lines in Inquiry'. In *Medieval Villages*, edited by Della Hooke, 47–60. Oxford, 1985.

Murray, Thomas Boyles. *Chronicles of a City Church, an Account of the Parish Church of St. Dunstan in the East*. London, 1859.

New, Elizabeth. 'Signs of Community or Marks of the Exclusive? Parish and Guild Seals in Later Medieval England'. In *The Parish in Late Medieval England*, edited by Clive Burgess and Eamon Duffy, 112–28. Donington, 2006.

Newman, J. E. 'Greater and Lesser Landowners and Parochial Patronage: Yorkshire in the Thirteenth Century'. *The English Historical Review* 92, no. 363 (1 April 1977): 280–308.

Newman, Paul. *Somerset Villages*. London, 1986.

Nicholls, J. F, and John Taylor. *Bristol Past and Present*. Vol. 2. Bristol, 1881.

Nightingale, Pamela. 'The Lay Subsidies and the Distribution of Wealth in Medieval England, 1275–1334'. *The Economic History Review*, 57, no. 1 (February 2004): 1–32.

Normington, Katie. *Gender and Medieval Drama*. Woodbridge, 2004.

Oliver, George. *The History and Antiquities of the Town and Minster of Beverley*. London, 1829.

Olson, Vibeke. 'Colonnette Production and the Advent of the Gothic Aesthetic'. *Gesta* 43, no. 1 (1 January 2004): 17–29.

——— 'The Significance of Sameness: An Overview of Standardization and Imitation in Medieval Art'. *Visual Resources: An International Journal of Documentation* 20, no. 2–3 (2004): 161–78.

Orme, Nicholas. 'Church and Chapel in Medieval England'. *Transactions of the Royal Historical Society* 6 (1 January 1996): 75–102.

——— *The Saints of Cornwall*. Oxford, 2000.

Ormerod, George. *The History of the County Palatine and City of Chester*. 2nd ed. Vol. 1. London, 1882.

Ormrod, W. M. 'Barnet, John (d. 1373)'. In *Oxford Dictionary of National Biography*. Oxford, 2004. http://dx.doi.org/10.1093/ref:odnb/1476.

——— *Edward III*. New Haven, 2011.

——— 'The English State and the Plantagenet Empire, 1259–1360: A Fiscal Perspective'. In *The Medieval State: Essays Presented to James Campbell*, edited by John Robert Maddicott and D. M. Palliser, 197–214. London, 2000.

Owen, Dorothy Mary. *Church and Society in Medieval Lincolnshire*. Lincoln, 1971.

Owen, Virginia Lee. 'The Economic Legacy of Gothic Cathedral Building: France and England Compared'. *Journal of Cultural Economics* 13, no. 1 (1989): 89–100.

——— 'Gothic Cathedral Building as Public Works'. In *Essays in Economic and Business History*, edited by James H. Soltow, 283–92. East Lancing, 1979.

Pacey, Arnold. *The Maze of Ingenuity: Ideas and Idealism in the Development of Technology*. Cambridge, 1992.

Page, Frances Mary. *The Estates of Crowland Abbey, a Study in Manorial Organisation*. Cambridge, 1934.

Page, William. ed. *VCH Bedfordshire*. Vol. 2. London, 1908.

——— ed. *VCH Bedfordshire*. Vol. 3. London, 1912.

——— ed. *VCH Buckinghamshire*. Vol. 3. London, 1925.

——— ed. *VCH Hertfordshire*. Vol. 3. London, 1912.

Bibliography

ed. *VCH Sussex*. Vol. 2. London, 1973.

ed. *VCH Yorkshire North Riding*. Vol. 1. London, 1914.

Page, William, and P. H. Ditchfield, eds. *VCH Berkshire*. Vol. 4. London, 1924.

Page, William, Granville Proby, and S. Inskipp Ladds, eds. *VCH Huntingdonshire*. Vol. 3. London, 1936.

Palmer, Anthony. *Tudor Churchwardens' Accounts*. Braughing, 1985.

Palmer, W. M. *John Layer (1586–1640) of Shepreth, Cambridgeshire; a Seventeenth-Century Local Historian*. Cambridge, 1935.

William Cole of Milton. Cambridge, 1935.

Palmer, William Mortlock. 'The Village Guilds of Cambridgeshire'. In *Transactions of the Cambridgeshire and Huntingdonshire Archaeological Society*, edited by C. H. Evelyn White, 330–402. Ely, 1904.

Panofsky, Erwin, ed. *Abbot Suger on the Abbey Church of St. Denis and Its Art Treasures*. Princeton, NJ, 1946.

Parker, John Henry. *Some Remarks upon the Church of Fotheringhay*. Oxford, 1841.

Parker, William. *The History of Long Melford*. London, 1873.

Parsons, David. 'Stone'. In *English Medieval Industries: Craftsmen, Techniques, Products*, edited by John Blair and Nigel Ramsay, 1–27. London, 1991.

Payling, Simon. *Political Society in Lancastrian England*. Oxford, 1991.

Pearson, Sarah. 'The Chronological Distribution of Tree-Ring Dates, 1980–2001: An Update'. *Vernacular Architecture* 32, no. 1 (1 June 2001): 68–69.

'Tree-Ring Dating: A Review'. *Vernacular Architecture* 28, no. 1 (1 June 1997): 25–39.

Pegge, Samuel, and John Nichols. *Illustrations of the Manners and Expences of Antient Times in England*. London, 1797.

Penn, Simon A. C., and Christopher Dyer. 'Wages and Earnings in Late Medieval England: Evidence from the Enforcement of the Labour Laws'. *The Economic History Review* 43, no. 3 (1 August 1990): 356–76.

Peters, Christine. *Patterns of Piety: Women, Gender and Religion in Late Medieval and Reformation England*. Cambridge, 2003.

Pevsner, Nikolaus. *Cambridgeshire*. 2nd ed. Harmondsworth, 1970.

Pevsner, Nikolaus, and John Harris. *Lincolnshire*. 2nd ed. London, 1989.

Phelps Brown, E. H., and Sheila V. Hopkins. 'Seven Centuries of Building Wages'. *Economica*, 22, no. 87 (August 1955): 195–206.

Phythian-Adams, Charles. *Desolation of a City: Coventry and the Urban Crisis of the Late Middle Ages*. Cambridge, 1979.

Platt, Colin. *Medieval England: A Social History and Archaeology from the Conquest to A.D. 1600*. London, 1978.

The Architecture of Medieval Britain: A Social History. New Haven, 1990.

The Parish Churches of Medieval England. 2nd ed. London, 1995.

Pollitt, William. *Southchurch and Its Past*. Southend, 1949.

Pollock, Frederick, and Frederic William Maitland. *The History of English Law: Before the Time of Edward I*. 2nd ed. Vol. 1. Cambridge, 1923.

Poos, L. R. *A Rural Society After the Black Death: Essex 1350–1525*. Cambridge, 1991.

'The Social Context of Statute of Labourers Enforcement'. *Law and History Review* 1, no. 1 (1983): 27–52.

Bibliography

Postan, M. M. *Essays on Medieval Agriculture and General Problems of the Medieval Economy*. Cambridge, 1973.

———. *Mediaeval Trade and Finance*. Cambridge, 2002.

———. *The Medieval Economy and Society: An Economic History of Britain in the Middle Ages*. London, 1972.

Poulson, George. *Beverlac: Or, The Antiquities and History of the Town of Beverley*. Vol. 1. London, 1829.

Pound, J. 'Clerical Poverty in Early Sixteenth-Century England: Some East Anglian Evidence'. *Journal of Ecclesiastical History* 37 (1986): 389–96.

Pounds, Norman John Greville. *A History of the English Parish*. Cambridge, 2000.

Powell, W. R. ed. *VCH Essex*. Vol. 4. London, 1956.

———. ed. *VCH Essex*. Vol. 7. London, 1978.

Pugh, R. B., ed. *VCH Cambridgeshire*. Vol. 4. London, 2002.

Putnam, Bertha Haven. 'Maximum Wage-Laws for Priests after the Black Death, 1348–1381'. *The American Historical Review* 21, no. 1 (1915): 12–32.

———. *The Enforcement of the Statutes of Labourers During the First Decade After the Black Death, 1349–1359*. New York, 1908.

Radford, G. H. 'Tavistock Abbey'. *Reports and Transactions of the Devonshire Association* 46 (1914): 119–55.

Raftis, J. A. *A Small Town in Late Medieval England: Godmanchester, 1278–1400*. Toronto, 1982.

———. 'Social Structure. The East Midlands'. In *AHEW*, edited by H. E. Hallam, 2: 634–50. Cambridge, 1988.

———. 'Social Structures in Five East Midland Villages: A Study of Possibilities in the Use of Court Roll Data'. *The Economic History Review*, 18, no. 1 (1 January 1965): 83–100.

———. *Tenure and Mobility: Studies in the Social History of the Mediaeval English Village*. Toronto, 1964.

———. 'The Concentration of Responsibility in Five Villages'. *Mediaeval Studies* 28, no. 1 (1 January 1966): 92–118.

Raine, James. *Catterick Church*. London, 1834.

Randall, Gerald. *The English Parish Church*. London, 1988.

Ravensdale, J. R. *Liable to Floods: Village Landscape on the Edge of the Fens, AD 450–1850*. Cambridge, 1974.

Rawcliffe, Carole. 'Chichele, Robert (d.1439), of London'. In *The History of Parliament: The House of Commons 1386–1421*, edited by J. S. Roskell, L. Clark, and C. Rawcliffe. Woodbridge, 1993. http://www.historyofparliamentonline.org/volume/1386-1421/member/chichele-robert-1439.

Razi, Zvi. 'Family, Land and the Village Community in Later Medieval England'. *Past & Present*, no. 93 (1 November 1981): 3–36.

———. *Life, Marriage and Death in a Medieval Parish: Economy, Society and Demography in Halesowen 1270–1400*. Cambridge, 1980.

———. 'The Toronto School's Reconstitution of Medieval Peasant Society: A Critical View'. *Past & Present*, no. 85 (1 November 1979): 141–57.

Rea, C. F. 'Building of Totnes Parish Church'. *Transactions of the Devon Association* 57 (1925): 273–84.

Rees Jones, Sarah. *York: The Making of a City 1068–1350*. Oxford, 2013.

310

Bibliography

Reynes, Robert. *The Commonplace Book of Robert Reynes of Acle*. Edited by Cameron Louis. New York, 1980.

Reynolds, Susan. *An Introduction to the History of English Medieval Towns*. Oxford, 1977.

——— 'Medieval Urban History and the History of Political Thought'. *Urban History Yearbook*, (1982): 14–23.

Richardson, H. G. 'The Parish Clergy of the Thirteenth and Fourteenth Centuries'. *Transactions of the Royal Historical Society*, 6 (1 January 1912): 89–128.

Richmond, Colin. *John Hopton: A Fifteenth Century Suffolk Gentleman*. Cambridge, 1981.

——— 'Religion and the Fifteenth Century English Gentleman'. In *The Church, Politics, and Patronage in the Fifteenth Century*, edited by Barrie Dobson, 193–208. Gloucester, 1984.

——— 'The English Gentry and Religion, c. 1500'. In *Religious Beliefs and Ecclesiastical Careers in Late Medieval England*, edited by Christopher Harper-Bill, 121–50. Woodbridge, 1991.

——— *The Paston Family in the Fifteenth Century: Fastolf's Will*. Cambridge, 1996.

Rickman, Thomas. *An Attempt to Discriminate the Styles of English Architecture*. London, 1817.

Rigby, Stephen H. 'Boston and Grimsby in the Middle Ages: An Administrative Contrast'. *Journal of Medieval History* 10 (1984): 51–66.

——— *English Society in the Later Middle Ages: Class, Status and Gender*. Basingstoke, 1995.

——— 'Urban "Oligarchy" in Late Medieval England'. In *Towns and Townspeople in the Fifteenth Century*, edited by J. A. F. Thomson, 62–86. Gloucester, 1988.

——— 'Urban Population in Late Medieval England: The Evidence of the Lay Subsidies'. *Economic History Review* 63, no. 2 (May 2010): 393–417.

Rigby, Stephen H., and Elizabeth Ewan. 'Government, Power and Authority 1300–1540'. In *The Cambridge Urban History of Britain*, edited by D. M. Palliser, 1:291–312. Cambridge, 2000.

Rodes, Robert E. *Ecclesiastical Administration in Medieval England*. Notre Dame, 1977.

Rogers, James E. Thorold. *A History of Agriculture and Prices in England*. Vol. 1. Oxford, 1866.

Rosenthal, Joel Thomas. *The Purchase of Paradise; Gift Giving and the Aristocracy, 1307–1485*. London, 1972.

Rosser, Gervase. 'Communities of Parish and Guild in the Late Middle Ages'. In *Parish, Church and People. Local Studies in Lay Religion 1350–1750*, edited by S. J. Wright, 29–55. London, 1988.

——— *Medieval Westminster: 1200–1540*. Oxford, 1989.

——— *The Art of Solidarity in the Middle Ages: Guilds in England 1250–1550*. Oxford, 2015.

Roundell, Charles. 'Tollemaches of Helmingham'. *Suffolk Institute of Archaeology Proceedings* xii (1904): 100–12.

Russell, Percy. *The Good Town of Totnes*. Exeter, 1964.

Rylands, W. H. '[No Title]'. *Ars Quatuor Coronatorum* VI (1893): 188.

Salter, H. E., and Mary D. Lobel. eds. *VCH Oxfordshire*. Vol. 3. London, 1954.

Salzman, L. F. *Building in England down to 1540: A Documentary History*. Second edition. Oxford, 1967.

Salzman, L. F. 'Etchingham Church'. *Sussex Notes & Queries* 3 (1930): 53–54.
  ed. *VCH Cambridgeshire*. Vol. 2. London, 1948.
  ed. *VCH Northamptonshire*. Vol. 4. London, 1937.
  ed. *VCH Sussex*. Vol. 7. London, 1940.
Sand, Alexa. *Vision, Devotion, and Self-Representation in Late Medieval Art*. Cambridge, 2014.
Sandars, Samuel. *Historical and Architectural Notes on Great Saint Mary's Church, Cambridge*. Cambridge, 1869.
Saul, Nigel. 'Chivalry and Art: The Camoys Family and the Wall Paintings in Trotton Church'. In *Soldiers, Nobles and Gentlemen: Essays in Honour of Maurice Keen*, edited by Peter R. Coss and Christopher Tyerman, 97–111. Woodbridge, 2009.
  Death, Art, and Memory in Medieval England: The Cobham Family and Their Monuments, 1300–1500. Oxford, 2001.
  English Church Monuments in the Middle Ages: History and Representation. London, 2009.
  'Language, Lordship, and Architecture: The Brass of Sir Thomas and Lady Walsh at Wanlip, Leicestershire, and Its Context'. *Midland History* 37, no. 1 (1 March 2012): 1–16.
  Scenes from Provincial Life: Knightly Families in Sussex 1280–1400. Oxford, 1986.
  'Shottesbrooke Church: A Study in Knightly Patronage'. In *Windsor: Medieval Archaeology, Art and Architecture of the Thames Valley*, edited by L. Keen and E. Scarff, 264–81. Norwich, 2002.
  'The Lovekyns and the Lovekyn Chapel at Kingston upon Thames'. *Surrey Archaeological Collections* 96 (2011): 85–108.
  'The Religious Sympathies of the Gentry in Gloucestershire, 1200–1500'. *Transactions of the Bristol and Gloucestershire Archaeological Society* 98 (1980): 99–112.
Saul, Nigel, Jonathan Mackman, and Christopher Whittick. 'Grave Stuff: Litigation with a London Tomb-Maker in 1421'. *Historical Research* 84, no. 226 (1 November 2011): 572–85.
Scaife, R. H. 'Civic Officials of York and Parliamentary Representatives'. York City Library, n.d.
Scarfe, Norman. *Suffolk in the Middle Ages*. Woodbridge, 1986.
Scarisbrick, J. J. *The Reformation and the English People*. Oxford, 1984.
Schofield, Phillipp R. 'Endettement et Credit Dans La Campagne Anglaise Au Moyen Age'. In *Endettement Paysan et Crédit Rural Dans l'Europe Médiévale et Moderne*, edited by M. Berthe, 69–97. Toulouse, 1998.
  'England: The Family and the Village Community'. In *A Companion to Britain in the Later Middle Ages*, edited by S. H. Rigby, 26–46. Oxford, 2003.
  'Tenurial Developments and the Availability of Customary Land in a Later Medieval Community'. *The Economic History Review*, 49, no. 2 (1 May 1996): 250–67.
Schofield, R. S. 'The Geographical Distribution of Wealth in England, 1334–1649'. *The Economic History Review*, 18, no. 3 (1 January 1965): 483–510.
Seaward, P. 'Gilbert Sheldon, the London Vestries, and the Defence of the Church'. In *The Politics of Religion in Restoration England*, edited by T. Harris, P. Seaward, and M. Goldie, 49–73. Oxford, 1990.

Bibliography

Serjeantson, R. M., and W. R. D. Adkins, eds. *VCH Northamptonshire*. Vol. 2. London, 1906.
Serjeantson, R. M., and H. I. Longden. 'The Parish Churches and Religious Houses of Northamptonshire: Their Dedications, Altars, Images and Lights'. *Archaeological Journal* 70 (1913): 217–452.
Shagan, Ethan H. *Popular Politics and the English Reformation*. Cambridge, 2003.
Sheail, John. *The Regional Distribution of Wealth in England as Indicated in the 1524/5 Lay Subsidy Returns*. Edited by R. W. Hoyle. Vol. 1. Kew, 1998.
——— *The Regional Distribution of Wealth in England as Indicated in the 1524/5 Lay Subsidy Returns*. Edited by R. W. Hoyle. Vol. 2. Kew, 1998.
Shelby, Lon R. 'Mediaeval Masons' Templates'. *Journal of the Society of Architectural Historians* 30, no. 2 (1 May 1971): 140–54.
——— 'The Contractors of Chartres'. *Gesta* 20, no. 1 (1 January 1981): 173–78.
——— 'The Role of the Master Mason in Mediaeval English Building'. *Speculum* 39, no. 3 (July 1964): 387–403.
Shorrocks, D. M. M. 'The Custom of Hogling'. *Somerset and Dorset N&Q* 28 (1967): 341–42.
Short, Philip. 'The Fourteenth-Century Rows of York'. *Archaeological Journal* 137 (1979): 86–136.
Shrewsbury, J. F. D. *A History of Bubonic Plague in the British Isles*. Cambridge, 2005.
Simpson, Alfred William Brian. *A History of the Common Law of Contract: The Rise of the Action of Assumpsit*. Oxford, 1975.
Smith, D. M. *A Guide to the Archives of the Company of Merchant Adventurers of York*. York, 1990.
Smith, Edwin, Graham Hutton, and Olive Cook. *English Parish Churches*. London, 1976.
Smith, H. Maynard. *Pre-Reformation England*. London, 1963.
Smith, Richard M. 'Families and Their Property in Rural England 1250–1800'. In *Land, Kinship and Life-Cycle*, edited by Richard M. Smith, 1–86. Cambridge, 1984.
Smith, Sally V. 'Towards a Social Archaeology of the Late Medieval English Peasantry: Power and Resistance at Wharram Percy'. *Journal of Social Archaeology* 9, no. 3 (1 October 2009): 391–416.
Snyder, Janet. 'Standardisation and Innovation in Design'. In *New Approaches to Medieval Architecture*, edited by Robert Odell Bork, William W. Clark, and Abby McGehee. Farnham, 2011.
Spraggon, Julie. *Puritan Iconoclasm during the English Civil War*. Woodbridge, 2003.
Spufford, Margaret. *Contrasting Communities: English Villagers in the Sixteenth and Seventeenth Centuries*. Stroud, 2000.
Spufford, Peter. *Money and Its Use in Medieval Europe*. Cambridge, 1988.
St. John Hope, W. H. 'Notes on the Architectural History of the Parish Church of High Wycombe'. *Records of Buckinghamshire* ix (1909): 7–50.
Staples, Kathryn Kelsey. *Daughters of London: Inheriting Opportunity in the Late Middle Ages*. Leiden, 2011.
Steed, Christopher. *Let the Stones Talk: Glimpses of English History Through the People of the Moor*. Milton Keynes, 2011.
Steer, Christian. 'The Language of Commemoration'. In *Language in Medieval Britain*, edited by Mary Carruthers, 240–51. Donington, 2015.

Steers, J. A, ed. *The Cambridge Region 1965*. Cambridge, 1965.
Steffen, Gustaf Fredrik. *Studien Zur Geschichte Der Englischen Lohnarbeiter*. Vol. 1. Stuttgart, 1901.
Stokes, J. 'The Hoglers: Evidences of an Entertainment Tradition in Eleven Somerset Parishes'. *Somerset and Dorset N&Q* 32 (1990): 807–16.
Stone, David. *Decision-Making in Medieval Agriculture*. Oxford, 2005.
Stow, John. *A Survey of London*. Edited by Charles Lethbridge Kingsford. Oxford, 1908.
Stratford, Neil. 'Romanesque Sculpture in Burgundy: Reflections on Its Geography, on Patronage, on the Status of Sculpture, and on the Working Methods of Sculptors'. In *Artistes, Artisans, et Production Artistique Au Moyen Age*, edited by X. Altet and I. Barral, 3:235–63. Paris, 1990.
Swaby, John. *A History of Louth*. London, 1951.
Swanson, Heather. 'Artisans in the Urban Economy: The Documentary Evidence from York'. In *Work in Towns*, edited by P. Corfield and D. Keene, 42–56, 1990.
  Building Craftsmen in Late Medieval York. York, 1983.
  Medieval Artisans: An Urban Class in Late Medieval England. Oxford, 1989.
Swanson, R. N. *Church and Society in Late Medieval England*. Oxford, 1989.
Tanner, Norman P. *The Church in Late Medieval Norwich, 1370–1532*. Toronto, 1984.
Taylor, Alison. 'Churches out of Use in Cambridgeshire'. *Proceedings of the Cambridge Antiquarian Society* LXXII (March 1982): 31–38.
Taylor, Peter Alfred, and Joseph Lemuel Chester. *Some Account of the Taylor Family (Originally Taylard)*. London, 1875.
The Story of the Parish Church of St. Petroc, Bodmin. 6th ed. Gloucester, n.d.
Thompson, A. Hamilton. 'Diocesan Organisation in the Middle Ages: Archdeacons and Rural Deans'. *Proceedings of the British Academy* 29 (1943): 153–94.
Thompson, J. D. A. *Inventory of British Coin Hoards, AD 600–1500*. London, 1956.
Titow, J. Z. *English Rural Society, 1200–1350*. London, 1969.
Tittler, Robert. *The Reformation and the Towns in England: Politics and Political Culture, c. 1540–1640*. Oxford, 1998.
Tollemache, Edward Devereux Hamilton. *The Tollemaches of Helmingham and Ham*. Ipswich, 1949.
Tompkins, Matthew. '"Let's Kill All the Lawyers": Did Fifteenth Century Peasants Employ Lawyers When They Conveyed Customary Land?' In *Identity and Insurgency in the Late Middle Ages*, edited by Linda Clark, 73–87. Woodbridge, 2006.
Trachtenberg, Marvin. *Building-in-Time from Giotto to Alberti and Modern Oblivion*. New Haven, 2010.
Truman, Nevile. 'Medieval Glass in Holme-by-Newark Church'. *Transactions of the Thoroton Society* 39 (1935): 92–118.
  'Medieval Glass in Holme-by-Newark Church, II'. *Transactions of the Thoroton Society* 43 (1939): 27–32.
  'The Barton Family of Holme-by-Newark'. *Transactions of the Thoroton Society* 40 (1936): 1–17.
Turnbull, David. *Masons, Tricksters and Cartographers: Comparative Studies in the Sociology of Scientific and Indigenous Knowledge*. London, 2000.

Bibliography

'The Ad Hoc Collective Work of Building Gothic Cathedrals with Templates, String, and Geometry'. *Science, Technology, & Human Values* 18, no. 3 (1 July 1993): 315–40.

Turner, Laurence. 'The Masons' Marks in the Church of St Mary, Over, Cambridgeshire'. *Proceedings of the Cambridge Antiquarian Society* 51 (1958): 67–77.

Tyack, Geoffrey, Simon Bradley, and Nikolaus Pevsner. *Berkshire*. New ed. New Haven, 2010.

Vale, Malcolm Graham Allan. *Piety, Charity, and Literacy among the Yorkshire Gentry, 1370–1480*. York, 1976.

Vallance, Aymer. *English Church Screens*. London, 1936.

——— 'R.N., with an Appendix on the Rood Screen'. *Archaeologia Cantiana* 44 (1932): 253–68.

von Simson, Otto G. 'Letters to the Editor'. *The Art Bulletin* 37, no. 3 (1955): 235–36.

——— *The Gothic Cathedral*. London, 1956.

Vroom, W. H. *Financing Cathedral Building in the Middle Ages: The Generosity of the Faithful*. Translated by Elizabeth Manton. Amsterdam, 2010.

Wake, Joan. 'Communitas Villae'. *The English Historical Review* 37, no. 147 (1 July 1922): 406–13.

Walker, Robert. 'William Dowsing in Cambridgeshire'. In *The Journal of William Dowsing: Iconoclasm in East Anglia during the English Civil War*, 34–46. Woodbridge, 2001.

Walls, Jerry L. *Purgatory: The Logic of Total Transformation*. Oxford, 2011.

Wareham, A. F., and A. P. M. Wright, eds. *VCH Cambridgeshire*. Vol. 10. London, 2002.

Warner, Peter. 'Walberswick: The Decline and Fall of a Coastal Settlement'. *Medieval Settlement Research Group Annual Report* 16 (2001): 12–13.

Wasson, John M. *Records of Early English Drama. Devon*. Toronto, 1986.

Watkin, Hugh Robert. *The History of Totnes Priory & Medieval Town*. 3 vols. Torquay, 1914.

Welby, Alfred. 'Chancel of Surfleet Church Re-Built 1420'. *Lincolnshire N&Q* 17 (1922): 110–11.

Wharton, Henry. *Anglia Sacra*. Vol. 1. London, 1691.

Whiting, Robert. *The Reformation of the English Parish Church*. Cambridge, 2010.

Whittle, Jane. *The Development of Agrarian Capitalism: Land and Labour in Norfolk, 1440–1580*. Oxford, 2000.

Willard, James F. *Parliamentary Taxes on Personal Property, 1290 to 1334*. Cambridge, MA, 1934.

Williams, Jane Welch. *Bread, Wine & Money: The Windows of the Trades at Chartres Cathedral*. Chicago, 1993.

Willis, Robert. *The Architectural History of Canterbury Cathedral*. London, 1845.

——— *The Architectural History of the University of Cambridge, and of the Colleges of Cambridge and Eton*. Edited by John Willis Clark. Vol. 1. Cambridge, 1886.

——— *The Architectural History of York Cathedral*. London, 1848.

Willmore, Frederic W. *A History of Walsall and Its Neighbourhood*. New ed. Wakefield, 1972.

Wilson, Christopher. 'Origins of the Perpendicular Style and Its Development to c. 1360'. PhD, University of London, 1979.
Wood, E. A. *A History of Thorpe-Le-Soken to the Year 1890*. Thorpe-le-Soken, 1975.
Woodman, Frances. 'The Writing on the Wall'. *Proceedings of the Suffolk Institute of Archaeology and History*. 42, no. 2 (2010): 185–98.
Woodman, Francis. 'Hardley, Norfolk, and the Rebuilding of Its Chancel'. In *Studies in Medieval Art and Architecture Presented to Peter Lasko*, edited by David Buckton and T. A. Heslop, 203–10. Stroud, 1994.
The Architectural History of Canterbury Cathedral. London and Boston, 1981.
The Architectural History of King's College Chapel. London, 1986.
Woodward, Donald. *Men at Work: Labourers and Building Craftsmen in the Towns of Northern England, 1450–1750*. Cambridge, 1995.
Wright, A. P. M., ed. *VCH Cambridgeshire*. Vol. 6. London, 1978.
ed. *VCH Cambridgeshire*. Vol. 8. London, 1982.
Wright, A. P. M., and C. P. Lewis, eds. *VCH Cambridgeshire*. Vol. 9. London, 1989.
Wright, S. M. *The Derbyshire Gentry in the Fifteenth Century*. Chesterfield, 1983.
Wrightson, Keith. 'Medieval Villagers in Perspective'. *Peasant Studies* 7 (1978): 203–16.
Wrightson, Keith, and David Levine. *Poverty and Piety in an English Village: Terling, 1525–1700*. Oxford, 1995.
Zell, M. L. 'Economic Problems of the Parochial Clergy in the Sixteenth Century'. In *Princes and Paupers in the English Church, 1500–1800*, edited by R. O'Day and Felicity Heal, 19–43. Leicester, 1981.
Ziegler, Philip. *The Black Death*. Stroud, 1990.

UNPUBLISHED THESES

Dale, M. K. 'Birch, Richard (by 1489–1527 or Later), of Chipping Wycombe, Bucks'. In *The House of Commons 1509–1558*, edited by S. T. Bindoff. London, 1982. http://www.historyofparliamentonline.org/volume/1509-1558/member/birch-richard-1489-1527-or-later.
Kissack, Paul. 'The London Parish Vestry, c. 1560–1640'. MPhil Thesis. Cambridge, 1998.
Sear, Joanne. 'Consumption and Trade in East Anglian Market Towns and Their Hinterlands in the Late Middle Ages'. Unpublished PhD Thesis, University of Cambridge, 2015.

ELECTRONIC SOURCES

Bain, Kristi. 'Community Conflict and Collective Memory in the Late Medieval Parish Church'. *Martin Marty Center-Religion and Culture Web Forum*, 2014. https://divinity.uchicago.edu/sites/default/files/imce/pdfs/webforum/042014/Bain_Conflict%20and%20Memory_Final.pdf.
Cole, Kate J. 'Great Dunmow's Local History: Henry VIII's 1523–4 Lay Subsidy Tax'. In *Essex Voices Past* (2012). http://www.essexvoicespast.com/henry-viiis-1523-4-lay-subsidy-tax/. Accessed 20 July 2016.

Bibliography

Kirby, J. L. 'Say, Sir John (D. 1478)'. In *Oxford Dictionary of National Biography*. Oxford, 2004. http://dx.doi.org/10.1093/ref:odnb/24764.

Marks, Richard. 'Brass and Glass: Rector Thomas Patesley and Great Shelford Church (Cambridgeshire)'. In *Vidimus* (2014). http://vidimus.org/issues/issue-76/feature/. Accessed 2 January 2017.

INDEX

Absenteeism, 131
Adderbury, Oxfordshire, 89, 233–36
Affordability
    gentry, 134, 135
    gentry, after the Black Death, 124–26
    gentry, before the Black Death, 122–24
    peasantry, after the Black Death, 92
    peasantry, before the Black Death, 84–86
Aldrych, Thomas, 253, 258
Ales. *See* Fundraising, ales
Alresford, Surrey, 132
Archdeacon, 170–71
Arlingham, Gloucestershire, 92, 178, 183
Arms, 65, 81, 112, 114, 115, 116, 134
Ash, Kent, 272
Ashburton, Devon, 77, 156
Assembly, 24, 25, 78, 137, 139, 169, 191, 205, 281
Attleborough, Norfolk, 80, 82
Audit, 24, 47, 92, 121, 161, 169, 192, 199, 211, 222, 225, 280
Aylsham, Norfolk, 80, 81

Bailiffs, manorial, 59, 152, 233, 236, 242
Balsham, Cambridgeshire, 114
Bardwell, Wiltshire, 47
Barrington, Cambridgeshire, 105
Bassingbourn, Cambridgeshire, 72, 75, 106
Bath, St Michael, 89, 157
Berry chapel, Bodmin, Cornwall, 54, 201–2
Bethersden, Kent, 185
Beverley, Yorkshire
    St Mary, 81
    the Bar, 189
Biddenham, Bedfordshire, 116, 119, 228–31, 253

Bideford, Devon, 131
Bishop's Stortford, Hertfordshire, 154, 273
Black Death, 13, 30, 31, 101, 125, 130, 250
Bodmin, Cornwall, 52, 53, 73, 77, 131, 192, 206
    churchwardens, 156
    collection, 69, 76
    fabric accounts, 199–200
    fabric wardens, 194, 196
    pledges, 271
Bolney, John, 1, 54, 134, 222–24, 242, 269
Bolney, Sussex, 53, 54, 68, 115, 121–22, 177, 221–26
    churchwardens, 157
Borrowed money, 84, 273–76
    churchwardens, 160, 162
    delayed payment, 275
    fabric committee, 185
    gentry, 126
    informal loans, 275
Bottisham, Cambridgeshire, 105
Brampton, Northamptonshire, 78
Brasses, 20, 93, 110, 112–13, 114, 117, 128, 219
Bray, Henry de, 122, 124, 126
Bredon, Worcestershire, 206
Bridgwater, Somerset, 19, 52, 54, 62, 75, 92, 162, 169, 192, 274
    fabric wardens, 194, 197, 199
Bristol
    All Saints, 244
    St Ewen, 55, 193, 206, 274
    St Nicholas, 272
    St Philip and St James, 163
Broxbourne, Hertfordshire, 218
Buckingham, St Romwold, 112, 126
Buckland, Hertfordshire, 113

Index

Bull, Edward, 163, 164, 167
Bunbury, Cheshire, 113
Bunwell, Norfolk, 271
Burwell, Cambridgeshire, 106, 128
Bury St Edmunds, St-John-atte-Hill, 221
Butler, William, 116, 119, 134, 229

Cambridge
  building work in, 107
  King's College chapel, 35, 136
  St Bene't, 151, 152
  St Mary the Great, 89, 151, 171–72, 180, 206, 210, 237
Cambridgeshire
  administration, 96
  appropriation, 132
  building work, post Black Death, 103–4
  chapelries, 36
  clerical patrons, 128
  economy after the Black Death, 102
  economy before the Black Death, 97, 100
  gentry, 116–18
  gentry patronage, 111
  land and building work, 99
  rectorial incomes, 129, 133
  wealth and building work, 101
Canterbury
  cathedral, 35, 249
  St Andrew, 63, 72, 156
  St John's Hospital, 220
  statutes (1279–92), 23
  wealth, 73
Carlton Scroop, Lincolnshire, 116
Catterick, Yorkshire, 219
Cawston, Norfolk, 68, 81, 269
Chagford, Devon, 47, 95, 193
  masters, 197
Chancel repair, 99, 128, 129, 131, 132, 208, 232, 233, 234, 236, 239, 240, 245, 272
Chapels of ease, 63, 75, 96
  destruction of, 36
  parish churches, 9
  quantity, 36
Chelmsford, 63
Chester, St Mary-on-the-Hill, 216
Chesterton, Cambridgeshire, 83, 106
Churchwardens
  accounts, 45, 46, 168–69
  accumulating funds, 270
  bells, 154–55
  borrowing, 274
  Burgess' revision, 138
  careers, 163
  'chief executive' thesis, 137
  contracts, 152, 153
  delegation, 142, 167
  limited power of, 159, 170–71
  origins, 22–23
  powers of the, 159–61
  regular income, 65
  resilience of, 150
  rood screens, 155–56
  running projects, 141
  separate accounts, 166
  'strong' and 'weak', 139
Cirencester, Gloucestershire, 33
Clerical Income. See Rectorial Income
Clerical patronage, 122, 127–33, 135, 140, 180, 208, 232, 233, 240, 245, 276
Clerk, parish, 77, 208, 225
Clopton, John, 126
Cockfield, Suffolk, 79, 122
Colby, Norfolk, 80
Collaboration, 80
  clergy and laity, 131, 178
  elites, 86, 279
  gentry and tenantry, 79, 122, 134, 178, 180, 224, 226–28, 229–31, 242–43, 245, 280
  institutional and local, 237
Collections. See Fundraising, collections
Comberton, Cambridgeshire, 107
Community cohesion, 279
Compton Pauncefoot, Somerset, 79
Consent, 169, 206, 207, 209, 243
Consultation, 206, 207, 213, 244, 280
Contractor masons, 250–51, 253–55, 257–58, 259–60, 261, 265, 275, 276
Contracts, 41, 211
  aristocratic, 119–20, 215
  background to, 46
  Biddenham, 228–31
  Bodmin, 203
  bonuses, 257
  clergy, 232
  contractors, 253–55
  financial planning, 265
  fraud, 259
  guarantees, 257
  Helmingham, 226–28
  legal action, 261

319

Index

Contracts (cont.)
  mason contractors, 255–56
  negotiating, 177
  non-aristocractic, 221
  oral, 221, 260
  parish government, 206
  quality control, 258
  reserved duties, 183
  style, 260
  the Black Death, 250
Cost of building work, 32, 84, 89, 115, 123, 125, 234, 280
  great churches, 264
Cottesbrooke, Northamptonshire, 176
Court of Requests, 23, 207
Coveney, Cambridgeshire, 130
Cracall, Richard, 253
Cranbrook, Kent, 79
Cratfield, Suffolk, 67
Croscombe, Somerset, 55, 60, 62, 66, 163, 221, 270
  chapel of St George, 148
Croxton, Norfolk, 80
Cuddington, Walter, 238, 269
Curteys, John, 126

Debt. *See* Borrowed money
Delegation
  churchwardens, 137, 142, 151, 152, 167
  fabric wardens, 203, 204, 212
  individual tasks, 150, 166
  masters, 211
  patterns in, 150
  project manager, 144–48
Denys, Roger, 253
Destruction of churches, 36
Devizes, St Mary, 116
Dunster, Somerset, 176, 184, 269

East Harling, Norfolk, 116
Economy
  after the Black Death, 13–17, 279
  before the Black Death, 11–13
Eltisely, Cambridgeshire, 117
Etchingham, Sussex, 110
Exbourne, Devon, 221
Executrixes, 95, 187, 221, 260
Exeter statutes (1287), 22
Exeter, St Petrock, 77
Eye, Suffolk, 63, 81, 140, 162, 274

Fabric accounts, 46, 52
  Adderbury, 234
  clergy, 232
  Merton College, Oxford, 239
  private gentry fabric accounts, 221–22
  separate account books, 77
Fabric wardens, 24
  executors, 220
  fabric committees, 184, 209
  for aristocratic projects, 216
  limitations on authority of, 210
  parochial government, 204
Fairford, Gloucestershire, 120, 126
Farnham, Surrey, 128
Fenstanton, Cambridgeshire, 127
Folkestone, Kent, 118, 244
Forthe, Thomas, 79
Fotheringhay College, Northamptonshire, 216–18
Fowler, Richard, 112, 126
Foxton, Cambridgeshire, 104
Fundraising
  ales, 9, 26, 64, 67, 93, 108, 206, 224, 279, 280
  chronology, 63
  collections, 9, 16, 20, 56, 62, 63, 64, 68–69, 76, 90, 92, 94, 104, 106, 108, 165, 196, 204, 206, 224, 264, 279
  financial models, 64
  future income, 272
  gifts in kind, 59, 62, 70
  levies, 54, 75–78, 92, 206
  offerings and oblations, 63
  pilgrimage, 63
  plays, 62, 68, 93, 207, 279, 280

Gamlingay, Cambridgeshire, 106
Garboldisham, Norfolk, 82, 116
Gentry
  accounts, 121–22
  affordability, 122–24
  affordability, after the Black Death, 124–26
  borrowed money, 274
  Cambridgeshire, 106, 111, 116–18
  collaboration. *See* Collaboration
  contractees, 219–20
  contracting committees, 177, 180
  economy, 134
  economy, after the Black Death, 21–22
  economy, before the Black Death, 20–21
  fabric accounts, 2, 221–22

Index

inscriptions, 111–16
privatisation thesis, 6–7
stockpiling, 269
the parish church, 5, 6, 242–43
wills, 118–20
Glapwell, Derbyshire, 208
Glastonbury, Somerset, 151, 274
Gloucester, John of, 255
Golant, Cornwall, 82
Grantchester, Cambridgeshire, 106, 133
Great church building, 7, 34, 35, 255, 262
Great Coxwell, Berkshire, 93
Great Dunmow, Essex, 71, 73, 76, 141, 146–48, 163
Great Eversden, Cambridgeshire, 104
Great Shelford, Cambridgeshire, 128
Great Sherston, Wiltshire, 89, 180, 183
Grimsby, Lincolnshire, 81
Guilds, 9
　Cambridgeshire, 106
　careers, 163, 165
　fabric wardens, 201–2
　female wardens, 95
　fundraising, 53, 54, 65, 108, 139
　history, 24–25
　inscriptions, 81
　loans, 273
　membership, 83, 94
　patronage, 82
　Reformation, 26

Hackington, Kent, 232, 251
Haddenham, Cambridgeshire, 128, 130
Halesowen, Worcestershire, 12, 67, 151
Halesworth, Suffolk, 113
Halstead, Essex, 241
Hardley, Norfolk, 236
Harlestone, Northamptonshire, 112, 122
Harmondsworth, Middlesex, 236
Harston, Cambridgeshire, 106
Harvey, John, 39
Hawkhurst, Kent, 118, 220
Heanton Punchardon, Devon, 220, 268
Hedon, Yorkshire, 54, 192
　churchwardens, 157
　fabric wardens, 197, 199
Helmingham, Suffolk, 181, 183, 226–28
Henley-on-Thames, Oxfordshire, 270
Heybridge, Essex, 62
Hildersham, Cambridgeshire, 128

Hinxton, Cambridgeshire, 106
Holme, Nottinghamshire, 120, 127
Hornby, Yorkshire, 89, 219
Horwode, William, 253
Hundred Rolls, 12, 84, 97

Indulgences, 49, 54, 69, 104
Inscriptions, 65, 80–81, 93, 94
　Cambridgeshire, 127
　collaboration, 63, 68, 82, 131, 207
　executors, 186
　gentry, 110, 115–16, 134, 244, 279
　gentry patronage, 112–13
　terminology, 113
Instalments. *See* Part-payment
Institutional building projects
　bailiffs, 236
　contracting, 239–42
　oversight, 235
　proctors, 237
　specialist officers, 239
　steward, 236
Isleham, Cambridgeshire, 106

Kilmersdon, Somerset, 140, 166, 209
Kingston upon Thames, Surrey, 126
Kingston, Cambridgeshire, 104
Kirby Muxloe Castle, 217

Labour services, 127
Lavenham, Suffolk, 18, 33, 126
Laverok, John, 229, 253, 254
Lay subsidy. *See* Taxation
Leverington, Cambridgeshire, 116, 130
Leverton, Lincolnshire, 55, 60, 76, 154, 167, 268
　Cope and bell, 170
Lewisham, Kent, 79, 272
Linton, Cambridgeshire, 106, 118
Little Shelford, Cambridgeshire, 117
Llanfairwaterdine, Shropshire, 80, 131
Local economies and church building, 64, 107, 262–64
London
　All Hallows, London Wall, 56, 62, 68, 70, 141, 152, 274
　economy, 18
　St Andrew Hubbard, 77, 141, 155, 163, 167
　St Andrew Undercroft, 114
　St Bartholomew-Exchange, 175
　St Dunstan, 218–19

Index

London (cont.)
  St Mary-at-Hill, 47, 65, 78, 81, 141, 153, 156, 157, 174, 189–91, 211, 274
  St Michael, Cornhill, 115, 170
  St Mildred, 81
  St Nicholas Cole Abbey, 272
  St Peter, Westcheap, 141, 144
Long Melford, Suffolk, 81, 92, 93, 126, 186
Lordly economy. *See* Seignurial economy
Louth, Lincolnshire, 19, 56, 66, 141, 148–50, 160, 162, 168, 273
  pledges, 271
Ludham, Norfolk, 80, 93
Ludlow, Shropshire, 55, 59, 144, 148, 269
Lydd, Kent, 156
Lyminge, Kent, 79

Mancetter, Warwickshire, 116
Marholm, Cambridgeshire, 119
Marsham, Norfolk, 116
Masters, 23–24, 26, 139, 193, 280, 281
  contracting committees, 177
  fabric committees, 210
  North Petherwin, 157, 197
  St Mary the Great, Cambridge, 171, 180
  St Mary-at-Hill, London, 174
  Tavistock, 208
  the churchwardens, 139
  wills, 244
Melbourn, Cambridgeshire, 105, 107, 133
Meldreth, Cambridgeshire, 106
Memory, communal, 71, 93, 115
Merton College chapel. *See* Oxford, St John the Baptist
Methwold, Norfolk, 80
Money shortages, 28, 32, 45, 275, 276
Morebath, Devon, 139, 141

Newbury, Berkshire, 120, 126
Newton, Cambridgeshire, 106
North Burlingham, Norfolk, 80
North Petherwin, Cornwall, 53
  churchwardens, 157
  fabric wardens, 197
North Repps, Norfolk, 80
North Walsham, Norfolk, 82
North Weald Bassett, Essex, 80
Northallerton, North Yorkshire, 270
Norwich
  guildhall, 189

St Mary Coslany, 244
St Peter Mancroft, 140
Nynehead, Somerset, 221

Oakham, Rutland, 244
Ockbrook, Derbyshire, 77
Orby, Lincolnshire, 181, 268
Orwell, Cambridgeshire, 128
Oxford
  All Saints, 272
  New College, 234
  St John the Baptist, 238, 269

Papworth St Agnes, Cambridgeshire, 106
Parishes
  definition of, 9
  government, 22–24, 209, 281
  government of, 169
  history, 94
  parish identity, 10, 279
  quantity, 36
  social structure, 16, 18, 90, 93, 108, 278
Part-payment, 53, 125, 146, 155, 156, 171–72, 218, 265–67, 272
Paston Hall, 219
Paston, Agnes, 219
Paston, John, 118
Pauncefoot, Sir Walter, 79
Peasant budgets
  c. 1300, 83
  c. 1475, 88
Peterborough, 208
Piers Plowman, 114
Plays. *See* Fundraising, plays
Pledges, 77, 121, 200, 264, 270–72, 277
Pluralism, 131–32, 135, 240
Prices
  after the Black Death, 31
  before the Black Death, 28
  glass, 29
  increases, 90
  increasing, 263, 276
  metals, 30
  rising, 11, 22, 250, 256, 261
  transport, 32
Priests. *See* Clergy
Purgatory, 49, 50, 278

Quantifying building work, 34–35, 40

322

Index

Ramsey, Huntingdonshire, 76, 272
Reading, 64, 73
　St Lawrence, 72, 155, 157
Rectorial incomes, 69, 232
　after the Black Death, 130–31
　before the Black Death, 128–30
Reformation, 26, 50
Rickman, Thomas, 33
Rippingale, Lincolnshire, 63
Risk, 251
Ropsley, Lincolnshire, 81
Roughton, Lincolnshire, 244

Saffron Walden, Essex, 55, 64, 68, 136, 162, 164
　fabric committee, 191
Sailholme, Lincolnshire, 63
Salisbury
　St Edmund, 69
　St Thomas, 81, 112, 208
Sandon, Hertfordshire, 239
Sandwich, 220
　St Clement, 148
Sawston, Cambridgeshire, 130
Seals, 176, 177
Seignurial economy
　after the Black Death, 22
　before the Black Death, 20–21
Serfdom, 13, 21
Shepreth, Cambridgeshire, 116
Shottesbrooke, Berkshire, 124, 274
Slump, mid-fifteenth-century, 9, 39, 40, 45, 102, 106, 215
Soham, Cambridgeshire, 105, 130
Southchurch, Essex, 84, 88, 89, 112, 123, 220, 255
Speed of completion, 267–68
St Erth, Cornwall, 233
St Neot, Cornwall, 82
Stambourne, Essex, 80
Star Chamber, 23
Statute of Labourers, 31
Steeple Ashton, Wiltshire, 79, 113
Stockpiling, 28, 32, 84, 126, 228, 239, 269–70, 273, 277
Stoke, Kent, 79
Stow, John, 114
Stratton, Cornwall, 180, 206
Sureties, 31, 170, 241, 257
Surfleet, Lincolnshire, 180
Swaffham Prior, Cambridgeshire, 106, 118

Swaffham, Norfolk, 37, 39, 58, 73, 73, 81, 141, 158, 162, 164, 168, 271
　guilds, 25

Tame, John, 126
Tavistock, Devon, 154, 169, 207–8
Taxation, 12, 32, 73, 76, 87, 90, 100, 103, 121, 125
Tempsford, Bedfordshire, 232
Thame, Oxfordshire, 56, 67, 71, 73, 76, 141, 142, 162
Thanet Minster, Kent, 115
Thornham Parva, Suffolk, 181
Thorpe-le-Soken, Essex, 82
Tintinhull, Somerset, 156
Tombs, 20, 93, 112–13, 122, 134, 150, 219
Toronto School, 16
Totnes, Devon, 19, 77, 78, 187, 190, 206, 211
Towns
　churchwardens, 45
　contracts, 175, 205
　control over churchwardens, 169, 172
　economies after the Black Death, 18
　economies before the Black Death, 17–18
　fundraising, 24, 63, 65, 165
　government, 18–19, 24, 25, 141, 163, 165, 208–9, 211, 280, 281
　social structure, 19–20
　office holding, 182–83, 193–96, 267
　oversight of building work, 191, 192–93, 207, 261
Trowbridge, 92
Trumpington, Cambridgeshire, 106
Trunch, Norfolk, 80
Tunbridge, Kent, 140, 155

Urban. *See* Towns

Valor Ecclesiasticus, 35, 130, 232
Vestry, 23, 26, 175

Wages
　after the Black Death, 30–31, 250
　before the Black Death, 26–28
Walberswick, Suffolk, 82, 141, 158, 181, 183, 269
Walsall, St Matthew, 141, 144–46
Wanlip, Leicestershire, 112
Warehorne, Kent, 244
Waterbeach, Cambridgeshire, 105, 111, 133

Index

Waterstoke, Oxfordshire, 221
Weasenham, Norfolk, 80
Wellingham, Norfolk, 80
Wells, St Cuthbert, 25
West Malling, Kent, 271
Westhall, Suffolk, 80
Westminster, St Margaret, 39, 73, 89, 140
Whittlesford, Cambridgeshire, 118
Wigginhall, Norfolk, 80
Wills, 40–44, 46, 267
   bequests to churchwardens, 140, 155
   Cambridgeshire, 106
   clerical, 131, 232
   consultation, 244
   cooperation, 26–28, 94
   direct contributions, 118–19
   fabric wardens, 186
   gentry, 134, 245
   pledges, 271
   Somerset, 44
   West Kent, 43
Wilmslow, Cheshire, 132
Wimborne, Dorset, 243, 269
Wimington, Bedfordshire, 112, 126

Winchcombe, Gloucestershire, 243, 268
Wingfield, Suffolk, 22
Wisbech, Cambridgeshire, 107
   Holy Trinity Guild, 25
Wiverton, Nottinghamshire, 78
Wolverhampton, 176
Wolvey, Warwickshire, 113
Women in parish administration, 94
Woodbridge, Suffolk, 113
Wool Gothic, 8
Worstead, Norfolk, 82
Wycombe, Buckinghamshire, 177, 182, 183

Yatton, Somerset, 155
   St Christopher image, 170
Yeomen, 14, 80, 93, 127, 162, 192, 245, 271
   Cambridgeshire, 103, 106–7
Yeovil, Somerset, 232
Yeovilton, Somerset, 140
Yevele, Henry, 35, 218
York
   houses in, 182
   statutes (c. 1306), 23

Lightning Source UK Ltd.
Milton Keynes UK
UKHW020700091220
374671UK00019B/443